FOUNDATIO
INTERNATIC
LAW AND POLITICS

By

OONA A. HATHAWAY

Associate Professor of Law
Yale Law School

HAROLD HONGJU KOH

Dean and Gerard C. and Bernice Latrobe Smith
Professor of International Law
Yale Law School

FOUNDATION PRESS
New York, New York
2005

395 Hudson Street
New York, NY 10014
Phone Toll Free 1–877–888–1330
Fax (212) 367–6799
fdpress.com

Printed in the United States of America
ISBN 1–58778–725–3

PREFACE

Until recently, international law and international politics have been two disciplines divided by a common subject matter. International law rarely found its way into the curriculum of political science departments. Law school courses only occasionally touched upon international relations. Scholarship in the two disciplines proceeded on separate tracks.

In recent years, the chasm between these disciplines has narrowed as international law and international relations theorists have finally begun to share insights. This book seeks to cement these gains and to provide a foundation for further interchange between the disciplines. We present the readings in this book with two main aims: first, to lay out several of the most central and current theoretical approaches found in international law and international relations scholarship, with an eye toward creating a common framework upon which both sets of scholars can build; and second, to offer a series of practical applications to spark discussion and debate.

To those ends, the first seven sections of this book provide an introduction to the core scholarly debate and survey the primary schools of international theory: what we call the "interest-based" and "norm-based" approaches to international studies. In the theory sub-sections, we include writings by both political scientists and legal scholars to convey a sense of the different ways in which the two sets of scholars perceive and use their theories. The final six sections provide a series of applications of the theories. In each of the applications, we seek to provide at least two contrasting perspectives on the subject matter. Our goal is to enrich discussion by demonstrating how the broader theoretical disagreements outlined in the earlier, theoretical parts generate contrasting approaches to, and predictions about, particular areas of state behavior.

Of course, this introduction to current theoretical scholarship in international law and politics remains just that: an introduction. It is intended only to serve as a starting point for those seeking to learn about international law and politics. Of necessity, many important works are omitted from the text (though virtually all schools of thought are touched upon somewhere in the volume, particularly in the Notes and Comments sections).

We intend for this book to be used in a variety of ways. It might serve as a companion volume to a book of case materials in an introductory course in international or transnational law. It could also serve as the central reader in a more advanced law school course or seminar on international law. Finally, it could be used in political science departments in a variety of courses to add legal content to the study of international relations or globalization in the 21st Century.

Over time, this field will only expand, and we expect to update this volume to address the changes. We welcome suggestions as to how the volume might be improved to incorporate new developments. More than half a century ago, our predecessors here at Yale, Myres McDougal and Harold Laswell, pioneered the modern collaboration between international law and international relations and founded the "New Haven School of International Law." We are pleased, in this new millennium, to continue their worthy efforts to work from New Haven to promote this critical dialogue between two burgeoning sibling disciplines.

OONA A. HATHAWAY

HAROLD HONGJU KOH

ACKNOWLEDGEMENTS

We are grateful to many for their assistance at every stage of this book's preparation. Dean Anthony Kronman, who served as Dean of Yale Law School from 1994–2004, gave us warm encouragement and unstinting support in our research efforts. Kris Kavanaugh and Deborah Sestito provided excellent administrative assistance, and Gene Coakley of Yale Law School's library staff was immensely creative and helpful in collecting the materials for the book. Our colleague Roberta Romano, the general editor of this series, and our publisher Steve Errick guided the book to publication with grace and patience and provided a great deal of encouragement and immensely helpful feedback along the way. Keith Darden offered generous feedback on the reader as it developed and co-taught a class with Oona Hathaway that formed a starting point for part of this reader. Several Yale students served as the first readers of the book manuscript and offered detailed assistance in its revision, including Aditi Banerjee, Rebecca Charnas, Dennis Clare, Anver Emon, Christian Ford, Seth Green, Heloisa Griggs, Joshua Hawley, Gretchen Hoff, Ellen Jooyeon Kang, SatKartar Khalsa, Eunice Lee, Felicia Medina, Christine Parker, Dakota Rudesill, Joanne Savage, and Boris Sokurov. We also benefited immensely from the thoughtful help of several diligent research assistants, including Ivana Cingel, David Newman, Galit Sarfaty, Derek Smith, and Natalie Wigg. Nor could this book have been completed without the superb assistance of Ariel Lavinbuk and Elizabeth Nathan, whose scholarly skill and knowledge are evident throughout the book.

Finally, it should be noted that as we worked on this volume, Harold Koh was named Dean of Yale Law School, and Oona Hathaway assumed the vast bulk of the responsibility for bringing this work to completion. There should be no mistaking, then, that as editors, we are listed in an order that reflects not just the alphabet, but also our relative substantive contributions to this volume.

O. A. H.

H. H. K.

*

ABOUT THE AUTHORS

Oona A. Hathaway is an Associate Professor of Law at Yale Law School. She earned her B.A. at Harvard University and her J.D. at Yale Law School. Before joining the faculty at Yale, she served as a Law Clerk for Justice Sandra Day O'Connor and for the D.C. Circuit Judge Patricia Wald, held fellowships at Harvard University's Carr Center for Human Rights Policy and Center for the Ethics and the Professions, and served as an Associate Professor at Boston University School of Law. Her current research focuses on how international law shapes countries' behavior. A 2004 Carnegie Scholar, she is working on a book on the promise and limits of international law.

Harold Hongju Koh is Dean and Gerard C. and Bernice Latrobe Smith Professor of International Law at Yale Law School. He holds a B.A. and J.D. from Harvard University, an MA from Magdalen College, Oxford, and seven honorary degrees. From 1998–2001 he served as Assistant Secretary of State for Democracy, Human Rights and Labor. Before joining the faculty at Yale, he served as a Law Clerk for Justice Harry A. Blackmun and for D.C. Circuit Judge Malcolm Richard Wilkey, and worked in private practice and in the Justice Department. He is a Fellow of the American Academy of Arts and Sciences, and Honorary Fellow of Magdelen College, Oxford, and has served on the Board of Editors of the American Journal of International Law and Foundation Press Casebook Series. He has written widely on international law and international relations.

FOUNDATIONS OF LAW SERIES

ROBERTA ROMANO, GENERAL EDITOR

Foundations of Administrative Law
Edited by Peter H. Schuck, Yale Law School

Foundations of Contract Law
Edited by Richard Craswell, Stanford Law School and Alan Schwartz, Yale Law School

Foundations of Corporate Law
Edited by Roberta Romano, Yale Law School

Foundations of Criminal Law
Edited by Leo Katz, Michael S. Moore and Stephen J. Morse, all of the University of Pennsylvania Law School

Foundations of The Economic Approach to Law
Edited by Avery Wiener Katz, Columbia Law School

Foundations of Employment Discrimination Law
Edited by John Donohue, III, Stanford Law School

Foundations of Environmental Law and Policy
Edited by Richard L. Revesz, New York University Law School

Foundations of Intellectual Property
Edited by Robert P. Merges, University of California Berkeley and Davis Schools of Law and Jane C. Ginsburg, Columbia University School of Law

Foundations of International Income Taxation
Edited by Michael J. Graetz, Yale Law School

Foundations of International Law and Politics
Edited by Oona A. Hathaway and Harold Hongju Koh, Yale Law School

Foundations of Labor and Employment Law
Edited by Samuel Estreicher, New York University Law School and Stewart J. Schwab, Cornell Law School

Foundations of the Law and Ethics of Lawyering
Edited by George M. Cohen, University of Virginia School of Law and Susan P. Koniak, Boston University School of Law

Foundations of Tort Law
Edited by Saul Levmore, University of Chicago Law School

CONTENTS

FOUNDATIONS OF INTERNATIONAL LAW AND POLITICS

*

I

International Law and International Relations: An Introduction

In the years following World War II, the study of international law and international relations became deeply divided. Although covering much of the same intellectual territory, the two fields evolved independently, pursuing different analytic missions, and adopting an unspoken division of labor regarding the intellectual projects each would pursue. International lawyers largely devoted their energies to description of international legal norms; application of these norms to particular cases; and occasional prescription of what the rule of law should be. International relations scholars tended instead to focus on the tasks of causal explanation and prediction.

While scholars of international relations proposed broad theories of war, peace, and economic progress, international legal academics were largely concerned with narrower issues pertaining to the formation, promulgation, and codification of treaties and customary international law. Both told incomplete stories. International lawyers paid relatively little attention to the broad economic and political environments that condition the making of international law and nations' responses to it. By contrast, international relations literature centered on this environment, yet international relations scholars almost never explored whether and how international law fit into this environment. In fact, international relations scholars tended simply to ignore international law and international legal scholarship altogether.

All of this began to change in the 1970s and 1980s, as international relations scholars began to confront the reality that, despite Cold War antipathies, international regimes and institutions had continued to grow in number, breadth, and authority. At the same time, legal scholars began to acknowledge and respond to the challenge mounted by the skeptics who viewed any reliance on international law as so idealistic as to be not simply unrealistic, but dangerous. Interest in interdisciplinary discussion began to flourish in academic journals in both realms.

By the end of the 1980s, this development had proved prescient. The fall of the Berlin Wall and the rise of U.S. hegemony as "the world's only superpower" ushered in grand proclamations of the end of history and focused attention on the shape of a new world order. By the end of the millennium, the law and politics of international cooperation had firmly taken center stage. The terrorist attacks of September 11, 2001—in retrospect, the real start of the 21st century—abruptly ended the post-Cold War euphoria, and made developing effective strategies of global cooperation seem an even more pressing necessity.

Today, international law and international relations are increasingly viewed as a single discipline. Yet significant differences remain. To date, most existing efforts to examine international law and international relations literature have placed the two side-by-side, thus emphasizing the disciplinary divide. By contrast, this book focuses on a conceptual divide that interweaves the work of legal scholars and political scientists. The divide stands between those theories that tend to portray states primarily as unitary actors that engage in instrumental behavior designed to promote exogenously given national interests—which we term *"interest-based" theories*—and those that tend to view states instead as motivated as much by ideas (or "norms") that help to construct their perceived self-interest—grouped here together under the general heading of *"norm-based" theories*.

A significant difference between these two approaches lies in the role played by sanctions in motivating state compliance with international law. Most interest-based accounts of international law argue that sanctions are essential to compliance. Under this view, where there are no material consequences for noncompliance, international law is unlikely to change state behavior. Norm-based scholarship, by contrast, argues that ideas and norms play a central role in motivating state behavior. This school argues that the single-minded focus on rational calculations of self-interest leads interest-based scholars to miss important features of the international legal and political arena.

Of course, this divide is far from absolute. Many interest-based scholars argue that if the relevant actors truly care about norms and ideas and are motivated by them, these interests can be easily captured within their frameworks. And norm-based scholars generally do not deny that states often pursue self-interest or that sanctions can serve to mold state behavior. Yet the core focus—and central insights—of the two approaches remain distinct.

More important, the prescriptive conclusions to which the theories point are entirely different. Interest-based scholars tend to encourage greater reliance on explicit costs and benefits in the effort to create more effective international laws. Norm-based scholars, on the other hand, argue that international laws can be made more effective through inculcation of shared normative frameworks and through the internalization of the ideas and norms embodied in international law into domestic legal, political, and social life. To draw an analogy to domestic criminal law, interest-based scholars would change the law to alter violators' perceptions of the costs and benefits of compliance and to reduce the costs of enforcement. Norm-based scholars, by contrast, would devote greater energy to designing social, political and institutional frameworks that help internalize norms of obedience into the value sets of potential violators.

At a time when the world is increasingly looking to international law to maintain world order, this difference is not simply academic. It is central to the future of international law and politics. It affects the way that we think about the role of international organizations, the goals of U.S. foreign policy, the relationship between international and domestic adjudication, and the value of drafting and ratifying international treaties.

Of course, these are age-old questions. To understand where scholarship on international law and politics is going, it is first necessary to examine where it has been. To that end, the two pieces excerpted below trace major developments in international relations and international law over the past half century. Both share a common set of facts: the rise of the Cold War, the establishment of the United Nations, Vietnam, the fall of the Berlin Wall, and the explosion of ethnic conflict, to name a few. Nevertheless, each tells a different story, emphasizes different developments, and acknowledges different legacies. However blurry the line between the study of law and politics may seem today, these two overlapping but distinct histories reveal that this has not always been the case. At the same time, these overviews serve to provide a brief introduction to each of the theoretical frameworks covered in much greater depth later in this book. The readings may prove difficult on first reading, as they introduce many new terms and theories. It is our hope, however, that this first introduction will help the reader place the interest-based and norm-based theories within a broader historical context, before proceeding to further reading on both theory and practice.

International Organization and The Study of World Politics*

PETER J. KATZENSTEIN, ROBERT O. KEOHANE, and STEPHEN D. KRASNER

In this article we tell the story of the ... evolution of [the field of international relations].... Our story ... goes as follows. In the late

* Reprinted by permission from 52 INTERNATIONAL ORGANIZATION 645 (1998).

1960s and mid–1970s some young political scientists studying international relations seized an opening created both by events in the world and in the social sciences. Growing levels of international interdependence pointed to by a few economists helped in the conceptualization of transnational relations theory. This analytical approach provided an alternative to the state-centric, realist approach then dominating the study of international relations.... In the 1980s neoliberal institutionalism and ... neorealism became the principal interlocutors—institutionalists emphasized the potential for interstate cooperation, whereas realists stressed the importance of state power. Since the late 1980s a new debate between constructivism and rationalism (including both realism and liberalism) has become more prominent as constructivists have built on epistemological challenges rooted in sociological perspectives emphasizing shared norms and values.[1]

...

Realism ...

Realism has been at the center of the theoretical debates of U.S. international relations scholarship for a long time. Historically, realism was a breed alien to the liberal and progressive intellectual and political sensibilities of the United States. At its inception in the early twentieth century, the discipline of international relations was part of the progressive movement that sought to build a systematic social science for the betterment of mankind in the United States and, by implication, worldwide. World War II and the Holocaust, experienced and interpreted by a generation of brilliant intellectuals closely linked to Europe, changed this. And so did the protracted Cold War that held the world in its grip for four decades. Prudent statecraft, realism argued, required a space for diplomacy and strategy that was uncontested by normal domestic politics. The grand debates in the field ... are products of this distinctive historical legacy....

For most American students of international politics, at least through the 1980s, realism was the perspective against which new ideas had to be tested.... Hans Morgenthau's Politics Among Nations was the most important text. Kenneth Waltz had published his first book in 1959 in which he initiated the intellectual project that culminated in his influential exposition of what came to be termed neorealism twenty years later....

Realism's core assumptions can be variously classified, but four are particularly important: (1) states are the key actors in world politics; (2) states can be treated as homogeneous units acting on the basis of self-

1. [Editors' note: This article identifies a debate in the international relations literature that overlaps in significant part with the bifurcation identified in this book. What the article terms "rationalism" is subsumed in our own classification under the heading of "interest-based theories." These theories include realism (In Part II.A.), institutionalism (Part II.B.), and liberalism (In Part II.C.). By contrast, constructivism (Part III.A.) is identified as a "norm-based theory," along with legitimacy-centered theories (Part III.B.) and legal process theories (Part III.C.).]

interest; (3) analysis can proceed on the basis of the assumption that states act as if they were rational; and (4) international anarchy—the absence of any legitimate authority in the international system—means that conflict between self-interested states entails the danger of war and the possibility of coercion. . . .

In the mid–1970s a new liberal challenge to realism began to emerge. This challenge focused on the concept of "international regime," drawn from a long-standing tradition of international law and first used in the political science literature by John Ruggie and subsequently elaborated by [Robert] Keohane and [Joseph] Nye. Ruggie defined regimes as sets of "mutual expectations, rules and regulations, plans, organizational energies and financial commitments, which have been accepted by a group of states." Keohane and Nye treated them simply as "governing arrangements that affect relationships of interdependence." Ruggie's understanding was sociological or constructivist, emphasizing the importance of intersubjective, shared understanding that defines rather than just reflects the preferences of actors; Keohane and Nye understood regimes as devices for enhancing the utility of actors whose interests were taken as given. Students of international regimes did not challenge one of the meanings of "anarchy": that no institutional hierarchy capable of enforcing rules exists in world politics. They did question the frequent implication that anarchy in this sense implied the absence of institutions based on rules.

. . .

By the end of the 1970s students of international regimes had introduced a potentially important new dependent variable into the analysis of world politics. At that time, however, this new dependent variable was not linked with a distinctive set of explanatory variables through an articulated causal mechanism and, therefore, did not seriously threaten the well-articulated explanatory project of realism based on interests, power, and anarchy. . . .

When Ronald Reagan won the presidency, realist analysis still held pride of place in the United States; it was still the theory that had to be refuted before a convincing intellectual challenge could be offered. Realism maintained its dominant position despite alternative arguments that appeared more accurately to describe actors, and despite the fact that its empirical validation had always been problematic. Realism continued to be *primus inter pares* because liberalism did not offer an alternative research program that specified causality and operationalized variables clearly enough to be falsifiable. The renewal of the Cold War after the Soviet invasion of Afghanistan at the end of 1979 seemed to reinforce realism's intellectual triumph.

Neoliberal Institutionalism

The development of neoliberal institutionalism posed a serious challenge for realist analysis. . . . [Drawing on his regime theory work,] Robert Keohane developed a rationalist argument to explain the existence of international institutions. Drawing an analogy to problems of market failure in economics, he argued that high transaction costs and asymmetrical uncertainty could lead, under conditions such as those modeled by Prisoners' Dilemma (PD) games, to suboptimal outcomes. Chiefly by providing information to actors (not by enforcing rules in a centralized manner), institutions could enable states to achieve their own objectives more efficiently. Institutions would alter state strategies by changing the costs of alternatives; institutionalization could thus promote cooperation. Keohane argued that institutions mattered because they could provide information, monitor compliance, increase iterations, facilitate issue linkages, define cheating, and offer salient solutions. Keohane did not deny the importance of power, but within the constraints imposed by the absence of hierarchical global governance, states could reap gains from cooperation by designing appropriate institutions....

Where the neoliberal institutionalism research program differed with realist arguments was not on its assumptions about actors, but rather on the nature of the exemplary problem in the international system: were states primarily concerned with market failure or with relative gains and distributional conflicts? Could issues be resolved through the voluntary acceptance of institutions that left all actors better off, or would coercion and power be more important for determining outcomes? ...

Neoliberal institutionalism has offered a set of heuristically powerful deductive arguments that could eventually be made more precise.... Hypotheses generated by neoliberal institutionalism were applied to a wide range of empirical problems, such as bargaining between the United Kingdom and the other members of the European Community over the Falklands or the evolution of international regimes for debt rescheduling. The appeal of neoliberal institutionalism was enhanced by its affinity with the reigning king of the social sciences in the United States—economics.

...

Globalization and Domestic Politics ...

Increasing levels of transboundary movements and their associated effects, what has come to be termed globalization, encourage a more intimate analytic relationship between international and domestic politics.... Globalization draws our attention to the increasing political salience of transboundary activities. Is the growing enmeshment of polities in the international political economy making institutions and policies, groups and individuals more alike, or are they retaining most of their differences? Is globalization altering "inter" national relations marginally, or is it fundamentally transforming them to "trans" national relations? Those who emphasize how globalization is remaking world politics stress how policy preferences and political coalitions at home change as a result of changing international pressures. Conversely, analyses ... that emphasize the persistence of distinctive national practices have shown how domestic institutions block price signals, freeze existing political coalitions and policies, and shape the national response to global change.

Both of these arguments focus on domestic political institutions, firms, interest groups, and economic sectors as units of analysis. An alternative conceptualization focuses not on the units themselves, but rather on the relationships among them and makes problematic the nature of these units in the first place. Households, communities, regions, and social movements, among others, reconstitute themselves in a global setting. This conceptualization points to processes of "globalization" that are transforming the identities, interests, and strategies of actors through a combination of global and local processes and are thus adding new political actors and processes to an increasingly global politics.

Globalization, however conceived, is a reflection of a phenomenon that scholars ... have recognized since the inception of the field: international and domestic politics cannot be isolated from each other. Neorealists and neoliberals did not incorporate domestic politics into their theoretical formulations, but they never denied its importance. States did not all respond in the same way to the opportunities and constraints presented by the international system. Studies of domestic politics enhanced our understanding of what neorealists and neoliberals took for granted in their theories in the 1980s: "state preferences." Domestic structure analysis suggested that preferences could be understood in two possibly complementary ways: either as the result of institutionalized norms or as the aggregations of the preferences of individuals, firms, and groups. Historical-institutional research on the reciprocal effects of domestic structures and the international political economy has been complemented by a decidedly economic and materialist variant that pays virtually no attention to the role of ideas, norms, and institutions. Different interpretations of the process of globalization reflect this difference in orientation.

A Post-Cold War Opening: Rationalism and Sociology Revisited

Even during the Cold War, there was substantial dissatisfaction with reigning realist and liberal approaches to international relations, especially outside the United States and in the related field of comparative politics. The end of the Cold War was a catalyst in several ways. It raised new issues for the ongoing rationalist debate, which pitted realists, who stressed the role of coercion, against liberals, who emphasized contractual relationships. The end of the Cold War also opened up space for cultural and sociological perspectives, often referred to as "constructivist," that had been neglected by both realists and liberals. And the discussions that ensued highlighted conceptual differences between possible points of complementarity of rationalism and constructivism.

Rationalism: Realism and Liberalism After the Cold War

Realism has been not only a salient general theoretical orientation but also part of a more enduring normative discourse, like liberalism and constructivism, about the most appropriate way to secure peace, stability, and justice in human society. Its self-conscious intellectual pedigree is long and impressive.

However, recent developments in world politics and within specific research programs have confronted realism with much greater challenges than it has faced since [the early 1970s]. For realism, power and conflict are inherent aspects of international politics. The interests of states will differ. Force and coercion are always available options. The astonishingly peaceful end of the Cold War and the collapse of the Soviet Union are not what a realist would have expected. Realism has not been silent, of course. The simplest explanation for the end of the Cold War is that Soviet power declined; the Soviet Union was a challenger that could no longer challenge. Predictions about relative changes in state capability have rarely been incorporated into realist research programs, and realism did not predict this decline. Realists, especially Waltz, have emphasized the importance of nuclear weapons in altering the likelihood of war. With secure second-strike capability, it is more evident now than at any other time in human history that a conflict among the major powers would reduce the well-being of all states. At least some observers view this situation as a change in the nature of the international system itself, not just an alteration in the characteristics of individual states. From a realist perspective, in a nonnuclear world it would have been much riskier for the Soviet Union to abandon its empire in eastern Europe and for any leader to break up the Soviet Union itself, acts that would have left even Russia's core territory more vulnerable to invasion.

Nevertheless, in the 1980s analysts working within a realist framework were arguing that bipolarity would continue. And they assumed that neither pole could disappear peacefully. When the Soviet Union did collapse, realists were skeptical about the robustness of international institutions, especially those related to international security, such as NATO, and the prospects for continued cooperation in the international economy. Over the last decade things have turned out much better than realists had any right to expect....

The burgeoning of ethnic conflict in the last decade has presented the kinds of problems that realist perspectives were designed to analyze, although not necessarily with states as the most salient actors. Ethnic conflicts have arisen between states and among groups within states, albeit groups operating in environments where authority structures have eroded or disappeared and where security dilemmas operate at the substate level. However, this return to a focus on the importance of variations in state objectives (of which ethnic conflict is only one example), as a result of factors exogenous to the distribution of power in the system as a whole, confronts realist analysis with the challenge of explaining why such variations should exist—a challenge that can only be met through a more systematic integration of realism with domestic politics. . . .

Neoliberal institutionalism correctly anticipated that the end of the Cold War would not undermine such institutions as NATO and the European Union, so it did not go through an "agonizing reappraisal" such as that experienced by some realists. Indeed, institutionalists began to apply their theory to security institutions such as alliances and to interpret post-Cold War politics in institutionalist terms. . . .

Institutionalist thinking has made a big impact on [international relations] during the last fifteen years, stimulating a set of research programs that have illuminated relationships among interests, power, and institutions. But it was of less value in understanding shifting identity politics afterwards. Advocates of domestic structure approaches had for several decades criticized international relations research, including neoliberal institutionalism, for taking for granted the preferences or identities of the actors whom it studied. Neoliberal institutionalism paid virtually no attention, for example, to the phenomenon of nationalism. And it could not capture the fact that during the 1980s increased interest in human rights and environmental issues seemed driven largely by normative concerns. After 1989, some rationalists began to think of ideas as variables that affected the solutions to games—for instance, by reducing uncertainty or providing focal points. Ideas could be incorporated into an institutional framework by emphasizing how particular conceptions become institutionalized and, therefore, persist over time. Since it was not wedded exclusively to a materialist conception of structure, neoliberalism could engage some of the issues of changing beliefs or identities posed by end of the Cold War.

The Revival of Sociological and Cultural Perspectives [Constructivism]

Sociological perspectives have always been important for comparative politics and have never been completely absent from international studies. In Europe, where the boundary between international and domestic politics was never particularly salient, the sociological bent of scholarship differed from prevailing American perspectives [and] . . . remained uninterested in the debates between the general theoretical orientations that dominated American scholarship, such as realism and liberalism. These schools of thought were at odds with the emphasis in American international relations scholarship on clearly stated causal propositions and their systematic exploration in methodologically rigorous ways.

In the United States [John] Ruggie published a series of papers demonstrating the value of a sociological orientation. He argued that the postwar international economic regime reflected what he termed embedded liberalism, identified by a shared intersubjective understanding that open international markets would be tempered by the need to maintain social stability. He criticized Waltz's [neorealist] theory for its lack of sociological content and for failing to explain systemic change. And, together with Friedrich Kratochwil, he pointed out that analysts had failed to investigate the shared understandings that led to the convergence of actor expectations on which, by some accounts, regime stability depended. They argued also that the treatment of principles and norms as "independent" or "intervening" variables, linking material structures to outcomes, was not easily accommodated within the epistemological foundations of institutional and normative analysis. . . .

Both the differences and complementarities between constructivism and rationalism promise to make the interaction between these two theoretical orientations a productive point of contestation. Both are concerned with what in ordinary language are called beliefs, but they understand this concept in different ways and use different terms in their analyses. The key terms for rationalists are preferences, information, strategies, and common knowledge. The key terms for constructivists are identities, norms, knowledge, and interests. Rationalist orientations do not offer a way to understand common knowledge. Constructivist arguments do not provide a way to analyze strategies. Yet both strategy and common knowledge are usually necessary to understand political outcomes. . . .

All rationalists rely on the assumption of instrumental rationality to provide the crucial link between the environment and actor behavior. . . . All rationalists use the assumption of rationality to provide the crucial link between features of the environment—power, interests, and institutional rules—and actor behavior. But on the issue of the importance of information, they are divided. Rationalists who subscribe to a materialist view of how to study the international political economy . . . assume preferences for more wealth and infer strategies from structure, especially the competitive positions of factors, sectors, or firms in the world political economy. Variations in information are unimportant in their analysis. These authors expect actors to understand the world accurately, and they do not conceptualize actors' choices in terms of game theory involving interdependent decisions. In contrast, rationalists whose thinking is more indebted to game theory emphasize the importance of imperfect information and strategic interaction. They stress how changes in information can account for variations in strategies, even if the preferences of actors remain unchanged. Small changes in information can have a profound impact on equilibrium outcomes. Institutions or rules can be consequential because they can alter information and empower players to set the agenda, make amendments, and accept or reject the final package.

Constructivists insist on the primacy of intersubjective structures that give the material world meaning. These structures have different components that help in specifying the interests that motivate action: norms, identity, knowledge, and culture. Norms typically describe collective expectations with "regulative" effects on the proper behavior of actors with a given identity. In some situations norms operate like rules that define the identity of actors; they have "constitutive" effects that specify the actions that will cause relevant others to recognize a particular identity.... [C]ulture is a broad label that denotes collective models of authority or identity, carried by custom or law. Culture refers to both evaluative standards (such as norms and values) and cognitive standards (such as rules and models) that define the social actors that exist in a system, how they operate, and how they relate to one another.

...

The differences and complementarities between rationalism and constructivism are illustrated by their treatments of persuasion. Rationalists interpret persuasion in the language of incentives, strategic bargaining, and information. They analyze the provision of new information, sometimes through costly signaling, and appeals to audiences. For a consistent rationalist, it would be anomalous to think of persuasion in terms of changing others' deepest preferences. Constructivists, by contrast, insist on the importance of social processes that generate changes in normative beliefs, such as those prompted by the antislavery movement of the nineteenth century, the contemporary campaign for women's rights as human rights, or nationalist propaganda. For constructivists, persuasion involves changing preferences by appealing to identities, moral obligations, and norms conceived of as standards of appropriate behavior.

The different styles of analysis—"thin" information for rationalists versus "thick" norms and identities for constructivists—to some extent reflect the familiar contest in social science between economic and sociological traditions. Constructivism is ideographic, whereas rationalism is nomothetic. Neither perspective is adequate to cover all aspects of social reality. But at one critical point they are joined. Both recognize—constructivism as a central research project and rationalism as a background condition—that human beings operate in a socially constructed environment, which changes over time. Hence, both analytical perspectives focus in one way or another on common knowledge—constructivism on how it is created, rationalism on how it affects strategic decision making. The core of the constructivist project is to explicate variations in preferences, available strategies, and the nature of the players, across space and time. The core of the rationalist project is to explain strategies, given preferences, information, and common knowledge. Neither project can be complete without the other.

...

Conclusion

[International relations is] built on a rich intellectual tradition that developed in the 1940s, 1950s, and 1960s. Many of the major lines of arguments that have preoccupied scholars ... for the last three decades were developed during these years. Then as now scholars continue to analyze the interaction between power, wealth, and social purpose.... For ease of presentation ... our story has followed two distinctive strands: the interplay between realist and liberal currents of theory ... and the analysis of domestic politics....

We have argued that in the 1990s some of the major points of contestation shifted. Influenced by strong currents in economics and cultural studies, debates between rationalism and constructivism are becoming more important. They offer contrasting analytical orientations for research in the social sciences at large and in international relations. . . . Nevertheless, we know a great deal more than we did thirty years ago about a number of processes that are central to how the world political economy works, such as how power is deployed under various conditions of vulnerability, how international regimes affect government policies, and how domestic institutions and world politics affect each other through institutional processes.

In international politics and in the world of scholarship well-established boundaries are being blurred and new ones are being created. World politics is witnessing enormous change in the wake of the collapse of the Berlin Wall, the end of strategic bipolarity, and the peaceful disintegration of the Soviet Union. We are observing different types of democratization processes in different world regions, ethnic conflicts over the control of territory, and growing conflicts over the spread of weapons of mass destruction to regional powers. We are also seeing far-reaching experiments with economic integration in some world regions and continuing marginalization in others, expanded trade under the auspices of a revamped World Trade Organization, and the redefinition of the role of the International Monetary Fund and other governance mechanisms in the wake of Asia's financial crisis. At the same time, religious fundamentalism is gaining ground in much of the Muslim world. And strong secular social movements championing environmentalism, feminism, and human rights are active worldwide. . . . All of these developments illustrate the complexity of contemporary world politics and the opportunity to draw new connections across generic theoretical orientations and between specific research programs.

Why Do Nations Obey International Law?*

HAROLD HONGJU KOH

. . .

The Era of Institutions

In the wake of the Allied victory in World War II, the architects of the postwar system replaced the preexisting loose customary web of state-centric rules with an ambitious positivistic order, built on institutions and constitutions: international institutions governed by multilateral treaties organizing proactive assaults on all manner of global problems. These global "constitutions" sought both to allocate institutional responsibility and to declare particular rules of international law. Political conflict, for example, was to be regulated by the United Nations

* Reprinted by permission from 106 YALE LAW JOURNAL 2599 (1997) (review essay).

and its constituent organs—the Security Council, the General Assembly, and the World Court—under the aegis of a United Nations Charter premised on abstinence from unilateral uses of force. The United Nations system was supplemented by an alphabet soup of specialized, functional political organs and regional political and defense pacts based on respect for sovereignty and territorial integrity. Destructive economic conflicts, by contrast, were to be mitigated through the Bretton Woods system, which provided that the World Bank would supervise international reconstruction and development, the International Monetary Fund would monitor balance of payments, and the General Agreements on Tariffs and Trade (GATT) would manage international principles of economic liberalism and market capitalism. These global economic institutions were buttressed by regional economic communities such as the European Economic Community, each governed by its own constitution-like treaty.

This complex positive law framework reconceptualized international law as a creative medium for organizing the activities and relations of numerous transnational players, a category that now included intergovernmental organizations with independent decisionmaking capacity. Within this intensely regulatory global framework, it was imagined, legal rules would reflect international systemic concerns, rather than parochial interests. The globalization of economic regulation made sharp inroads into now-established distinctions between public and private law. Meanwhile, the prospect of European regional integration of domestic and international law, along with the post-Nuremberg growth of international human rights law and its potentially deep incursion into domestic jurisdiction, posed powerful theoretical challenges to the dualistic municipal-international distinction. One of the best-known legal tracts of this era, Grenville Clark and Louis Sohn's World Peace Through World Law, even proposed a criminal law enforcement model to enforce international rules, with the great powers of the United Nations acting jointly as the policemen of the world. Yet almost immediately, the intense bipolarity of the Cold War era rendered this positivistic vision a Potemkin Village. With respect especially to the use of force, the Cold War order soon resembled a "revolutionary system," one "wracked by inexpiable power rivalries and ideological conflicts ... in which international organization [was] reduced to impotence as a force of its own." The system remained dualistic, particularly in the United States, as international and domestic law continued as separated systems.

During these years, international law fell into tremendous public disrepute. Particularly in the United States, the positivistic, realist strand came to dominate thinking on the compliance issue. Meanwhile, the Kantian strand fell into particular disrepute, dismissed as a kind of utopian moralizing about world government, which, like the strategy of appeasement, played into the hands of the Communist bloc. One leading critic, George F. Kennan, memorably attacked "the legalistic-moralistic approach to international problems," that is, "the belief that it should be possible to suppress the chaotic and dangerous aspirations of governments in the international field by the acceptance of some system of legal rules and restraints," as an approach that "runs like a red skein through our foreign policy of the last fifty years."

Particularly in the United States, the realists' Cold War disdain for the utopianism of international law helped trigger the odd estrangement between the fields of international law and international relations. Although the two fields cover much of the same intellectual territory, they began to evolve independently, pursuing different analytic missions, and reaching different conclusions about the influence of law in international affairs. Over time, the fields came to adopt an unspoken division of labor regarding the intellectual projects that they would pursue. International relations scholars, suffused with realism, treated international law as naive and virtually beneath discussion. International lawyers, meanwhile, shifted their gaze toward modest tasks: description of international legal norms; application of these norms to particular cases; and occasional prescription of what the rule of law should be. Legal scholars therefore largely avoided the difficult tasks of causal explanation and prediction.

. . .

Within the American legal academy, a new defense of international law arose, based less on Kant or Grotius than on emerging American notions of legal process. This defense followed two distinct paths: the so-called Policy Science or New Haven School of International Law, pioneered at Yale by Myres McDougal, Harold Lasswell, and their associates, and a lawyering approach founded at Harvard, crystallized in the International Legal Process School of Abram Chayes, Thomas Ehrlich, and Andreas Lowenfeld. Both strands argued that transnational actors' compliance with transnational law could be explained by reference to the process by which these actors interact in a variety of public and private fora. Through this interactive process, they suggested, law helps translate claims of legal authority into national behavior.

The two schools of legal process theory grew from disparate roots. The New Haven School grew from the American theory of legal realism, which focused on the interplay between rules and social process in enunciating the law. The School sought to develop "a functional critique of international law in terms of social ends ... that shall conceive of the legal order as a process and not as a condition." "Within the decision-making process," McDougal and Lasswell wrote, "our chief interest is in the legal process, by which we mean the making of authoritative and controlling decisions." In its modern incarnation as the "World Public Order" school, New Haven School leaders Myres McDougal and W. Michael Reisman argued that international law is itself a "world constitutive process of authoritative decision," not merely a set of rules, whose goal is a world public order of human dignity, designed to serve particular ends and values by establishing regimes of effective control.

Almost contemporaneously, Chayes, Ehrlich, and Lowenfeld published a series of case studies entitled International Legal Process, which sought to illustrate the role of law in the process of policy decisions in the international realm. Unlike the New Haven School, which drew on Yale's domestic school of policy science, Chayes and his colleagues drew explicitly upon Henry Hart and Albert Sacks's famous unpublished domestic materials on The Legal Process. The Chayes materials deliberately "cut across the categories of international legal studies as they are sometimes conceived—'public international law,' 'international organizations,' 'legal problems of international business,' and the like." They asked explicitly: "How and how far do law, lawyers and legal institutions operate to affect the course of international affairs? What is the legal process by which interests are adjusted and decisions are reached on the international scene?"

. . .

Thus by the end of this era, the process tradition had diverged into two distinct streams: the International Legal Process School's focus on process as policy constraint versus the New Haven School's focus on process as policy justification. The New Haven School viewed international law as itself a decisionmaking process dedicated to a set of normative values, while the International Legal Process School saw international law as a set of rules promulgated by a pluralistic community of states, which creates the context that cabins a political decisionmaking process.

. . .

Interdependence and Transnationalism

By the 1970s and '80s, the legal landscape had altered significantly. The growth of international regimes and institutions, the proliferation of nonstate actors, and the increasing interpenetration of domestic and international systems inaugurated the era of "transnational relations," defined by one scholar as "regular interactions across national boundaries ari[sing] when at least one actor is a non-state agent or does not operate on behalf of a national government or an intergovernmental organization." Multinational enterprises, nongovernmental organizations, and private individuals reemerged as significant actors on the transnational stage. In particular, the oil crisis of the early 1970s highlighted the interdependence of politics and economics in the new transnational economy, and created the discipline of international political economy. Instead of focusing narrowly on nation-states as global actors, scholars began to look as well at transnational networks among nonstate actors, international institutions, and domestic political structures as important mediating forces in international society.

The question now forced upon international relations scholars was why, despite the bipolarity of the Cold War regime, had interstate cooperation persisted? These scholars could not ignore the remarkable growth of formal and informal, public and nonpublic regimes, which promoted the evolution of norms, rules, and decisionmaking procedures in such "transnational issue areas" as international human rights, arms control, international economic law, and international environmental law. In response, liberal institutionalists and international political economists developed "regime theory," the study of principles, norms, rules, and decisionmaking procedures that converge in given issue areas. In so doing, they shifted the focus of inquiry from the functioning of international organizations per se to the broader phenomenon of international cooperation, as exemplified by the regimes of "international peacekeeping" or "debt management" as they transpire both within and without institutional settings.

In one fell swoop, this analysis created new theoretical space for international law within international relations theory, as political scientists came to recognize that legal rules do, in fact, foster compliance with regime norms by providing channels for dispute-settlement, signaling and triggering retaliatory actions, and requiring states to furnish information regarding compliance. The major theoretical work on compliance in this era was done by political scientists Robert Keohane, Robert Axelrod, and Oran Young. But as [Abram Chayes and Antonia Handler Chayes] wryly note, what strikes an international lawyer reading this literature is the political scientists' persistent reluctance ever "to say the 'L-word,'" (law) even though "'principles, norms, rules and decisionmaking procedures' are what international law is all about." Moreover, regime theorists chose to explain cooperation almost entirely in rationalistic terms: They understood compliance with international law to result almost entirely from the functional benefits such compliance provides.

The rationalists dominated international relations theory in the 1980s with their functionalist analysis of why nations obey international law. Yet in the United States, the study of legal process continued to dominate the study of international law. Following the lead of Chayes, Ehrlich, and Lowenfeld, legal scholars began to eschew, as artificially constraining, the traditional public/private, domestic/international categories in favor of what Philip Jessup called "transnational law," defined to embrace "all law which regulates actions or events that transcend national frontiers" and including "[b]oth public and private international law . . . [plus] other rules which do not wholly fit into such standard categories."

. . .

After the Cold War: The New World Order

The end of the Cold War and the ensuing collapse of bipolarity initiated the era of global law in which we now live. In the heady days after the Berlin Wall fell, the future seemed unusually bright for the new "New World Order." Democracy was breaking out all over. Multilateralism and international law seemed resurgent with the United Nations's defeat of Saddam Hussein in Operation Desert Storm. The Soviet Union did a remarkable about-face, first embracing international law, then disintegrating, leaving the United States as "the world's indispensable nation." The conclusion of the Uruguay Round of the GATT, the North

American Free Trade Agreement (NAFTA), and the Maastricht Treaty all signalled new vitality for regional organization and trade liberalization.

But the euphoria faded, as reality dampened the possibilities for new global law. As Communism collapsed, states fragmented, triggering violent waves of ethnic nationalism and brutal war and genocide in the former Yugoslavia. Regional organizations like NAFTA and the European Union and global regimes of trade and the environment faced difficult challenges brought on by the global recession. The dissolution of failed states like Somalia, Rwanda, and Haiti triggered refugee outflows that challenged compassion and vexed policymakers.

The post-Cold War era has seen international law, transnational actors, decisional fora, and modes of regulation mutate into fascinating hybrid forms. International law now comprises a complex blend of customary, positive, declarative, and "soft" law, which seeks not simply to ratify existing practice, but to elevate it. As sovereignty has declined in importance, global decisionmaking functions are now executed by a complex rugby scrum of nation-states, intergovernmental organizations, regional compacts, nongovernmental organizations, and informal regimes and networks. The system has become "neomonistic," with new channels opening for the interpenetration of international and domestic law through judicial decision, legislation and executive action. New forms of dispute resolution, executive action, administrative decisionmaking and enforcement, and legislation have emerged as part of a transnational legal process that influences national conduct, transforms national interests, and helps constitute and reconstitute national identities.

In the last five years, these developments have returned the compliance question to center stage in the journals of international theory. A significant number of international relations scholars have tackled pieces of the problem, particularly in the environmental and arms control areas. International ethicists have continued to examine the question, usually from a Kantian/Rawlsian perspective. A small but increasing number of international law scholars have come to explore compliance issues from an interdisciplinary perspective. Among international law and relations scholars interested in norms, much of the recent talk has been of interdisciplinary collaboration, with some even suggesting an emerging "joint discipline" to examine the compliance question and related issues.

The compliance literature has followed three distinct explanatory pathways, each having origins in one of the historical roots of compliance theory. The first, not surprisingly, is a rationalistic instrumentalist strand that views international rules as instruments whereby states seek to attain their interests in wealth, power, and the like. International relations scholars such as Robert Keohane, Duncan Snidal, and Oran Young, and legal scholars such as Kenneth Abbott and John Setear, have applied increasingly sophisticated techniques of rational choice theory to argue that nation-states obey international law when it serves their short- or long-term self-interest to do so. Under this rationalistic account, pitched at the level of the international system, nations employ cooperative strategies to pursue a complex, multifaceted long-run national interest, in which compliance with negotiated legal norms serves as a winning long-term strategy in a reiterated "prisoner's dilemma" game. While hard-core rationalists tend generally to embrace some variant of Henkin's "cynic's formula," the more sophisticated instrumentalists are willing to disaggregate the state into its component parts, to introduce international institutions and transnational actors, to incorporate notions of long-term self-interest, and to consider the issue within the context of massively iterated multiparty games.

A second explanatory pathway follows a Kantian, liberal vein. The Kantian thread divides into two identifiable strands: one based on Franck's notion of rule-legitimacy, and another that makes more expansive claims for the causal role of national identity. "Liberal international relations" theorists, such as Andrew Moravcsik and Anne-Marie Slaughter, have argued that the determinative factor for whether nations obey can be found, not at a systemic level, but at the level of domestic structure. Under this view, compliance depends significantly on whether or not the state can be characterized as "liberal" in identity, that is, having a form of representative government, guarantees of civil and political rights, and a judicial system dedicated to the rule of law. Flipping the now-familiar Kantian maxim that "democracies don't fight one another," these theorists posit that liberal democracies are more likely to "do law" with one another, while relations between liberal and illiberal states will more likely transpire in a zone of politics.

The third strand is a "constructivist" strand, based broadly on notions of both identity-formation and international society. Unlike interest theorists, who tend to treat state interests as given, "constructivists" have long argued that states and their interests are socially constructed by "commonly held philosophic principles, identities, norms of behavior, or shared terms of discourse." Rather than arguing that state actors and interests create rules and norms, constructivists argue that "[r]ules and norms constitute the international game by determining who the actors are, what rules they must follow if they wish to ensure that particular consequences follow from specific acts, and how titles to possessions can be established and transferred." Thus constructivists see norms as playing a critical role in the formation of national identities.

The predominantly American constructivist school has close familial ties to the English "international society" school of Grotian heritage. Like the constructivists (and unlike sophisticated instrumentalists), the international society scholars see the norms, values, and social structure of international society as helping to form the identity of actors who operate within it. Nations thus obey international rules not just because of sophisticated calculations about how compliance or noncompliance will affect their interests, but because a repeated habit of obedience remakes their interests so that they come to value rule compliance. In Andrew Hurrell's words, "[a] good deal of the compliance pull of international rules derives from the relationship between individual rules and the broader pattern of international relations: states follow specific rules, even when inconvenient, because they have a longer-term interest in the maintenance of law-impregnated international community."

Notes and Comments

1. The first explicit proposal to reintegrate the study of international law and international relations can be traced to a foundational essay by Kenneth W. Abbott, *Modern International Relations Theory: A Prospectus for International Lawyers*, 14 Yale Journal of International Law 335 (1989). In arguing for greater interaction between the disciplines, Abbott began to sketch the form and function of a joint research program:

> The opportunity to integrate IL and IR stems ... from the analytical approaches, insights and techniques of modern IR theory, which can readily be applied to a variety of legal norms and institutions.... Consider the Limited Test Ban Treaty (LTBT) and the Nuclear Non-Proliferation Treaty (NPT), related sets of norms designed to restrict the development and spread of nuclear weapons. The traditional IL approach would focus on the lawfulness of state conduct under these conventional norms or under customary norms arguably derived from them. Modern IR theory would supplement that approach with a broader scholarly perspective based on a rational choice model of state interaction.
>
> First, an analyst using modern IR theory might inquire into the incentives that lead rational states to cooperate in the formation of regimes like the LTBT and NPT: what do states gain from such regimes that makes them willing to restrain the development of important weapons and the export of valuable technology? One might begin by examining the structure of the relationship between the United States and the Soviet Union, the prime movers behind both conventions; game models would be well suited to this task. In analyzing the widespread adoption of the LTBT and NPT, economic models might be more useful: both conventions can be interpreted as institutional arrangements designed to improve the outcome of unregulated market-like interactions.
>
> Second, one might extend this functional analysis to more detailed characteristics of the two regimes. One of the salient institutional features of the NPT, for example, is its reliance on the International Atomic Energy Agency (IAEA), particularly for the application of "safeguards" to peaceful uses of nuclear energy. Exactly what functions does the IAEA perform, and what arrangements, if any, take its place in the LTBT?
>
> Third, one might inquire into the conditions that favored U.S.-Soviet agreement and widespread participation in conventions gov-

> erning these two issue areas, when other bilateral and multilateral security regimes have been difficult to form. One might also pursue the negative of this inquiry: why have important near-nuclear states refused to ratify the NPT? Can any lessons be learned that would assist in designing regimes to restrict biological and chemical weapons, ballistic missiles, or battlefield nuclear weapons? Could conditions in those areas be modified by joint or unilateral action to make cooperation easier?
>
> Fourth, one might ask related questions about compliance, for both the Soviet Union and the United States have seemingly modified their conduct to conform with LTBT and NPT norms. What factors in these areas encourage compliance with international rules in the face of obvious short-run incentives to cheat? How do the LTBT and NPT regimes themselves encourage compliance?

Id. at 340–41. Notice that while Abbott urges a broad integration of international law and international relations scholarship, he views international relations theory as deriving primarily from a "rational choice" framework.

2. Progress in generating interdisciplinary dialogue between law and political science has been slow but steady on both sides since Abbott's essay. Witness the Summer 2000 issue of *International Organization*, the flagship publication of international relations scholarship, which was devoted to international relations approaches to international law, and the *American Journal of International Law*, which has devoted several articles to charting the burgeoning interdisciplinary scholarship, including an essay by Abbott. Kenneth W. Abbott, *International Relations Theory, International Law, and the Regime Governing Atrocities in Internal Conflicts*, 93 American Journal of International Law 361 (1999). For further commentary, see *The Role of Law in International Politics* (Michael Byers ed., 2000); and the American Society of International Law's 2002 annual conference, "The Legalization of International Relations/The Internationalization of Legal Relations." For a critique of the September 2000 issue of *International Organization*, see Martha Finnemore and Stephen J. Toope, *Alternatives to "Legalization": Richer Views of Law and Politics*, 55 International Organization 743 (2001).

3. Anne-Marie Slaughter, a political scientist and lawyer, has been at the forefront of efforts to integrate international law and international relations scholarship. Her work includes two articles (the second with co-authors Andrew Tulumello and Stepan Wood) that provide a comprehensive overview of the state of the process of integration. Anne-Marie Slaughter Burley, *International Law and International Relations Theory: A Dual Agenda*, 87 American Journal of International Law 205 (1993); Anne-Marie Slaughter et al., *International Law and International Relations Theory: A New Generation of Interdisciplinary Scholarship*, 92 American Journal of International Law 367 (1998). She offers a liberal perspective—which is outlined in more detail in Part II—as a response to the "Realist Challenge" to international law. As Slaughter puts it:

The discipline of international relations was born after World War I in a haze of aspirations for the future of world government. These were quickly dimmed by World War II. The fledgling discipline was thus weaned on Political Realism, articulated and systematized by scholars such as Hans Morgenthau, Georg Schwarzenberger, E.H. Carr and George Kennan. These seasoned observers of the interwar period reacted against Wilsonian liberal internationalism, which presumed that the combination of democracy and international organization could vanquish war and power politics. They believed instead in the polarity of law and power, opposing one to the other as the respective emblems of the domestic versus the international realm, normative aspiration versus positive description, cooperation versus conflict, soft versus hard, idealist versus realist. Regardless of their domestic colors, states in the international realm were champions only of their own national interest. "Law," as understood in the domestic sense, had no place in this world. The only relevant laws were the "laws of politics," and politics was "a struggle for power."

. . .

This, then, was the Realist challenge to international lawyers: a challenge to establish the "relevance" of international law. International legal theorists had long grappled with the theoretical conundrum of the sources of international legal obligation—of law being simultaneously "of" and "above" the state. Yet the endless debates on this question nevertheless assumed that international legal rules, however derived, had some effect on state behavior, that law and power interacted in some way, rather than marking opposite ends of the domestic-international spectrum. Political Realists, by contrast, gave no quarter. Their challenge struck at the heart of the discipline, claiming that international law was but a collection of evanescent maxims or a "repository of legal rationalizations."

The Realist challenge was not merely academic posturing. It was mounted by one of the major architects of postwar foreign policy and formulated in terms of policy prescriptions that ignored law and lawyers. The efforts to answer it shaped the evolution of postwar international legal scholarship.

Slaughter Burley, *supra*, at 207–08.[2]

4. The so-called "New Haven School" of Yale Law Professor Myres McDougal and his political science colleague Harold Laswell represents one of the early efforts in international law theory to integrate the disciplines of law and politics. As McDougal's and Laswell's collaborator and successor Michael Reisman, also of Yale Law School, wrote in his essay, *A Theory about Law from the Policy Perspective, in* LAW AND POLICY 75 (1976):

2. Reprinted by permission from 87 AMERICAN JOURNAL OF INTERNATIONAL LAW 205 (1993). © The American Society of International Law.

> In the desperate drive to develop an autonomous discipline or specialization, many theorists purport to find a distinction between law and politics. I do not find this distinction realistic, cogent, or useful. The contemporary lawyer, as I see him, is a specialist in advising, making or appraising social choices or decisions. He views both the regular flow of decisions or choices as well as the entire environment that he calls "legal" as a complex of policy choices, sustained by effective power in a community. To the affected human being or to the lawyers he engages in his interest, it makes little difference if a decision emanates from a "legal" or a "political" institution; the critical question is whether it meets his needs. Similarly, for the individual committed to world order it makes no difference if decisions flow from political or legal institutions. Here again the critical question is whether the decisions approximate and contribute to the needs of a world order meeting his value demands.

Id. at 75–76.

5. There is a significant body of scholarship that cuts across the divide outlined here between norm-based and interest-based approaches to international law. See, e.g., ALEC STONE SWEET, WAYNE SANDHOLTZ & NEIL FLIGSTEIN, THE INSTITUTIONALIZATION OF EUROPE, (2001). Moreover, the split between political science and law is not nearly as pronounced in the work of those commonly associated with the "English School" of international relations (also called the "international society tradition," the "Grotian tradition," or "British Realism"), which continues to hold sway among English scholars. The approach begins from a position close to American realism (which is covered in more depth in the next chapter). But unlike realism, it begins not with individual states but with international society. This leads scholars of the English school to take law much more seriously than do American realists. As a recent paper put it:

> The general stance of the school towards international law may be described as follows. International law is a real body of law, no less binding than domestic law, and therefore no less deserving of the name "law" than domestic law. Although the main bases of international order are to be found elsewhere, international law is certainly not without efficacy in this regard. Importantly, international law provides a normative framework, an essential ingredient for the successful operation of any large and complex social arrangement. By providing a reasonably clear guide as to what is the done thing and what is not in any given set of circumstances, of what can be expected and what not, and what will be tolerated and what will likely be met with a disapproving, perhaps vociferous, perhaps even violent, response, law helps to reduce the degree of unpredictability in international affairs. While lacking a central legislature to make new and modify existing law, international society nonetheless has its own mechanisms for changing the law and keeping it "up-to-date." . . . [I]t should be seen as a body of rules, deemed by those to whom it applies as binding, the purpose of which is to facilitate

regular, continuous, and generally orderly international relationships.

Peter Wilson, *The English School and the Sociology of International Law: Strengths and Limitations* (unpublished manuscript) (presented to the annual British International Studies Association conference, University of Birmingham, December 2003). Significantly, English scholars were less driven by Cold War politics than their American counterparts, and so, perhaps, less attracted by the adversarial image provided by realism. Important works in the English School tradition include HEDLEY BULL, THE ANARCHICAL SOCIETY: A STUDY OF ORDER IN WORLD POLITICS (1977); and C.A.W. MANNING, THE NATURE OF INTERNATIONAL SOCIETY (1962). Other useful sources include HEDLEY BULL ON INTERNATIONAL SOCIETY (Kai Alderson and Andrew Hurrell, eds. 2000); Stanley Hoffmann, *Hedley Bull and His Contribution to International Relations*, 62 INTERNATIONAL AFFAIRS 179 (1977); THE BASES OF INTERNATIONAL ORDER: ESSAYS IN HONOUR OF C. A. W. MANNING (Alan James, ed. 1973); and Barry Buzan, The English School: A Bibliography (unpublished manuscript) (March 2003), available at http://www.leeds.ac.uk/polis/englishschool/bibliomarch03.doc.

6. The aforementioned "English School," or "international society" approach traces its roots to the work of Dutch international lawyer Hugo Grotius—considered by many to be the father of international relations theory. For more detailed discussions on Grotian thought, see Hersch Lauterpacht, *The Grotian Tradition in International Law*, 23 BRITISH YEARBOOK OF INTERNATIONAL LAW (1946); Benedict Kingsbury and Adam Roberts, *Introduction: Grotian Thought in International Relations*, *in* HUGO GROTIUS AND INTERNATIONAL RELATIONS (Hedley Bull et al. eds, 1990). In his treatise on the law of war and peace, Grotius put forward a vision of international law—strongly influenced by the Spanish naturalists of the sixteenth and early seventeenth centuries—that draws no sharp distinction between international law and international relations theory. In his view, international law can only be law if it passes a moral test provided by nature. Witness this excerpt from Grotius's classic, *The Law of War and Peace*:

> Nothing is more common than the assertion of antagonism between law and arms.... Man is, to be sure, an animal.... But among the traits characteristic of man is an impelling desire for society ...; this social trend the Stoics called "sociableness." ... This maintenance of the social order, which ... is consonant with human intelligence, is the source of law properly so called....
>
> [T]here is no state so powerful that it may not some time need the help of others outside itself, either for purposes of trade, or even to ward off the forces of many foreign nations united against it. In consequence we see that even the most powerful peoples and sovereigns seek alliances....,
>
> Least of all should that be admitted which some people imagine, that in war all laws are in abeyance. On the contrary war ought not to be undertaken except for the enforcement of rights; when once

> undertaken, it should be carried on only within the bounds of law and good faith. . . .

HUGO GROTIUS, *Prolegomena to* THE LAW OF WAR AND PEACE ¶ ¶ 3, 6, 22, 25 (1925). Compare Grotius' words with these from the English international theorist Hedley Bull, in *The Anarchical Society:*

> *A society of states* (or international society) exists when a group of states, conscious of certain common interests and common values, form a society in the sense that they conceive themselves to be bound by a common set of rules in their relations with one another, and share in the working of common institutions. If states today form an international society . . . this is because, recognising certain common interests and perhaps some common values, they regard themselves as bound by certain rules in their dealings with one another, such as that they should respect one another's claims to independence, that they should honour agreements into which they enter, and that they should be subject to certain limitations in exercising force against one another. At the same time they cooperate in the working of institutions such as the forms of procedures of international law, the machinery of diplomacy and general international organisation, and the customs and conventions of war. . . .
>
> What has been called the Grotian or internationalist tradition stands between the realist tradition and the universalist tradition. The Grotian tradition describes international politics in terms of a society of states or international society. As against the Hobbesian tradition, the Grotians contend that states are not engaged in simple struggle, like gladiators in an arena, but are limited in their conflicts with one another by common rules and institutions. But as against the Kantian or universalist perspective the Grotians accept the Hobbesian premise that sovereigns or states are the principal reality in international politics; the immediate members of international society are states rather than individual human beings. International politics, in the Grotian understanding, expresses neither complete conflict of interest between states nor complete identity of interest; it resembles a game that is partly distributive but also partly productive. The particular international activity which, on the Grotian view, best typifies international activity as a whole is neither war between states, nor horizontal conflict cutting across the boundaries of states, but trade—or, more generally, economic and social intercourse between one country and another.
>
> The Grotian prescription for international conduct is that all states, in their dealings with one another, are bound by the rules and institutions of the society they form. As against the view of the Hobbesians, states in the Grotian view are bound not only by rules of prudence or expediency but also by imperatives of morality and law. But, as against the view of the universalists, what these imperatives enjoin is not the overthrow of the system of states and its replacement by a universal community of mankind, but rather

> acceptance of the requirements of coexistence and co-operation in a society of states.... [T]he Grotian idea of international society has always been present in thought about the states system....

HEDLEY BULL, THE ANARCHIAL SOCIETY: THE STUDY OF ORDER IN WORLD POLITICS 13, 25–26 (2d ed. 1995). As you read the chapters that follow, notice the similarities between the "international society" or "Grotian" approach and the modern international relations school of "constructivism."

7. For a thoughtful overview of international law and political science scholarship that identifies a divide between "instrumentalist" and "normative" optics see Robert O. Keohane, *International Relations and International Relations and International Law: Two Optics*, 38 HARVARD INTERNATIONAL LAW JOURNAL 487 (1997). See also James G. March & Johan P. Olsen, Rediscovering Institutions: The Organizational Basis of Politics 160–62 (1989) (using the terms "logic of consequences" and "logic of appropriateness" to describe two forms of reasoning drawn from cognitive psychology); Oona A. Hathaway, *Do Human Rights Treaties Make a Difference?*, 111 YALE LAW JOURNAL 1935, 1942–1962 (2002). For an accessible review of the primary theoretical traditions in the study of international relations, see Stephen Walt, *International Relations: One World, Many Theories*, 110 FOREIGN POLICY 29 (1998). Finally, for a recent work that offers a theory of international law that draws on insights gained from the international law and international relations literature, see Oona A. Hathaway, *Between Power and Principle: A Political Theory of International Law,* 71 UNIVERSITY OF CHICAGO LAW REVIEW (forthcoming May 2005).

II

Interest-Based Theories of State Behavior[1]

"Interest-based" theories have at their heart a shared belief that states and the individuals that guide them are rational self-interested actors that calculate the costs and benefits of alternative courses of action in the international realm and act accordingly. In this view, international law does not hold a privileged position. It is only one of a series of tools available to the relevant actors in their ongoing battle to achieve their self-interested ends. Compliance with international law does not occur unless it furthers the self-interest of the parties by, for example, improving their reputation, enhancing their geopolitical power, furthering their ideological ends, avoiding conflict, or avoiding sanction by a more powerful state.

The three variants of the interest-based model outlined in this book differ primarily in the types and sources of interests that they claim motivate country decisions. In the *realist* view, states are viewed as unified principal actors that are motivated first and foremost by a desire for power. In the realist framework, international law exists and is complied with only when it is in the interests of the most powerful states, which then coerce less powerful states into accepting the law and complying with it. The *institutionalist* model shares with realism the assumption that states act as unified principal actors in pursuit of self-interest. It departs from realism, however, by viewing system-wide

1. Portions of the text of this introduction and others in this book include material adapted from Oona A. Hathaway's article, *Do Human Rights Treaties Make a Difference?* They are reprinted by permission of The Yale Law Journal Company and William S. Hein Company from YALE LAW JOURNAL, 1935–2041 (2002).

institutions—including legal institutions—as having the potential to influence state behavior. In this perspective, international law can make it possible for countries to achieve long-term goals by restraining short-term power maximization. Finally, *liberal* theory also argues that states pursue their own self-interest, but differs from realism and institutionalism in that it looks within states to find the domestic sources of that self-interest. Liberal theorists argue that societal ideas, interests, and institutions shape state preferences and thereby influence state behavior. They claim that it is not possible to understand state decisions without understanding the domestic politics that drive them.

A. Realism

In the wake of the Second World War, Political Realism came to the fore as the principal tradition for the analysis of international relations. Reacting in part to what they regarded as the failed idealism of the interwar period, realist scholars sought to explain international politics as it really is, rather than how it ought to be. These scholars argued that the international system is anarchic—that it lacks any central authority that governs state relations—and hence they focused their attention primarily on states as the central actors in international politics. In their view, states are rational unitary actors who, in Kenneth Waltz's now famous words, "at a minimum, seek their own preservation and, at a maximum, drive for universal domination." The central conclusion of these theories—what some have called the realist *problematique*—is that the existence of several states in an anarchical system renders each state's security uncertain, leading states to compete with each other for power and security.

The classical realist tradition can be traced back centuries to the works of Thucydides, Niccolo Machiavelli, and Thomas Hobbes, among others. Yet the advent in America of what is often referred to as "classical realist theory" traces to more recent sources: E.H. Carr's classic attack on "utopian" theory on the eve of the Second World War, *The Twenty Years' Crisis*, and the subsequent publication of Hans J. Morgenthau's immensely influential *Politics Among Nations* in 1948. Utopians, Carr argued, are inclined "to ignore what was and what is in contemplation of what should be."[2] Realists, by contrast, are inclined "to deduce what should be from what was and what is."[3] In the wake of the Second World War, which many felt had demonstrated the failure of Wilsonian idealism, the realist approach took hold in foreign policy circles and continued to guide American policymakers (particularly diplomats George Kennan and Henry Kissinger) for decades.

Even in its early years, the approach was not without its detractors. The realist approach came under heavy attack almost immediately for providing an insufficiently nuanced (and, some argue, wholly inaccurate) account of state behavior. Contemporary realist theory, sometimes called

2. E.H. Carr, The Twenty Years' Crisis 12 (2001) (1939).

3. *Id.*

"neorealist theory," provides a response to some of these complaints. In his reconceptualization of realist theory in *Theory of International Politics*, excerpted below, Kenneth Waltz gives a more rigorous and systematic approach to political realism that is heavily influenced in particular by neoclassical microeconomic theory. The approach differs from those that come before it in its emphasis on the *structure* of the international system as an independent force. Moreover, this neorealist view relaxes assumptions about the ends that states pursue and the means they use to pursue them, acknowledging that states may seek a broader set of interests than classical theory indicates and recognizing that states might sometimes make strategic decisions to engage in international cooperation. This revision of realist theory was itself far from impervious to attack, as we shall see. Nonetheless, it remains for many the starting point for any effort to understand relations between and among states.

The Twenty Years' Crisis*

E.H. CARR

The foundations of realism

[R]ealism enters the field far behind utopianism and by way of reaction from it. The thesis that "justice is the right of the stranger" was, indeed, familiar in the Hellenic world, but it never represented anything more than the protest of an uninfluential minority, puzzled by the divergence between political theory and political practice. Under the supremacy of the Roman Empire, and later of the Catholic Church, the problem could be regarded as identical with moral good. It was only with the break-up of the mediaeval system that the divergence between political theory and political practice became acute and challenging. Machiavelli is the first important political realist.

Machiavelli's starting point is a revolt against the utopianism of current political thought:

> It being my intention to write a thing which shall be useful to him who apprehends it, it appears to me more appropriate to follow up the real truth of a matter than the imagination of it; for many have pictured republics and principalities which in fact have never been seen and known, because how one lives is so far distant from how one ought to live that he who neglects what is done for what ought to be done sooner effects his ruin than his preservation.

The three essential tenets implicit in Machiavelli's doctrine are the foundation-stones of the realist philosophy. In the first place, history is a sequence of cause and effect, whose course can be analysed and understood by intellectual effort, but not (as the utopians believe) directed by "imagination." Secondly, theory does not (as the utopians assume) create practice, but practice theory. In Machiavelli's words, "good counsels, whencesoever they come, are born of the wisdom of the prince, and

* Reprinted by permission from E.H. Carr, The Twenty Years' Crisis (2001) (1939).

not the wisdom of the prince from good counsels." Thirdly, politics are not (as the utopians pretend) a function of ethics, but ethics of politics. Men "are kept honest by constraint." Machiavelli recognized the importance of morality, but thought that there could be no effective morality where there was no effective authority. Morality is the product of power.

. . .

The relativity of thought

The outstanding achievement of modern realism, however, has been to reveal, not merely the determinist aspects of the historical process, but the relative and pragmatic character of thought itself. In the last fifty years, thanks mainly though not wholly to the influence of Marx, the principles of the historical school have been applied to the analysis of thought; and the foundations of a new science have been laid, principally by German thinkers, under the name of the "sociology of knowledge." The realist has thus been enabled to demonstrate that the intellectual theories and ethical standards of utopianism, far from being the expression of absolute and *a priori* principles, are historically conditioned, being both products of circumstances and interests and weapons framed for the furtherance of interests. "Ethical notions," as Mr. Bertrand Russell has remarked, "are very seldom a cause, but almost always an effect, a means of claiming universal legislative authority for our own preference, not, as we fondly imagine, the actual ground of those preferences." This is by far the most formidable attack which utopianism has to face; for here the very foundations of its belief are undermined by the realist critique.

. . .

National interest and the universal good

. . .

It will not be difficult to show that the utopian, when he preaches the doctrine of the harmony of interests, is innocently and unconsciously adopting Walewski's maxim,[4] and clothing his own interest in the guise of a universal interest for the purpose of imposing it on the rest of the world. "Men come easily to believe that the arrangements agreeable to themselves are beneficial to others," as Dicey observed; and theories of the public good, which turn out on inspection to be an elegant disguise for some particular interest, are as common in international as in national affairs. The utopian, however eager he may be to establish an absolute standard, does not argue that it is the duty of his country, in conformity with that standard, to put the interest of the world at large before its own interest; for that would be contrary to his theory that the interest of all coincides with the interest of each. He argues that what is

4. [Editors' note: Carr notes earlier in the book, "Bismarck records the remark made to him by Walewski, the French Foreign Minister, in 1857, that it was the business of a diplomat to cloak the interests of his country in the language of universal justice." CARR at 69.]

best for the world is best for his country, and then reverses the argument to read that what is best for his country is best for the world, the two propositions being, from the utopian standpoint, identical.... British writers of the past half-century have been particularly eloquent supporters of the theory that the maintenance of British supremacy is the performance of a duty to mankind. "If Great Britain has turned itself into a coal-shed and blacksmith's forge," remarked The Times ingenuously in 1885, "it is for the behoof of mankind as well as its own." ...

The first world war carried this conviction to a pitch of emotional frenzy. A bare catalogue, culled from the speeches of British statesmen, of the services which British belligerency was rendering to humanity would fill many pages. In 1917, Balfour told the New York Chamber of Commerce that "since August 1914, the fight has been for the highest spiritual advantages of mankind, without a petty thought or ambition." The Peace Conference and its sequel temporarily discredited these professions and threw some passing doubt on the belief on British supremacy as one of the moral assets of mankind. But the disillusionment and modesty was short. Moments of international tension, and especially moments when the possibility of war appears on the horizon, always stimulate this identification of national interest with morality....

In recent times, the same phenomenon has become endemic in the United States. The story of how McKinley prayed for divine guidance and decided to annex the Phillipines is a classic of modern American history; and this annexation was the occasion of a popular outburst of moral self-approval hitherto more familiar in the foreign policy of Great Britain than of the United States. Theodore Roosevelt, who believed more firmly than any previous American President in the doctrine of *L'etat, c'est moi*, carried the process a step further. The following curious dialogue occurred in his cross-examination during a libel action brought against him in 1915 by a Tammany leader:

> Query: How did you know that substantial justice was done?
>
> Roosevelt: Because I did it, because ... I was doing my best.
>
> Query: You mean to say that, when you do a thing, thereby substantial justice is done.
>
> Roosevelt: I do. When I do a thing, I do it so as to do substantial justice. I mean just that.

Woodrow Wilson was less naively egotistical, but more profoundly confident of the identity of American policy and universal justice. After the bombardment of Vera Cruz in 1914, he assured the world that "the United States had gone down to Mexico to serve mankind." During the first world war, he advised American naval cadets "not only always to think first of America, but always, also, to think first of humanity"—a feat rendered slightly less difficult by his explanation that the United States had been "founded for the benefit of humanity." Shortly before the entry of the United States into the war, in an address to the Senate on war aims, he stated the identification still more categorically: "These are American principles, American policies.... They are the principles of mankind and must prevail."

. . .

The realist critique of internationalism

. . .

The exposure of the real basis of the professedly abstract principles commonly invoked in international politics is the most damning and most convincing part of the realist indictment of utopianism. The nature of the charge is frequently misunderstood by those who seek to refute it. The charge is not that human beings fail to live up to their principles.... What matters is that these supposedly absolute and universal principles were not principles at all, but the unconscious reflexions of national policy based on a particular interpretation of national interest at a particular time. There is a sense in which peace and co-operation between nations or classes or individuals is a common and universal end irrespective of conflicting interests and politics. There is a sense in which a common interest exists in the maintenance of order, whether it be international order or "law and order" within the nation. But as soon as the attempt is made to apply these supposedly abstract principles to a concrete political situation, they are revealed as the transparent disguises of selfish vested interests. The bankruptcy of utopianism resides not in its failure to live up to its principles, but in the exposure of its inability to provide any absolute and disinterested standard for the conduct of international affairs. The utopian, faced by the collapse of standards whose interested character he has failed to penetrate, takes refuge in condemnation of a reality which refuses to conform to these standards....

Politics Among Nations*

H.J. MORGENTHAU

A Realist Theory of International Politics

The main signpost that helps political realism find its way through the landscape of international politics is the concept of interest defined in terms of power. This concept provides the link between reason trying to understand international politics and the facts to be understood. It sets politics as an autonomous sphere of action and understanding apart from other spheres, such as economics (understood in terms of interest defined as wealth), ethics, aesthetics, or religion. Without such a concept a theory of politics, international or domestic, would be altogether impossible, for without it we could not distinguish between political and

* Reprinted by permission from H.J. MORGENTHAU, POLITICS AMONG NATIONS (6th ed. 1985) (revised by Kenneth W. Thompson).

nonpolitical facts, nor could we bring at least a measure of systematic order to the political sphere.

We assume that statesmen think and act in terms of interest defined as power, and the evidence of history bears that assumption out. That assumption allows us to retrace and anticipate, as it were, the steps a statesman—past, present, or future—has taken or will take on the political scene. We look over his shoulder when he writes his dispatches; we listen in on his conversation with other statesmen; we read and anticipate his very thoughts. Thinking in terms of interest defined as power, we think as he does, and as disinterested observers we understand his thoughts and actions perhaps better than he, the actor on the political scene, does himself.

The concept of interest defined as power imposes intellectual discipline upon the observer, infuses rational order onto the subject matter of politics, and thus makes the theoretical understanding of politics possible. On the side of the actor, it provides for rational discipline in action and creates that astounding continuity in foreign policy which makes American, British, or Russian foreign policy appear as in intelligible, rational continuum, by and large consistent with itself, regardless of the different motives, preferences, and intellectual and moral qualities of successive statesmen. A realist theory of international politics, then, will guard against two popular fallacies: the concern with motives and the concern with ideological preferences.

. . .

What is Political Power?

As Means to the Nation's Ends

International politics, like all politics, is a struggle for power. Whatever the ultimate aims of international politics, power is always the immediate aim. Statesmen and peoples may ultimately seek freedom, security, prosperity, or power itself. They may define their goals in terms of a religious, philosophic, economic, or social ideal. They may hope that this ideal will materialize through its own inner force, through divine intervention, or through the natural development of human affairs. They may also try to further its realization through nonpolitical means, such as technical co-operation with other nations or international organizations. But whenever they strive to realize their goal by means of international politics, they do so by striving for power. The Crusaders wanted to free the holy places from domination by the infidels; Woodrow Wilson wanted to make the world safe for democracy; the Nazis wanted to open Eastern Europe to German colonization, to dominate Europe, and to conquer the world. Since they all chose power to achieve these ends, they were actors on the scene of international politics.

Two conclusions follow from this concept of international politics. First, not every action that a nation performs with respect to another nation is of a political nature. Many such activities are normally undertaken without any consideration of power, nor do they normally affect the power of the nation undertaking them. Many legal, economic, humanitarian, and cultural activities are of this kind. Thus a nation is not normally engaged in international politics when it concludes an extradition treaty with another nation, when it exchanges goods and services with other nations, when it co-operates with other nations in providing relief from natural catastrophes, and when it promotes the distribution of cultural achievements throughout the world. In other words, the involvement of a nation in international politics is but one among many types of activities in which a nation can participate on the international scene.

Second, not all nations are at all times to the same extent involved in international politics. The degree of their involvement may run all the way from the maximum at present attained by the United States and the Soviet Union, through the minimum involvement of such countries as Switzerland, Luxembourg, or Venezuela, to the complete noninvolvement of Liechtenstein and Monaco. Similar extremes can be noticed in the history of particular countries. Spain in the sixteenth and seventeenth centuries was one of the main active participants in the struggle for power on the international scene, but plays today only a marginal role in it. The same is true of such countries as Austria, Sweden, and Switzerland. On the other hand, nations like the United States, the Soviet Union, and China are today much more deeply involved in international politics than they were fifty or even twenty years ago. In short, the relation of nations to international politics has a dynamic quality. It changes with the vicissitudes of power, which may push a nation into the forefront of the power struggle, or may deprive a nation of the ability to participate actively in it. It may also change under the impact of cultural transformations, which may make a nation prefer other pursuits, for instance commerce, to those of power. . . .

The Depreciation of Political Power

The aspiration for power being the distinguishing element of international politics, as of all politics, international politics is of necessity power politics. While this fact is generally recognized in the practice of international affairs, it is frequently denied in the pronouncements of scholars, publicists, and even statesmen. Since the end of the Napoleonic Wars, ever larger groups in the Western world have been persuaded that the struggle for power on the international scene is a temporary phenomenon, a historical accident that is bound to disappear once the peculiar historic conditions that have given rise to it have been eliminated. Thus Jeremy Bentham believed that the competition for colonies was at the root of all international conflicts. "Emancipate your colonies!" was his advice to the governments, and international conflict and war would of necessity disappear. Adherents of free trade, such as Cobden and Proudhon, were convinced that the removal of trade barriers was the only condition for the establishment of permanent harmony among nations, and might even lead to the disappearance of international politics altogether. "At some future election," said Cobden, "we may probably see the test 'no foreign politics' applied to those who offer to become the representatives of free constituencies." For Marx and his followers, capitalism is at the root of international discord and war. They maintain that international socialism will do away with the struggle for power on the international scene and will bring about permanent peace. During the nineteenth century, liberals everywhere shared the conviction that power politics and war were residues of an obsolete system of government, and that the victory of democracy and constitutional government over absolutism and autocracy would assure the victory of international harmony and permanent peace over power politics and war. Of this liberal school of thought, Woodrow Wilson was the most eloquent and most influential spokesman.

In recent times, the conviction that the struggle for power can be eliminated from the international scene has been connected with the great attempts at organizing the world, such as the League of Nations and the United Nations. Thus Cordell Hull, then U.S. Secretary of State, declared in 1943 on his return from the Moscow Conference, which laid the groundwork for the United Nations, that the new international organization would mean the end of power politics and usher in a new era of international collaboration. Mr. Philip Noel–Baker, then British Minister of State, declared in 1946 in the House of Commons that the British government was "determined to use the institutions of the United Nations to kill power politics, in order that, by the methods of democracy, the will of the people shall prevail."

[I]t is sufficient to state that the struggle for power is universal in time and space and is an undeniable fact of experience. It cannot be denied that throughout historic time, regardless of social, economic, and political conditions, states have met each other in contests for power. Even though anthropologists have shown that certain primitive peoples seem to be free from the desire for power, nobody has yet shown how their state of mind and the conditions under which they live can be recreated on a worldwide scale so as to eliminate the struggle for power from the international scene. It would be useless and even self-destructive to free one or the other of the peoples of the earth from the desire for power while leaving it extant in others. If the desire for power cannot be abolished everywhere in the world, those who might be cured would simply fall victims to the power of others.

The position taken here might be criticized on the ground that conclusions drawn from the past are unconvincing, and that to draw such conclusions has always been the main stock in trade of the enemies of progress and reform. Though it is true that certain social arrangements and institutions have always existed in the past, it does not necessarily follow that they must always exist in the future. The situation is, however, different when we deal not with social arrangements and institutions created by man, but with those elemental bio-psychological drives by which in turn society is created. The drives to live, to propagate, and to dominate are common to all men. Their relative strength is dependent upon social conditions that may favor one drive and tend to repress another, or that may withhold social approval from certain manifestations of these drives while they encourage others. Thus, to take examples only from the sphere of power, most societies condemn killing as a means of attaining power within society, but all societies encourage the killing of enemies in that struggle for power which is called war. Dictators look askance at the aspirations for political power among their fellow citizens, but democracies consider active participation in the competition for political power a civic duty. Where a monopolistic organization of economic activities exists, competition for economic power is absent, and in competitive economic systems certain manifestations of the struggle for economic power are outlawed, while others are encouraged. Ostrogorsky, invoking the authority of Tocqueville, states that "the passions of the American people are not of a political, but of a commercial, nature. In that world awaiting cultivation, the love of power aims less at men than at things."

Regardless of particular social conditions, the decisive argument against the opinion that the struggle for power on the international scene is a mere historic accident must be derived from the nature of domestic politics. The essence of international politics is identical with its domestic counterpart. Both domestic and international politics are a struggle for power, modified only by the different conditions under which this struggle takes place in the domestic and in the international spheres.

The tendency to dominate, in particular, is an element of all human associations, from the family through fraternal and professional associations and local political organizations, to the state. On the family level, the typical conflict between the mother-in-law and her child's spouse is in its essence a struggle for power, the defense of an established power position against the attempt to establish a new one. As such it foreshadows the conflict on the international scene between the policies of the status quo and the policies of imperialism. Social clubs, fraternities, faculties, and business organizations are scenes of continuous struggles for power between groups that either want to keep what power they already have or seek to attain greater power. Competitive contests between business enterprises as well as labor disputes between employers and employees are frequently fought not only, and sometimes not even primarily, for economic advantages, but for control over each other and over others; that is, for power. Finally, the whole political life of a nation, particularly of a democratic nation, from the local to the national level, is a continuous struggle for power. In periodic elections, in voting in legislative assemblies, in lawsuits before courts, in administrative decisions and executive measures—in all these activities men try to maintain or to establish their power over other men. The processes by which legislative, judicial, executive, and administrative decisions are reached are subject to pressures and counterpressures by "pressure groups" trying to defend and expand their positions of power....

. . .

The Struggle for Power: Policy of the Status Quo

Domestic and international politics are but two different manifestations of the same phenomenon: the struggle for power. Its manifestations differ in the two different spheres because different moral, political, and social conditions prevail in each. Western national societies show a much greater degree of social cohesion within themselves than among themselves. Cultural uniformity, technological unification, external pressure, and, above all, a hierarchic political organization combine to make the national society an integrated whole set apart from other national societies. In consequence, the domestic political order is, for instance, more stable and less subject to violent change than is the international order.

All history shows that nations active in international politics are continuously preparing for, actively involved in, or recovering from organized violence in the form of war. In the domestic politics of Western democracies, on the other hand, organized violence as an instrument of political action on an extensive scale has become a rare exception. Yet as a potentiality it exists here, too, and at times the fear of it in the form of revolution has exerted an important influence upon political thought and action. The difference between domestic and international politics in this respect is one of degree and not of kind.

All politics, domestic and international, reveals three basic patterns; that is, all political phenomena can be reduced to one of three basic types. A political policy seeks either to keep power, to increase power, or to demonstrate power.

To these three typical patterns of politics, three typical international policies correspond. A nation whose foreign policy tends toward keeping power and not toward changing the distribution of power in its favor pursues a policy of the status quo. A nation whose foreign policy aims at acquiring more power than it actually has, through a reversal of existing power relations—whose foreign policy, in other words, seeks a favorable change in power status—pursues a policy of imperialism. A nation whose foreign policy seeks to demonstrate the power it has, either for the purpose of maintaining or increasing it, pursues a policy of prestige. It should be noted that these formulations are of a provisional nature and are subject to further refinement.

The concept "status quo" is derived from *status quo ante bellum*, a diplomatic term referring to the usual clauses in peace treaties which provide for the evacuation of territory by enemy troops and its restoration to the prewar sovereignty. Thus the peace treaties with Italy and Bulgaria terminating the Second World War provide that "all armed forces of the Allied and Associated Powers shall be withdrawn" from the territory of the particular nation "as soon as possible and in any case not later than ninety days from the coming into force of the present Treaty." That is, within this time limit the *status quo ante bellum* shall be reestablished with regard to this territory.

The policy of the status quo aims at the maintenance of the distribution of power which exists at a particular moment in history. One might say that the policy of the status quo fulfills the same function for international politics that a conservative policy performs for domestic affairs. The particular moment in history which serves as point of reference for a policy of the status quo is frequently the end of a war, when the distribution of power has been codified in a treaty of peace. This is so because the main purpose of peace treaties is to formulate in legal terms the shift in power which victory and defeat in the preceding war have brought about, and to insure the stability of the new distribution of power by means of legal stipulations. Thus it is typical for a status quo policy to appear as defense of the peace settlement that terminated the last general war. The European governments and political parties that pursued a policy of the status quo from 1815 to 1848 did so in defense of the peace settlement of 1815, which terminated the Napoleonic Wars. The main purpose of the Holy Alliance, which these governments concluded in 1815, was the maintenance of the status quo as it existed at the conclusion of the Napoleonic Wars. In consequence it functioned mainly as a guarantor of the peace treaty, that is, the Treaty of Paris of 1815.

In this respect, the relation between the policy in defense of the status quo of 1815, the Treaty of Paris, and the Holy Alliance is similar to the relation between the policy in favor of the status quo of 1918, the peace treaties of 1919, and the League of Nations. The distribution of power as it existed at the end of the First World War found its legal expression in the peace treaties of 1919. It became the main purpose of the League of Nations to maintain peace by preserving the status quo of 1918 as it had been formulated in the peace treaties of 1919. Article 10 of the Covenant of the League, obligating its members "to respect and preserve as against external aggression the territorial integrity and existing political independence of all members of the League," recognized as one of the purposes of the League the maintenance of the territorial status quo as established by the peace treaties of 1919. Consequently, in the period between the two world wars the struggle for and against the status quo was in the main fought either by defending or opposing the territorial provisions of the Treaty of Versailles and their guarantee in Article 10 of the Covenant of the League. It was, therefore, only consistent from their point of view that the nations chiefly opposed to the status quo established in 1919 should sever their connections with the League of Nations—Japan in 1932, Germany in 1933, Italy in 1937. . . .

The manifestation of the policy of the status quo which has had the greatest importance for the United States and has been the cornerstone of its foreign relations is the Monroe Doctrine. A unilateral declaration made by President Monroe in his annual message to Congress on December 2, 1823, the Doctrine lays down the two essential principles of any status quo policy. On the one hand, it stipulates respect on the part of the United States for the existing distribution of power in the Western

Hemisphere: "With the existing colonies or dependencies of any European power we have not interfered and shall not interfere." On the other hand, it proclaims resistance on the part of the United States to any change of the existing distribution of power by any non-American nation: "But with the governments who have declared their independence, and maintain it ... we could not view any interposition for the purpose of oppressing them, or controlling in any other manner their destiny, by any European power, in any other light than as the manifestation of an unfriendly disposition towards the United States." As President Franklin D. Roosevelt expressed it in an address before the Governing Body of the Pan–American Union on April 12, 1933: "it [the Monroe Doctrine] was aimed and is aimed against the acquisition in any manner of the control of additional territory in this hemisphere by any non-American power."

We have said that the policy of the status quo aims at the maintenance of the distribution of power as it exists at a particular moment in history. This does not mean that the policy of the status quo is necessarily opposed to any change whatsoever. While it is not opposed to change as such, it is opposed to any change that would amount to a reversal of the power relations among two or more nations, reducing, for instance, A from a first-rate to a second-rate power and raising B to the eminent position A formerly held. Minor adjustments in the distribution of power, however, which leave intact the relative power positions of the nations concerned, are fully compatible with a policy of the status quo. For instance, the purchase of the territory of Alaska by the United States in 1867 did not then affect the status quo between the United States and Russia, since, in view of the technology of communications and warfare at the time, the acquisition by the United States of this then inaccessible territory did not affect to any appreciable extent the distribution of power between the United States and Russia.

Similarly, by acquiring the Virgin Islands from Denmark in 1917, the United States did not embark upon a policy aiming at a change of the status quo with regard to the Central American republics. While the acquisition of the Virgin Islands greatly improved the strategic position of the United States in so far as the defense of the approaches to the Panama Canal was concerned, it did not change the relative power positions of the United States and the Central American republics. The acquisition of the Virgin Islands may have strengthened the already dominant position of the United States in the Caribbean, yet it did not create it and, therefore, was compatible with a policy of the status quo. One might even say that, by strengthening the preponderance of the United States over the Central American republics, it actually reinforced the existing distribution of power and thus served the purposes of a policy of the status quo....

...

The Main Problems of International Law

The General Nature of International Law

. . .

[D]uring the four hundred years of its existence international law has in most instances been scrupulously observed. When one of its rules was violated, it was, however, not always enforced and, when action to enforce it was actually taken, it was not always effective. Yet to deny that international law exists at all as a system of binding legal rules flies in the face of all the evidence. This misconception as to the existence of international law is at least in part the result of the disproportionate attention that public opinion has paid in recent times to a small fraction of international law, while neglecting the main body of it. Public opinion has been concerned mainly with such spectacular instruments of international law as the Briand–Kellogg Pact, the Covenant of the League of Nations, and the Charter of the United Nations. These instruments are indeed of doubtful efficacy (that is, they are frequently violated), and sometimes even of doubtful validity (that is, they are often not enforced in case of violation). They are, however, not typical of the traditional rules of international law concerning, for instance, the limits of territorial jurisdiction, the rights of vessels in foreign waters, and the status of diplomatic representatives.

To recognize that international law exists is, however, not tantamount to asserting that it is as effective a legal system as the national legal systems are and that, more particularly, it is effective in regulating and restraining the struggle for power on the international scene. International law is a primitive type of law resembling the kind of law that prevails in certain preliterate societies, such as the Australian aborigines and the Yurok of northern California. It is a primitive type of law primarily because it is almost completely decentralized law.

The decentralized nature of international law is the inevitable result of the decentralized structure of international society. Domestic law can be imposed by the group that holds the monopoly of organized force; that is, the officials of the state. It is an essential characteristic of international society, composed of sovereign states, which by definition are the supreme legal authorities within their respective territories, that no such central lawgiving and law-enforcing authority can exist there. International law owes its existence and operation to two factors, both decentralized in character: identical or complementary interests of individual states and the distribution of power among them. Where there is neither community of interest nor balance of power, there is no international law. Whereas domestic law may originate in, and be enforced by, the arbitrary will of the agencies of the state, international law is overwhelmingly the result of objective social forces.

That the balance of power is such a social force was recognized by one of the foremost modern teachers of international law. L. Oppenheim calls the balance of power "an indispensable condition of the very existence of International Law." . . . :

> [A] Law of Nations can exist only if there be an equilibrium, a balance of power, between the members of the Family of Nations. If the Powers cannot keep one another in check, no rules of law will

> have any force, since an overpowerful State will naturally try to act according to discretion and disobey the law. As there is not and never can be a central political authority above the Sovereign States that could enforce the rules of the Law of Nations, a balance of power must prevent any member of the Family of Nations from becoming omnipotent.

The balance of power operates as a decentralizing force only in the form of a general deterrent against violations of international law and in the exceptional cases when a violation of international law calls for a law enforcement action. On the other hand, identical and complementary interests as decentralizing agents are continuously at work; they are the very lifeblood of international law. They exert their decentralizing influence upon three basic functions that any legal system must fulfill: legislation, adjudication, and enforcement.

The Legislative Function of International Law

Its Decentralized Character

In our contemporary domestic societies, the most important rules of law are created by legislators and courts; that is to say, by centralized agencies that create law either for all members of the national community, as do Congress and the Supreme Court of the United States, or for certain regional groups, as do state legislatures, city councils, and regional and local courts. In the international sphere there are but two forces creating law: necessity and mutual consent. International law contains a small number of rules concerning, for instances, the limits of national sovereignty, the interpretation of its own rules, and the like, which are binding upon individual states regardless of their consent; for without these rules there could be no legal order at all or at least no legal order regulating a multiple-state system. Aside from this small number of rules of what one might call common or necessary international law, the main bulk of rules of international law owe their existence to the mutual consent of the individual subjects of international law themselves—the individual nations. Each nation is only bound by those rules of international law to which it has consented. . . .

The Enforcement of International Law

Its Decentralized Character

. . . When individual A violates the rights of individual B within the national community, the law-enforcement agencies of this state will intervene and protect B against A and compel A to give B satisfaction according to the law. Nothing of the kind exists in the international sphere. If State A violates the rights of State B, no enforcement agency will come to the support of B. B has the right to help itself if it can; that is to say, if it is strong enough in comparison with A to meet the infringement of its rights with enforcement actions of its own. Only under very exceptional and narrow conditions, in the forms of self-help and self-defense, does domestic law give the victim of a violation of the law the right to take the law into his own hands and enforce it against the violator. What is a narrowly circumscribed exception in domestic law is the principle of law enforcement in international law. According to this principle, the victim, and nobody but the victim, of a violation of the law has the right to enforce the law against the violator. Nobody at all has the obligation to enforce it.

There can be no more primitive and no weaker system of law enforcement than this; for it delivers the enforcement of the law to the vicissitudes of the distribution of power between the violator of the law and the victim of the violation. It makes it easy for the strong both to violate the law and to enforce it, and consequently puts the rights of the weak in jeopardy. A great power can violate the rights of a small nation without having to fear effective sanctions on the latter's part. It can afford to proceed against the small nation with measures of enforcement under the pretext of a violation of its rights, regardless of whether the alleged infraction of international law has actually occurred or whether its seriousness justifies the severity of the measures taken.

The small nation must look for the protection of its rights to the assistance of powerful friends; only thus can it hope to oppose with a chance of success an attempt to violate its rights. Whether such assistance will be forthcoming is a matter not of international law but of the national interest as conceived by the individual nations, which must decide whether or not to come to the support of the weak member of the international community. In other words, whether or not an attempt will be made to enforce international law and whether or not the attempt will be successful do not depend primarily upon legal considerations and the disinterested operation of law-enforcing mechanisms. Both attempt and success depend upon political considerations and the actual distribution of power in a particular case. The protection of the rights of a weak nation that is threatened by a strong one is then determined by the balance of power as it operates in that particular situation. Thus the rights of Belgium were safeguarded in 1914 against their violation by Germany, for it so happened that the protection of those rights seemed to be required by the national interests of powerful neighbors. Similarly, when in 1950 South Korea was attacked by North Korea, their concern with the maintenance of the balance of power in the Far East and of territorial stability throughout Asia prompted the United States and some of its allies, such as France and Great Britain, to come to the aid of South Korea. On the other hand, the rights of Colombia, when the United States supported the revolution in 1903 which led to the establishment of the Republic of Panama, and the rights of Finland, when attacked by the Soviet Union in 1939, were violated either with impunity or, as in the case of Finland, without the intervention of effective sanctions. There was no balance of power which could have protected these nations.

It must be pointed out, however, that the actual situation is much less dismal than the foregoing analysis might suggest. The great majority of the rules of international law are generally observed by all nations without actual compulsion, for it is generally in the interest of all nations concerned to honor their obligations under international law. A nation will hesitate to infringe upon the rights of foreign diplomats residing in its capital; for it has an interest, identical with the interests of all other nations, in the universal observance of the rules of international law which extend their protection to its own diplomatic representatives in foreign capitals as well as the foreign diplomats in its own capital. A nation will likewise be reluctant to disregard its obligations under a commercial treaty, since the benefits that it expects from the execution of the treaty by the other contracting parties are complementary to those anticipated by the latter. It may thus stand to lose more than it would gain by not fulfilling its part of the bargain. This is particularly so in the long run, since a nation that has the reputation of reneging on its commercial obligations will find it hard to conclude commercial treaties beneficial to itself.

Most rules of international law formulate in legal terms such identical or complementary interests. It is for this reason that they generally enforce themselves, as it were, and that there is generally no need for a specific enforcement action. In most cases in which such rules of international law are actually violated despite the underlying community of interests, satisfaction is given to the wronged party either voluntarily or in consequence of adjudication. And it is worthy of note that of the thousands of such judicial decisions which have been rendered in the last century and a half, voluntary execution was refused by the losing party in fewer than ten cases.

Thus the great majority of rules of international law are generally unaffected by the weakness of its system of enforcement, for voluntary compliance prevents the problem of enforcement from arising altogether. The problem of enforcement becomes acute, however, in that minority of important and generally spectacular cases, particularly important in the context of our discussion, in which compliance with international law and its enforcement have a direct bearing upon the relative power of the nations concerned. In those cases, as we have seen, considerations of power rather than of law determine compliance and enforcement.

Theory of International Politics*

KENNETH WALTZ

Anarchic Orders and Balances of Power

. . . Ever since Machiavelli, interest and necessity—and *raison d'etat*, the phrase that comprehends them—have remained the key concepts of *Realpolitik*. From Machiavelli through Meinecke and Morgenthau the elements of the approach and the reasoning remain constant. Machiavelli stands so clearly as the exponent of *Realpolitik* that

* Reprinted by permission from KENNETH WALTZ, THEORY OF INTERNATIONAL POLITICS (1979).

one slips into thinking that he developed the closely associated idea of balance of power as well. Although he did not, his conviction that politics can be explained in its own terms established the ground on which balance-of-power theory can be built.

Realpolitik indicates the methods by which foreign policy is conducted and provides a rationale for them. Structural constraints explain why the methods are repeatedly used despite differences in the persons and states who use them. Balance-of-power theory purports to explain the result that such methods produce. Rather, that is what the theory should do. If there is any distinctively political theory of international politics, balance-of-power theory is it. And yet one cannot find a statement of the theory that is generally accepted. Carefully surveying the copious balance-of-power literature, Ernst Haas discovered eight distinct meanings of the term, and Martin Wight found nine. Hans Morgenthau, in his profound historical and analytic treatment of the subject, makes use of four different definitions. Balance-of-power is seen by some as being akin to a law of nature; by others, as simply an outrage. Some view it as a guide to statesmen; others as a cloak that disguises their imperialist policies. Some believe that a balance of power is the best guarantee of the security of states and the peace of the world; others, that it has ruined states by causing most of the wars they have fought.

. . . A balance-of-power theory, properly stated, begins with assumptions about states: They are unitary actors who, at a minimum, seek their own preservation and, at a maximum, drive for universal domination. States, or those who act for them, try in more or less sensible ways to use the means available, in order to achieve the ends in view. Those means fall into two categories: internal efforts (moves to increase economic capability, to increase military strength, to develop clever strategies) and external efforts (moves to strengthen and enlarge one's own alliance or to weaken and shrink an opposing one). The external game of alignment and realignment requires three or more players, and it is usually said that balance-of-power systems require at least that number. The statement is false, for in a two-power system the politics of balance continue, but the way to compensate for an incipient external disequilibrium is primarily by intensifying one's internal efforts. To the assumptions of the theory we then add the condition for its operation: that two or more states coexist in a self-help system, one with no superior agent to come to the aid of states that may be weakening or to deny to any of them the use of whatever instruments they think will serve their purposes. The theory, then, is built up from the assumed motivations of states and the actions that correspond to them. It describes the constraints that arise from the system that those actions produce, and it indicates the expected outcome: namely, the formation of balances of power. Balance-of-power theory is microtheory precisely in the economist's sense. The system, like a market in economics, is made by the actions and interactions of its units and the theory is based on assumptions about their behavior.

A self-help system is one in which those who do not help themselves, or who do so less effectively than others, will fail to prosper, will lay themselves open to dangers, will suffer. Fear of such unwanted consequences stimulates states to behave in ways that tend toward the creation of balances of power. Notice that the theory requires no assumptions of rationality or of constancy of will on the part of all of the actors. The theory says simply that if some do relatively well, others will emulate them or fall by the wayside. Obviously, the system won't work if all states lose interest in preserving themselves. It will, however, continue to work if some states do, while others do not, choose to lose their political identities, say, through amalgamation. Nor need it be assumed that all of the competing states are striving relentlessly to increase their power. The possibility that force may be used by some states to weaken or destroy others does, however, make it difficult for them to break out of the competitive system.

. . .

The theory leads us to expect states to behave in ways that result in balances forming. To infer that expectation from the theory is not impressive if balancing is a universal pattern of political behavior, as is sometimes claimed. It is not. Whether political actors balance each other, or climb on the bandwagon depends on the system's structure. Political parties, when choosing their presidential candidates, dramatically illustrate both points. When nomination time approaches and no one is established as the party's strong favorite, a number of would-be leaders contend. Some of them form coalitions to check the progress of others. The maneuvering and balancing of would-be leaders when the party lacks one is like the external behavior of states. But this is the pattern only during the leaderless period. As soon as someone looks like the winner, nearly all jump on the bandwagon rather than continuing to build coalitions intended to prevent anyone from winning the prize of power. Bandwagoning, not balancing, becomes the characteristic behavior.

Bandwagoning and balancing behavior are in sharp contrast. Internally, losing candidates throw in their lots with the winner. Everyone wants someone to win; the members of a party want a leader established even while they disagree on who it should be. In a competition for the position of leader, bandwagoning is sensible behavior where gains are possible even for the losers and where losing does not place their security in jeopardy. Externally, states work harder to increase their own strength, or they combine with others, if they are falling behind. In a competition for the position of leader, balancing is sensible behavior where the victory of one coalition over another leaves weaker members of the winning coalition at the mercy of the stronger ones. Nobody wants anyone else to win; none of the great powers wants one of their number to emerge as the leader.

If two coalitions form and one of them weakens, perhaps because of the political disorder of a member, we expect the extent of the other coalition's military preparation to slacken or its unity to lessen. The classic example of the latter effect is the breaking apart of a war-winning coalition in or just after the moment of victory. We do not expect the strong to combine with the strong in order to increase the extent of their power over others, but rather to square off and look for allies who might help them. In anarchy, security is the highest end. Only if survival is assured can states safely seek such other goals as tranquility, profit, and power. Because power is a means and not an end, states prefer to join the weaker of two coalitions. They cannot let power, a possibly useful means, become the end they pursue. The goal the system encourages them to seek is security. Increased power may or may not serve that end. Given two coalitions, for example, the greater success of one in drawing members to it may tempt the other to risk preventive war, hoping for victory through surprise before disparities widen. If states wished to maximize power, they would join the stronger side, and we would see not balances forming but a world hegemony forged. This does not happen because balancing, not bandwagoning, is the behavior induced by the system. The first concern of states is not to maximize power but to maintain their positions in the system.

Secondary states, if they are free, to choose, flock to the weaker side; for it is the stronger side that threatens them. On the weaker side, they are both more appreciated and safer, provided, of course, that the coalition they join achieves enough defensive or deterrent strength to dissuade adversaries from attacking. Thus Thucydides records that in the Peloponnesian War the lesser city states of Greece cast the stronger Athens as the tyrant and the weaker Sparta as, their liberator, (circa 400 B.C., Book v, Chapter 17). According to Werner Jaeger, Thucydides thought this "perfectly natural in the circumstances," but saw "that the parts of tyrant and liberator did not correspond with any permanent moral quality in these states but were simply masks which would one day be interchanged to the astonishment of the beholder when the balance of power was altered." This shows a nice sense of how the placement of states affects their behavior and even colors their characters. It also supports the proposition that states balance power rather than maximize it. States can seldom afford to make maximizing power their goal. International politics is too serious a business for that.

The theory depicts international politics as a competitive realm. Do states develop the characteristics that competitors are expected to display? The question poses another test for the theory. The fate of each state depends on its responses to what other states do. The possibility that conflict will be conducted by force leads to competition in the arts and the instruments of force. Competition produces a tendency toward the sameness of the competitors. Thus Bismarck's startling victories over Austria in 1866 and over France in 1870 quickly led the major continental powers (and Japan) to imitate the Prussian military staff system, and the failure of Britain and the United States to follow the pattern simply indicated that they were outside the immediate arena of competition. Contending states imitate the military innovations contrived by the country of greatest capability and ingenuity. And so the weapons of major contenders, and even their strategies, begin to look much the same all over the world. Thus at the turn of the century Admiral Alfred von Tirpitz argued successfully for building a battleship fleet on the grounds that Germany could challenge Britian at sea only with a naval doctrine and weapons similar to hers.

The effects of competition are not confined narrowly to the military realm. Socialization to the system should also occur. Does it? Again, because we can almost always find confirming examples if we look hard, we try to find cases that are unlikely to lend credence to the theory. One should look for instances of states conforming to common international practices even though for internal reasons they would prefer not to. The behavior of the Soviet Union in its early years is one such instance. The Bolsheviks in the early years of their power preached international revolution and flouted the conventions of diplomacy. They were saying, in effect, "we will not be socialized to this system." The attitude was well expressed by Trotsky, who, when asked what he would do as foreign minister, replied, "I will issue some revolutionary proclamations to the peoples and then close up the joint." In a competitive arena, however, one party may need the assistance of others. Refusal to play the political game may risk one's own destruction. The pressures of competition were rapidly felt and reflected in the Soviet Union's diplomacy. Thus Lenin, sending foreign minister Chicherin to the Genoa Conference of 1922, bade him farewell with—this caution: "Avoid big words." Chicherin, who personified the carefully tailored traditional diplomat rather than the simply uniformed revolutionary, was to refrain from inflammatory rhetoric for the sake of working deals. These he successfully completed with that other pariah power and ideological enemy, Germany.

The close juxtaposition of states promotes their sameness through the disadvantages that arise from a failure to conform to successful practices. It is this "sameness," an effect of the system, that is so often attributed to the acceptance of so-called rules of state behavior. Chiliastic rulers occasionally come to power. In power, most of them quickly change their ways. They can refuse to do so, and yet hope to survive, only if they rule countries little affected by the competition of states. The socialization of nonconformist states proceeds at a pace that is set by the extent of their involvement in the system. And that is another testable statement.

The theory leads to many expectations about behaviors and outcomes. From the theory, one predicts that states will engage in balancing behavior, whether or not balanced power is the end of their acts. From the theory, one predicts a strong tendency toward balance in the system. The expectation is not that a balance, once achieved, will be maintained, but that a balance, once disrupted, will be restored in one way or another. Balances of power recurrently form. Since the theory depicts international politics as a competitive system, one predicts more specifically that states will display characteristics common to competitors:

namely, that they will irritate each other and become socialized to their system....

Notes and Comments

1. E.H. Carr is widely regarded along with Morgenthau as one of the founders of modern realist international relations theory. Carr's path toward realism is itself revealing. He resigned from the British Foreign Office in 1936, after nearly 20 years of service, disillusioned with the liberalism that guided British foreign policy during the interwar period—a liberalism that he had himself shared but which he eventually came to believe had made the recurrence of war all but inevitable. He went on to write the classic realist text, *The Twenty Years' Crisis* (1939), in which he sought to put forward a new vision of international relations based not on the high-sounding moral rhetoric of Wilson but on an unvarnished examination of state interests. Originally entitled "Utopia and Reality," Carr's book sought to reveal the ineptitude of the "utopian" vision of international relations, which he believed disregarded the facts in favor of "visionary projects for the attainment of the ends which they have in view." CARR, *supra*, at 6. In its place, he offered a more "realist" conception based on what he saw as the true facts and analysis of the world as it really is. For more on Carr's background, see Michael Cox's introduction to *The Twenty Years' Crisis* (Palgrave 2001).

2. Realism has come under attack from scholars of diverse perspectives. Some from the left have criticized it for its pretensions to neutrality, arguing that it is in fact pervasively normative and privileges particular conceptions of state interest, power, and security. See, e.g., Martti Koskenniemi, *The Place of Law in Collective Security*, 17 MICHIGAN JOURNAL OF INTERNATIONAL LAW 455 (1996). Feminist scholars have noted that traditional international relations theory and international law—and realist approaches in particular—are unnecessarily gendered disciplines and are based on a patriarchal, normative structure that lies in opposition to much of feminist theory. See, e.g., Hilary Charlesworth et al., *Feminist Approaches to International Law*, 85 AMERICAN JOURNAL OF INTERNATIONAL LAW 613 (1991); J. Ann Tickner, *You Just Don't Understand: Troubled Engagements between Feminist and IR Theorists*, 41 INTERNATIONAL STUDIES QUARTERLY 611 (1997); Hilary Charlesworth, *Feminist Methods in International Law*, 93 AMERICAN JOURNAL OF INTERNATIONAL LAW 379 (1999). Those who focus on the developing world have argued that realism fails to capture the interests of developing nations and relies on normative foundations accepted by powerful, resource-rich nations that are not widely accepted outside the West. See, e.g., Deepa Ollapally, *Third World Nationalism and the United States After the Cold War*, 110 POLITICAL SCIENCE QUARTERLY 417 (1995); Robert H. Jackson, *Quasi-States, Dual Regimes, and Neo-Classical Theory: International Jurisprudence and the Third World*, 41 INTERNATIONAL ORGANIZATIONS 519 (1987). Critical legal scholars, too, have long argued against what they see as the intellectual poverty of the absolutist realist position. See, e.g., David

Kennedy, *Theses About International Law Discourse*, 23 GERMAN YEAR BOOK OF INTERNATIONAL LAW 353, 361 (1980); David Kennedy, *A New Stream of International Law Scholarship*, 7 WISCONSIN INTERNATIONAL LAW JOURNAL 1 (1988). Finally, the theory has come under untold number of critiques for its failure to account for the more cooperative shape of international relations in the post Cold–War era, even from neoconservatives who share many of the realists' concerns. See, e.g., ROBERT KAGAN, OF PARADISE AND POWER: AMERICA AND EUROPE IN THE NEW WORLD ORDER (2004). A concise collection of the varied critiques of neorealist theory can be found in NEOREALISM AND ITS CRITICS (Robert Keohane ed. 1986).

3. Although it has been much criticized as the relic of a Cold War mentality, the realist tradition remains influential. As Stephen Walt wrote in his 2002 essay, "The Enduring Relevance of the Realist Tradition":

> Realist theories are still widely criticized, but the realist tradition has yet to be supplanted by an alternative perspective with similar range or explanatory power. Although critics were quick to announce the obsolescence of realist theory in the wake of the cold war . . ., the real world has paid scant attention to these academic obituaries. Major powers remain acutely sensitive to the distribution of power, are wary of developments that might leave them vulnerable, and still strive to enhance their positions at the expense of potential rivals. Although states do cooperate in a variety of ways, they continue to guard their autonomy jealously and find extensive collaboration difficult to sustain. Military force remains a depressingly constant feature of political life. . . .
>
> . . . By identifying the core problem of international politics—the insecurity and competition induced by the existence of independent states in anarchy—the realist tradition has set the terms of debate even for those thinkers who do not accept its generally pessimistic conclusions.
>
> In short, the basic elements of the realist tradition are akin to the theory of universal gravitation. On earth, gravity is a force that heavier-than-air objects must overcome in order to fly. One can think of several ways to overcome this force (aircraft, balloons, rockets, etc.), but the fact that gravity can be countered does not mean it has ceased to exist or that knowledge of its role is not essential for designing a working flying machine.

Stephen M. Walt, *The Enduring Relevance of the Realist Tradition*, *in* POLITICAL SCIENCE: THE STATE OF THE DISCIPLINE (2002).

4. Realism had a profound effect on American foreign policy in the decades immediately following the Second World War. George Kennan, John Herz, Walter Lippman, and Henry Kissinger are just a few of the many American thinkers and policymakers during this period who took a world view drawn from realism. In a famous statement of his views, George Kennan—who worked for a time as chief of mission in the American Embassy in Moscow and became one of the primary architects of U.S. foreign policy during the Truman Administration—published an article under the pseudonym "X." The article, an earlier version of which he had written as what became famously known as "The Long Telegram," advanced a view that deeply influenced the U.S. Cold War policy toward the Soviet Union. "The main element of any United States policy toward the Soviet Union," Kennan wrote, "must be that of a long-term, patient but firm and vigilant containment of Russian expansive tendencies." To that end, he called for countering "Soviet pressure against the free institutions of the Western world" through the "adroit and vigilant application of counter-force at a series of constantly shifting geographical and political points, corresponding to the shifts and maneuvers of Soviet policy." See X [George F. Kennan], *The Sources of Soviet Conduct*, 25 FOREIGN AFFAIRS 566 (1947); see also Henry A. Kissinger, *Reflections on American Diplomacy*, 35 FOREIGN AFFAIRS 37 (1956); HENRY KISSINGER, DIPLOMACY (1994). The article became the intellectual touchstone of the "containment policy" that governed nearly the next half-century of U.S. foreign policy. In the days after the terrorist attacks of September 11, 2001, did the administration of George W. Bush return the United States to a new "containment policy" against terrorism? In what obvious ways does an American strategy to contain terror necessarily differ from a strategy to check Soviet expansive tendencies?

5. What are the perceived shortcomings of "utopianism" in the realist view?

6. What are the central differences between the realist (Carr and Morgenthau) and neorealist (Waltz) theories of state behavior?

7. Notice Morgenthau's acknowledgement that "[t]he great majority of the rules of international law are generally observed by all nations without actual compulsion, for it is generally in the interest of all nations concerned to honor their obligations under international law." What empirical basis do you suppose that he had for making that assertion. Is it testable? If so, how?

8. Waltz draws a sharp contrast between states' "bandwagoning and balancing behavior." Are they really in sharp contrast? Or can both be described as a form of coordinated, or even cooperative, state behavior?

9. What role does international law play in realist and neorealist theory? What is the nature of international law, in these views?

B. Institutionalism

Institutionalism emerged as a distinctive view of international relations a decade before the Cold War began to draw to a close. Many scholars who were trained in the realist tradition began to question realism's ability to account for flourishing of international institutions in the face of ongoing Cold War hostilities. Their approach, which soon came to be known as "institutionalism," focused overdue attention on what was then regarded as a puzzling feature of international politics: the existence of apparently influential international institutions. Built on neorealist foundations, institutionalism views states largely as unified principal actors that behave on the basis of self-interest. It also shares neorealist assumptions that anarchy and the distribution of power among states are the underlying principles of world politics.

In the institutionalist view—which has been variously recast as "modified structural realism," "intergovernmental institutionalism," "neoliberal institutionalism," and "new institutionalism,"—regimes (including treaty regimes) exist in order to facilitate agreements. They are complied with largely because of the rational utility-maximizing activity of states pursuing their self-interest. As political scientist Robert Keohane explains below in an excerpt from one of his many cogent and careful articulations of institutional theory, regimes allow countries to engage in cooperative activity by restraining short-term power maximization in pursuit of long-term goals. When compliance with international legal rules occurs, it can be explained as a winning long-term strategy to obtain self-interested ends.

The increased attention to international regimes by international relations scholars during the late seventies and early eighties did not, at least initially, signal a new focus on international law. Early on, political scientists defined "regimes" as "principles, norms, rules and decision-making procedures around which actors' expectations converge in a given area"[1] and as "sets of governing arrangements" that include "networks of rules, norms, and procedures that regularize behavior and control its effects."[2] Notice that the word "law" was entirely omitted. Regimes required neither formal institutions nor enforcement powers, and hence much of the ensuing literature on regimes focused on informal cooperation and largely ignored traditional international organizations and international law. Yet the most recent work in this vein has adopted a broader view of institutions that encompasses law as well as international legal institutions. In this view, legal institutions, like other institutions, are seen as "rational, negotiated responses to the problems international actors face."[3]

This reconceptualization of institutionalism among international relations scholars to include international law is one of many signs of the increasing convergence of international law and international relations. In the last decade, a few legal scholars have adopted the interests-based approach of institutionalism, while now placing law at the center of the analysis. In a recent paper, excerpted below, Andrew T. Guzman puts forward a comprehensive institutionalist view of state action in the international realm as a function of interests and power rather than legitimacy or ideology. In Guzman's framework, countries take into account both direct sanctions and more indirect sanctions in the form of reputational costs in deciding whether to comply with international legal

1. Stephen D. Krasner, *Structural Causes and Regime Consequences: Regimes as Intervening Variables*, in INTERNATIONAL REGIMES 1, 2 (Stephen D. Krasner ed., 1983).

2. ROBERT O. KEOHANE & JOSEPH S. NYE, POWER AND INTERDEPENDENCE 19 (1977).

3. Barbara Koremenos et al., *The Rational Design of International Institutions*, 55 INTERNATIONAL ORGANIZATION 761, 768 (2001) (emphasis omitted).

rules. They weigh these costs against the benefits they will obtain from compliance, and, based on this calculus, decide how to act.

Institutional Theory and the Realist Challenge After the Cold War*

ROBERT O. KEOHANE, JR.

Institutional Theory and the Issue of Relative Gains

Rational institutionalist theory begins with the assumption, shared with realism, that states, the principal actors in world politics, are rational egoists. . . . Institutionalists do not elevate international regimes to mythical positions of authority over states: on the contrary, such regimes are established by states to achieve their purposes. Facing dilemmas of coordination and collaboration under conditions of interdependence, governments demand international institutions to enable them to achieve their interests through limited collective action. These institutions serve state objectives not principally by enforcing rules (except when they coordinate rule-enforcement by the strong against the weak, as in the International Monetary Fund—IMF), but by facilitating the making and keeping of agreements through the provision of information and reductions in transactions costs. Even if such costs remain substantial, states will create and use such institutions as long as the institutions enable states to achieve valued objectives unattainable through unilateral or bilateral means. Cooperation will never be perfect and is intimately associated with discord. Nevertheless, those institutions that succeed in facilitating mutually beneficial cooperation will become valued for the opportunities they provide to states, they will therefore acquire a certain degree of permanence, and their rules will constrain the exercise of power by governments. Governments will still seek to attain their ends, including increasing their shares of the gains from cooperation, through the use of political influence. However, the exercise of influence will depend not merely on their material capabilities but also on the relationship between their ends and means, on the one hand, and the rules and practices of the international institution, on the other.

. . .

Realist and Institutionalist Forecasts After the Cold War

During the Cold War, it was difficult to evaluate the relative merits of institutionalist and realist theories of cooperation, because both approaches seemed broadly consistent with observation. Institutionalists such as myself pointed to the increasing visibility and specificity of international institutions such as the IMF and World Bank, GATT, NATO, and the European Community as evidence for a functional

* Reprinted by permission from ROBERT O. KEOHANE, JR., NEOREALISM & NEOLIBERALISM 269 (David A. Baldwin ed., 1993).

theory of international regimes: when attaining their interests required systematic and durable cooperation, governments were able to establish such institutions on the basis of mutual self-interest. Institutions helped them to overcome collective action problems by providing information and reducing the costs of transactions. Hegemony was not essential to the maintenance of regimes based on mutual interest, although American hegemony had been an important factor in establishing many of them in the first place. And although military force played an indirect role in U.S. relations with its closest allies, "changes in relations of military power have not been the major factors affecting patterns of cooperation and discord among the advanced industrialized countries since the end of World War II."

Realists, on the other hand, emphasized that the strongest international regimes were constructed in a bipolar world in the shadow of U.S. hegemony, and most of them were led at least initially by the United States. Some versions of these arguments are compatible with institutionalist views. Joanne Gowa, for instance, argues on both theoretical and historical grounds that "the security externalities of agreements to open borders to trade imply that these agreements are more likely to occur within than between military alliances." That is, the security externalities of trade are positive for allies, negative for adversaries; the utility of trade regimes will therefore be enhanced for the former, diminished for the latter. Agreement with this proposition does not entail a belief that "relative gains are more important than absolute gains"; only an awareness of enduring realities of competitive security politics.

Gowa's argument suggests that as military alliances become less important, the security externalities that have reinforced liberal trade regimes will become less significant as well, and the regimes themselves may suffer. Institutionalist theories are ambiguous on the future of liberal economic regimes, since in the absence of a specification of interests (which will depend in part on domestic politics), institutionalist predictions about cooperation are indeterminate. That is, institutional theory takes states' conceptions of their interests as exogenous: unexplained within the terms of the theory. Unlike naive versions of commercial or republican liberalism, institutionalist theory does not infer a utility function for states simply from their material economic interests or the alleged values common to democracies. The key question with respect to global economic regimes such as GATT, therefore, is whether their principal members will regard their continuation or strengthening (whether in liberal or illiberal directions) as in their interests. Institutional theory makes no prediction about these interests, and therefore has no well-defined view on their evolution. Nor does realism predict interest. This weakness of systemic theory, of both types, denies us a clear test of their relative predictive power.

Other patterns of change, however, may help to illuminate the value of the theories. Institutionalist theory has claimed to account for the increase in the number of international organizations from about one hundred in 1945 to over six hundred by 1980 by referring to increasing levels of economic and ecological interdependence, which are alleged to create demand for both rules and organizations. Insofar as realism offers an account of this phenomenon, it is seen as a result of bipolarity and American hegemony. Hence realist theory should expect a decline in the number of international institutions after the Cold War, as the world returns to more traditional patterns of multipolar competition under anarchy. Institutionalism, by contrast, sees increased economic and ecological interdependence as secular trends, and therefore expects that as long as technological change prompts increased economic interdependence, and as long as threats to the global environment grow in severity, we will observe a continuing increase in the number and complexity of international institutions, and in the scope of their regulation. It is important to point out, however, that these institutions will not necessarily be liberal: it is quite possible for strong illiberal institutions, such as the Multifiber Arrangements for textiles, to be devised. The rate of growth in their numbers and in the scope of their action may also slow down; but if institutionalist theory is correct, they should not suffer a sharp decline.

Institutionalism also expects existing organizations to adapt quite easily to new purposes, within limits set by basic interests. Existing organizations should adopt new tasks more easily than new organizations can be created; incremental institutional change should prevail over both continual improvisation and radical institutional innovation. As I said in 1984, "It would count against my theory if most agreements made among governments were constructed not within the framework of international regimes, but on an ad hoc basis."

So far, in Europe, most but not all evidence is consistent with institutionalist expectations. On issues of trade and the environment, the European Community is playing the predominant role, moving into new geographical or functional areas, as institutionalists would expect. With respect to debt management and public international finance, however, the European Bank for Reconstruction and Development (EBRD) is an apparent anomaly for institutionalists, since the IMF and World Bank already operate in this area. Institutionalist theory would have led us to expect that the IMF and World Bank, perhaps in conjunction with the European Community's European Investment Bank, would dominate this issue area, expanding to East Europe and crowding out newcomers. Realist theory, with its emphasis or, distinct national interests, is better suited to understanding why the West European countries, led by France, wanted to establish the EBRD. Looking toward the future, institutionalist forecasts are ambiguous. On the one hand, institutionalist theory attributes considerable staying power to organizations such as the EBRD, once established; on the other hand, the IMF and World Bank are much stronger entities with better-entrenched networks.

If institutionalists are disturbingly vague in their forecasts on economic questions, realists are also annoyingly ambiguous in their preferred domain, that of security. Kenneth Waltz said at the 1990 American Political Science Association convention that "NATO's days are not numbered, but its years are." His sophisticated realist view acknowledged that institutions often persist beyond the conditions of their creation, but led him to believe that structural change would undermine NATO. However, another realist could point out that one of the unstated purposes of NATO has always been to inhibit independent action by Germany, and that this interest of Germany's NATO partners has only been enhanced by the end of the Cold War. Institutionalists would expect NATO to use its organizational resources to persist, by changing its tasks. And indeed NATO is shifting from the mission of deterring a Soviet threat to a variety of different political and lower-level military tasks, including co-opting East European governments in a NATO Cooperation Council, just as the March of Dimes, when polio was conquered in the United States, turned its attention to birth defects. So far, so good, for institutionalists. But institutionalists cannot tell us precisely "how sticky" organizations are in the face of changes in interests. Will NATO persist indefinitely, or should we only amend Waltz's comment to indicate that "its years are numbered on more than the fingers of one hand?" Once again, weak theory leads to ambiguous prediction.

The most doctrinaire version of realism (which Charles Lipson at the 1992 meeting of the American Political Science Association referred to as "hyper-realism") generates more definite predictions. But its visions are disturbingly and often implausibly apocalyptic. John Mearsheimer has argued that bipolarity, an equal military balance, and nuclear weapons kept the peace in Europe during the Cold War, and that the reunification of Germany and the likely removal of the American guarantee—of both external protection and interalliance peace—will lead to intensified political rivalry and perhaps even military conflict among major European powers. "The root cause of the problem," he claims, "is the anarchic nature of the international system," which means that "all other states are potential threats" and "relative power, not absolute levels of power, matters most to states."

One reason for being skeptical of such realist pessimism is that "anarchy," a constant for realists, cannot explain variation in patterns of conflict and cooperation among states. Although anarchy in the sense of lack of common government has been a constant throughout the history of the interstate system, cooperation among states has varied substantially. The proliferation of international institutions during the Cold War, and most notably the history of the European Community, show that anarchy does not necessarily prevent cooperation. Mearsheimer's argument really rests not on broad generalizations about anarchy but on more specific worries about hypernationalism in Eastern Europe and the effects of multipolarity (resulting both from the end of the Cold War and the decline of American dominance over Europe and Japan).

In the absence of stabilizing institutions, multipolarity and hypernationalism are indeed dangerous. States will expect conflict and seek to protect themselves through self-help, as discussed by generations of realist writers. Where effective means of power are at stake, and a small number of highly competitive states is involved, they will seek relative gains. Alliances will form, providing a context in which nationalistic conflicts can set off large-scale war. The scenario is familiar: it is the story of 1914.

The underlying framework of analysis leading to this conclusion is shared by both realists and rational institutionalists such as myself: state action is based on rational calculation, meaning that leaders seek to maximize subjective expected utility. Calculations of expected utility incorporate both estimates of others' capabilities and their likely intentions; hence the decisions of leaders depend on their expectations about other states' likely actions. But focusing on expectations brings us back to institutions. International institutions exist largely because they facilitate self-interested cooperation by reducing uncertainty, thus stabilizing expectations. It follows that the expectations of states will depend in part on the nature and strength of international institutions. Hence a valid analysis of rational state policy in an area such as Europe, which is institutionally dense, must take international institutions into account.

The continued salience of international institutions after the end of the Cold War is quite evident from an examination of state strategies. All five major powers used international institutions in their strategies of adaptation to the structural changes of 1989–91. Germany sought to reassure its partners by its attachment to NATO as well as to the EC; the Soviet Union tried to use the Conference on Security and Cooperation in Europe (CSCE) to cover its military withdrawal from Eastern Europe, and to join Western economic organizations in order to integrate itself with the capitalist world economy. The United States, which had developed a highly successful strategy of working through international institutions in Europe, sought not to diminish but to reinforce those organizations and rules, NATO in particular. France used the EC to try to help control the process of German reunification, which it feared; even Britain, with its dislike of supranationalism, resorted to international institutions—in this case NATO—to counter attempts by Germany and France to strengthen EC security arrangements.

The propensity of states to use existing international institutions, at least in the short run, hardly refutes sophisticated realist arguments, although it does suggest that claims . . . that "international institutions are unable to mitigate anarchy's constraining effects on inter-state cooperation" are misleading. . . . The absence of supranational enforcement, overcoming anarchy, does not imply the insignificance of international institutions.

As Mearsheimer suggests, the European Community provides fairly clear grounds for a comparative test between strong realist contentions, based on anarchy and relative gains, and institutionalist arguments. Mearsheimer argues that the European Community will be weakened by the end of the Cold War. In his words, "the Cold War provided a hothouse environment in which the EC could flourish. If the Cold War ends and the stable order it produced collapses, the EC is likely to grow weaker, not stronger with time."

My view is just the opposite, since my version of institutionalist theory embeds it selectively in a larger framework of neoliberal thought. As commercial liberalism or interdependence theory emphasizes, the EC has provided substantial economic and political gains for its members. Its members are all resolutely democratic, in their social as well as their political institutions: republican liberalism stresses the significance of this fact. As "sociological liberalism" would emphasize, extensive transnational ties and coalitions criss-cross the Continent. Finally, the institutions of the EC are firmly entrenched, and it continues to perform crucial functions. Thus there is a "synergy" among these four aspects of liberalism, which are arguably mutually reinforcing.

Within the European Community, commitment to its institutions is an essential condition for Germany to be able to pursue its interests and to exercise the influence that its economic strength and political coherence create, without unduly alarming its partners. Those of its partners that follow coherent domestic policies and realistic foreign policies may be able to use the institutional constraints of the EC to exercise some influence over policies, such as monetary policy, that would otherwise (given the level of economic interdependence in Europe) be determined unilaterally by Germany. Externally, the EC reinforces Europe's power vis-a-vis the United States, on the one hand, and the now-fragmented states to the East on the other. Europe has become a magnet for peripheral states. Those that are ready, such as Austria and Sweden, seek to join the EC; others, such as the Czech Republic, Hungary, and Poland, attempt to adapt their laws and practices in anticipation of future membership. If the former Soviet Union becomes a conflict-ridden zone of hypernationalism (which in the absence of institutions based on common interests would not be surprising to an institutionalist), the EC will, in my view, have even stronger motivations to stick together.

The Maastricht agreement, negotiated in December 1991, was a patchwork of provisions that satisfied no one. Its provisions for monetary union implied a transition period in which exchange rates would be fixed in the Community but capital would move freely across borders and national governments and central banks would retain control over monetary as well as fiscal policy. In December 1992, after a series of currency crises, the President of the Bundesbank labeled this "exchange rate mechanism" as "a powerful incentive for speculation." Britain's opting-out of the Social Charter created anomalies in the Treaty, as well as contributing to the parliamentary controversy over ratification. Debates on the treaty have revealed both the gulf between elite and popular views in Europe and the widespread resistance to centralization at the European level. The controversy over ratification of Maastricht, exemplified in 1992 by the close Danish "No" vote and the almost equally close French "Yes," seems to make it unlikely that the most ambitious aspirations of advocates of European union will be met. It should also remind us both that elected officials in Europe still depend for their tenure on national electorates, not technocrats in Brussels, and that Europe's progress toward greater unity has never been either smooth or linear.

Increasing the size of the European Community is likely to take precedence over increasing the authority of EC institutions; the EC will continue to be run by states in a system of pooled sovereignty, not by a Commission of international civil servants or by a supranational government responsible to the European Parliament; authority will not be concentrated in Brussels. Discord among members of the European Community will persist and is even likely to intensify as the EC engages in more important activities (such as monetary policy) and controls greater resources. But discord and cooperation go together in bargaining relationships: cooperation is political, and closer in many ways to discord than to harmony. Since common interests are likely to persist, and the institutions of the European Community are well-entrenched, institutionalist theory implies at a minimum that the EC will remain a durable and important entity, at least as long as continued cooperation will help governments to attain their economic and political interests. Even taking prospects of tough bargaining into account, I am willing to predict that the EC will be larger and have greater impact on its members' policies in the year 2000 than it was when the Berlin Wall came down in November 1989.

. . .

Conclusions

The double dialectic of international relations theory continues to operate. In its latest cycle, institutionalists have attempted to explain the unprecedented institutionalization of aspects of world politics since 1945, and realists have subjected their claims to critical scrutiny. Perhaps this volume will contribute to wider agreement on a new synthesis of these views. Since rationalistic approaches to international institutions build on realism by trying to specify conditions under which institutions will be significant, such a synthesis would not be a contradiction in terms. And since both modern realists such as Joseph Grieco and Kenneth Waltz, and institutionalists such as myself and Duncan Snidal, believe that theories should be systematically tested with evidence, there is some prospect that increased scholarly consensus might emerge from further empirical work.

The end of the Cold War has overtaken the academic debate between institutionalists and realists, thus adding a dialectic between theory and practice to that between academicians. This change in world politics is fortunate for social scientists seeking to evaluate the quality of different interpretations, since realism and institutionalism have different implications. Strict realism should lead one to expect a decline in the number and significance of international institutions; institutionalists such as myself expect no such decline. Institutionalists expect existing international institutions to adapt and to persist more easily than new institutions, formed by states on the basis of changing interests, can be created. Realists make no such prediction. Most dramatically, some realists such as John Mearsheimer forecast a collapse or at least weakening of the European Community, due to the demise of bipolarity. However, I expect the European Community to become larger and more significant, although the reaction to Maastricht in 1992 shows that the EC may again take a step backward before it moves forward. . . .

When we use our weak theories to offer predictions about the future, we must be humble, since during the last several years we have failed to anticipate major changes in world politics. Mearsheimer has made an important contribution by clearly offering his own forecasts and challenging others to do likewise. As he says, "We will then wait and see whose analysis proves most correct." Those of us who make forecasts may well be embarrassed by the results, but we can hope, at least, that our imperfect efforts will not only provide amusement for our colleagues and students but also help some of them to do better.

A Compliance Based Theory of International Law*

ANDREW GUZMAN

Without an understanding of the connection between international law and state actions, scholars cannot hope to provide useful policy advice with respect to international law. Improving the functioning of the international legal system and developing a workable theory of international legal and regulatory cooperation also require a coherent theory of compliance with international law. At present, the best theories relevant to international law and compliance come not from legal scholarship, but from international relations scholarship. The scholars developing these theories, however, are often skeptical of international law's relevance to the international system, or ignore international law altogether.

This Article draws on international relations theory to develop a better theory of compliance with international law. Unlike traditional international law scholarship, the theory developed here explains compliance using a model of rational, self-interested states. It argues that compliance occurs due to state concern about both reputational and direct sanctions triggered by violations of the law. This theory explains not only why nations comply, but also why and when they violate international law. Furthermore, this Article responds to the argument that international law is merely epiphenomenal by constructing a model of rational, self-interested states in which international law does, in fact, matter.

. . .

* Reprinted by permission from the University of California, Berkeley from 90 California Law Review 1823 (2002). © California Law Review.

A Theory of Compliance

This Part presents a theoretical model of compliance that explains both how international law can affect state behavior and why states sometimes violate that law. First, it develops a one-period model to demonstrate how the irrelevance of international law is modeled. Second, the assumption of a single period is relaxed, showing how in a model with repeated state interactions, one can develop a theory in which international law matters.

With respect to government behavior, the model makes standard assumptions about states: they are rational, they act in their own self-interest, and they are aware of the impact of international law on behavior. Although it is assumed that states act in a self-interested fashion, no assumption is made regarding the way in which states identify their self-interest.

A Theory of the Irrelevance of International Law

The first step in understanding this Article's theory of compliance is to understand the theory of the irrelevance of international law. As shown below, the simplest rational-actor model of country behavior leads to the conclusion that international law does not matter. Once that basic model is understood, it is possible to identify the assumptions that generate the irrelevance result and then relax those assumptions to develop a model of compliance in which international law matters.

The most basic model of country behavior is a one-shot game in which states decide whether or not to comply with a particular rule of international law. For concreteness, suppose that two countries have agreed to a ban on satellite-based weapons and the decision at hand is whether or not to comply with that agreement. Assume that (1) each country is better off if it violates the agreement while the other country complies, and (2) both are better off if they both comply than if they both violate. This game, a simple prisoner's dilemma,[4] is presented in Figure A, and the well-known equilibrium is for both countries to violate their international obligation.

Figure A

		Country 2	
		Comply	Violate
Country 1	Comply	5, 5	2, 6
	Violate	6, 2	3, 3

If this game is a fair representation of international relations, we would expect to see a world of chaos in which cooperation and compliance with international law are nonexistent. Such an observation is clearly at odds with what we observe.

4. [Editors' Note: See Note 5 at the end of this section for a description of a prisoner's dilemma.]

Though international law scholars have cited the widespread compliance with international commitments as evidence that international law matters, a simple extension of the above model shows that a high level of compliance need not imply that international law affects national behavior. Adding an additional round to the game explains how countries can regularly act in a manner consistent with their international obligations even if those obligations have no impact on state behavior. In an extension of the above model, the game is unchanged, but represents only a portion of a larger game. In the larger game, there is an initial period in which the state of nature is determined. Assume that there are two possible states of nature labeled "good" and "bad." Figure A, and the related discussion, represent the bad state of nature. In the satellite-based weapons treaty example given above, the bad state of nature corresponds to a situation in which the parties have an incentive to develop space-based weapons in spite of their treaty obligations.

The good state of nature, represented by Figure B below, corresponds to the situation in which the parties have an incentive to comply with treaty provisions independent of their international obligations. Suppose that the technology for the construction of a satellite-based weapons system is too primitive to make the system effective and that the cost is prohibitive, making it a poor use of government resources. In this situation, neither party would develop satellite-based weapons, even in the absence of an international agreement.

Figure B

		Country 2	
		Comply	Violate
Country 1	Comply	10, 10	6, 8
	Violate	8, 6	4, 4

In Figure B, if both countries violate the treaty, they are both worse off because they would have expended resources on an unreliable system. If Country 1 violates the treaty, that country is worse off as a result of the expended resources, and Country 2 also suffers a loss because even an unreliable weapons system in the hands of a potential enemy is undesirable. If both comply with the treaty, however, both enjoy the maximum possible payoff. More importantly, compliance is the dominant strategy for both parties. In other words, each country is better off if it complies with the treaty, regardless of the action taken by the other party.

Combining the good and bad outcomes yields a theory of national behavior consistent with the observation that countries obey their international obligations much of the time. Further, the analysis is also consistent with the view that international law does not matter. At times, a state's behavior happens to coincide with its international obligations, as in the example of states choosing not to develop satellite-based weapons because the technology is inadequate. At other times, states violate their obligations, as in the example of states choosing to develop such weapons despite the presence of a treaty. In neither case does the existence of an international agreement affect behavior.

This model in which international law is irrelevant has been advanced by the neorealist school in international relations. Though it is simple and elegant, and may explain instances of both observed compliance with international obligations and violations thereof, this theory cannot explain other observed behavior. It cannot explain, for example, why countries enter into treaties in the first place. The negotiation of international treaties and other agreements consumes resources that a state could use in other ways. If international law does not have any impact on behavior, there is no reason for a country to waste resources on international legal conventions and negotiations. Similarly, this simple model is unable to explain why countries invest resources to demonstrate that they are in compliance with international law; if the model is correct that international law has no impact on behavior, countries should ignore it. What we observe, however, are attempts by countries to justify their actions under international law. The model also fails to explain the existence of international law dispute-resolution processes to which nations sometimes submit their disputes. If international law does not matter, there is no reason for such procedures. Finally, the theory is contradicted by empirical data suggesting that international law does, indeed, influence state behavior.

In a finitely repeated prisoner's dilemma like the one presented above, the irrelevance of international law is inevitable. By adopting a finitely repeated game, one ensures that the equilibrium in a prisoner's dilemma context is noncooperative behavior ("defection"). This amounts to an assumption that cooperation will fail and that international law does not matter.

A Theory of the Relevance of International Law

In a domestic setting, even one-shot prisoner's dilemmas can yield the cooperative outcome through the use of contract. Suppose, for example, that two individuals agree to swap vacation homes for the summer. They each agree to care for the other's home, including the performance of certain regular maintenance chores. While on vacation, however, maintenance is time consuming, expensive, and boring, so there is an incentive to avoid it. The standard prisoner's dilemma model predicts that neither party will honor their promise to care for the other's home. Despite this tendency towards shirking, if their agreement is legally enforceable, a shirking party must pay damages which, if high enough, will induce the parties to carry out the promised maintenance. Law changes the payoffs and solves the prisoner's dilemma by imposing a penalty against the shirking party. To change the equilibrium, the penalty must change the payoffs enough to make cooperation a dominant strategy for each party.

Just as compliance with promises at the domestic level requires the existence of damages, a model of compliance with international law requires a mechanism through which nations that violate an agreement are sanctioned. The finitely repeated game of the previous Section can generate a model of effective international law only if there exists an entity that can sanction those who violate international law, much like courts sanction domestic violations. Those who argue that international law has little or no impact on national behavior, therefore, are implicitly claiming that the existing penalties for violations of international law are insufficient to change the equilibrium of the game. As mentioned, the use of a finitely repeated game without a coercive compliance mechanism is equivalent to assuming that result.

To generate a model in which international law matters, then, it is necessary to identify a mechanism through which violations are sanctioned. Even those who believe that international law plays an important role in regulating conduct in the international community must concede that there is, at best, a weak system of meting out punishments for violations of law. Nevertheless, a sound model of international law must turn on the impact of sanctions. It is important to note, however, that the term "sanction" must encompass more than just direct punishments resulting from a failure to live up to one's international obligations. Sanctions include all costs associated with such a failure, including punishment or retaliation by other states, and reputational costs that affect a state's ability to make commitments in the future.

To take the role of reputation into account, it is useful to remember one of the most basic elements of contract theory: in the absence of transaction costs, parties to a contract will negotiate to the most efficient outcome. This implies that the best possible rule, both for individuals in the domestic context and for states in the international context, is one in which the parties have complete freedom of contract, including the ability to make irrevocable commitments. In the domestic setting, the power to commit oneself exists because the courts stand ready to enforce contracts. In the international setting, states must rely on the imperfect system of international sanctions and reputational effects. Although states are not able to make fully irrevocable commitments, the greater a state's ability to commit itself, the better off it is.

The model of international law presented in this Article is an infinitely repeated game that operates as follows. Any given international obligation is modeled as a two-stage game. In the first stage, states negotiate over the content of the law and the level of commitment. In the second stage, states decide whether or not to comply with their international obligations. International law affects a state's self-interest, and thus its compliance decision, in two ways. First, it can lead to the imposition of direct sanctions such as trade, military, or diplomatic sanctions. Second, it can lead to a loss of reputational capital in the international arena. If the direct and reputational costs of violating international law are outweighed by the benefits thereof, a state will violate that law.

In the first period, states decide whether or not to enter into a legal obligation. For present purposes, an obligation is defined as a promise to other states; it could be a treaty, an informal agreement, or any other form of promise. If no promise is made, the state is free to engage in whatever conduct it chooses in the second period without suffering any sanction.

The second period reveals the state of the world. In the "good" state, the interests of the relevant countries converge and those that comply with the agreement receive a payoff higher than if they had violated the agreement. As a result, all countries comply in this period and in each period thereafter. In the good state, then, countries behave in the same way whether there is an agreement or not, and international law does not affect the behavior of states.

If the countries find themselves in the "bad" state, however, they face a prisoner's dilemma. If there is no agreement in place, countries behave in a noncooperative fashion (they "defect" in game-theoretic parlance), and receive a corresponding payoff. . . .

Reputation, however, can alter the above equilibrium. . . .

An Application of the Model: Bilateral Investment Treaties

. . .

Consider a country that has signed a BIT [bilateral investment treaty] in which it promises not to expropriate foreign investment. Assume for the purposes of this example that the country makes this promise because doing so increases the flow of foreign direct investment into the country. Even after making the promise, of course, the country could choose to expropriate the local assets of foreign firms. Assume that the available assets have a total value of $100 million to the country. This potential gain of $100 million must be weighed against the cost of an expropriation, which includes several components. First, the violating country loses the benefits currently being provided by foreign firms, including tax revenues, technological transfers, employment, and so on. Suppose that this loss amounts to $40 million. Second, the country is likely to suffer a reputational loss in the eyes of foreign investors. The act of expropriation signals a willingness to seize the assets of foreigners and reduces the attractiveness of the country to potential investors. Assume this translates into a loss of future investment, which the country values at $40 million. Finally, the country will suffer a loss of reputational capital with respect to other countries. Potential treaty partners will view the country as a less reliable partner and will be less willing to enter into future agreements. Assume that this loss is equivalent to $30 million. Taken together, then, the total cost of the expropriation will be $110 million.

In deciding whether or not to violate its international commitment, a country compares the total costs of doing so to the total benefits. Using the numbers given above, it is clear that the country would prefer to honor its commitment. A violation of the treaty would impose a loss of

$110 million and yield a gain of only $100 million—a net loss of $10 million. Notice also that the outcome can change as a result of international law. In the absence of a legal obligation, the expropriating country would not suffer a $30 million reputational loss in the eyes of other states, so its total loss from the expropriation would be no more than $80 million. Because the benefits from expropriation are $100 million, the expropriation would cause a net gain absent the international commitment. This example demonstrates that a reputational loss can affect decisions even when the loss is considerably less than the total potential gains from the action. This is so because there will typically be other costs that the country must consider. This simply illustrates that the reputational consequences of an action can alter the outcome if they are large enough to tip the balance of costs and benefits in favor of compliance.

If we make different assumptions about the numbers, of course, we can generate different results. For example, if the gain from expropriation is $200 million while the other numbers are unchanged, the country will choose to expropriate, even if doing so is a violation of international law.

Dynamic Issues

A country's decision to follow international law reflects a judgment that the costs of a violation outweigh the benefits. Because the opportunities and risks facing a country vary both over time and across contexts, however, a country may choose to follow a particular law at one time or in one context and violate it at another time or in another context.

. . . Suppose a country anticipates that the expropriation of foreign investment will lead to a complete halt in the flow of investment into the country. Assume that the expropriated investment is worth $100 million to the country if left in the hands of investors and $200 million if expropriated. The benefit from expropriation, therefore, is $100 million. To evaluate the cost of the expropriation, the decision-makers must also consider the value of future investment if it expropriates (which by assumption is zero) as compared to the value of future investment if it does not expropriate. If the expected value of future foreign investment changes over time, a country may choose to abide by its BITs for a period of time but, when conditions change, it may decide to violate those commitments.

Imagine that times are good and the country is enjoying high levels of foreign investment that are expected to increase further in the years to come. The present discounted value of future investment is $200 million. Under these conditions, expropriation is unattractive. The country can do better by encouraging more foreign investment and by treating that investment well. Benefits in the form of tax revenues, employment, technology transfers, and so on, are larger than the benefits from expropriation. Now suppose that the political mood in the country changes as the leader of a populist party gains widespread support by blaming the country's troubles on foreign capitalists. He points to the high level of foreign investment in the country and the substantial profits being made by investors, contrasting this with the low wages paid at some of the facilities of foreign firms. His actions generate feelings of hostility toward foreign interference in the local economy, and newly formed rebel groups target foreigners for kidnapping. Suppose further that despite its best efforts, the government cannot provide sufficient security to ensure the safety of all foreign residents and businesses.

From the perspective of a potential investor, these developments greatly reduce the country's appeal. Not only are employees at risk, but there is no way of knowing if the current pro-investor regime will win the next election or if the country will be consumed by violence and possibly even civil war. As a result of these events, the expected level and value of future investments fall to the point where the expected stream of benefits to the country is worth, say, $50 million rather than $200 million. This lower level of expected future investment affects the country's expropriation decision. The country still stands to gain $200 million by expropriating, as compared to $100 million from existing investment plus $50 million from future investment if it does not expropriate. The reduction in future investment has made expropriation the country's best strategy.

The same dynamic analysis applies in every case in which the present value of some future benefit changes based on the country's present choices. For instance, the history of Russian and Soviet debt in the twentieth century demonstrates exactly this sort of behavior. When the Soviet Union came into being, it immediately repudiated debts from the prior Russian czarist regime. The political philosophy of the new Soviet Union was hostile to the established sources of capital. Therefore, it stood little chance of securing large foreign loans in the foreseeable future. In that environment, a refusal to pay is easy to understand because the country had little to lose by offending international capital markets. When the Soviet Union collapsed, however, the situation changed. The new Russian government was in need of large capital infusions, including loans from other states and the International Monetary Fund. In an effort to improve its reputation among potential creditors, the Russian state pledged to repay not only Soviet debts, but also to compensate the holders of Russian bonds repudiated by the Soviet Union in 1918.

The Level of Commitment

The above discussion demonstrates that a model of rational states is consistent with the existence of international law. This result is important because, just as the ability to bind oneself through contract is valuable to private parties, the ability to commit to a particular action is valuable to states. A state's ability to signal its commitment more credibly through an international agreement, whether a treaty or other form of promise, increases welfare because it allows that state to enter into a broader range of potential agreements. In other words, the ability to make credible commitments makes states better off.

In the absence of transaction costs, the parties to an agreement would specify the precise conditions under which they would (or would not) perform. Agreements would list every possible state of the world and the obligations of the parties in each state. . . .

In practice, however, substantial transaction costs prevent international agreements from specifying every possible future contingency. First, it is often impossible to predict all potential future states of the world, let alone to list them all in an agreement. For example, in the mid–1980s it would have been difficult to predict the collapse of communism and the subsequent evolution of Eastern Europe and the former Soviet Union to market-based economies with democratic governments. Second, even if the range of possible states of the world is known, the probability of being in any given state of the world is not. For example, it is conceivable that a Free Trade Agreement of the Americas will be signed within the next ten years, but the probability of such an event is difficult to estimate. Third, identifying the state of the world at any given moment is difficult. Countries may disagree, for example, about whether certain practices constitute protectionist barriers or reasonable health measures, and this introduces questions of interpretation that can lead to a dispute even in the case of a well-specified treaty. Finally, a long list of contingencies and conditions can make ratification of international agreements much more difficult. Even where an agreement taken in its entirety is a good one, groups opposed to it would still have ammunition with which to rally public opinion in opposition.

As a result of these and other transaction costs, international agreements do not list every possible contingency. The parties to an agreement know that reservations, exceptions, escape clauses, and so on capture only some of the possible future situations. They recognize that there is a risk that they will violate a commitment, and that this may generate a loss of reputation. Consequently, a country that wants to make a promise, but recognizes a high probability that it will later violate that promise, may not want to put too much of its reputation on the line. Of course, if the reputational risk is too great, a country can always choose simply not to make the promise. This strategy is not ideal, however, because the country may want to make at least a weak promise to extract some form of concession from the other side.

Having the ability either to commit or not commit is valuable, then, but the ability to choose from a range of commitment levels is even more valuable. By varying the form of its promise, a state can choose its level of commitment and signal that commitment to other states. Suppose that a country is willing to share certain information regarding Internet-fraud schemes in exchange for a reciprocal promise of information sharing. The state may be concerned, however, that privacy issues will arise, become important to its citizens, and force the state to end the practice of sharing information. The treaty could expressly address this contingency, but the state may also be worried that other unanticipated or unforeseeable developments will make the country want to violate its promise. In this example, because violating a treaty carries reputational costs, a treaty may represent an excessive commitment. However, simply refusing to enter into any agreement frustrates the country's initial goal. The best solution, then, may be an intermediate level of commitment, which could take the form, for example, of an "accord" that falls short of a treaty but that specifies the commitments of each state.

It is possible to identify at least two dimensions along which international agreements can range in order to adjust the level of commitment: (1) the formality of the commitment and (2) the clarity of the agreement. When possible, countries that wish to increase the level of commitment prefer more formal and detailed agreements. For example, trade negotiations often feature schedules of commitments that provide a precise enumeration of commitments and obligations. At the other extreme, vague statements regarding national intent lead to relatively low levels of commitment, in part because it is difficult to determine when a country has violated the agreement.

The ability to modulate the level of obligation should not be mistaken for a system of truly enforceable promises. By choosing one form of international agreement over another, countries are varying the reputational stake that they have in the obligation. A violation will impose a higher reputational cost in the case of a treaty than it will in the case of a nonbinding agreement. In neither case should one conclude that the country cannot turn away from its obligation. The strength of reputation remains limited, and even the strongest commitments will sometimes be ignored. On the other hand, it is a mistake to discount the importance of reputation altogether.... [A] reputation for compliance with agreements is valuable to a country, so countries will only compromise that reputation if they receive something else of higher value in exchange.

. . .

Direct Sanctions

Up to this point, this Article has focused on the reputational impact of violations of international law, which is a markedly different approach from the way one ordinarily studies domestic rules. In the domestic setting, state-imposed sanctions receive the primary focus, while reputational effects, if any, are normally considered secondary. The weakness of direct sanctions in the international arena, however, makes reputational sanctions more important. That is not to say that direct sanctions are irrelevant. In certain instances they can have an important impact on a country's incentives and behavior. This Section examines direct sanctions and discusses when they are likely to be most effective.

If states face direct sanctions for violations of international law, optimal compliance is more likely because reputational sanctions are generally, though not always, weaker than optimal sanctions. Just as compliance with a contract is not always optimal, 100% compliance with international law is not the optimal level of compliance. Like individuals entering into contracts, states entering into agreements are unable to anticipate all possible situations in their agreements, and in certain circumstances the total costs associated with compliance outweigh the costs of violation. Violation of the law is preferable in these cases. This point is understood in contract law, where it is well established that expectation damages encourage "efficient breach." The same result holds in international law. When the total benefits of a violation of international law outweigh the benefits of performance, it is preferable that there be a violation. Consequently, a regime under which violations of international law trigger expectation damages will lead to violations only when they are efficient. In other words, expectation damages lead to optimal levels of deterrence.

Although direct sanctions could take a variety of forms, they most commonly consist of retaliatory measures taken by one or more states against a violator. For example, following the enactment of the Hawley–Smoot Tariff Act of 1930, which increased U.S. tariffs dramatically, other countries retaliated with tariff increases of their own.

In some cases, direct retaliation takes the form of a decision by the complying state to terminate its own compliance with the underlying agreement. These types of retaliation often have the advantage of imposing a cost on the offending state and being in the interest of the complying state. Whether a complying country will resort to this form of retaliation as opposed to another will be relevant to a country's decision to violate the agreement in the first place. Indeed, in some cases the threat of such retaliation will be enough to prevent a violation. In many cases, however, the simple abrogation of the treaty will not be enough to prevent a violation and, more importantly, will not be an optimal sanction. For instance, imagine that Country A and Country B each expect to receive gains of 5 as a result of an environmental agreement, but neither is certain of the actual gain. Both countries consent to the deal in good faith, but after the agreement is signed, Country A learns that it actually faces a loss of 1 as a result, rather than a gain of 5, while Country B stands to gain 5 from the agreement, as expected. If both countries honor the agreement, the total benefit is 4 (5 for Country B, −1 for Country A). If Country A violates its commitment, and Country B abrogates the treaty, the total gain is zero. Country A will nevertheless violate the agreement (assuming there is no sanction other than abrogation) precisely because it is better off without it. The threat of abrogation alone is insufficient to provide optimal deterrence because optimal deterrence would require that Country A face a sanction of 5 if it violates the agreement. Thus the mere withdrawal of benefits conferred by an agreement may be an inadequate sanction.

The inadequacy of withdrawal of one's own compliance may lead states to impose other sanctions intended to punish the offending state. For example, following the Persian Gulf War, an embargo on Iraqi oil was put in place. Punitive sanctions of this sort need not be directly related to the violation and can therefore more easily be tailored to resemble optimal sanctions. Thus, even though Iraq's actions were only indirectly related to its oil sales, the embargo represented an available and relatively powerful sanction.

There are two important problems with the imposition of this sort of penalty. First, without a dispute-settlement procedure, it is difficult to distinguish appropriate sanctions from inappropriate ones. While it is true that punitive sanctions have the potential to be used as optimal sanctions, they generally are not imposed by neutral third parties but unilaterally by injured states. There is, therefore, the risk that the sanctions will be excessive and will overdeter. Second, the imposition of these sanctions imposes costs on both sanctioned and sanctioning states. For instance, the embargo on Iraqi oil has certainly hurt Iraq, but it has also hurt countries participating in the embargo by reducing the number of potential suppliers of oil. Because imposing a sanction inflicts costs on a sanctioning country, the incentive to impose optimal sanctions is often weak, leading to penalties that may be too lenient.

Despite their shortcomings, punitive sanctions should not be dismissed too quickly, especially when compared to the alternative international mechanisms for compliance. In some situations it is possible to have such sanctions imposed and, as a result, to provide more efficient incentives to states.

Consider first a one-shot game in which Country A violates international law and Country B must decide whether or not to expend resources punishing Country A. Assuming that the punishment is the last play of the game, Country B has no incentive to impose the punishment. Country A realizes this, so it is not deterred from violating its obligations. In a one-shot game, therefore, countries will not impose sanctions on other countries when doing so is costly. It is elementary game theory that the same result holds for any finitely repeated game. The situation changes, however, in an infinitely repeated game. Where states interact repeatedly over time, it may be worthwhile for states to develop reputations for punishing offenders. By punishing offenders today, states increase the likelihood of compliance tomorrow because the threat of future punishment is credible. To sustain such an equilibrium by using punishment, it must be worthwhile for a state to punish today's violation in order to achieve future compliance. This condition will be met when (1) the states have relatively low discount rates; (2) the cost to the punishing state is not too large relative to the benefit received when other states follow the law; and (3) the benefits from violations of the law are not too large relative to the payoff from following the law.

. . .

Rethinking International Law

Up to this point, this Article has focused on developing a more complete theory of compliance with international law. This Part uses the theory to take a fresh look at the traditional sources of international law: treaties and CIL [customary international law]. . . .

Rethinking Treaties

. . .

At least two dimensions are critical to an understanding of treaty compliance. The first is the reputational impact of a violation, which has already been discussed. The second dimension is the cost of compliance, which is informed by the subject matter of the treaty. Treaties that implicate critical issues of national security and other issues of central importance to states are less likely to succeed in tipping the scales in favor of compliance. These treaties implicate issues of profound national importance, and it is unlikely that reputation will be enough to change a country's course of action from violation to compliance. In other words, the decision of whether to act in accordance with the treaty will most likely be made based on costs and benefits that have nothing to do with international law.

Rethinking Customary International Law

CIL is the second form of international law recognized by traditional scholars. Unlike treaties, however, CIL is not the product of explicit bargaining and formal ratification. Under the traditional interpretation, it arises instead from widespread state practice and opinio juris—a sense of legal obligation. . . .

An alternative interpretation of CIL, one that addresses the theoretical difficulties with the traditional approach without denying the existence of CIL, is suggested by the theory advanced in this Article. Under this theory, CIL represents a form of legal obligation that countries have toward one another, even without explicit agreement. That much is consistent with the traditional view of legal scholars. A reputational model also addresses CIL's critics and resolves the theoretical problems with the traditional definition. Indeed, under this view, the problems of CIL are not problems at all. Rather, they are factors that either cause CIL to be a weak form of commitment or represent the product of that weakness. For example, the ambiguity regarding the content of CIL makes it a relatively weak mechanism through which to pledge reputational collateral. Because CIL's content is uncertain, states can often claim to have complied even when they have ignored the content of CIL. In other words, the commitment to CIL is more easily avoided than the commitment to a treaty. Like a contract that can be revoked at any time, an international commitment that can be avoided has limited force. To demonstrate that even the limited force of CIL can matter, however, consider the example of diplomatic immunity. The immunity of diplomats from the jurisdiction of local courts was a longstanding principle of CIL, and was widely, though not universally, respected. One would expect this in a reputational model because the cost of providing diplomatic immunity is normally small when compared with the reputational cost of violating it.

The above discussion suggests a new definition of CIL: CIL consists of legal norms whose violation will harm a country's reputation as a law-abiding state. Compare this definition to the traditional one. The practice requirement, present in traditional accounts of CIL, is not an explicit factor under a reputational account of international law. The practice requirement becomes important indirectly, however, if it causes a particular norm to be seen as an obligation.

Unlike the traditional concept of opinio juris, what matters under the theory advanced in this Article is that countries other than the offending state believe that there is such an obligation. That is, a state faces a norm of CIL if other states believe that the state has such an obligation and if those other states will view a failure to honor that obligation as a violation. Only under these circumstances will a violation by the state lead to a reputational loss. If, for example, respect for the principles of diplomatic immunity is considered a legal obligation, then a violation of those rules will be viewed by other states (or perhaps only the offended state) in a negative light. This will cause those states to doubt the reliability of the offending state, making them less prone to trust it in the future.

. . .

Unfortunately, we simply do not know how much reputational capital is at stake with respect to CIL. It is clear that CIL is weaker than treaties in part because CIL is typically not clearly specified, making its boundaries ambiguous. There is often debate about whether a particular norm of CIL exists at all, and countries normally have not consented to CIL in an explicit way, making their commitment to it uncertain. For all of these reasons, the possibility that CIL is so weak as to be negligible cannot be dismissed until some form of empirical evidence becomes available.

Rethinking International Law

. . .

In domestic law, it makes sense to use the term "law" to distinguish obligations that are legally enforceable from those that are not. When using "law" in the international context, however, analogies to domestic contract law are difficult. In particular, it makes no sense to restrict the use of "law" to obligations that are legally enforceable because most international legal obligations exist without any sort of formal enforcement mechanism. The associated conclusion that very little of international law qualifies as law, however, does nothing to help us understand the operation of international law. A vocabulary is needed to distinguish those obligations of states that affect incentives and behavior, and the term law seems to be sufficient for that purpose.

The classical usage of "international law" refers only to treaties and CIL. This definition excludes promises made by states through instruments that fall short of full-scale treaties, such as memoranda of understanding, executive agreements, nonbinding treaties, joint declarations, final communiques, agreements pursuant to legislation, and so on. The place of such commitments, sometimes referred to as "soft law," within the framework of international law is uncertain. What is clear is that traditional international law scholarship considers soft law less "law" than the "hard law" of treaties and custom. The focus of international legal scholars is often exclusively on treaties and custom, as if soft law either does not exist or has no impact. Although only occasionally stated explicitly, the general presumption appears to be that soft law is less binding than the traditional sources of international law, and states are accordingly less likely to comply.

The Problem of Large Stakes

. . .

All else equal, it is reasonable to expect that the compliance pull of international law will be the weakest when the stakes at issue are large. . . .

. . . When the costs and benefits of a particular action are small, there is a good chance that the reputational consequences will tip the balance in favor of compliance with international law. Where the costs and benefits other than reputation are relatively large, however, it is less likely that reputational costs will be enough to alter the outcome.

The above discussion implicitly assumes that the reputational cost of violating an international obligation is fixed. Under this assumption, international law has less effect as the stakes get larger. Although convenient to demonstrate that the most important issues are less likely to be affected by international law, the assumption of a constant reputational cost for violations of such law is unrealistic. That being said, it remains true that reputation plays a more important role when the costs and benefits of a particular action are small. This is so for at least two reasons. First, there is an upper bound to the reputational cost that a country can suffer as a result of a decision. Even a complete loss of reputation has a limited cost for a country. Furthermore, a single decision to violate international law is unlikely to cause a complete loss of reputational capital. Faced with a matter of great importance, therefore, even the most severe reputational sanction is unlikely to affect state behavior.

Second, although the reputational cost of a violation of international law can vary based on the circumstances, it does not necessarily increase with the importance of the issue. For example, a country's decision to violate an arms control agreement may impose reputational costs only in the area of arms control. Other states may recognize that military and national security issues are central to a country's identity and that treaties in that area are not particularly reliable. As a result, the violation of this sort of treaty may not call into question the willingness of the state to honor a treaty in another area, such as economic matters. Remember that violations of international law impose a reputational cost because they have a negative impact on other countries' perception of a state's willingness to accept short-term costs in order to protect long-term relationships and trust. When compliance with international law would impose extreme losses on a country, violation of that law may not have much impact on reputation. Such a violation sheds little light on the willingness of a state to violate agreements when the costs of compliance are smaller. This helps to explain why analysis of the role of international law during the Cold War leads to a pessimistic set of conclusions—many issues were perceived to involve high stakes.

These implications are significant for the study of international law. Most obviously, the theory predicts that international law will have the smallest impact in those areas of greatest importance to countries. This observation suggests that many of the most central topics in traditional international law scholarship are the most resistant to influence. Thus, for example, the laws of war, territorial limits (including territorial seas), neutrality, arms agreements, and military alliances are among the areas least likely to be affected by international law. Although agreements with large stakes can be stable, this will rarely be the result of the obligations imposed by international law. Adherence to such agreements is more likely to be the result of a game in which international law plays no more than a small part. The existence of an international legal obligation may be consistent with the outcome, but it is unlikely to alter behavior.

The message for scholars is twofold. First, international law scholars may be focusing their efforts in the wrong place. Rather than concentrating on those topics that are of greatest importance to states, they might do better to devote more attention to those areas in which international law can yield the greatest benefits. The most promising fields of study, therefore, are those in which reputational effects are likely to affect behavior. Some international law scholars may be disheartened by this message. After all, international law is an interesting subject in part because it concerns itself with great questions of war, peace, alliances, human rights, and so on. A focus on more mundane questions might seem to diminish the grandeur of the field of study. On the other hand, there is also an optimistic side to this conclusion. International law is often criticized for being irrelevant. By turning the attention of scholars to areas in which international law matters most, the importance of the subject can be demonstrated. Furthermore, those areas in which international law matters are themselves of great importance. These include, for example, the entire range of international economic issues, from trade to the international regulation of competition law to environmental regulation. The livelihood and sometimes the lives of millions of people depend on the effective resolution of international economic issues. Surely this is a worthwhile subject for international law scholars.

This discussion is not intended to imply that international law scholars must or should completely abandon the field when it comes to the sort of large-stakes questions that have occupied so much of the discipline in the past. Scholars have a role to play in important international agreements because they are uniquely qualified to evaluate the structure of the related institutions and the manner in which agreements are struck. International law can be used to strengthen national commitments, but its value depends on the context. Scholars must focus not only on the legality of state actions, but also on the ways in which international law can be structured to improve compliance. Issues involving large stakes can sometimes be influenced by international law, but this is most likely to be achieved through an indirect use of international commitments. For example, an agreement not to develop nuclear weapons is, by itself, unlikely to have much relevance. If it is combined with obligations with stakes that are lower but that cumulatively achieve the desired goal, success is more likely. For example, if it is possible to monitor compliance through regular inspections, countries will be less likely to violate their obligations. Monitoring allows violations to be detected early, which both reduces the benefits of violation—a nuclear weapons program that is detected early provides fewer benefits to the violating state—and increases the costs—early detection might cause other countries to withdraw their own promises, denying the violating country the benefit of compliance by others. The point here is that scholars should approach large-stakes issues with compliance in mind, and they should be searching for institutions and agreements that achieve the desired objectives through a series of discrete, low-stakes compliance decisions rather than through a single large-stakes decision.

Second, there is a message for critics of international law. Following the lead of international law scholars, critics point to the failure of international law in areas where it is unrealistic to expect success. Because they use the easiest cases to criticize international law, their attacks on the subject are unpersuasive. These attacks should be aimed at those areas in which international law plays a larger role.

Conclusion

. . .

Taken seriously, a reputational model of compliance leads to important changes in the way we view international law. It forces us to reject the classical definition of international law, which considers only treaties and CIL to be law. Instead, it leads us to a more functional definition, which considers any international promise or commitment that has a substantial influence on national incentives to be law. It also forces us to recognize in an explicit way that not all international law is created equal. Some obligations are more binding than others, and states choose the level of their commitments against this background fact. We can no longer be satisfied with the simple conclusion that "treaties are to be obeyed."

Notes and Comments

1. Oona A. Hathaway elaborates on the implications of an institutionalist perspective on international law. She writes:

> This institutionalist view of international law can be seen as a necessary and overdue counterpart to the longstanding consent-based approach to international law. International lawyers have long

> pointed to state consent as the central basis for the binding nature of international law. The consent-based approach is centered, as its name suggests, on the notion that states can bear no obligation to which they have not consented. Proponents of this view of international law see international treaties as simply a means for states to consent to abide by certain well-specified obligations. Once a state has accepted such an obligation, the argument continues, the obligation becomes binding and a nation must comply with it. The institutionalist approach outlined above helps fill a gap in consent theory by offering a possible explanation for why, if international law binds only countries that consent to it, international law exists and has any force at all. International law exists and has force, the institutionalist would say, because it provides a means of achieving outcomes possible only through coordinated behavior. States consent to commit themselves because doing so is the only way to achieve certain goals. They then comply with obligations already made as long as the reputational costs and direct sanctions that would result from noncompliance outweigh the costs of continued compliance. In this view, then, law provides a real constraint, but only insofar as violating it entails real costs. Law carries no weight divorced from the quantifiable sanctions and costs imposed in the case of its violation.

Oona A. Hathaway, *Do Human Rights Treaties Make A Difference?,* 111 Yale Law Journal 1936 (2002).

2. Eric Posner and Jack Goldsmith have put forward a controversial new view of international law that draws on institutionalist theory. They summarize their theory as follows:

> Our theory gives pride of place to two elements of international politics usually neglected or discounted by international law scholars—state power, and state interest. And it uses a methodological tool infrequently used in international law scholarship, rational choice theory, to analyze these factors. Put briefly, our theory is that international law emerges from states acting rationally to maximize their interests, given their perceptions of the interests of other states and the relevant distribution of national power.

Jack L. Goldsmith & Eric A. Posner, The Limits of International Law 2 (Oxford 2005). How does this approach compare to that of Keohane and Guzman in the excerpts above? Under this approach, where do state interests come from?

3. Institutionalism, like realism, is not short on critics. (Indeed, as is apparent in coming chapters, much of modern international law and politics scholarship is framed as a reaction against institutionalism and realism.) A powerful realist critique of institutionalism is offered by Joseph M. Grieco:

> This essay's principal argument is that, in fact, neoliberal institutionalism misconstrues the realist analysis of international anarchy on the preferences and actions of states. Indeed, the new

liberal institutionalism fails to address a major constraint on the willingness of states to cooperate which is generated by international anarchy and which is identified by realism. As a result, the new theory's optimism about international cooperation is likely to be proven wrong.

Neoliberalism's claims about cooperation are based on its belief that states are atomistic actors. It argues that states seek to maximize their individual *absolute* against and are indifferent to the gains achieved by others. Cheating, a new theory suggests, is the greatest impediment to cooperation among rationally egoistic states, but international institutions, the new theory also suggests, can help states overcome this barrier to joint action. Realists understand that states seek absolute gains and worry about compliance. However, realists find that states are *positional*, not atomistic, in character, and therefore realists argue that, in addition to concerns about cheating, states in cooperative arrangements also worry that their partners might gain more from cooperation than they do. For realists, a state will focus both on its absolute and relative gains from cooperation, and a state that is satisfied with a partner's compliance in a joint arrangement might nevertheless exit from it because the partner is achieving relatively greater gains. Realism, then, finds that there are at least two major barriers to international cooperation: state concerns about cheating and state concerns about relative achievement of gains. Neoliberal institutionalism pays attention exclusively to the former, and is unable to identify, analyze or account for the latter.

Realism's identification of the relative gains problem for cooperation is based on its insight that states in anarchy fear for their survival as independent actors. According to realists, states worry that today's friend may be tomorrow's enemy in war, and fear that achievements of joint gains that advantage a friend in the present might produce a more dangerous *potential* foe in the future. As a result, states must give serious attention to the gains of partners. Neoliberals fail to consider the threat of war arising from international anarchy, and this allows them to ignore the matter of relative gains and to assume that states only desire absolute gains. Yet, in doing so, they fail to identify a major source of state inhibitions about international cooperation.

In sum, I suggest that realism, its emphasis on conflict and competition notwithstanding, offers a more complete understanding of the problem of international cooperation than does its latest liberal challenger. If that is true, then realism is still the most powerful theory of international politics.

Joseph M. Grieco, *Anarchy and the Limits of Cooperation: A Realist Critique of the Newest Liberal Institutionalism*, 42 INTERNATIONAL ORGANIZATION 485 (1988). Do you find this critique persuasive? How might an institutionalist respond?

4. Guzman uses a Prisoner's Dilemma to illustrate his argument. The Prisoner's Dilemma is a famous, short parable about two prisoners who are both individually offered an opportunity to confess and offer evidence against the other prisoner ("defect") in return for a lighter sentence (leaving the other prisoner with a heavier sentence than if they had both remained silent). The players cannot communicate and coordinate their responses to the interrogator in advance, hence the situation is what is known as a "noncooperative game." The dilemma results from the fact that both prisoners can defect, and, if both do, both receive worse sentences than they would have had they both kept silent (though the sentence for each prisoner is less severe than it would have been had the prisoner remained silent when the other talked). The parable is often used as a model of noncooperation between two or more individuals where each individual is better off defecting, regardless of what the other party does, even though this strategy will lead to worse results than had they cooperated. In Guzman's illustration, Figure A presents a prisoner's dilemma, because the payoffs are structured so that a country does better by violating, regardless of what the other party does, leading both players to receive worse payoffs than had they cooperated. The game depicted in Figure B is not a prisoner's dilemma. Indeed, it is precisely the reverse: each player does better complying regardless of what the other player does. This leads the players to the ideal outcome (cooperation) in which both receive the highest possible payoffs. A similar result might be achieved with a prisoners' dilemma framework if the game is played over multiple periods. While the solution to a one-shot prisoners' dilemma is for both players to confess (noncooperation), cooperation is possible in a longer term game. What consequences might this have for the application of the prisoners' dilemma to the international law context? For more on the prisoners' dilemma, see DOUGLAS G. BAIRD, ROBERT H. GERTNER, AND RANDAL C. PICKER, GAME THEORY AND THE LAW 33–34 (1994); ERIC RASMUSSEN, GAMES AND INFORMATION 20–21, 111 (3d ed. 2001).

5. What does Grieco's critique suggest for Andrew Guzman's argument? In a repetitive game, will actors appraise the value gained by others when they choose whether to comply or not? How might they know what benefits the other players stand to gain?

6. What are the central differences between institutional theory and realism? And neorealism? In what ways are they similar? In this respect, what would Carr and Morgenthau say in response to Guzman's discussion of the role of reputation in international law? Should Keohane embrace Guzman's view as complementary to his own?

7. How does institutional theory account for change over time? How does this explanation compare to that offered by Realism? (Consider the same question with regard to the other theories as you proceed through this book.) Alec Stone Sweet's work provides an account of the sources and consequences of institutional change, focusing in particular on how social norms evolve, with what effects. See, e.g., MARTIN SHAPIRO & ALEC STONE SWEET, GOVERNING WITH JUDGES: CONSTITUTIONAL POLITICS IN EUROPE (2000). As such, his work—sometimes characterized as a "modified neofunctionalism"—operates at the intersection of norm-based and interest-based accounts. Can institutional theory provide a convincing account of change without such a reference to norms?

8. Why do states behave as they do in the institutionalist view? What role does international law play? How does international law come about? When and why does it genuinely constrain state behavior?

C. Liberal Theory

A third approach to international law and politics, like the realist and institutional theories on which it builds, assumes that states act in pursuit of self-interest. The source of this self-interest, however, is distinct. Liberal theory (sometimes termed "institutional liberalism" or "liberal institutionalism"), discards the assumption of realism and institutionalism that states are properly viewed as unitary rational agents. Instead, the theory disaggregates the state and places the focus on domestic political processes.

This approach finds its intellectual antecedents in the work of Immanuel Kant, in particular his essay *Perpetual Peace*. In the essay, Kant argues that the first condition of perpetual peace is that "the civil construction of every nation should be republican," because republican governments (i.e., representative democracies) rely on the consent of the citizens to engage in war and must therefore "consider all its calamities before committing themselves to so risky a game." Kant's claim was later taken up by international relations scholars, most notably Michael Doyle and Bruce Russett, who claimed that although "liberal" states engage in war, they do not engage in war with one another. In its modern iteration, Liberal international relations theory has come to stand for the straightforward proposition that domestic politics matter.

The Liberal approach holds that interstate politics are much more complex than realists and institutionalists acknowledge. States are the sum of many different parts. Understanding those parts—the political institutions, interest groups, and state actors—is essential to fully understanding state action on the world stage. As political scientist Andrew Moravcsik puts it in the article excerpted below: "Societal ideas, interests, and institutions influence state behavior by shaping state preferences, that is, the fundamental social purposes underlying the strategic calculations of governments." In other words, one cannot fully understand state decisions in the international realm without understanding the domestic politics that underlie them.

Anne–Marie Slaughter has taken the lead in bringing this version of the Liberal view to the attention of legal scholars. In the article excerpted below, she outlines the tenets of the theory and demonstrates how they illuminate the study of international law. As she notes, the Liberal framework—in contrast with many traditional accounts of international law—focuses not on interactions between states but instead on interactions between individuals and government institutions. In the commentary that follows, legal scholar Jose Alvarez focuses on the implications of Slaughter's Liberal approach for international law. In particular, he criticizes what he sees as the implied distinction—made more expressly in Slaughter's earlier work (cited in the Notes below)—between liberal and non-liberal states. He proceeds to enumerate what he sees as four incorrect and inappropriate underlying assumptions of Liberal theory, as applied to international law.

Taking Preferences Seriously: A Liberal Theory of International Politics*

ANDREW MORAVCSIK

... Postwar realist critics such as Hans Morgenthau and E. H. Carr took rhetorical advantage of liberalism's historical role as an ideology to contrast its purported altruism ("idealism," "legalism," "moralism," or "utopianism") with realism's "theoretical concern with human nature as it actually is [and] historical processes as they actually take place." Forty years later, little has changed. Robert Gilpin's influential typology in international political economy juxtaposes a positive mercantilist view ("politics determines economics") against a narrower and conspicuously normative liberal one ("economics *should* determine politics"). Kenneth Waltz, a realist critic, asserts that "if the aims ... of states become matters of ... central concern, then we are forced back to the descriptive level; and from simple descriptions no valid generalizations can be drawn...."

... Robert Keohane, an institutionalist sympathetic to liberalism, maintains that "in contrast to Marxism and Realism, Liberalism is not committed to ambitious and parsimonious structural theory." ...

I seek to move beyond this unsatisfactory situation by proposing a set of core assumptions on which a general restatement of positive liberal IR [international relations] theory can be grounded.... I argue that the basic liberal insight about the centrality of state-society relations to world politics can be restated in terms of three positive assumptions, concerning, respectively, the nature of fundamental social actors, the state, and the international system.

Drawing on these assumptions, I then elaborate three major variants of liberal theory—each grounded in a distinctive causal mechanism linking social preferences and state behavior. Ideational liberalism stresses the impact on state behavior of conflict and compatibility among collective social values or identities concerning the scope and nature of public goods provision. Commercial liberalism stresses the impact on state behavior of gains and losses to individuals and groups in society from transnational economic interchange. Republican liberalism stresses the impact on state behavior of varying forms of domestic representation and the resulting incentives for social groups to engage in rent seeking.

* Reprinted by permission from 51 INTERNATIONAL ORGANIZATION 513 (1997).

Core Assumptions of Liberal IR Theory

Liberal IR theory's fundamental premise—that the relationship between states and the surrounding domestic and transnational society in which they are embedded critically shapes state behavior by influencing the social purposes underlying state preferences—can be restated in terms of three core assumptions. These assumptions are appropriate foundations of any social theory of IR: they specify the nature of societal actors, the state, and the international system.

Assumption 1: The Primacy of Societal Actors

The fundamental actors in international politics are individuals and private groups, who are on the average rational and risk-averse and who organize exchange and collective action to promote differentiated interests under constraints imposed by material scarcity, conflicting values, and variations in societal influence.

Liberal theory rests on a "bottom-up" view of politics in which the demands of individuals and societal groups are treated as analytically prior to politics. Political action is embedded in domestic and transnational civil society, understood as an aggregation of boundedly rational individuals with differentiated tastes, social commitments, and resource endowments. Socially differentiated individuals define their material and ideational interests independently of politics and then advance those interests through political exchange and collective action. Individuals and groups are assumed to act rationally in pursuit of material and ideal welfare.

For liberals, the definition of the interests of societal actors is theoretically central. Liberal theory rejects the utopian notion that an automatic harmony of interest exists among individuals and groups in society; scarcity and differentiation introduce an inevitable measure of competition. Where social incentives for exchange and collective action are perceived to exist, individuals and groups exploit them: the greater the expected benefits, the stronger the incentive to act. . . .

Assumption 2: Representation and State Preferences

States (or other political institutions) represent some subset of domestic society, on the basis of whose interests state officials define state preferences and act purposively in world politics.

In the liberal conception of domestic politics, the state is not an actor but a representative institution constantly subject to capture and recapture, construction and reconstruction by coalitions of social actors. Representative institutions and practices constitute the critical "transmission belt" by which the preferences and social power of individuals and groups are translated into state policy. Individuals turn to the state to achieve goals that private behavior is unable to achieve efficiently. Government policy is therefore constrained by the underlying identities, interests, and power of individuals and groups (inside and outside the state apparatus) who constantly pressure the central decision makers to pursue policies consistent with their preferences.

This is not to adopt a narrowly pluralist view of domestic politics in which all individuals and groups have equal influence on state policy, nor one in which the structure of state institutions is irrelevant. No government rests on universal or unbiased political representation; every government represents some individuals and groups more fully than others. In an extreme hypothetical case, representation might empower a narrow bureaucratic class or even a single tyrannical individual, such as an ideal-typical Pol Pot or Josef Stalin. Between theoretical extremes of tyranny and democracy, many representative institutions and practices exist, each of which privileges particular demands; hence the nature of state institutions, alongside societal interests themselves, is a key determinant of what states do internationally.

. . .

Societal pressures transmitted by representative institutions and practices alter "state preferences." This term designates an ordering among underlying substantive outcomes that may result from international political interaction. Here it is essential—particularly given the inconsistency of common usage—to avoid conceptual confusion by keeping state "preferences" distinct from national "strategies," "tactics," and "policies," that is, the particular transient bargaining positions, negotiating demands, or policy goals that constitute the everyday currency of foreign policy. State preferences, as the concept is employed here, comprise a set of fundamental interests defined across "states of the world." Preferences are by definition causally independent of the strategies of other actors and, therefore, prior to specific interstate political interactions, including external threats, incentives, manipulation of information, or other tactics. By contrast, strategies and tactics—sometimes also termed "preferences" in game-theoretical analyses—are policy options defined across intermediate political aims, as when governments declare an "interest" in "maintaining the balance of power," "containing" or "appeasing" an adversary, or exercising "global leadership." Liberal theory focuses on the consequences for state behavior of shifts in fundamental preferences, not shifts in the strategic circumstances under which states pursue them.

. . .

Taken together, assumptions 1 and 2 imply that states do not automatically maximize fixed, homogeneous conceptions of security, sovereignty, or wealth per se, as realists and institutionalists tend to assume. Instead they are, in Waltzian terms, "functionally differentiated"; that is, they pursue particular interpretations and combinations of security, welfare, and sovereignty preferred by powerful domestic groups enfranchised by representative institutions and practices. As Arnold Wolfers, John Ruggie, and some others have observed, the nature and intensity of national support for any state purpose—even apparently fundamental concerns like the defense of political and legal sovereignty, territorial integrity, national security, or economic welfare—varies decisively with the social context. It is not uncommon for states knowingly to surrender sovereignty, compromise security, or reduce aggregate economic welfare. In the liberal view, trade-offs among such goals, as well as cross-national differences in their definition, are inevitable, highly varied, and causally consequential.

Assumption 3: Interdependence and the International System

The configuration of interdependent state preferences determines state behavior.

For liberals, state behavior reflects varying patterns of state preferences. States require a "purpose," a perceived underlying stake in the matter at hand, in order to provoke conflict, propose cooperation, or take any other significant foreign policy action. The precise nature of these stakes drives policy. This is not to assert that each state simply pursues its ideal policy, oblivious of others; instead, each state seeks to realize its distinctive preferences under varying constraints imposed by the preferences of other states. Thus liberal theory rejects not just the realist assumption that state preferences must be treated as if naturally conflictual, but equally the institutionalist assumption that they should be treated as if they were partially convergent, compromising a collective action problem. To the contrary, liberals causally privilege variation in the configuration of state preferences, while treating configurations of capabilities and information as if they were either fixed constraints or endogenous to state preferences.

The critical theoretical link between state preferences, on the one hand, and the behavior of one or more states, on the other, is provided by the concept of policy interdependence. Policy interdependence is defined here as the set of costs and benefits created for foreign societies when dominant social groups in a society seek to realize their preferences, that is, the pattern of transnational externalities resulting from attempts to pursue national distinctive purposes.[1] Liberal theory assumes that the pattern of interdependent state preferences imposes a binding constraint on state behavior.

. . .

For liberals, the form, substance, and depth of cooperation depends directly on the nature of these patterns of preferences. Hence where "Pareto-inefficient" outcomes are observed—trade protection is a commonly cited example—liberals turn first to countervailing social preferences and unresolved domestic and transnational distributional conflicts, whereas institutionalists and realists, respectively, turn to uncertainty and particular configurations of interstate power.

Liberal Theory as Systemic Theory

These liberal assumptions, in particular the third—in essence, "what states want is the primary determinant of what they do"—may

1. [Editors' Note: The economic concept of an "externality" is a cost or benefit imposed on those outside a system by the actions of those acting within the system.]

seem commonsensical, even tautological. Yet mainstream IR theory has uniformly rejected such claims for the past half-century. At the heart of the two leading contemporary IR theories, realism and institutionalism, is the belief that state behavior has ironic consequences. Power politics and informational uncertainty constrain states to pursue second- and third-best strategies strikingly at variance with their underlying preferences. Thus varying state preferences should be treated as if they were irrelevant, secondary, or endogenous. In his classic definition of realism Morgenthau contrasts it to "two popular fallacies: the concern with motives and the concern with ideological preferences." Neorealist Waltz's central objection to previous, "reductionist" theories is that in world politics "results achieved seldom correspond to the intentions of actors"; hence "no valid generalizations can logically be drawn" from an examination of intentions. Though the interests it assumes are different, Keohane's institutionalism relies on a similar as if assumption: it "takes the existence of mutual interests as given and examines the conditions under which they will lead to cooperation." In short, Powell observes that "structural theories ... lack a theory of preferences over outcomes." What states do is primarily determined by strategic considerations—what they can get or what they know—which in turn reflect their international political environment. In short, variation in means, not ends, matters most.

Liberal theory reverses this assumption: Variation in ends, not means, matters most. Realists and institutionalists, as well as formal theorists who seek to integrate the two, criticize this core liberal assumption because it appears at first glance to rest on what Waltz terms a "reductionist" rather than a "systemic" understanding of IR. In other words, liberalism appears to be a purely "domestic" or "unit-level" theory that ignores the international environment. In particular, realists are skeptical of this view because it appears at first glance to be grounded in the utopian expectation that every state can do as it pleases. This commonplace criticism is erroneous for two important reasons.

First, state preferences may reflect patterns of transnational societal interaction. While state preferences are (by definition) invariant in response to changing interstate political and strategic circumstances, they may well vary in response to a changing transnational social context. In the political economy for foreign economic policy, for example, social demands are derived not simply from "domestic" economic assets and endowments, but from the relative position of those assets and endowments in global markets. Similarly, the position of particular values in a transnational cultural discourse may help define their meaning in each society. In this regard, liberalism does not draw a strict line between domestic and transnational levels of analysis.

A second and more Waltzian reason why the charge of "reductionism" is erroneous is that according to liberal theory the expected behavior of any single state—the strategies it selects and the systemic constraints to which it adjusts—reflect not simply its own preferences, but the configuration of preferences of all states linked by patterns of significant policy interdependence. National leaders must always think systemically about their position within a structure composed of the preferences of other states. Since the pattern of and interdependence among state preferences, like the distribution of capabilities and the distribution of information and ideas, lies outside the control of any single state, it conforms to Waltz's own definition of systemic theory, whereby interstate interactions are explained by reference to "how [states] stand in relation to one another." Hence the causal preeminence of state preferences does not imply that states always get what they want.

One implication of liberalism's systemic, structural quality is that, contra Waltz, it can explain not only the "foreign policy" goals of individual states but the "systemic" outcomes of interstate interactions. That systemic predictions can follow from domestic theories of preferences should be obvious simply by inspecting the literature on the democratic peace. In addition, by linking social purpose to the symmetry and relative intensity of state preferences, liberalism offers a distinctive conception of political power in world politics—something traditionally considered unique to realist theory.

The liberal conception of power is based on an assumption more consistent with basic theories of bargaining and negotiation than those underlying realism: namely that the willingness of states to expend resources or make concessions is itself primarily a function of preferences, not capabilities. In this view—the foundation of Nash bargaining analysis, which has been extended to IR by Albert Hirshman, Keohane, Joseph Nye, and others—bargaining outcomes reflect the nature and relative intensity of actor preferences. The "win-set," the "best alternative to negotiated agreement," the pattern of "asymmetrical interdependence," the relative opportunity cost of forgoing an agreement—all these core terms in negotiation analysis refer to different aspects of the relationship of bargaining outcomes on the preference functions of the actors. The capability-based power to threaten central to realism enters the equation in specific circumstances and only through linkage to threats and side-payments. Even where capability-based threats and promises are employed, preference-based determinants of the tolerance for bearing bargaining costs, including differential temporal discount rates, risk-acceptance, and willingness to accept punishment, remain central.

The liberal claim that the pattern of interdependence among state preferences is a primary determinant not just of individual foreign policies, but of systemic outcomes, is commonsensical. Nations are rarely prepared to expend their entire economic or defense capabilities, or to mortgage their entire domestic sovereignty, in pursuit of any single foreign policy goal. Few wars are total, few peaces Carthaginian. Treating the willingness of states to expend resources in pursuit of foreign policy goals as a strict function of existing capabilities thus seems unrealistic. On the margin, the binding constraint is instead generally "resolve" or "determination"—the willingness of governments to mobilize and expend social resources for foreign policy purposes.

Extensive empirical evidence supports this assumption. Even in "least likely" cases, where political independence and territorial integrity are at stake and military means are deployed, relative capabilities do not necessarily determine outcomes. A "strong preference for the issue at stake can compensate for a deficiency in capabilities," as demonstrated by examples like the Boer War, Hitler's remilitarization of the Rhineland, Vietnam, Afghanistan, and Chechnya. In each case the relative intensity of state preferences reshaped the outcome to the advantage of the "weak." Such examples suggest that the liberal view of power politics, properly understood, generates plausible explanations not just of harmony and cooperation among nations, but of the full range of phenomena central to the study of world politics, from peaceful economic exchange to brutal guerrilla warfare.

Variants of Liberal Theory

Like their realist and institutionalist counterparts, the three core liberal assumptions introduced earlier are relatively thin or content-free. Taken by themselves, they do not define a single unambiguous model or set of hypotheses, not least because they do not specify precise sources of state preferences. Instead they support three separate variants of liberal theory, termed here ideational, commercial, and republican liberalism. Each rests on a distinctive specification of the central elements of liberal theory: social demands, the causal mechanisms whereby they are transformed into state preferences, and the resulting patterns of national preferences in world politics. Ideational liberalism focuses on the compatibility of social preferences across fundamental collective goods like national unity, legitimate political institutions, and socioeconomic regulation. Commercial liberalism focuses on incentives created by opportunities for transborder economic transactions. Republican liberalism focuses on the nature of domestic representation and the resulting possibilities for rent-seeking behavior.

Ideational Liberalism: Identity and Legitimate Social Order

Drawing on a liberal tradition dating back to John Stuart Mill, Giuseppe Mazzini, and Woodrow Wilson, ideational liberalism views the configuration of domestic social identities and values as a basic determinant of state preferences and, therefore, of interstate conflict and cooperation. "Social identity" is defined as the set of preferences shared by individuals concerning the proper scope and nature of public goods provision, which in turn specifies the nature of legitimate domestic order by stipulating which social actors belong to the polity and what is owed them. Liberals take no distinctive position on the origins of social identities, which may result from historical accretion or be constructed through conscious collective or state action, nor on the question of whether they ultimately reflect ideational or material factors.

Three essential elements of domestic public order often shaped by social identities are geographical borders, political decision-making processes, and socioeconomic regulation. Each can be thought of as a public or club good; the effectiveness of each typically requires that it be legislated universally across a jurisdiction. Recall that for liberals, even the defense of (or, less obvious but no less common, the willing compromise of) territorial integrity, political sovereignty, or national security is not an end in itself, but a means of realizing underlying preferences defined by the demands of societal groups. According to assumption 2, social actors provide support to the government in exchange for institutions that accord with their identity-based preferences; such institutions are thereby "legitimate." Foreign policy will thus be motivated in part by an effort to realize social views about legitimate borders, political institutions, and modes of socioeconomic regulation.

The consequences of identity-based preferences for IR depend, according to assumption 3, on the nature of transnational externalities created by attempts to realize them. Where national conceptions of legitimate borders, political institutions, and socioeconomic equality are compatible, thus generating positive or negligible externalities, harmony is likely. Where national claims can be made more compatible by reciprocal policy adjustment, cooperation is likely. Where social identities are incompatible and create significant negative externalities, tension and zero-sum conflict is more likely. Parallel predictions about international politics follow from each of the three essential sources of ideational preferences: national, political, and socioeconomic identity. Let us briefly consider each.

The first fundamental type of social identity central to the domestic legitimacy of foreign policy comprises the set of fundamental societal preferences concerning the scope of the "nation," "which in turn suggest the legitimate location of national borders and the allocation of citizenship rights." The roots of national identity may reflect a shared set of linguistic, cultural, or religious identifications or a shared set of historical experiences—often interpreted and encouraged by both private groups and state policy. In explaining conflict and cooperation over borders and citizenship, realism stresses the role of relative power, and institutionalism stresses the role of shared legal norms, whereas ideational liberalism stresses the extent to which borders coincide with the national identities of powerful social groups. Where borders coincide with underlying patterns of identity, coexistence and even mutual recognition are more likely. Where, however, inconsistencies between borders and underlying patterns of identity exist, greater potential for interstate conflict exists. In such circumstances, some social actors and governments are likely to have an interest in uniting nationals in appropriate jurisdictions, perhaps through armed aggression or secession; other governments may intervene militarily to promote or hinder such efforts. . . .

Strong empirical evidence supports the proposition that disjunctures between borders and identities are important determinants of international conflict and cooperation. In early modern Europe, interstate conflict reflected in part the competition between two communal religious identities—each of which, at least until domestic and international norms of tolerance spread, was perceived as a threat to the other. Over the last century and a half, from mid-nineteenth-century nationalist uprisings to late-twentieth-century national liberation struggles, the desire for national autonomy constitutes the most common issue over which wars have been fought and great power intervention has taken place; the Balkan conflicts preceding World War I and succeeding the Cold War are only the most notorious examples. The post-World War II peace in Western Europe and the reintegration of Germany into Europe were assisted by the reestablishment of borders along ethnic lines in the Saar and Alsace–Lorraine, as well as much of Eastern Europe. Even leading realists now concede though it in no way follows from realist premises—that disputes between "intermingled or divided nationalities" are the most probable catalyst for war in Eastern Europe and the former Soviet Union.

A second fundamental type of social identity central to foreign policymaking is the commitment of individuals and groups to particular political institutions. Realism accords theoretical weight to domestic regime type only insofar as it influences the distribution of capabilities, institutionalism only insofar as it contributes to the certainty of coordination and commitment. Ideational liberalism, by contrast, maintains that differences in perceptions of domestic political legitimacy translate into patterns of underlying preferences and thus variation in international conflict and cooperation. Where the realization of legitimate domestic political order in one jurisdiction threatens its realization in others, a situation of negative externalities, conflict is more likely. Where the realization of national conceptions of legitimate decision making reinforce or can be adjusted to reinforce one another, coexistence or cooperation is more likely.

Plausible examples abound. Thucydides accords an important role to conflict between oligarchs and democrats in alliance formation during the Peloponnesian War. In the seventeenth and eighteenth centuries, absolutist kings fought to establish dynastic claims and religious rule; in the nineteenth century, they cooperated to preserve monarchical rule against societal pressures for reform. The twentieth century has witnessed a struggle between governments backing fascist, communist, and liberal ideologies, as well as more recently a resurgence of religious claims and the emergence of a group of developed countries that share democratic norms of legitimate dispute resolution—a plausible explanation for the "democratic peace" phenomenon. A more complex pattern, consistent with the preceding assumptions, may emerge when individual domestic actors—most often national executives—exploit the legitimacy of particular international policies as a "two-level" instrument to increase their influence over the domestic polity. This is a constant theme in modern world politics, from Bismarck's manipulation of domestic coalitions to the current use of monetary integration by today's European leaders to "strengthen the state" at home.

A third fundamental type of social identity central to foreign policy is the nature of legitimate socioeconomic regulation and redistribution. Modern liberal theory (as opposed to the laissez faire libertarianism sometimes invoked by critics as quintessentially "liberal") has long recognized that societal preferences concerning the nature and level of regulation impose legitimate limits on markets. In a Polanyian vein, Ruggie recently reminds us that domestic and international markets are embedded in local social compromises concerning the provision of regulatory public goods. Such compromises underlie varying national regulations on immigration, social welfare, taxation, religious freedom, families, health and safety, environmental and consumer protection, cultural promotion, and many other public goods increasingly discussed in international economic negotiations.

In the liberal view, state preferences concerning legitimate socioeconomic practices shape interstate behavior when their realization imposes significant transborder externalities. Evidence from the European Community (EC) suggests that substantial prior convergence of underlying values is a necessary prerequisite for cooperation in regulatory issue areas like environmental and consumer protection, many tax and social policies, immigration, and foreign policy, as well as for significant surrenders of sovereign decision making to supranational courts and bureaucracies. Regulatory pluralism limits international cooperation, in particular economic liberalization. Courts, executives, and parliaments mutually recognize "legitimate differences" of policy in foreign jurisdictions. Concerns about the proper balance between policy coordination and legitimate domestic regulation are giving rise to even more complex forms of cooperation. Hence regulatory issues play an increasingly important role in international economic negotiations such as the 1992 initiative of the EC, the Uruguay Round of GATT, NAFTA, and the U.S.-Japan Structural Impediments Initiative.

Commercial Liberalism: Economic Assets and Cross-Border Transactions

Commercial liberalism explains the individual and collective behavior of states based on the patterns of market incentives facing domestic and transnational economic actors. At its simplest, the commercial liberal argument is broadly functionalist: Changes in the structure of the domestic and global economy alter the costs and benefits of transnational economic exchange, creating pressure on domestic governments to facilitate or block such exchanges through appropriate foreign economic and security policies.

It is tempting, particularly for critics, to associate commercial liberal theory with ideological support for free trade. Yet as theory rather than ideology, commercial liberalism does not predict that economic incentives automatically generate universal free trade and peace—a utopian position critics who treat liberalism as an ideology often wrongly attribute to it—but instead stresses the interaction between aggregate incentives for certain policies and obstacles posed by domestic and transnational distributional conflict. The greater the economic benefits for powerful private actors, the greater their incentive, other things being equal, to press governments to facilitate such transactions; the more costly the adjustment imposed by economic interchange, the more opposition is likely to arise. Rather than assuming that market structure always creates incentives for cooperation among social actors as well as states, or focusing exclusively on those issue areas where it does, as do some liberal ideologies, liberal IR theory focuses on market structure as a variable creating incentives for both openness and closure.

Accordingly, many commercial liberal analyses start with aggregate welfare gains from trade resulting from specialization and functional differentiation, then seek to explain divergences from foreign economic and security policies that would maximize those gains. To explain the rejection of aggregate gains, commercial liberals from Adam Smith to contemporary "endogenous" tariff theorists look to domestic and international distributional conflicts. The resulting commercial liberal explanation of relative gains seeking in foreign economic policy is quite distinct from that of realism, which emphasizes security externalities and relative (hegemonic) power, or that of institutionalism, which stresses informational and institutional constraints on interstate collective action.

One source of pressure for protection is domestic distributional conflict, which arises when the costs and benefits of national policies are not internalized to the same actors, thus encouraging rent-seeking efforts to seek personal benefit at the expense of aggregate welfare. In this view, uncompetitive, monopolistic, or undiversified sectors or factors lose the most from liberalization and have an incentive to oppose it, inducing a systematic divergence from laissez faire policies. Smith himself reminds us that "the contrivers of [mercantilism are] the producers, whose interest has been so carefully attended to . . . our merchants and manufacturers"—a view echoed by many liberals since. Recent research supports the view that protectionist pressure from rent-seeking groups is most intense precisely where distributional concerns of concentrated groups are strongest, for example, when industries are uncompetitive or irreversible investments (asset specificity) impose high adjustment costs on concentrated interests. Free trade is more likely where strong competitiveness, extensive intra-industry trade, or trade in intermediate goods, large foreign investments, and low asset specificity internalize the net benefits of free trade to powerful actors, thus reducing the influence of net losers from liberalization.

The distributional consequences of global market imperfections create a second sort of disjuncture between the aggregate benefits of economic interdependence and national policies. Modern trade theory identifies incentives for strategic behavior where increasing returns to scale, high fixed costs, surplus capacity, or highly concentrated sources of supply render international markets imperfectly competitive. Firms hoping to create (or break into) a global oligopoly or monopoly, for example, may have an incentive to engage in predatory dumping abroad while seeking domestic protection and subsidization at home, even though this imposes costs on domestic consumers and foreign producers. Such policies can create substantial international conflict, since government intervention to assist firms can improve welfare for society as a whole, though usually not for all societies involved.

Commercial liberalism has important implications for security affairs as well. Trade is generally a less costly means of accumulating wealth than war, sanctions, or other coercive means, not least due to the minimization of collateral damage. Yet governments sometimes have an incentive to employ coercive means to create and control international markets. To explain this variation, domestic distributional issues and the structure of global markets are again critical. Commercial liberals argue that the more diversified and complex the existing transnational commercial ties and production structures, the less cost-effective coercion is likely to be. Cost-effective coercion was most profitable in an era where the main sources of economic profit, such as farmland, slave labor, raw materials, or formal monopoly, could be easily controlled in conquered or colonial economies. Yet economic development tends to increase the material stake of social actors in existing investments, thereby reducing their willingness to assume the cost and risk of coercion through war or sanctions. As production becomes more specialized and efficient and trading networks more diverse and complex, political extraction (for example, war and embargoes) become more disruptive, and profitable monopolies over commercial opportunities become more difficult to establish. Both cross-cultural anthropological evidence and modern cross-national evidence link warfare to the existence of monopolizable resources; over the past century, it has remained the major determinant of boundary disputes. Yet the advent of modern industrial networks, particularly those based on postindustrial informational exchange, has increased the opportunity costs of coercive tactics ranging from military aggression to coercive nationalization.

Republican Liberalism: Representation and Rent Seeking

While ideational and commercial liberal theory, respectively, stress demands resulting from particular patterns of underlying societal identities and economic interests, republican liberal theory emphasizes the ways in which domestic institutions and practices aggregate those demands, transforming them into state policy. The key variable in republican liberalism is the mode of domestic political representation, which determines whose social preferences are institutionally privileged. When political representation is biased in favor of particularistic groups, they tend to "capture" government institutions and employ them for their ends alone, systematically passing on the costs and risks to others. The precise policy of governments depends on which domestic groups are represented. The simplest resulting prediction is that policy is biased in favor of the governing coalition or powerful domestic groups.

A more sophisticated extension of this reasoning focuses on rent seeking. When particularistic groups are able to formulate policy without necessarily providing offsetting gains for society as a whole, the result is likely to be inefficient, suboptimal policies from the aggregate perspective—one form of which may be costly international conflict. While many liberal arguments are concerned with the seizure of state institutions by administrators (rulers, armies, and bureaucracies), similar arguments apply to privileged societal groups that "capture" the state, according to assumption 2, or simply act independently of it. If, following assumption 1, most individuals and groups in society, while acquisitive, tend also to be risk-averse (at least where they have something to lose), the more unbiased the range of domestic groups represented, the less likely they will support policies that impose high net costs or risks on a broad range of social actors. Thus, aggressive behavior—the voluntary recourse to costly or risky foreign policy—is most likely in undemocratic or inegalitarian polities where privileged individuals can easily pass costs on to others.

This does not, of course, imply the existence of a one-to-one correspondence between the breadth of domestic representation and international political or economic cooperation, for two reasons. First, in specific cases, elite preferences may be more convergent than popular ones. If commercial or ideational preferences are conflictual, for example where hypernationalist or mercantilist preferences prevail, a broadening of representation may have the opposite effect—a point to which I will return. Elites, such as those leaders that constructed the Concert of Europe or similar arrangements among African leaders today, have been attributed to their convergent interests in maintaining themselves in office. Second, the extent of bias in representation, not democratic participation per se, is the theoretically critical point. Direct representation may overrepresent concentrated, organized, short-term, or otherwise arbitrarily salient interests. Predictable conditions exist under which governing elites may have an incentive to represent long-term social preferences more unbiasedly than does broad opinion.

Despite these potential complexities and caveats, republican liberalism nonetheless generates parsimonious predictions where conflictual policies impose extremely high costs and risks on the majority of individuals in domestic society. With respect to extreme but historically common policies like war, famine, and radical autarky, fair representation tends to inhibit international conflict. In this way, republican liberal theory has helped to explain phenomena as diverse as the "democratic peace," modern anti-imperialism, and international trade and monetary cooperation. Given the prima facie plausibility of the assumption that major war imposes net costs on society as a whole, it is not surprising that the prominent republican liberal argument concerns the "democratic peace," which one scholar has termed "as close as anything we have to a law in international relations"—one that applies to tribal societies as well as to modern states. Liberal democratic institutions tend not to provoke such wars because influence is placed in the hands of those who must expend blood and treasure and the leaders they choose.

Often overlooked is the theoretical corollary of "democratic peace" theory: a republican liberal theory of war that stresses abnormally risk-acceptant leaders and rent-seeking coalitions. Substantial evidence shows that the aggressors who have provoked modern great power wars tend either to be risk-acceptant individuals in the extreme or individuals well able to insulate themselves from the costs of war or both. Most leaders initiating twentieth-century great power wars lost them; Adolf Hitler and Saddam Hussein, for example, initiated conflicts against coalitions far more powerful than their own. In the same vein, Jack Snyder has recently deepened Hobson's classic rent-seeking analysis of imperialism—whereby the military, uncompetitive foreign investors and traders, jingoistic political elites, and others who benefit from imperialism are particularly well-placed to influence policy—by linking unrepresentative and extreme outcomes to logrolling coalitions. Consistent with this analysis, the highly unrepresentative consequences of partial democratization, combined with the disruption of rapid industrialization and incomplete political socialization, suggest that democratizing states, if subject to these influences, may be particularly war prone. Such findings may challenge some variants of liberal ideology but are consistent with liberal theory.

The link between great-power military aggression and small-group interests in nonrepresentative states implies neither unceasing belligerence by autocratic regimes nor unquestioning pacifism by democratic ones. Enlightened despotism or democratic aggression remains possible. The more precise liberal prediction is thus that despotic power, bounded by neither law nor representative institutions, tends to be wielded in a more arbitrary manner by a wider range of individuals, leading both to a wider range of expected outcomes and a more conflictual average. Nonetheless, liberal theory predicts that democratic states may provoke preventive wars in response to direct or indirect threats, against very weak states with no great power allies, or in peripheral areas where the legal and political preconditions for trade and other forms of profitable transnational relations are not yet in place.

Scholars also often overlook precise analogs to the "democratic peace" in matters of political economy. The liberal explanation for the persistence of illiberal commercial policies, such as protection, monetary instability, and sectoral subsidization, where such policies manifestly undermine the general welfare of the population, is pressure from powerful domestic groups. Thus in the liberal view the creation and maintenance of regimes assuring free trade and monetary stability result not primarily from common threats to national security or appropriate international institutions, but from the ability of states to overcome domestic distributional conflicts in a way supportive of international cooperation. This may ultimately reflect the economic benefits of doing so, as commercial liberal theory suggests, but it can also be decisively helped or hindered by biases in representative institutions. Where such biases favor sheltered groups, and substantial misrepresentation of this type is seen as endemic to most contemporary representative institutions, rent-seeking groups are likely to gain protection through tariffs, subsidies, favorable regulation, or competitive devaluation. Where policymakers are insulated from such pressures, which may involve less democratic but more representative institutions, or where free trade interests dominate policy, open policies are more viable.

. . .

Liberalism as a General Theory: Parsimony and Coherence

. . .

Liberal theory also illuminates at least three major phenomena for which realism and institutionalism offer few, if any, predictions.... First, *liberal theory provides a plausible theoretical explanation for variation in the substantive content of foreign policy.* Neither realism nor institutionalism explains the changing substantive goals and purposes over which states conflict and cooperate; both focus instead on formal causes, such as relative power or issue density, and formal consequences, such as conflict and cooperation per se. By contrast, liberal theory provides a plausible explanation not just for conflict and cooperation, but for the substantive content of foreign policy. Major elements of international order emphasized, but not explained, in recent criticisms of realism and institutionalism include the difference between Anglo–American, Nazi, and Soviet plans for the post-World War II world; U.S. concern about a few North Korean, Iraqi, or Chinese nuclear weapons, rather than the greater arsenals held by Great Britain, Israel, and France; the substantial differences between the compromise of "embedded liberalism" underlying Bretton Woods and arrangements under the Gold Standard; divergences between economic cooperation under the EC and the Council for Mutual Economic Assistance; and the greater protectionism of the Organization for Economic Cooperation and Development's agricultural policy, as compared to its industrial trade policy. Liberal IR theory offers plausible, parsimonious hypotheses to explain each of these phenomena.

Second, *liberal theory offers a plausible explanation for historical change in the international system.* The static quality of both realist and institutionalist theory—their lack of an explanation for fundamental long-term change in the nature of international politics—is a recognized weakness. In particular, global economic development over the past five hundred years has been closely related to greater per capita wealth, democratization, education systems that reinforce new collective identities, and greater incentives for transborder economic transactions. Realist theory accords these changes no theoretical importance. Theorists like Waltz, Gilpin, and Paul Kennedy limit realism to the analysis of unchanging patterns of state behavior or the cyclical rise and decline of great powers. Liberal theory, by contrast, forges a direct causal link between economic, political, and social change and state behavior in world politics. Hence, over the modern period the principles of international order have been decreasingly linked to dynastic legitimacy and increasingly tied to factors directly drawn from the three variants of liberal theory: national self-determination and social citizenship, the increasing complexity of economic integration, and liberal democratic governance.

Third, *liberal theory offers a plausible explanation for the distinctiveness of modern international politics*. Among advanced industrial democracies, a stable form of interstate politics has emerged, grounded in reliable expectations of peaceful change, domestic rule of law, stable international institutions, and intensive societal interaction. This is the condition Deutsch terms a "pluralistic security community" and Keohane and Nye term "complex interdependence."

Whereas realists (and constructivists)[2] offer no general explanation for the emergence of this distinctive mode of international politics, liberal theory argues that the emergence of a large and expanding bloc of pacific, interdependent, normatively satisfied states has been a precondition for such politics. Consider, for example, the current state of Europe. Unlike realism, liberal theory explains the utter lack of competitive alliance formation among the leading democratic powers today. For example, the absence of serious conflict among Western powers over Yugoslavia—the "World War I scenario"—reflects in large part a shared perception that the geopolitical stakes among democratic governments are low. Similarly, liberalism makes more sense of the sudden reversal of East–West relations, a shift made possible by the widespread view among Russian officials (so interview data reveal) that Germany is ethnically satisfied, politically democratic, and commercially inclined.

. . .

Conclusion: The Virtues of Theoretical Pluralism

Liberal IR theory is not simply an ideological foil for more realistic and rigorous theories, as its critics claim, nor an eclectic collection of hypotheses linked only by common intellectual history and normative commitment, as its proponents are currently forced to concede. It is instead a logically coherent, theoretically distinct, empirically generalizable social scientific theory—one that follows from explicit assumptions and generates a rich range of related propositions about world politics that reach far beyond cases of cooperation among a minority of liberal states. By reformulating liberalism as theory rather than ideology, we have repeatedly seen that what are often treated as liberal failures become liberal predictions.

Moreover, liberalism exhibits considerable potential for theoretical extension. Aside from the myriad opportunities for empirical testing and theoretical refinement of specific hypotheses, a number of broader areas are poised for theoretical innovation. Relaxing the assumption of unitary state behavior would support a range of "two level" hypotheses about

2. [Editors' Note: For more on constructivism, see Part III.A.]

the differential ability of various domestic state and societal actors to pursue semiautonomous transnational activities. Relaxing the assumption that decision making is static would support analyses of change over time. Greater attention to feedback from prior decisions mediated by intervening liberal factors like domestic ideas, institutions, and interests might provide firmer microfoundations for theories of regime stability and change—an area of potential collaboration with constructivists and historical institutionalists. Finally, the rich interaction among domestic and transnational ideas, interests, and institutions is only beginning to be explored.

. . .

A Liberal Theory of International Law*

ANNE-MARIE SLAUGHTER

. . .

The Sources and Relative Impact of Rules Regulating International Order

Public international law, as traditionally taught and practiced, assumes its own pride of place in the rules contributing to international order. International law is defined as "inter-state" law. International society is a society of states; international law seeks to achieve the goals and values of that society; it does so primarily by regulating states. The tables of contents of international law casebooks tell the story. The unmistakable message is that international order is created from the top down.

A Liberal approach to international law assumes that international order is created from the bottom up. It identifies multiple bodies of rules, norms and processes that contribute to international order, beginning with voluntary codes of conduct adopted by individual and corporate actors operating in transnational society and working up through transnational and transgovernmental law to traditional public international law. Some of these bodies of rules are already covered in existing casebooks on international and transnational law, but typically as peripheral or interstitial phenomena. Others are largely invisible. Voluntary codes of conduct adopted by transnational enterprises, for instance, simply do not fit into a state-centric, top-down framework. The Liberal approach, by contrast, brings them into the center of the discipline and provides an overarching theory linking them to one another.

In addition to identifying and integrating these different types and levels of law within a unified framework, the Liberal approach reorders their relative priority as sources of international order. If the sources of state behavior lie in the formation and representation of individual and

* Reprinted by permission from 94 American Society of International Law Proceedings 240 (2000). © The American Society of International Law.

group preferences, then the key to international order lies in shaping those preferences and regulating the individual and collective ability to achieve them. On this metric, traditional international treaties imposing obligations on states without direct links to individuals other than the standard implementing requirements presumptively fall behind national, transnational, transgovernmental and even "voluntary" rules and norms that directly regulate individual and group behavior.

Three "Levels of Law"

The three core assumptions of Liberal IR theory suggest three levels of law, or at least of lawmaking. First, individuals and groups operating in domestic and transnational society make rules governing themselves. Second, governments make rules regulating individuals and groups operating in domestic and transnational society; parts of governments may also cooperate with one another to make rules binding themselves on matters of common concern. Third, states make rules governing their mutual relations.

. . . The distinctive contribution of Liberal IR theory is its emphasis on interaction between individuals operating in society and the "state," meaning an aggregation of government institutions, and the way in which that interaction shapes state behavior at the international level. As applied to law, the theory's power lies not in a static typology of levels of law, but in a dynamic account of lawmaking, implementation and enforcement.

As developed to date in the IR literature, Liberal IR theory focuses more on politics than on law, emphasizing preference formation among individuals and groups and the way in which state governments represent some subset of those preferences and bargain with each other in inter-state relations. Extended to law, the relationship between governments and society becomes more complex, involving regulation as well as representation. Indeed, the twin processes of representation and regulation take place simultaneously and interactively, structuring and shaping both state and society. In classic liberal contractarian theory, individuals in the state of nature create the state to establish order among themselves and thus to create the conditions necessary for society. In a democracy, however, individuals elect the officials who comprise the state and make the law that establishes order.

Liberal IR theory thus assumes a relationship between individuals and some kind of "state" authority, consistent with the classical liberal view of a social contract and of the need for a state to provide both legitimacy and effective governance. This relationship takes many forms: individual and group action spurs state action; state action, or even the possibility of state action, can spur individual and group action; state support can underpin and encourage individual and group action. It is a traditional liberal assumption, however, that "law" requires some kind of state involvement. Thus, the Liberal account of international law offered here searches always for the seam of individual-state interaction running through all three levels of the international system.

From this perspective, the three "levels" of law that a Liberal theory highlights could be reinterpreted to reflect three standard and frequent types of individual-state interaction. Individuals and groups interact with each other in the shadow of government institutions, directly through government institutions, and through government institutions with the individuals and groups of other states. These are not the exclusive sites of interaction, however; state authority can be delegated directly to international institutions, which can then interact directly with individuals and groups independent of national government institutions, as discussed further below. But the three levels discussed here are the dominant sites.

The first level of law is the voluntary law of individuals and groups in transnational society. The Liberal focus on state-society relations leads first to an examination of rules arising out of the interactions of individuals, private groups and organizations across borders. These actors regulate themselves in a variety of ways, from decentralized choice of national laws and fora to regulate private commercial transactions to the adoption of both civic and corporate codes of conduct designed to substitute for or supplement state regulation. Although much of the literature on this growing body of rules and norms treats them as entirely "private," the state is never far away.

The voluntary law governing transnational society further subdivides into several categories. First is a category of protolaw generated by a wide range of business and professional organizations. In the domestic context, Robert Cooter has described these rules as the "new law merchant," voluntary norms adopted by corporate networks, self-regulating professions and business associations. Many of these networks and associations extend transnationally as well, generating an accompanying network of transnational voluntary norms, or, as political scientists call them, private regimes.

The content of these regimes also extends beyond purely commercial matters, at least as traditionally defined. Many human rights and environmental nongovernmental organizations (NGOs) have been working hard to give substance to the concept of "corporate accountability" by convincing multinational corporations to adopt specific codes governing their responsibilities to their workers and the social and environmental conditions of the societies in which they operate. NGOs, in turn, face growing challenges to their accountability, to which they are responding by adopting codes of conduct on their own. These codes and norms may not seem like law at all. Yet scholars and practitioners seeking to predict actual behavior must take them into account as empirical facts that guide action. Further, as will be discussed below, these bodies of rules may be templates for future law.

A second category of rules governing transnational commerce is the law selected by individual actors to govern the interpretation and application of bilateral commercial agreements and the mode of resolving disputes arising out of those agreements. The actors enter into contractual relations. Their interaction is to be governed by the contract. But they also determine what law shall govern the contract and where and how disputes arising out of or related to the contract will be resolved. They can choose either a judicial or an arbitral forum. If they choose arbitration, they can also write their own rules of procedure governing the dispute resolution process.

A final example is the "other" new lex mercatoria, the rules developed by arbitration. Within international commercial arbitration, individuals and groups may find themselves, either by specification or not, governed by an independent body of law developed by international commercial arbitrators on the basis of customary transnational business practices. These rules have also been referred to as "the new law merchant," or lex mercatoria. The arbitrators derive their authority from the arbitral agreement. They themselves form an informal network, such that they can effectively draw on their collective experience in distilling and applying these rules. Formally, this body of law has no more status than voluntary norms developed and adopted by professional associations. It similarly evolves from social and economic practice in transnational society.

Thus far, the law of transnational society has been presented as essentially stateless. This is an accurate depiction in that individuals and groups are the primary actors; state functions are ancillary to the functioning of the system. But the state appears in several guises.

First, social norms can simply coexist alongside more formal legal rules, with the state acquiescing in or even welcoming the arrangement. Virginia Haufler finds that officials in the United States and Europe welcome voluntary corporate initiatives as a complement to traditional regulation and public law. States also provide the bodies of rules available for selection by individual and corporate actors in arbitration agreements. The lex mercatoria of international commercial arbitration coexists with formal bodies of national and international law governing arbitral procedures.

Second, governments can play an active role in the development of private regimes. They can underpin them with the assured exercise of public authority to enforce private arrangements. The best traditional example is the way in which private commercial arbitration agreements depend on the framework provided by the New York Convention, which secures the coercive power of national courts to make such agreements transnationally enforceable. Governments can also trigger private regimes by threatening state action in the absence of changed behavior through self-regulation. From this perspective, many of these private regimes may be better understood as privatized law. Finally, as many law and economics scholars have urged, states can allow private actors to develop their own codes of conduct and then incorporate those codes into official regulation, thereby purportedly ensuring the efficiency of the rules that are adopted.

Third, state law is likely to be needed to regulate conflicts between different private actors in transnational society. When one side or the other—corporations or NGOs—perceives a major power imbalance, it is likely to appeal for state intervention. Many NGOs are already rediscovering the value of state power over international talking shops; many corporations on the receiving end of NGO-organized consumer boycotts are likely to seek some kind of government redress. The result will be more traditional direct regulation of private actors in various ways, with deliberate transnational or global intent.

These sources of law barely appear in international law treatises and casebooks; they are marginal at best. But from the perspective of a Liberal theory of international relations, they may be the most important and effective sources of law, since they directly regulate the primary actors in the international system without intermediation.

The second level of law is transnational and transgovernmental law. A focus on state-society relations also leads to a focus on the activities of different government agencies as they respond to the increased ability of the individuals and groups they regulate to move, and to conduct transactions, across borders. The result is a growing body of transnational and "transgovernmental" law. Transnational law has many definitions. I mean to include here simply national law that is designed to reach actors beyond national borders: the assertion of extraterritorial [judicial] jurisdiction. Extraterritorial jurisdictional provisions are often the first effort a national government is inclined to make to regulate activity outside its borders with substantial effects within its borders. The United States has pioneered this "effects" jurisdiction, notably in antitrust, but increasingly in every area of law. Its efforts have produced a great deal of conflict but have also increasingly spawned imitation.

A more cooperative approach, and one often developed as a way of trying to resolve the conflict caused by assertion of extraterritorial jurisdiction, is the conclusion of agreements and understandings between government institutions and their foreign counterparts. The "memorandum of understanding," the typical vehicle of transgovernmental regulation, is the fastest growing legal instrument of the past decade. Such instruments codify agreements to share information, coordinate regulatory efforts, and cooperate in the development of joint regulatory approaches. They are agreements made by parts of states, although one of their major advantages, at least from the perspective of the regulatory agencies that conclude them, is that they do not have to be ratified by the state as a whole.

An additional source of transgovernmental law is the rules adopted by transgovernmental regulatory organizations such as the Basel Committee, the International Organization of Securities Commissioners and the International Association of Insurance Supervisors. These are more formalized transgovernmental relations, but the resulting promulgations and model codes have no formal binding power. Nevertheless, they often have considerable impact on state behavior, as they can be used by investors and international institutions as indicators of government performance in a particular issue area.

Finally, at the third level, a Liberal approach to international law would also incorporate the traditional sources of public international law—treaties and customary law. States here are conceived of as agents of individuals and groups. The resulting rules are thus at least at one remove, and often at two removes, from the actors whose behavior they seek to modify. The interesting questions in this category concern those relatively infrequent cases in which states create international institutions to which they delegate enough power to interact autonomously and effectively with individuals.

Reordering International Order

Parts of the first two levels of law may be found scattered across the pages of international law casebooks. But they are peripheral, or at least secondary, to the third level. This traditional ordering reflects implicit value judgments about the relative impact of these three levels of law on international order.

As discussed above, Liberal IR theory not only supplies a different ontology of the international system, in terms of changing our conception of relative actors and activity; it also provides the foundation for a theory of international order that reorders the relative impact of these different bodies of rules. Global problems have domestic roots. Law that directly regulates individuals and groups thus is more likely to get at the root of the problem. Law that has a direct impact on individuals and groups will thus have the greatest impact on international order.

Whether pride of place belongs to transnational voluntary law, traditional transnational law or transgovernmental law depends on the relative impact of self-regulation and social norms versus at least the threat of coercive power. But both these levels of law should have a greater impact than public international law, except to the extent that national-level authorities delegate real power to supranational authorities. Alternatively, international law and institutions can explicitly target individual and group behavior or the nature and quality of state-society relations. That project is the subject of the next two sections.

The Functions of Public International Law

The traditional function of public international law is to allow states to solve coordination and collective-action problems in relations with one another, or arising from the need to regulate their common geographical space. But, again from the perspective of Liberal IR theory, many if not most "international" problems have domestic roots. War, environmental degradation, protectionism—all spring from either adverse individual and group preferences or distortions in the representation of those preferences by governments. Alternatively put, the levers of progressive change in the international system lie in state-society relations—the plethora of ways in which domestic institutions interact with individuals and groups in domestic and transnational society. In a shorthand formulation, the global rule of law depends on the domestic rule of law.

It follows that, from a Liberal perspective, a—if not the—primary function of public international law is not to create international institutions to perform functions that individual states cannot perform by themselves, but rather to influence and improve the functioning of domestic institutions. This function is increasingly evident in international legal life, as the following examples will demonstrate, but it is again regarded as exceptional, problematic, or marginal. A Liberal theory of international law would privilege these issue areas, doctrines, and developments as the core of the discipline and as most likely to achieve its substantive goals.

Human Rights Law

From the perspective of Liberal theory, human rights law is the core of international law. Human rights lawyers such as Louis Henkin have long maintained this position, of course, but from a normative rather than a positive perspective. Many international lawyers and policymakers still see human rights law as an exception to the fundamental proposition of state sovereignty and nonintervention—a specialized area that is apart from the core discipline. Yet human rights law is precisely about structuring state-society relations to ensure at least minimal individual flourishing. We can justify that function from a moral perspective; Liberal IR theory would also argue that governments that oppress their citizens are more likely to resent [sic] a threat to other governments or to the international system.

Humanitarian Intervention

Humanitarian intervention is also very much on the current international agenda; UN Secretary-General Kofi Annan made it the centerpiece of his address to the General Assembly this year. Many international lawyers are deeply worried about the move away from the "classicist" doctrine of nonintervention. However, from a Liberal IR perspective, the legitimization of humanitarian intervention is a natural concomitant of human rights law. It is necessitated by some radical breakdown in the functioning of domestic institutions—the failure of a state of provide essential services such as food and shelter to its citizens or the active mass oppression of its citizens. In such circumstances, international action is justified to substitute for and in some cases even rebuild basic state institutions to the extent such efforts have a reasonable chance of success. Again, the justification is not moral, although it can certainly be, but instrumental, in terms of the likely impact of the humanitarian disaster on other states.

At the same time, however, the Liberal approach advocates extreme caution. If the justification for humanitarian intervention is the need to restore and rebuild institutions within a state to reduce the impact of the failure of those institutions on other states, then the task facing would-be intervenors is a complex and difficult one. To do the job halfway is likely only to exacerbate the situation and may well be worse than inaction. Thus, in the majority of cases, the policy prescriptions grounded in Liberal IR theory are likely to support only a very limited doctrine of humanitarian intervention.

. . .

Enhancing the Effectiveness of International Institutions

International institutions must be embedded in domestic society in some way to be maximally effective. The best examples are international tribunals, which are proliferating. Those that have the maximum impact are those in which individuals can initiate cases, preferably directly as in the European Court of Justice or the European Court of Human Rights, and parts of the North American Free Trade Agreement, or else indirectly, as in the World Trade Organisation dispute resolution system, in which corporations often have direct channels for pressuring their governments to initiate litigation. At the other end of the spectrum is pure inter-state litigation, not because governments do not comply with many of the resulting judgments, but because the tribunals involved cannot develop genuine domestic and transnational constituencies both to bring cases and to press for compliance.

Courts need cases, and states simply have too many incentives not to bring them against one another. If allowed access to individuals (a reversal of the normal assumption that individuals should be allowed access to them), courts can develop constituencies in both domestic and transnational society. Nor is this strategy limited to courts. Kofi Annan has been assiduously courting a transnational constituency of NGOs and corporations alike. At Davos, he urged corporations to take advantage of UN knowledge about how to be good global citizens; elsewhere he encourages NGOs to monitor corporations. This phenomenon and strategy could be called embedded internationalization. However, the capacity of international institutions will in turn depend on differences in the nature of state-society relations among the states comprising or subject to the jurisdiction of a particular international institution.

. . . We should not explicitly limit global institutions to liberal states or develop domestic and international doctrines that explicitly categorize or label entire states as such. Regional organizations, such as the European Union and the European Council, are free to require attributes of democracy and respect for human rights, as they do. But as a global strategy it is likely to do more harm than good, at least at this juncture.

On the other hand, Liberal IR theory insists that differences in domestic regime type drive differences in positive behavior. Thus, I do subscribe to a distinction between liberal and non-liberal states as a positive predictor of how states are likely to behave in a variety of circumstances, including within or toward international institutions.

However, I would also distinguish between theocracies and kleptocracies, and between weak and strong democracies. For instance, although strong empirical data support the proposition that mature democracies are unlikely to go to war with one another, it also appears that democratizing countries are more likely to go to war with one another. Further, in many cases the democracy/nondemocracy distinction will be simply too crude to be useful. Overall, however, who is being represented and how differs considerably in the different domestic systems: these differences will matter in international institutions.

... Let me leave you with the following paradox: On the one hand, tribunals that do have access to individuals with strong domestic legal systems and liberal rule-of-law cultures have found it easier to become established and expand their power. On the other hand, it is precisely those states with the strongest domestic legal systems and rights traditions that are likely most strenuously to resist strong enforcement mechanisms.

Conclusions

First, Liberal IR theory provides a new ontology of what international law is and how different bodies of law subsumed under that rubric contribute to international order. Second, it offers a perspective on the functions of public international law that moves areas that have been on the periphery or on the margin of the discipline to the center. Third, it offers an account of how to maximize the effectiveness of international institutions by embedding them in domestic and transnational society and tailoring our expectations of their performance to what we know about how domestic regime type affects international behavior.

Interliberal Law: Comment*

JOSE E. ALVAREZ

... To date, most of the published work on liberal theory has relied on drawing distinctions between "liberal" and "non-liberal" states. Both inside the beltway and within critical legal circles, liberal theory has been reduced to a bumper sticker: "Democracies do law better—especially with each other." What people have been drawn to in liberal theory is the premise that since liberal states do not make war on each other, they are more apt to cooperate with one another to make international rules—and that non-liberal nations are outside this emerging zone of interliberal law.

According to this version of liberal theory, if we want to achieve perpetual peace, we need to create a world of nations in the image of the United States and Europe, that is, states with periodic elections that respect both human rights and free markets; states that have shown that they can create truly effective treaty regimes (like the European Union

* Reprinted by permission from 94 AMERICAN SOCIETY OF INTERNATIONAL LAW PROCEEDINGS 249 (2000). © The American Society of International Law.

and the European human rights system) as well as expeditious and effective transnational regulatory networks like the Basel Committee of central bankers.

I am extremely skeptical of any attempt to draw distinctions between the treaty or other regulatory regimes of "liberal" and "non-liberal" states—especially if the goal or the unintended, result is, as one panelist has suggested at this conference, to introduce a "new standard of civilization" into the Article 38 sources of law. As Brad Roth, Susan Marks, and Harold Koh have argued, the problems begin with definitions and assumptions. How "liberal" have liberal states been anyway, given their illiberal exclusions of distant groups throughout history? How do we handle the historical peculiarities of self-described "democracies" across time? What do we do with states that do not stay "liberal" or that elect illiberal leaders?

But even assuming that we can distinguish between liberal/non-liberal regimes, there are four other assumptions that trouble me.

Assumption (1): that the future of effective international regulation lies not with traditional treaties that are subject only to horizontal forms of enforcement but with transnational networks of government regulators (like the Basel Committee) or "vertically enforced" treaties (like the European Convention of Human Rights) that arise among liberal nations.

Many of the regulatory schemes that exist today, including many transnational networks, are nestled within traditional treaty regimes and draw their legitimacy in part from the fact that they have arisen within the context of pluralist regimes that have been formally approved by domestic processes. The world of arbitration remains reliant on formal treaties such as the New York Convention and dependent on traditional rules of treaty interpretation as well as custom and general principles. As the probable establishment of the International Criminal Court and the recent institutionalization of the GATT—to cite but a few examples—suggests, the age of intergovernmental institutions aspiring to universal participation is not past. There is no sign that states are entering into fewer formal treaties and considerable evidence that many of the developments that liberal theorists describe (such as the increased support for the concept of universal jurisdiction for some crimes, including terrorist acts) rely on developments initiated within universalist institutions (such as ICAO's [International Civil Aviation Organization's] anti-terrorism conventions). We should also be careful about extolling transnational forms of administration regulation in a world where there are growing critiques of the administrative state. It is premature to suggest that transgovernmental regulation along the lines of the Basel Committee is invariably more flexible, faster, more amenable to the application of technical expertise or to forms of domestic implementation likely to lead to deeper forms of cooperation—especially when we consider the many needs to create successful cooperation across the liberal/non-liberal divide and the relatively successful treaty regimes in place to deal with such issues. Formal treaty arrangements, including managerial framework conventions, come in all shapes and sizes and many lead to very deep cooperation indeed. Further, there is a risk that in disaggregating the state we lose sight of the continuing significance of power. In a world that appears to be increasingly dominated by rules imposed by the north, many are not ready to rejoice in rule by the north's central bankers.

The possibly unique case of the European Union aside, I see little evidence that liberal membership automatically facilitates deep international cooperation. For every successful regulatory effort by OECD [Organisation for Economic Co-operation and Development] nations (as with respect to antitrust cooperation), there are counter-examples of failure, including the OECD's multiple efforts to deepen multilateral cooperation concerning investment issues. The collapse of the third such effort within the OECD, the ill-fated Multilateral Agreement on Investment, suggests the difficulties for international regulation posed by disaggregated interests within liberal nations. Liberal theorists need to focus more attention on how traditions of democratic governance or other aspects of domestic civil society can back the assumption of international obligations or efforts to deepen them—as through concerns stemming from "separation of powers," the need for "checks and balances," or the values of "federalism." As the triumvirate of Curtis Bradley, Jack Goldsmith, and John Yoo suggests, it is easy to don democratic garb while exhibiting a fundamental hostility to international law. The absence of "democratic" concerns, or their radical reconfiguration within the context of "non-liberal" states, may sometimes hasten the acceptance of international regulation or its enforcement.

Assumption (2): transjudicial communication is most likely to occur among liberal courts.

Liberal theory has focused valuable attention on a growing phenomenon but the world of transjudicial communication is a great deal more complex. Courts in "liberal" nations may avoid citing to international or foreign authorities precisely because they need to respond to liberal civil society. The recent Israeli torture case is an instance of a court that goes out of its way to avoid explicit citation to any international or foreign sources of authority because of a perceived need to ground its holding in the legitimacy of local law. Liberal judges have elaborated many doctrines of avoidance to use for such purposes. Liberal courts do not paradigmatically distinguish between the laws of liberal and non-liberal. The analysis of when transjudicial communication is most likely to occur—when judges from liberal nations see themselves as dissagregated independent actors engaged in a common enterprise with their liberal brethren abroad—is simplistic and potentially misleading. As Keck and Sikkink have noted, much transjudicial communication occurs when activists within non-liberal states reach for transnational allies to exert a boomerang pattern of influence within such states. As their analysis suggests, the most effective forms of transjudicial influence may be felt in fragile democracies, not stable ones, and the most common examples may arise not through citations to foreign or international tribunal judgments but through the reinterpretation of local law (such as the scope of Chile's amnesty law) while avoiding direct reference to "foreign" sources of law. This approach to transjudicial communication recognizes its genuine constructivist potential. It regards these judicial efforts not as a conveyor belt transmitting liberal values to the unenlightened but as a part of a truly transformative dialogue.

Assumption (3): we should expect and ought to be able to secure better compliance and enforcement of virtually any kind of treaty when the parties to these agreements consist of liberal states since such states are more likely to be monist, are more likely to comply with international forms of dispute settlement, and are more amenable to "vertical" enforcement of treaty obligations through domestic courts.

This does not describe either the treaty relations of liberal states or those of non-liberals, much less the treaties both types of states have with each other. Monist constitutional provisions have, historically, told us little; they certainly do not tell us whether a real defendant is likely to have a remedy in a real court. The United States, the ostensible prime example of a liberal nation, as is well known, does not generally provide for vertical enforcement of international legal obligations for human rights treaties and when it does provide for vertical enforcement of treaty obligations, it has not historically done so in the context of a "liberal" regime. Throughout U.S. history, the prime examples of vertically enforced treaty obligations, including treaties of Friendship, Commerce and Navigation, bilateral investment treaties, and Chapter 11 of the NAFTA, have been undertaken with nations that, when the treaty was concluded, were, more often than not, illiberal. As we all know the United States has not been particularly amenable to accepting the jurisdiction of international tribunals such as the International Court of Justice or of the Inter–American Court of Human Rights and there is no evidence that this would change if the supranational institution were within a liberal regime. No one believes that the United States refrains from joining the Inter–American system of human rights because some of its members are not stable democracies. The world of international arbitration includes liberal and non-liberal and many non-liberal nations appear more amenable to going to the International Court of Justice than is the United States. Further, many states, not merely those regarded as non-liberal, seem to have considerable difficulties in providing for the domestic judicial enforcement of treaty obligations.

There is no evidence that liberal states change their behavior more often as a result of entering into international obligations than do non-liberal states. The most thorough empirical study of treaty compliance—Jacobson's and Weiss's study of a number of environmental conventions—suggests that the success of rich democratic states in this regard is over-determined. These states comply better for many reasons, including the fact that they are rich. It is arbitrary to focus on regime type as the explanatory factor.

That states defined to be non-liberal in part because they fail to respect human rights fail to comply with human rights conventions tells us nothing about the non-liberal world's compliance record on other subjects. In the end we might conclude, with Professor Louis Henkin, that almost all states comply with almost all of their international obligations almost all of the time but even if Professor Henkin is wrong, we have little basis at present to conclude that compliance divides along liberal/non-liberal lines.

Assumption (4): drawing distinctions between liberal and non-liberal will lead to perpetual peace.

I am more inclined to believe that any attempt to draw such lines, to shrink law's domain, is a recipe for conflict. The subjectivity of the "liberal peace" undermines the prescriptive claims made in its behalf. The "liberal peace" appears to measure the disinclination of one state to make war on another state that it considers to be, for subjective and sometimes arbitrary reasons, a "friend." By the second half of the 20th century, we have chosen to call such friends "fellow democracies." But even if we accept the proposition that liberal friends do not make war on each other, those who have discovered this also tell us that liberal democracies are particularly susceptible to making war on "the other"—and have scarcely needed encouragement when convinced that "the other" is non-democratic. Others have found that democratizing states are more likely to go to war than either stable autocracies or stable democracies. We need to pursue democratization efforts with our eyes open. We should not sell democratization as a recipe for "peace" when it may provoke considerable conflict, both within states and between them, for many years to come.

Liberal theory, if read to emphasize distinctions between liberal and non-liberal regimes, is, first too pessimistic about the likelihood of effective international cooperation among non-liberal nations and between liberal and non-liberal; and, second, too optimistic about international cooperation in the liberal world. Read in the way my bumper sticker suggests, liberal theory is triumphalist when it ought to be wary about rule of law by sole superpower; messianic about cosmetic democracy when it ought to be more concerned about economic and social stratification; and complacent about the consistency between a liberal zone of law and perpetual peace at a time of increased tensions produced by, among other things, intensified globalization.

Liberal theory should adhere to its central insight: investigating the complex consequences of the disaggregated state. Drawing lines between liberal and non-liberal betrays this insight. A preoccupation with the supposedly distinctive regulatory methods pursued by the liberal world threatens liberal theory's refutation of the realist billiard ball analogy. It makes it appear that liberals are not really giving up on billiards; they are just interested in playing with a smaller number of "democratic" balls.

Liberal theorists have to work hard to convince people that they are really interested in what goes on within all types of regimes and not just within the regulatory bureaucracies of the transatlantic. Until then, liberals' talk of justified "humanitarian intervention," for example, will continue to scare people, and not just those unfashionably enamored of sovereignty or the principle of sovereign equality. Once the liberal/non-liberal dichotomy is abandoned for good and for real, liberal theory will stop drawing the harsh, but predictable, critique that it is intolerant of those states and peoples not regarded as democratic, narrow in its conception of the ideal society, and ill disposed to the possibility of real reform within the world we have, namely, institutions and regimes of mixed membership.

Once liberal theory begins to truly engage the disaggregated interests and actors that exist even within the ostensibly non-liberal world, I will be proud to call myself a "liberal" theorist. For now I am content to remain an international, and not an interliberal, lawyer.

Notes and Comments

1. Liberal theory is grounded in the work of neo-Kantians, who argue that democracies do not engage in war with one another—the so-called "democratic peace" hypothesis. The most prominent proponent of this view is Michael Doyle. See Michael Doyle, *Liberalism and World Politics*, 80 American Political Science Review 1151 (1986). The topic continues to be a source of ongoing debate. See, for example, the contributions by Michael W. Doyle, Bruce Russett, and others in Michael E. Brown, et al eds., Debating the Democratic Peace (1996).

2. As Alvarez's critique demonstrates, one of the more powerful—and controversial—claims that arises out of a liberal theory of international law is that liberal and nonliberal states have different propensities to engage in law. In an early piece in this vein, Anne–Marie Slaughter argues that just as liberal states act differently toward one another in waging war, they act differently toward one another in the legal realm. She writes:

> ... I draw a distinction between "liberal" and "nonliberal" states and use that distinction to analyze transnational legal relations among private individuals and between individuals and state entities. "Liberal" states, for these purposes, are defined broadly as states with juridical equality, constitutional protections of individual rights, representative republican governments, and market economies based on private property rights. "Nonliberal" states, by contrast, are defined as those states lacking these characteristics.

> This distinction between liberal and nonliberal states first emerged in empirical political science research demonstrating that liberal states have created "a separate peace." Liberal states are not inherently pacific, as demonstrated by their record of conflict, even aggressive conflict, with nonliberal states. But they do not make war on one another.
>
> I contend that the distinctive nature of political-military relations among liberal states has an analog in the legal relations among liberal states. By applying and extending the Kantian theory of liberal internationalism, I construct a "liberal internationalist model" of transnational legal relations that specifies how such relations among liberal states might be expected to differ from those between liberal and nonliberal states. In brief, I hypothesize that liberal states operate in a "zone of law," in which domestic courts regulate transnational relations under domestic law. Courts within this zone evaluate and apply the domestic law of foreign states in accordance with general pluralist principles of mutual respect and interest-balancing. Nonliberal states, by contrast, operate in a "zone of politics," in which domestic courts either play no role in the resolution of transnational disputes or allow themselves to be guided by the political branches. The intersection of these two zones gives rise to an interesting paradox: in many circumstances the courts of liberal states are more likely to evaluate and sometimes reject or override the laws of other liberal states than the laws of nonliberal states.

Anne–Marie Burley, *Law Among Liberal States: Liberal Internationalism and the Act of State Doctrine*, 92 COLUMBIA LAW REVIEW 1907 (1992). In a more recent article, Slaughter and her coauthor Laurence Helfer make a similar argument with regard to the effectiveness of international or "supranational" adjudication. See Laurence R. Helfer & Anne–Marie Slaughter, *Toward a Theory of Effective Supranational Adjudication*, 107 YALE LAW JOURNAL 273, 278 (1997). Oona Hathaway finds some empirical support for the claim that democracies act differently with regard to international law in Oona A. Hathaway, *Do Human Rights Treaties Make a Difference?*, 111 YALE LAW JOURNAL 1935 (2002); and in Oona A. Hathaway, *The Cost of Commitment*, 55 STANFORD LAW REVIEW 1821 (2003).

3. Are you persuaded by Alvarez's critique of Slaughter's liberal approach to international law? (A more detailed critique of the Liberal Theory as applied to law is found in Jose E. Alvarez, *Do Liberal States Behave Better? A Critique of Slaughter's Liberal Theory*, 12 EUROPEAN JOURNAL OF INTERNATIONAL LAW 183 (2001).) Is the distinction between liberal and non-liberal states a necessary aspect of liberal theory? Both Slaughter and Moravcsik go to some length in their recent work to emphasize the positive—as opposed to normative—nature of the Liberal theory they espouse. Is the normative content that Alvarez ascribes to the theory an inescapable consequence of its descriptive approach?

4. Some have argued that Liberal theory is susceptible to the charge that although it can provide explanations for government actions after the fact, it has difficulty generating predictions *ex ante*. Do you agree? How does Liberal theory differ in this respect from the other theories presented herein?

5. Liberal democracies have emerged in waves over the course of history: the old-line democracies such as the United States and France emerged in the late eighteenth century, more democracies emerged with the decline of colonial empires, and even more emerged at the end of the Cold War, particularly in Central and Eastern Europe. At what point can and should we categorize a state as having crossed the line from "illiberal" to "liberal"?

6. Many political scientists view what Moravcsik and Slaughter label "liberal theory" as a subset of a broader liberal theory (sometimes labeled "neoliberal theory") that encompasses institutional theory as well. What are the central similarities and differences between Moravcsik's and Slaughter's liberal theory and institutional theory? (For more on their perspective on international law and politics, see, e.g., Andrew Moravcsik, *Liberal International Relations Theory: A Scientific Assessment*, *in* PROGRESS IN INTERNATIONAL RELATIONS THEORY: APPRAISING THE FIELD 159–204 (Colin Elman and Miriam Fendius Elman, eds. 2003); ANNE-MARIE SLAUGHTER, A NEW WORLD ORDER (2004).) Still others suggest that the term "liberal theory" should broadly embrace not just theories of international relations that encompass domestic structure, but also broader theories of fairness and legitimacy as sources of legal obligation, another element of a Kantian perspective. These theories are discussed in Part III.B. below.

7. Numerous scholars have looked to domestic society in constructing sophisticated arguments about state behavior in a wide range of areas, using approaches that might be broadly labeled as "liberal." A few examples include: Peter Gourevitch, *Squaring the Circle: The Domestic Sources of International Relations*, 50 INTERNATIONAL ORGANIZATION (1996); HELEN MILNER, INTERESTS, INSTITUTIONS, AND INFORMATION: DOMESTIC POLITICS AND INFORMATION (1997); BETH SIMMONS, WHO ADJUSTS: DOMESTIC SOURCES OF FOREIGN ECONOMIC POLICY DURING THE INTERWAR YEARS (1994); Jeffry Frieden, *Actors and Preferences in International Relations*, *in* STRATEGIC CHOICE AND INTERNATIONAL RELATIONS (David Lake & Robert Powell, eds. 1999); and LISA MARTIN, DEMOCRATIC COMMITMENTS: LEGISLATURES AND INTERNATIONAL COOPERATION (2000). Indeed, much recent scholarship on international law and politics pays close attention to the influence of domestic political institutions and actors. As we turn to constructivism in the next part, compare the constructivist conception of when and how domestic society shapes state action to that offered by liberal scholars.

III

Norm-Based Theories of State Behavior

The theories of state behavior that we collect under the wide umbrella of "norm-based theories" share the conviction that the interest-based models overlook the persuasive power of legitimate legal obligations. Scholars adopting this approach argue that many state decisions cannot be explained simply by calculations of geopolitical or economic interests or even the relative power of domestic political groups. A complete description of state action in the international realm, they argue, requires an understanding of the influence and importance of ideas and norms.

How and why ideas matter, and the extent to which they influence international relations and international law, remains a source of disagreement. This section highlights three major normative approaches in international law and international relations. The first, which primarily draws on recent scholarship in political science is generally referred to as "*constructivism.*" This approach focuses on how ideas not only matter, but in fact construct the social environment which, in turn, constitutes the identities and interests of states. The second and third approaches arise primarily from legal scholarship. The *"fairness" model* emphasizes the crucial role of the ideas of legitimacy and fairness in inducing compliance with international rules. *Legal process theories* address the ways that the process of making and enforcing international law itself generates or enhances compliance. The legal process approach encompasses two main strands, one emphasizing intergovernmental legal process, or legal process among nation-states and intergovernmental organizations ("*horizontal legal process*") and the other detailing how states themselves domesticate international law, or "bring international law home," by internalizing international norms into domestic law over time through a series of legal interactions (*"transnational legal process"*). Despite their differences, all of these approaches agree that norms and ideas are a critically important factor in the conduct of international law and politics.

A. Constructivism

In political science, most norm-based scholarship centers on what has come to be called "constructivist" theory. In this view, transnational actors and their interests are not fully formed or unchanging. Rather, they are constituted or "constructed" by and through interaction with one another.

This section draws from three leading exponents of the constructivist approach to international relations theory. Martha Finnemore explains that constructivists may agree with rationalist scholars that states pursue their interests. But she argues that rationalists are wrong to assume that all states seek the same thing—some combination of power, security, and wealth. Instead, she argues that "we cannot understand what states want without understanding the international social structure of which they are a part." She takes an empirical approach to exploring the origins of social structures that determine state preferences, focusing in particular on how international organizations "teach" states to have new interests. International law can change state action, in this view, "not by constraining states with a given set of preferences from acting, but by changing their preferences." Like Finnemore, John Ruggie indicts both neorealism and neoliberal institutionalism—engaging them together as "neo-utilitarianism"—for taking the interests and identities of states as exogenously given. As the article excerpted below demonstrates, an important starting point for constructivists is that actors do not view the world objectively, but instead derive their interests and even their identities from their social surroundings. Shared ideas—or "intersubjective" meanings—are thus a crucial basis for social order. Finally, Alexander Wendt applies this social approach to the neorealist conclusion that a "self-help" system is the inevitable byproduct of anarchy. He finds that it is not at all inevitable that states end up in the Hobbesian world so central to realist thought.

National Interests in International Society*

MARTHA FINNEMORE

Chapter 1: Defining State Interests

How do states know what they want? One might think that this would be a central question for international relations scholars. After all, our major paradigms are all framed in terms of power and interests. The sources of state interests should matter to us. In fact, they have not—or not very much. Aspirations to develop a generalizable theory of international politics modeled on theories in the natural sciences and economics have led most international relations scholars in the United States since the 1960s to assume rather than problematize state interests. Interests across the states system had to be treated as both stable and roughly identical if systemic-level theory of this kind was to proceed. Thus neorealist and neoliberal scholars currently dominating the field make parsimonious assumptions about what all states want. States are assumed to want some combination of power, security, and wealth. With these few assumptions, these scholars seek to explain, as Kenneth Waltz put it, "a small number of big and important things."

... It is all fine and well to assume that states want power, security, and wealth, but what kind of power? Power for what ends? What kind of security? What does security mean? How you ensure or obtain it? Similarly, what kind of wealth? Wealth for whom? How do you obtain it? Neorealists and neoliberals have no systemic answers for these questions. If external threats and power constraints are not determinative, such questions can be dealt with only on a case-by-case basis by country specialists or foreign policy analysts. International-level theory is helpless and mute.

This book addresses that silence. In it I develop a systemic approach to understanding state interests and state behavior by investigating an international structure, not of power, but of meaning and social value. We cannot understand what states want without understanding the international social structure of which they are a part. States are embedded in dense networks of transnational and international social relations that shape their perceptions of the world and their role in that world. States are *socialized* to want certain things by the international society in which they and the people in them live.

Ultimately, power and wealth are means, not ends. States must decide what to do with them. States may not always know what they want or how to use their resources. Foreign policy debates after the Cold War make this clear. Interests are not just "out there" waiting to be discovered; they are constructed through social interaction. States want to avoid invasion, extinction, and economic collapse, but for most states most of the time these negative interests do not narrow the set of possible wants very much. There remains a wide range of goals and values states could espouse in a wide variety of policy areas. Domestic politics can play a large, sometimes determining, role in defining national goals and interests, but as the cases here make clear, domestic politics and local conditions cannot explain many of the interests articulated and policy choices made.

State interests are defined in the context of internationally held norms and understandings about what is good and appropriate. That normative context influences the behavior of decisionmakers and of mass publics who may choose and constrain those decisionmakers. The normative context also changes over time, and as internationally held norms and values change, they create coordinated shifts in state interests and behavior across the system. It is these patterns of coordinated, system-wide redefinition of interests that look odd from conventional perspectives and that this book addresses. . . .

Where do preferences come from?

The claim of this book—that states are socialized to accept new norms, values, and perceptions of interest by international organizations—has important implications for the way we think about the international political world and the way we do research. It reverses traditional causal arrows. We have usually taken states as the starting point for analysis and examined the ways in which they create and interact with the various bits of furniture in the international system—international organizations, treaties, legal structures, multinational corporations, other states. This analysis looks at the way the international system, here in the form of IOs [International Organizations], changes and reconstitutes states. We are used to speaking a language of constraint. The international system is said to be important because it constrains states from taking actions they would otherwise take. The argument here is different. The international system can change what states *want*. It is constitutive and generative, creating new interests and values for actors. It changes state action, not by constraining states with a given set of preferences from acting, but by changing their preferences.

The claims made here about the importance of norms and values also shift attention from the largely material conceptions of international politics espoused by neorealists and neoliberals to a more social and ideational conception. Material facts acquire meaning only through human cognition and social interaction. My defensive measure is your security threat; my assault on free trade is your attempt to protect jobs at home. We have long understood that different social meanings assigned to the same set of facts can create different behaviors and even lead to conflict. We have paid much less attention to ways in which shared understandings of the material world create similar behaviors, and we have not thought much about what the implications of such shared understandings and similar behavior might be. Material facts do not speak for themselves, and attempts to make them do so have limited utility.

. . .

Preferences in Empirical Research

. . .

Preferences Supplied Externally: Learning versus Teaching

Much of international relations theory rests on the assumption that states know what they want. Preferences are treated as inherent in states; they come from within the state as a result of material conditions and functional needs. The changes detailed in this study suggest, however, that preferences may not be inherent in states and may not be wedded to material conditions. Instead, state preferences are malleable. States may not always know what they want and are receptive to teaching about what are appropriate and useful actions to take. How would we think about such a process theoretically?

Adherents to an internal demand-driven view of state preference formation might argue that the "learning" of preferences documented here can be explained within the more conventional learning frameworks used in foreign policy analysis. The international system is, after all, an environment full of uncertainty, and states, like most actors, suffer from bounded rationality. Boundedly rational actors operating in environments of uncertainty frequently look for solutions to their problems in the solutions tried by other, apparently successful actors. Imitation, in a world of uncertainty, is often a perfectly rational strategy to adopt. . . .

These processes differ from the phenomena I document in this study. In the cases [of conventional learning], state officials change policies because they are under pressure to solve some already-identified problem. . . . The problem for state administrators is how to respond to these demands. The impetus for action comes from within the state, even if the solution does not. By contrast, in the cases I investigate, state officials were not responding to any pressing demands or obvious crises. They were not looking for a solution to a problem. Both the "problem" and the solution were supplied to states by outside actors. Prior to the actions of UNESCO [United Nations Educational, Scientific, and Cultural Organization], most states, especially less developed countries (LDCs), had no notion that they needed or wanted a state science bureaucracy. Similarly, European heads of state were not particularly concerned about treatment of the war wounded until Henr[i] Dunant and the International Committee of the Red Cross made it an issue. Global poverty alleviation, while long considered desirable in the abstract, was not considered a pressing responsibility of states, particularly of developed states, until the World Bank under Robert McNamara made it a necessary part of development.

. . . In the cases presented in this study, however, there *are* active teachers with well defined lesson plans for their pupils. Other actors are setting agendas, defining tasks, and shaping interests of states. . . .

Receptivity to the teaching of preferences implies a more social character for states than is generally acknowledged in international relations theory. It implies that the international environment is more than a "billiard table" constraining state action. It implies that states are embedded in a social structure and are "socialized" to a degree not allowed for by the more conventional, self-contained conceptions of the state. The role of "teacher" for international organizations similarly implies a more active and causal character than most theories currently allow. . . . It would embed states in a more diverse context of causal factors and push beyond "the limits of realism." . . .

Structure Versus Agents

The debate between theoretical frameworks in which states are treated as autonomous actors and those in which they are embedded in global structures is an old one and reflects the more general agent-structure debate that has been bubbling through social science for some years. At issue here is essentially what is at issue there, and that is whether, analytically, one treats actors (i.e., agents), capabilities, and preferences as given and derives social structures from their interaction, or whether one takes the social structures as given and treats actors, their preferences and powers, as defined by the social system(s) in which they are embedded.

Political science has been dominated by actor- or agent-oriented approaches. Analysis generally proceeds by positing both preferences and powers for some group of actors, be they voters, members of Congress, firms, social classes, or nation-states. Macro-level political outcomes are then derived from the sum of micro-level behaviors by these actors pursuing their pre-specified preferences. In international relations, neo-realism proceeds in this way. While Waltz in his *Theory of International Politics* argues for the constraining force of international structure on state actors, the structure itself is an epiphenomenon of the preferences and powers of the constituent states. It has no independent ontological status. More to the point, it is not generative. It does not create and constitute actors and interests. Instead it is constituted by them.

Structure-oriented approaches, by contrast, treat social structures as causal variables and derive actors and interests from them. Structures, not agents, are ontologically primitive and the starting point for analysis....

There is no reason why the structure in a structural argument must be material and economic. Structures of shared knowledge and intersubjective understandings may also shape and motivate actors. Socially constructed rules, principles, norms of behavior, and shared beliefs may provide states, individuals, and other actors with understandings of what is important or valuable and what are effective and/or legitimate means of obtaining those valued goods. These social structures may supply states with both preferences and strategies for pursuing those preferences.

...

The best-known of these [social-structural] approaches in mainstream American political science has come to be called "constructivism." As the name suggests, scholars working in this vein share a general interest in social construction processes and their effects. They are concerned with the impact of cultural practices, norms of behavior, and social values on political life and reject the notion that these can be derived from calculations of interests. They emphasize the importance of intersubjective understandings in structuring the ways in which actors understand what kinds of actions are valuable, appropriate, and necessary. These authors part ways with the more conventional actor-oriented approaches that Robert Keohane has called "rationalist" in that they elevate socially constructed variables—commonly held philosophic principles, identities, norms of behavior, or shared terms of discourse—to the status of basic causal variables that shape preferences, actors, and outcomes. In this way, they endogenize preferences. Preferences are strongly influenced and often constituted by social norms, culturally dominated roles and rules, and historically contingent discourse.

. . .

Chapter 5: Politics in International Society

. . .

The Politics of International Norms

Tensions and contradictions among normative principles in international life mean that there is no set of ideal political and economic arrangements toward which we are all converging. There is no stable equilibrium, no end of history. All good things do not and probably cannot go together. Instead, social institutions are continually being contested, albeit to varying degrees at different times. Unresolved normative tensions in a set of social compromises at one time may be the mobilizing force for attacks on that set of social arrangements later, as people articulate normative claims that earlier were pushed aside.

These contestation processes are political. In fact, normative contestation is in large part what politics is all about: competing values and understandings of what is good, desirable, and appropriate in our collective, communal life. Debates about civil rights, affirmative action, social safety nets, regulation and deregulation, and the appropriate degree of government intrusion into the lives of citizens are all debates precisely because there is no clear stable normative solution. . . .

Assuming a normative structure that contains competing and contradictory elements forces constructivists to attend to both politics and process. Norms of international society may create similar structures and push both people and states toward similar behavior, but the body of international norms is not completely congruent. Certainly, it is not congruent enough to produce homogeneity or equifinality. Tensions and contradictions among the norms leave room for different solutions and different arrangements, each of which makes legitimacy claims based on the same norms. The compromises arrived at may be contingent on local circumstances and personalities and are likely to reflect the local norms and customs with which international norms have had to compromise. International norms may have persuaded all states that they needed science bureaucracies, but the bureaucracies in Germany, Romania, and Botswana look quite different from one another. More generically, international norms may dictate that the state is *the* appropriate form of political organization, yet there is room for wide variety in the form of governing arrangements within those acceptable international normative parameters. The particular form of any state is a result of both international and local factors.

These local variations are not simply oddities of interest only to area specialists. Some contingent, local results may become internationalized and institutionalized as part of the global normative structure in important ways, thus influencing the content of international normative structure at a later time....

It is this interaction between international structures and local agents of change that interests constructivists. It is not enough for constructivists to look only at international normative structures and their effects. They must also focus on the origins and dynamics of these norms, a focus which inevitably takes them into a world of agents. ... I have demonstrated the widespread effects of the norms in question and presented analyses of the origins and dynamics of these norms that highlight political contestation and agency. The agents investigated here were transnational-level actors, both IOs and the individuals in them. One could examine other agent relationships with these norms, focusing most obviously on the ways in which these norms worked their effects inside the many states of the system and, perhaps, the ways in which the norms were eventually affected by those individual state experiences....

Constructivism and International Law

The notion that norms, understandings, and discourse shape state behavior is hardly news to many outside political science. International legal scholars have always known this: norms are their bread and butter. At the international level norms *are* the law.... A constructivist approach in political science opens up possibilities for conversation with international legal scholars that were foreclosed under realist domination of our discipline....

... International legal scholarship should be interesting to constructivists in at least two ways. First, the nature of the analytical enterprise is similar. When lawyers argue and courts or tribunals decide matters of customary international law, they are looking for *opinio juris*—evidence that states share a belief that some principle is law. The methods for doing so look much like the methods used by constructivist scholars in political science to establish the existence of a norm. They look at behavior and ask whether states act as if there is, in fact, such a norm. Additionally, they look at discourse and ask if states justify actions by identifying and emphasizing the importance of the norm or principle. When adjudicating norm violations, they ask whether the conflict is at the level of a norm or fact, that is, whether violators are challenging the norm or challenging interpretations of fact (such as whether particular events occurred and if they occurred, whether they are prohibited under the norm). As investigatory efforts the two are similar.

Second, international legal scholarship is an interesting object of study for constructivists in that part of its mission is to make new norms. One of the functions of legal scholarship is to articulate and codify norms and rules for states. The status of scholarly writings as authoritative sources to be used in the efforts of courts to discern the law has been accepted for centuries. . . .

. . . [I]t is the arguments of lawyers and international jurists about the ways in which these agreements should be interpreted that shape outcomes in conflicts over international legal norms. The most serious and fundamental normative conflicts will only be settled politically, but much of the lower-level, day-to-day international normative conflict is fought out and settled by lawyers in national and international courts and tribunals. In these legal forums the decision rule is normative consistency as determined through logical argumentation. Normative claims become powerful and prevail by being persuasive; being persuasive means grounding claims in existing norms in ways that emphasize normative congruence and coherence. Persuasiveness and logical coherence of normative claims are important politically, but are essential and must be explicit in law.

Conventional IR theories cannot talk about persuasion. The consequentialist, utility-maximizing foundations of neorealism and neoliberalism leave no room for it. . . .

Law thus offers constructivists interesting avenues for research, but the relationship is reciprocal. Constructivism should be interesting for legal scholars because it engages the central social scientific debates with realism that have forced international law to defend its relevance, even its existence, for so many years. Drawing on social psychological and organization theory literatures, constructivism provides arguments about why, at the most basic level, behavior may be rule-driven. It seeks to provide a social theoretical foundation for law's claim that its norms and rules shape behavior in ways that are not simply epiphenomenal of interests. Linking law with behavior even in the absence of enforcement has been the critical missing component of law's response to realism.

. . .

At the heart of the realist challenge is the fact that international law has no social theoretical microfoundations. It is easy to prescribe: anyone can dream up desirable rules and happy futures. The hard job is to articulate a set of desirable rules that have some chance of being followed, given what we know about behavior. If prescription is not based on some fairly explicit understandings about behavior, about why international politics works as it does, law's prescriptions will be dismissed as the kind of "idealism" that was discredited in political science in the 1930s. By explaining why and how behavior may be norm-governed, constructivism deals precisely with issues that are microfoundational for international law and so can help law respond to the realists.

. . .

We can understand changes in this normative fabric of international politics only if we investigate the shared understandings that underlie it.

Doing so requires a fundamentally different approach from the actor-oriented, economistic approaches we have been using for 50 years. Taking a sociological turn and treating social relations as social realities that shape behavior as much as material realities allows us to do this.

What Makes the World Hang Together? Neo-utilitarianism and the Social Constructivist Challenge*

JOHN GERARD RUGGIE

Social constructivism rests on an irreducibly intersubjective dimension of human action. As Max Weber insisted at the turn of the century, "We are cultural beings, endowed with the capacity and the will to take a deliberate attitude towards the world and to lend it significance." This capacity gives rise to a class of facts that do not exist in the physical object world: social facts, or facts that, in the words of the linguistic philosopher John Searle, depend on human agreement that they exist and typically require human institutions for their existence. Social facts include money, property rights, sovereignty, marriage, football, and Valentine's Day, in contrast to such brute observational facts as rivers, mountains, population size, bombs, bullets, and gravity, which exist whether or not there is agreement that they do.

In short, constructivism is about human consciousness and its role in international life. In contrast to neo-utilitarianism,[1] constructivists contend that not only are identities and interests of actors socially constructed, but also that they must share the stage with a whole host of other ideational factors that emanate from the human capacity and will of which Weber wrote. The fact that human behavior at all levels of social aggregation is constrained is not in dispute. Nor is the likelihood that modal responses may exist to some types of structural constraints or situational exigencies. What social constructivists reject, however, is the presumption or pretense that their study constitutes the totality or even the main part of the social scientific enterprise.

. . .

The Emergence of Social Constructivism

. . .

Interests and Identities

Neorealism and neoliberal institutionalism treat the identity and interests of actors as exogenous and given. Some neorealists claim to

* Reprinted by permission from 52 International Organization 855 (1998).

1. [Editors' Note: The theories Ruggie refers to here as "neo-utilitarian" are the "interest-based" theories covered in Part II of this book. In addition, Ruggie, like many political scientists, includes what we have separately labeled "institutionalism" and "liberalism" under the collective label "neoliberalism."]

"derive" state interests from the condition of anarchy but, as Helen Milner has argued persuasively, anarchy is an exceedingly slippery concept, and the propositions one can derive from it are almost entirely indeterminate. Hence, interests are, in fact, handled by assumption, notwithstanding claims to the contrary. The power and elegance of the neo-utilitarian [neorealist and neoliberal] model rests on this point of departure. But so, too, do some of its limitations.

First, neo-utilitarianism provides no answer to the core foundational question: how the constituent actors—in international relations, territorial states—came to acquire their current identity and the interests that are assumed to go along with it. Similarly, any potential future change in this identity and in corresponding interests is beyond the scope of the theory. States and the system of states simply *are*: endowed with the ontological status of being, but not of becoming, to borrow a phrase from Nobel laureate Ilya Prigogine. Addressing these foundational issues requires the concept of constitutive rules, which I take up in a subsequent section.

Second, not only does neo-utilitarianism have no analytical means for dealing with the generic identities and interests of states *qua* states, it also excludes consideration of how specific identities of specific states shape their interests and, thereby, patterns of international outcomes. This is true even of treatments of the United States—the century's central great power and yet so atypical in its advantageous geopolitical position and internal political and ethnic makeup. I have indicated elsewhere how the postwar international order would have differed if the Soviet Union or Nazi Germany had ended up as its hegemon instead of the United States; indeed, important things would have differed if Britain had become the leading power. Thus, contra neorealism, I argued that *American* hegemony was every bit as important as American *hegemony* in shaping the postwar order. And, contra neoliberal institutionalism, I noted that America's choice of the specific features of the postwar institutional frameworks—be it the United Nations, indivisible security commitments in NATO, or nondiscriminatory norms in trade and monetary relations—cannot be rendered accurately merely in terms of marginal utility but also reflected America's sense of self as a nation.

What is more, the identity of the same state can change and pull its interests along. Thus, Thomas Berger argues that Germany and Japan today differ significantly from their pre–World War II predecessors. Antimilitarism, he maintains, has become integral to their sense of self as nations and is embedded in domestic norms and institutions. Peter Katzenstein makes a similar case for the police and military in postwar Japan and Germany. Robert Herman explains the Gorbachev revolution in the Soviet Union and its international aftermath in terms of an identity shift leading to a radical recalibration of interests. It may be true that constraints and opportunities led initially to changes in behavior, but in all three cases, the authors contend, a transformation of identity has taken place. Although it is possible that these changes are not irreversible, Katzenstein in particular identifies the specific normative and institutional practices in Japan and Germany that any move toward a reversal would have to contend with and overcome.

Third, there is growing empirical evidence that normative factors in addition to states' identities shape their interests, or their behavior, directly, which neo-utilitarianism does not encompass. Some of these factors are international in origin, others domestic.

. . .

More empirical work in the social constructivist vein is necessary, and the origins of identities and other normative factors need to be better theorized. But it is not an undue stretch to conclude, even at this point, that neo-utilitarianism's assumptions that the identities and interests of states are exogenous and given (in contrast to being treated as endogenous and socially constructed) pose potentially serious distortions and omissions, even as they provide the basis on which neo-utilitarianism's theoretical payoff rests.

Ideational Causation

Neo-utilitarianism has a narrowly circumscribed view of the role of ideas in social life. . . .

What is the social constructivist contribution to the ideational research program? Social constructivists have sought to understand the full array of roles that ideas play in world politics, rather than specifying a priori roles based on theoretical presuppositions and then testing for those specified roles, as neo-utilitarians do. Because there is no received theory of the social construction of international reality, constructivists have gone about their work partly in somewhat of a barefoot empiricist manner and partly by means of conceptual analysis and thick description. To briefly map constructivist research on ideational factors, I begin by using Goldstein and Keohane's own typology and then push beyond it.

As noted, a core constructivist research concern is what happens before the neo-utilitarian model kicks in. Accordingly, what Goldstein and Keohane call "world views" are of great interest: civilizational constructs, cultural factors, state identities, and the like, together with how they shape states' interests and patterns of international outcomes. I identified some of the empirical work on these subjects earlier. In addition, such world views include changing forms of nationalism in its constitutive and transformative roles, as Ernst Haas has studied it extensively, not merely as adjuncts to states and their power. They include the globalization of market rationality and its effects, which has been of particular interest to constructivists who work in the tradition of Antonio Gramsci, Karl Polanyi, as well as the sociological institutionalists. And they include emerging bonds of "we-feeling" among nations, such as appear to have taken effect within the transatlantic security community—much as Karl Deutsch predicted forty years ago—and, of course, in the European Union.

Constructivist empirical studies documenting the impact of principled beliefs on patterns of international outcomes include, among other subjects, decolonization, international support for the termination of apartheid, the growing significance of human rights, the role of multilateral norms in stabilizing the consequences of rapid international change, as well as the already-mentioned studies on increasingly nondiscriminatory humanitarian interventions and the emergence of weapons taboos. The most important feature differentiating constructivist from other readings of these and similar phenomena is that they make the case that principled beliefs are not simply "theoretical fillers," to use Mark Blyth's apt term, employed to shore up instrumentalist accounts, but that in certain circumstances they lead states to redefine their interests or even their sense of self.

One major route for constructivist explorations of the impact of causal beliefs has been through the roles played by transnational networks of knowledge-based experts, or "epistemic communities." Here, the empirical research seeks to relate the impact of the shared beliefs held by such communities on resolving particular policy problems, such as ozone depletion; specifying operational content to general and sometimes ambivalent state interests, as at Bretton Woods; and helping to redefine states' interests, including in the case of the antiballistic missile treaty as well as the Mediterranean pollution control regime. Disentangling strictly ideational from institutional impacts is difficult in practice, but that problem is not unique to the epistemic community literature.

. . .

Constitutive Rules

Perhaps the most consequential difference between neorealism and neoliberal institutionalism, on the one hand, and social constructivism, on the other, has to do with the distinction between constitutive and regulative rules. The distinction goes back to a seminal article by John Rawls. [John] Searle offers an easier point of entry.

Let us begin with a simple illustration. We can readily imagine the act of driving a car existing prior to the rule that specified "drive on the right(left)-hand side of the road." In an account perfectly consistent with neo-utilitarianism, the rule would have been instituted as a function of increased traffic and growing numbers of fender-benders. Specifying which side of the road to drive on is an example of a regulative rule; as the term implies, it regulates an antecedently existing activity. To this rule were soon added others, such as those requiring licenses, yielding at intersections, imposing speed limits, and forbidding driving while under the influence of alcohol.

Now imagine a quite different situation: playing the game of chess. "It is not the case," Searle notes sardonically, "that there were a lot of people pushing bits of wood around on boards, and in order to prevent them from bumping into each other all the time and creating traffic jams, we had to regulate the activity. Rather, the rules of chess create the very possibility of playing chess. The rules are constitutive of chess in the sense that playing chess is constituted in part by acting in accord with the rules." Regulative rules are intended to have causal effects—getting people to approximate the speed limit, for example. Constitutive rules define the set of practices that make up a particular class of consciously organized social activity—that is to say, they specify *what counts as* that activity.

This basic distinction permits us to identify an utterly profound gap in neo-utilitarianism: it lacks any concept of constitutive rules. Its universe of discourse consists entirely of antecedently existing actors and their behavior, and its project is to explain the character and efficacy of regulative rules in coordinating them. This gap accounts for the fact that, within their theoretical terms, neorealism and neoliberal institutionalism are capable of explaining the origins of virtually nothing that is constitutive of the very possibility of international relations: not territorial states, not systems of states, not any concrete international order, nor the whole host of institutional forms that states use, ranging from the concept of contracts and treaties to multilateral organizing principles. All are assumed to exist already or are misspecified.

Why is this the case, and is it inherent to the enterprise? The reason is not difficult to decipher: neo-utilitarian models of international relations are imported from economics. It is universally acknowledged that the economy is embedded in broader social, political, and legal institutional frameworks that make it possible to conduct economic relations—which are constitutive of economic relations. Modern economic theory does not explain the origins of markets; it takes their existence for granted. The problem arises because, when neo-utilitarian models are imported into other fields, they leave those constitutive frameworks behind.

This problem appears not to matter for some (as yet unspecified) range of political phenomena, domestic and international, which has been explored by means of microeconomic models and the microfoundations of which are now far better understood than before. But there are certain things that these models are incapable of doing. Accounting for constitutive rules—which they were not responsible for in economics—is among the most important.

Nor can this defect be remedied within the neo-utilitarian apparatus. Alexander James Field has demonstrated from within the neoclassical tradition, and Robert Brenner the neo-Marxist, that marginal utility analysis cannot account for the constitutive rules that are required to generate market rationality and markets—an insight that Weber had already established at the turn of the century and Polanyi demonstrated powerfully a half century ago. The terms of a theory cannot explain the conditions necessary for that theory to function, because no theory can explain anything until its necessary preconditions hold. So it is with modern economic theory.

Social constructivists in international relations have not yet managed to devise a theory of constitutive rules, but the phenomenon itself is of central concern to them. Take first the states system. The very concept of the modern state was made possible only when a new rule for differentiating the constituent units within medieval Christendom replaced the constitutive rule of heteronomy (interwoven and overlapping jurisdictions, moral and political). And the modern system of states became conceivable only when the constitutive rule of reciprocal sovereignty took hold.

Moreover, Hedley Bull of the English school has argued that norms regarding promise keeping and contracting are constitutive of order in the international realm no less than the domestic. But the concept of promises and the institution of contracts must be understood and enjoy legitimacy before there can be any talk of regulative rules designed to deal with problems of cheating on agreements or incomplete contracting. . . .

Constructivists do not claim to understand the extraordinarily complex processes regarding constitutive rules fully (or even mostly). But neorealists and neoliberal institutionalists lack even a place for them in their ontology. The scope of their theories, as a result, is confined to regulative rules that coordinate behavior in a preconstituted world.

Transformation

In light of the foregoing discussion, it follows almost axiomatically that neo-utilitarian models of international relations theory would have little to offer on the subject of systemic transformation: doing so would require them to have some concept of constitutive rules. Waltz's model, I have shown elsewhere, contains only a reproductive logic, but no transformative logic. Neorealists have made some effort to respond by claiming, in essence, that no such logic is necessary. Neoliberal institutionalism has remained relatively silent on the subject.

. . .

Here again, constructivists have not yet managed to devise a fully fledged theoretical formulation. But its general thrust has become evident. It consists of historicizing the concept of structure in international politics: that is to say, rescuing it from being treated as the reified residue left behind by long-ceased historical processes. Doing so involves addressing both macro and micro dimensions of international political life.

. . .

The Social Constructivist Project

. . .

Constructivism's Core Features

As noted at the outset, constructivism concerns the issue of human consciousness in international life: the role it plays and the implications for the logic and methods of inquiry of taking it seriously. Constructivists hold the view that the building blocks of international reality are ideational as well as material; that ideational factors have normative as well as instrumental dimensions; that they express not only individual but also collective intentionality; and that the meaning and significance of ideational factors are not independent of time and place.

... [A]t the level of individual actors constructivism seeks, first of all, to problematize the identities and interests of states and to show how they have been socially constructed. Neorealists come close to believing that states' identities and interests are, in fact, given and fixed. For neoliberal institutionalists, this premise is more likely to reflect a convenient assumption, intended to permit their analytical apparatus to function. When neoliberal institutionalists are pressed about the origins of either, however, they turn immediately to domestic politics. Social constructivists, in contrast, argue and have shown that even identities are generated in part by international interaction—both the generic identities of states qua states and their specific identities, as in America's sense of difference from the Old World. Still at the level of individual units, constructivism also seeks to map the full array of additional ideational factors that shape actors' outlooks and behavior, ranging from culture and ideology to aspirations and principled beliefs, onto cause-effect knowledge of specific policy problems.

At the level of the international polity, the concept of structure in social constructivism is suffused with ideational factors. There can be no mutually comprehensible conduct of international relations, constructivists hold, without mutually recognized constitutive rules resting on collective intentionality. These rules may be more or less "thick" or "thin," depending on the issue area or the international grouping at hand. Similarly, they may be constitutive of conflict or cooperation. But in any event, these constitutive rules prestructure the domains of action within which regulative rules take effect....

These ontological characteristics have implications for the logic and methods of constructivist inquiry. First, constructivism is not itself a theory of international relations, the way balance-of-power theory is, for example, but a theoretically informed approach to the study of international relations. Moreover, constructivism does not aspire to the hypothetico-deductive mode of theory construction. It is by necessity more "realistic," to use Weber's term, or inductive in orientation. Additionally, its concepts in the first instance are intended to tap into and help interpret the meaning and significance that actors ascribe to the collective situation in which they find themselves. It is unlikely that this function could be performed by concepts that represent a priori types derived from some universalizing theory-sketch or from purely nominal definitions.

. . .

Paradigmatic (Ir)Reconcilability

. . .

The strength of neo-utilitarianism lies in its axiomatic structure, which permits a degree of analytical rigor, and in neoliberal institutionalism's case also of theoretical specification, that other approaches cannot match. This is not an aesthetic but a practical judgment. Rigor and specificity are desirable on self-evident intellectual as well as policy grounds. At the same time, neo-utilitarianism's major weakness lies in the foundations of its axiomatic structure, its ontology, which for some purposes is seriously flawed and leads to an incomplete or distorted view of international reality. That problem is particularly pronounced at a time, such as today, when states are struggling to redefine stable sets of interests and preferences regarding key aspects of the international order.

The obverse is true of constructivism. It rests on a deeper and broader ontology, thereby providing a richer understanding of some phenomena and shedding light on other aspects of international life that, quite literally, do not exist within the neo-utilitarian rendering of the world polity. At the same time, it lacks rigor and specification—indeed, it remains relatively poor at specifying its own scope conditions, the contexts within which its explanatory features can be expected to take effect. Improvements are inevitable as work in the constructivist vein continues to increase in quantity and quality, but given its nature there are inherent limits.

Anarchy is What States Make of It: The Social Construction of Power Politics*

ALEXANDER WENDT

The debate between realists and liberals has reemerged as an axis of contention in international relations theory. Revolving in the past around competing theories of human nature, the debate is more concerned today with the extent to which state action is influenced by "structure" (anarchy and the distribution of power) versus "process" (interaction and learning) and institutions. Does the absence of centralized political authority force states to play competitive power politics? Can international regimes overcome this logic, and under what conditions? What in anarchy is given and immutable, and what is amenable to change?

. . .

My objective in this article is to build a bridge between these two [realist and liberal] traditions . . . by developing a constructivist argument, drawn from structurationist and symbolic interactionist sociology,

* Reprinted by permission from 46 INTERNATIONAL ORGANIZATION 391 (1992).

on behalf of the liberal claim that international institutions can transform state identities and interests. . . .

My strategy for building this bridge will be to argue against the neorealist claim that self-help is given by anarchic structure exogenously to process. Constructivists have not done a good job of taking the causal powers of anarchy seriously. This is unfortunate, since in the realist view anarchy justifies disinterest in the institutional transformation of identities and interests and thus building systemic theories in exclusively rationalist terms; its putative causal powers must be challenged if process and institutions are not to be subordinated to structure. I argue that self-help and power politics do not follow either logically or causally from anarchy and that if today we find ourselves in a self-help world, this is due to process, not structure. There is no "logic" of anarchy apart from the practices that create and instantiate one structure of identities and interests rather than another; structure has no existence or causal powers apart from process. Self-help and power politics are institutions, not essential features of anarchy. *Anarchy is what states make of it.*

. . .

Anarchy and Power Politics

. . .

Anarchy, self-help, and intersubjective knowledge

Waltz defines political structure on three dimensions: ordering principles (in this case, anarchy), principles of differentiation (which here drop out), and the distribution of capabilities. By itself, this definition predicts little about state behavior. It does not predict whether two states will be friends or foes, will recognize each other's sovereignty, will have dynastic ties, will be revisionist or status quo powers, and so on. These factors, which are fundamentally intersubjective, affect states' security interests and thus the character of their interaction under anarchy. In an important revision of Waltz's theory, Stephen Walt implies as much when he argues that the "balance of threats," rather than the balance of power, determines state action, threats being socially constructed. Put more generally, without assumptions about the structure of identities and interests in the system, Waltz's definition of structure cannot predict the content or dynamics of anarchy. Self-help is one such intersubjective structure and, as such, does the decisive explanatory work in the theory. The question is whether self-help is a logical or contingent feature of anarchy. In this section, I develop the concept of a "structure of identity and interest" and show that no particular one follows logically from anarchy.

A fundamental principle of constructivist social theory is that people act toward objects, including other actors, on the basis of the meanings that the objects have for them. States act differently toward enemies than they do toward friends because enemies are threatening and friends are not. Anarchy and the distribution of power are insufficient to tell us which is which. U.S. military power has a different significance for

Canada than for Cuba, despite their similar "structural" positions, just as British missiles have a different significance for the United States than do Soviet missiles. The distribution of power may always affect states' calculations, but how it does so depends on the intersubjective understandings and expectations, on the "distribution of knowledge," that constitute their conceptions of self and other. If society "forgets" what a university is, the powers and practices of professor and student cease to exist; if the United States and Soviet Union decide that they are no longer enemies, "the cold war is over." It is collective meanings that constitute the structures which organize our actions.

Actors acquire identities—relatively stable, role-specific understandings and expectations about self—by participating in such collective meanings. Identities are inherently relational: "Identity, with its appropriate attachments of psychological reality, is always identity within a specific, socially constructed world," Peter Berger argues. Each person has many identities linked to institutional roles, such as brother, son, teacher, and citizen. Similarly, a state may have multiple identities as "sovereign," "leader of the free world," "imperial power," and so on. The commitment to and the salience of particular identities vary, but each identity is an inherently social definition of the actor grounded in the theories which actors collectively hold about themselves and one another and which constitute the structure of the social world.

Identities are the basis of interests. Actors do not have a "portfolio" of interests that they carry around independent of social context; instead, they define their interests in the process of defining situations. As Nelson Foote puts it: "Motivation . . . refer[s] to the degree to which a human being, as a participant in the ongoing social process in which he necessarily finds himself, defines a problematic situation as calling for the performance of a particular act, with more or less anticipated consummations and consequences, and thereby his organism releases the energy appropriate to performing it." Sometimes situations are unprecedented in our experience, and in these cases we have to construct their meaning, and thus our interests, by analogy or invent them de novo. More often they have routine qualities in which we assign meanings on the basis of institutionally defined roles. When we say that professors have an "interest" in teaching, research, or going on leave, we are saying that to function in the role identity of "professor," they have to define certain situations as calling for certain actions. This does not mean that they will necessarily do so (expectations and competence do not equal performance), but if they do not, they will not get tenure. The absence or failure of roles makes defining situations and interests more difficult, and identity confusion may result. This seems to be happening today in the United States and the former Soviet Union: without the cold war's mutual attributions of threat and hostility to define their identities, these states seem unsure of what their "interests" should be.

An institution is a relatively stable set or "structure" of identities and interests. Such structures are often codified in formal rules and norms, but these have motivational force only in virtue of actors' socialization to and participation in collective knowledge. Institutions are fundamentally cognitive entities that do not exist apart from actors' ideas about how the world works. This does not mean that institutions are not real or objective, that they are "nothing but" beliefs. As collective knowledge, they are experienced as having an existence "over and above the individuals who happen to embody them at the moment." In this way, institutions come to confront individuals as more or less coercive social facts, but they are still a function of what actors collectively "know." Identities and such collective cognitions do not exist apart from each other; they are "mutually constitutive." On this view, institutionalization is a process of internalizing new identities and interests, not something occurring outside them and affecting only behavior; socialization is a cognitive process, not just a behavioral one. Conceived in this way, institutions may be cooperative or conflictual, a point sometimes lost in scholarship on international regimes, which tends to equate institutions with cooperation. There are important differences between conflictual and cooperative institutions to be sure, but all relatively stable self-other relations—even those of "enemies"—are defined intersubjectively.

Self-help is an institution, one of various structures of identity and interest that may exist under anarchy. Processes of identity-formation under anarchy are concerned first and foremost with preservation or "security" of the self. Concepts of security therefore differ in the extent to which and the manner in which the self is identified cognitively with the other, and, I want to suggest, it is upon this cognitive variation that the meaning of anarchy and the distribution of power depends. Let me illustrate with a standard continuum of security systems.

At one end is the "competitive" security system, in which states identify negatively with each other's security so that ego's gain is seen as alter's loss. Negative identification under anarchy constitutes systems of "realist" power politics: risk-averse actors that infer intentions from capabilities and worry about relative gains and losses. At the limit—in the Hobbesian war of all against all—collective action is nearly impossible in such a system because each actor must constantly fear being stabbed in the back.

In the middle is the "individualistic" security system, in which states are indifferent to the relationship between their own and others' security. This constitutes "neoliberal" systems: states are still self-regarding about their security but are concerned primarily with absolute gains rather than relative gains. One's position in the distribution of power is less important, and collective action is more possible (though still subject to free riding because states continue to be "egoists").

Competitive and individualistic systems are both "self-help" forms of anarchy in the sense that states do not positively identify the security of self with that of others but instead treat security as the individual responsibility of each. Given the lack of a positive cognitive identification on the basis of which to build security regimes, power politics within such systems will necessarily consist of efforts to manipulate others to satisfy self-regarding interests.

This contrasts with the "cooperative" security system, in which states identify positively with one another so that the security of each is perceived as the responsibility of all. This is not self-help in any interesting sense, since the "self" in terms of which interests are defined is defined in the community; national interests are international interests. In practice, of course, the extent to which states' identification with the community varies, from the limited form found in "concerts" to the full-blown form seen in "collective security" arrangements. Depending on how well developed the collective self is, it will produce security practices that are in varying degrees altruistic or prosocial. This makes collective action less dependent on the presence of active threats and less prone to free riding. Moreover, it restructures efforts to advance one's objectives, or "power politics," in terms of shared norms rather than relative power.

On this view, the tendency in international relations scholarship to view power and institutions as two opposing explanations of foreign policy is therefore misleading, since anarchy and the distribution of power only have meaning for state action in virtue of the understandings and expectations that constitute institutional identities and interests. Self-help is one such institution, constituting one kind of anarchy but not the only kind. Waltz's three-part definition of structure therefore seems underspecified. In order to go from structure to action, we need to add a fourth: the intersubjectively constituted structure of identities and interests in the system.

. . .

The state-centrism of this agenda may strike some, particularly postmodernists, as "depressingly familiar." The significance of states relative to multinational corporations, new social movements, transnationals, and intergovernmental organizations is clearly declining, and "postmodern" forms of world politics merit more research attention than they have received. But I also believe, with realists, that in the medium run sovereign states will remain the dominant political actors in the international system. Any transition to new structures of global political authority and identity—to "postinternational" politics—will be mediated by and path-dependent on the particular institutional resolution of the tension between unity and diversity, or particularism and universality, that is the sovereign state. In such a world there should continue to be a place for theories of anarchic interstate politics, alongside other forms of international theory; to that extent, I am a statist and a realist. I have argued in this article, however, that statism need not be bound by realist ideas about what "state" must mean. State identities and interests can be collectively transformed within an anarchic context by many factors—individual, domestic, systemic, or transnational—and as such are an important dependent variable. Such a reconstruction of state-centric international theory is necessary if we are to theorize adequately about the emerging forms of transnational political identity that sovereign states will help bring into being. To that extent, I hope that statism, like the state, can be historically progressive.

Notes and Comments

1. Ruggie, in the excerpt above, acknowledges at the outset an intellectual debt to the English (or Grotian) school (also discussed in the Notes to Part I of this book). The English school, with its emphasis on shared norms and social goals, can be thought of as an intellectual precursor to constructivism. While most scholars in the English tradition, including Hedley Bull, would probably still consider themselves realists, they share with constructivists a conviction that the social nature of man is an important feature of international relations. In this sense, the two traditions can be said to share an enduring and important feature of Hugo Grotius' work: "the affirmation of the social nature of man as the basis of the law of nature." Hersch Lauterpacht, *The Grotian Tradition in International Law*, 23 BRITISH YEAR BOOK OF INTERNATIONAL LAW 24 (1946).

2. The constructivist view of the central actors in international law and politics differs in important ways from that of rationalist theories. For example, one theme of much modern constructivist scholarship is the role of expert and activist communities in shaping international law and politics. John Ruggie argues that the literature on "epistemic communities"—transnational networks of experts who place issues on the the international agenda—provides an important key to explaining the transformation of societal interests and identities, and hence of the international system that they shape. Similarly, Martha Finnemore emphasizes the role of international organizations can play in "teaching" states new interests. For yet another perspective on the role of communities of experts in international law and politics, see Emmanuel Adler and Peter M. Haas, *Conclusion: Epistemic Communities*, 46 INTERNATIONAL ORGANIZATION 367 (1990).

Relatedly, constructivist scholars often focus closely on the role played by activist groups, or nongovernmental organizations, that they argue can help determine state behavior. As Martha Finnemore and Kathryn Sikkink observe, "These cases present attractive research puzzles because activists working for change often have few levers of conventional power relative to those controlling existing structures (often the state or corporations); to the extent that activists succeed, these situations are not easily explained by dominant utilitarian approaches; and they open spaces for constructivist alternatives." Martha Finnemore & Kathryn Sikkink, *Taking Stock: The Constructivist Research Program in International Relations and Comparative Politics*, 4 ANNUAL REVIEW OF POLITICAL SCIENCE 391, 400 (2001). Margaret Keck's and Kathryn Sikkink's discussion of the role of "transnational advocacy networks" is an excellent example of such work. See MARGARET E. KECK & KATHRYN SIKKINK, ACTIVISTS BEYOND BORDERS (1998). (A chapter of this book is excerpted in

Part IV.A., on Human Rights, *infra*.) See also THE POWER OF HUMAN RIGHTS: INTERNATIONAL NORMS AND DOMESTIC CHANGE (Thomas Risse, Stephan C. Ropp, and Kathryn Sikkink, eds. 1999). For a thoughtful commentary on the nature and rise of constructivism, see Christian Reus-Smit, *Constructivism, in* THEORIES OF INTERNATIONAL RELATIONS (Scott Burchill, ed. 1996).

3. What is the source of political change in the constructivist framework? Where do norms (and changes therein) come from? How do the excerpts above differ on this and on their conceptions of constructivism more generally?

4. In a footnote to the the article excerpted above, Wendt adds:

> Throughout this article, I assume that a theoretically productive analogy can be made between individuals and states. There are at least two justifications for this anthropomorphism. Rhetorically, the analogy is an accepted practice in mainstream international relations discourse, and since this article is an immanent rather than external critique, it should follow the practice. Substantively, states are collectivities of individuals that through their practices constitute each other as "persons" having interests, fears, and so on. A full theory of state identity-and interest-formation would nevertheless need to draw insights from the social psychology of groups and organizational theory, and for that reason my anthropomorphism is merely suggestive.

Wendt, supra, at 397 n. 21. What does it mean to anthropomorphize the state? Is this a useful (or necessary) assumption? How does constructivist work differ from the theories outlined in Part II of this book in its view of the state as the central actor in international politics? How is Wendt's view on this point similar to and different from that of Finnemore and Ruggie? Which view do you find most persuasive? How would each perspective account for a change in those in power in government and the effect of such a change on state policy?

5. Wendt argues that the anarchic international system need not necessarily lead inevitably to a Hobbesian world of self-help. In a subsequent book, SOCIAL THEORY OF INTERNATIONAL POLITICS, Wendt describes three possible "cultures" or realizations of anarchy: the familiar Hobbesian one, a Lockean world of rivalry, and a Kantian world of friendship (see Wendt, *supra*, ch. 6 ("Three Cultures of Anarchy")). How does this view, which admits the possibility of multiple possible outcomes in an anarchic world, differ from that of realism? Which view do you find more persuasive?

6. In the excerpt above, Finnemore highlights several connections between constructivism and international legal scholarship, noting how they might benefit from future collaboration. (For a more recent statement of her views, see Martha Finnemore & Stephen J. Toope, *Alternatives to "Legalization": Richer Views of Law and Politics*, 55 INTERNATIONAL ORGANIZATION 743 (2001)). As you read Harold Koh's work on transnational legal process (Part III.C.2.), consider how the constructivist "top-down" approach (which draws directly from sociology), is similar to and different from the transnational legal integration processes highlighted by Koh.

7. A persistent critique of constructivism is that it is difficult to falsify and hence is not truly a "theory" of state behavior. While it allows for explanations of state behavior after the fact, it has been critiqued for being less capable of producing specific predictions about state behavior *ex ante*. In 2001, Finnemore and Sikkink wrote that constructivism "is not a substantive theory of politics" and it "does not, by itself, produce specific predictions about political outcomes that one could test in social science research" (Finnemore & Sikkink, *Taking Stock*, at 393). Consider how constructivism compares in this respect to other theories of state behavior. Are "norms" inherently any less difficult to define than "power" or "interests"? As the constructivist research program has progressed over the last decade, those working within the constructivist paradigm have worked to respond to the critique that its claims are difficult to test. For example, Thomas Risse's 2000 article, *Let's Argue: Communicative Action in World Politics*, 54 INTERNATIONAL ORGANIZATION 1 (2000), claims that "Jürgen Habermas's critical theory of communicative action is helpful in conceptualizing the logic of arguing and can actually be brought to bear to tackle empirical questions in world politics." *Id.* at 2. The piece has spawned an array of empirical projects.

8. Constructivism, by emphasizing the role of ideas over interests and the malleability of international politics, creates space for scholars to consider how individuals and groups can bring about purposeful change. Hence many constructivist scholars have sought to move beyond the observation that norms influence state behavior to begin asking how individuals can transform the normative setting in which states act and thereby change state behavior. Several have also become practitioners, cooperating with NGOs or working with intergovernmental organizations. John Ruggie, for example, served as Special Advisor to U.N. Secretary–General Kofi Annan in planning the U.N.'s Millennium Summit and Global Compact, and has continued to work on issues of the corporate social responsibility of multinational enterprises. As Finnemore and Sikkink put it, constructivists are examining the process of "strategic social construction"—how individuals set out to and succeed in changing norms, identities, and perceived interests. *See, e.g.*, Martha Finnemore & Kathryn Sikkink, *International Norm Dynamics and Political Change*, 52 INTERNATIONAL ORGANIZATION 888 (1998). The growing scholarship on strategic social construction may add to the transformative and predictive capacities of constructivism, and spawn a new generation of theoretically informed activists.

9. Constructivism has been credited with creating theoretical space for other theories such as feminism to enter the field of international relations. As J. Ann Tickner observes:

> It is not coincidental that feminist theory came to IR at the same time as a fundamental questioning of its epistemological foundations that called for rethinking the ways in which we explain or understand world politics. Constructivists suggested that ideational as well as material forces could explain international politics and the

> "third debate" proclaimed the beginning of a "post-positivist era" in international relations ... [T]hese developments marked the appearance of a substantial body of scholarship, associated with critical theory, historical sociology, and postmodernism, that challenged both the epistemological and ontological foundations of a field dominated, in the United States at least, by rationalist methodologies.

J. Ann Tickner, *Feminist Perspectives on International Relations, in* Walter Carlsnaes, Thomas Risse, and Beth A. Simmons, eds., HANDBOOK OF INTERNATIONAL RELATIONS 276 (2002).

B. Theories of Fairness and Legitimacy

A defining difference between much of legal and political science scholarship on international law lies in the importance placed on sanctions. As prior sections have demonstrated, most political science accounts of international law argue that enforcement through sanctions plays the central role in motivating compliance. In this view, where sanctions are absent, international law is unlikely to change state behavior.

This section focuses on a theoretical approach to state behavior that is largely dominated by legal scholars—an approach that finds the source of support for and effectiveness of international regimes in the legitimacy of the norms and rules that compose them. In contrast with rationalist accounts of state behavior, this model points not to state calculations of self-interest as the source of state decisions to act consistently with international legal obligations, but instead to the perceived legitimacy of the legal obligations. Compliance with international law, in this view, is traced to the widespread normative acceptance of international rules, which in turn reflects the consistency of the rules with widely held values and the legitimacy of the rulemaking process.

The excerpts in this section begin with the work not of an international legal scholar or political scientist, but of a legal philosopher—H.L.A. Hart. The work of modern scholars who focus on procedural legitimacy finds its roots in the writings of H.L.A. Hart, among others. Connecting the debate over international law to a centuries' old tradition of debate among legal scholars over the source of legal obligation, Hart encourages us to consider when and why rules generate legally binding claims. He offers a legal positivist account of the law that places central emphasis on legal legitimacy. By contrast with the natural law theorists, such as Hugo Grotius, Hart argues that law is not a set of principles that transcend time and place, waiting to be found. Nor does he subscribe to "command theory" of law that is primarily associated with John Austin, according to which laws are commands—expressions of desire backed by threat. Instead, Hart argues that what is law is contingent neither on morality nor on sanctions but on a rule's legitimacy within the particular context in which it exists. To lay the groundwork for this claim, Hart, in the portion of his book excerpted below, focuses on refuting common challenges to the legally binding character of international law.

The second excerpt seeks to reconcile the legitimacy-based view with more traditional political science accounts of state behavior. In it, political scientist Ian Hurd argues that there are a number of reasons why an actor might obey a rule. Two of these reasons—coercion and self-interest—have traditionally been the focus of most political science scholarship on state behavior. An equally important and yet often ignored reason for law-abiding behavior, he argues, is the legitimacy of the rule. Compliance with international law cannot be explained by reference to only one of these features, he argues, but is instead due to some combination of these devices.

The final excerpt is from a book by the leading modern exponent of the legitimacy-centered view, Thomas Franck. It offers a comprehensive statement of an approach to international law that focuses on fairness and legitimacy as the source of legal obligation. The book excerpted below, *Fairness in International Law and Institutions*, continues a conversation Franck began in his earlier and equally influential book, *The Power of Legitimacy Among Nations*. In it, Franck asks, "Why do powerful nations obey powerless rules?" Building on the work of legal philosphers Ronald Dworkin and Jurgen Habermas, Franck answers that a variety of non-coercive factors—which he labeled as falling under the general term "legitimacy"—engender state obedience to international rules. Legitimacy is, he explains, "a property of a rule or rule-making institution which itself exerts a pull toward compliance on those addressed normatively because those addressed believe that the rule or institution has come into being and operates in accordance with generally accepted principles of right process."[1]

In the book excerpted below, Franck expands this framework. He now argues that the central element explaining treaty adherence and compliance is whether the law is "fair." Responding perhaps to critiques of his earlier work for its wholly procedural approach to legitimacy, Franck argues here that it is not enough for a rule to be legitimate, or, as he now puts it, "procedurally fair." It must also be substantively fair—its ends must lead to distributive justice. Rules that are both procedurally and substantively fair exert a "compliance pull" that leads states to abide by them even in the absence of coercion.

Concept of Law*

H.L.A. HART

International Law

Sources of doubt

. . .

Though we shall devote to it only a single chapter some writers have proposed an even shorter treatment for this question concerning the

1. THOMAS FRANCK, THE POWER OF LEGITIMACY AMONG NATIONS 24 (1990)

* Reprinted by permission from H.L.A. HART, CONCEPT OF LAW (1961).

character of international law. To them it has seemed that the question "Is international law really law?" has only arisen or survived, because a trivial question about the meaning of words has been mistaken for a serious question about the nature of things: since the facts which differentiate international law from municipal law are clear and well known, the only question to be settled is whether we should observe the existing convention or depart from it; and this is a matter for each person to settle for himself. But this short way with the question is surely too short. It is true that among the reasons which have led theorists to hesitate over the extension of the word "law" to international law, a too simple, and indeed absurd view, of what justifies the application of the same word to many different things has played some part. The variety of types of principle which commonly guide the extension of general classifying terms has too often been ignored in jurisprudence. Nonetheless the sources of doubt about international law are deeper, and more interesting than these mistaken views about the use of words. Moreover, the two alternatives offered by this short way with the question ("Shall we observe the existing convention or shall we depart from it?") are not exhaustive; for, besides them, there is the alternative of making explicit and examining the principles that have in fact guided the existing usage.

. . .

We shall consider two principal sources of doubt concerning the legal character of international law and, with them, the steps which theorists have taken to meet these doubts. Both forms of doubt arise from an adverse comparison of international law with municipal law, which is taken as the clear, standard example of what law is. The first has its roots deep in the conception of law as fundamentally a matter of orders backed by threats and contrasts the character of the *rules* of international law with those of municipal law. The second form of doubt springs from the obscure belief that states are fundamentally incapable of being the subjects of legal obligation, and contrasts the character of the *subjects of* international law with those of municipal law.

Obligations and Sanctions

The doubts which we shall consider are often expressed in the opening chapters of books on international law in the form of the question "How can international law be binding?" . . . Plainly the question, "Is international law binding?" and its congeners "How can international law be binding?" or "What makes international law binding?" . . . express a doubt not about the applicability, but about the general legal status of international law: this doubt would be more candidly expressed in the form "Can such rules as these be meaningfully and truthfully said ever to give rise to obligations?" As the discussions in the books show, one source of doubt on this point is simply the absence from the system of centrally organized sanctions. This is one point of adverse comparison with municipal law, the rules of which are taken to be unquestionably "binding" and to be paradigms of legal obligation. From this stage the further argument is simple: if for this reason the rules of international law are not "binding," it is surely indefensible to take seriously their classification as law; for however tolerant the modes of common speech may be, this is too great a difference to be overlooked. All speculation about the nature of law begins from the assumption that its existence at least makes certain conduct obligatory.

In considering this argument we shall give it the benefit of every doubt concerning the facts of the international system. We shall take it that neither Article 16 of the Covenant of the League of Nations nor Chapter VII of the United Nations Charter introduced into international law anything which can be equated with the sanctions of municipal law. In spite of the Korean war and of whatever moral may be drawn from the Suez incident, we shall suppose that, whenever their use is of importance, the law enforcement provisions of the Charter are likely to be paralysed by the veto and must be said to exist only on paper.

To argue that international law is not binding because of its lack of organized sanctions is tacitly to accept the analysis of obligation contained in the theory that law is essentially a matter of orders backed by threats. This theory ... identifies "having an obligation" or "being bound" with "likely to suffer the sanction or punishment threatened for disobedience." Yet ... this identification distorts the role played in all legal thought and discourse of the ideas of obligation and duty.... [O]nce we free ourselves from the predictive analysis and its parent conception of law as essentially an order backed by threats, there seems no good reason for limiting the normative idea of obligation to rules supported by organized sanctions.

We must, however, consider another form of the argument, more plausible because it is not committed to definition of obligation in terms of the likelihood of threatened sanctions. The sceptic may point out that there are in a municipal system, as we have ourselves stressed, certain provisions which are justifiably called necessary; among these are primary rules of obligation,[2] prohibiting the free use of violence, and rules providing for the official use of force as a sanction for these and other rules. If such rules and organized sanctions supporting them are in this sense necessary for municipal law, are they not equally so for international law? That they are may be maintained without insisting that this follows from the very meaning of words like "binding" or "obligation."

The answer to the argument in this form is to be found in those elementary truths about human beings and their environment which constitute the enduring psychological and physical setting of municipal law. In societies of individuals, approximately equal in physical strength

2. [Editors' Note: In Hart's terminology, "primary rules" are rules that tell those in a society how they ought to act in a given set of circumstances. They are distinguished from "secondary rules," "which specify the ways in which primary rules may be conclusively ascertained, introduced, eliminated, varied, and the fact of their violation conclusively determined." Hart, *supra*, at 94.]

and vulnerability, physical sanctions are both necessary and possible. They are required in order that those who would voluntarily submit to the restraints of law shall not be mere victims of malefactors who would, in the absence of such sanctions, reap the advantages of respect for law on the part of others, without respecting it themselves. Among individuals living in close proximity to each other, opportunities for injuring others, by guile, if not by open attack, are so great, and the chances of escape so considerable, that no mere natural deterrents could in any but the simplest forms of society be adequate to restrain those too wicked, too stupid, or too weak to obey the law. Yet, because of the same fact of approximate equality and the patent advantages of submission to a system of restraints, no combination of malefactors is likely to exceed in strength those who would voluntarily co-operate in its maintenance. In these circumstances, which constitute the background of municipal law, sanctions may successfully be used against malefactors with relatively small risks, and the threat of them will add much to whatever natural deterrents there may be. But, just because the simple truisms which hold good for individuals do not hold good for states, and the factual background to international law is so different from that of municipal law, there is neither a similar necessity for sanctions (desirable though it may be that international law should be supported by them) nor a similar prospect of their safe and efficacious use.

This is so because aggression between states is very unlike that between individuals. The use of violence between states must be public, and though there is no international police force, there can be very little certainty that it will remain a matter between aggressor and victim, as a murder or theft, in the absence of a police force, might. To initiate a war is, even for the strongest power, to risk much for an outcome which is rarely predictable with reasonable confidence. On the other hand, because of the inequality of states, there can be no standing assurance that the combined strength of those on the side of international order is likely to preponderate over the powers tempted to aggression. Hence the organization and use of sanctions may involve fearful risks and the threat of them add little to the natural deterrents. Against this very different background of fact, international law has developed in a form different from that of municipal law. In a population of a modern state, if there were no organized repression and punishment of crime, violence and theft would be hourly expected; but for states, long years of peace have intervened between disastrous wars. These years of peace are only rationally to be expected, given the risks and stakes of war and the mutual needs of states; but they are worth regulating by rules which differ from those of municipal law in (among other things) not providing for their enforcement by any central organ. Yet what these rules require is thought and spoken of as obligatory; there is general pressure for conformity to the rules; claims and admissions are based on them and their breach is held to justify not only insistent demands for compensation, but reprisals and counter-measures. When the rules are disregarded, it is not on the footing that they are not binding; instead efforts are made to conceal the facts. It may of course be said that such rules are efficacious only so far as they concern issues over which states are unwilling to fight. This may be so, and may reflect adversely on the importance of the system and its value to humanity. Yet that even so much may be secured shows that no simple deduction can be made from the necessity of organized sanctions to municipal law, in its setting of physical and psychological facts, to the conclusion that without them international law, in its very different setting, imposes no obligations, is not "binding," and so not worth the title of "law."

Obligation and the Sovereignty of States

Great Britain, Belgium, Greece, Soviet Russia have rights and obligations under international law and so are among its subjects. They are random examples of states which the layman would think of as independent and the lawyer would recognize as "sovereign." One of the most persistent sources of perplexity about the obligatory character of international law has been the difficulty felt in accepting or explaining the fact that a state which is sovereign may also be "bound" by, or have an obligation under, international law. This form of scepticism is, in a sense, more extreme than the objection that international law is not binding because it lacks sanctions. For whereas that would be met if one day international law were reinforced by a system of sanctions, the present objection is based on a radical inconsistency, said or felt to exist, in the conception of a state which is at once sovereign and subject to law.

Examination of this objection involves a scrutiny of the notion of sovereignty, applied not to a legislature or to some other element or person *within* a state, but to a state itself. Whenever the word "sovereign" appears in jurisprudence, there is a tendency to associate with it the idea of a person above the law whose word is law for his inferiors or subjects. . . . It is, of course, *possible* to think of a state along such lines, as if it were a species of Superman—a Being inherently lawless but the source of law for its subjects. From the sixteenth century onwards, the symbolical identification of state and monarch ("L'etat c'est moi") may have encouraged this idea which has been the dubious inspiration of much political as well as legal theory. But it is important for the understanding of international law to shake off these associations. The expression "a state" is not the name of some person or thing inherently or "by nature" outside the law; it is a way of referring to two facts: first, that a population inhabiting a territory lives under that form of ordered government provided by a legal system with its characteristic structure of legislature, courts, and primary rules; and, secondly, that the government enjoys a vaguely defined degree of independence.

. . . It is possible to imagine many different forms of international authority and correspondingly many different limitations on the independence of states. The possibilities include, among many others, a world legislature on the model of the British Parliament, possessing legally unlimited powers to regulate the internal and external affairs of all; a federal legislature on the model of Congress, with legal competence only over specified matters or one limited by guarantees of specific rights of the constituent units; a regime in which the only form of legal control consists of rules generally accepted as applicable to all; and finally a regime in which the only form of obligation recognized is contractual or self-imposed, so that a state's independence is legally limited only by its own act.

It is salutary to consider this range of possibilities because merely to realize that there are many possible forms and degrees of dependence and independence, is a step towards answering the claim that because states are sovereign they "*cannot*" be subject to or bound by international law or "can" only be bound by some specific form of international law. For the word "sovereign" means here no more than "independent"; and, like the latter, is negative in force: a sovereign state is one *not* subject to certain types of control, and its sovereignty is that area of conduct in which it is autonomous. Some measure of autonomy is imported, as we have seen, by the very meaning of the word state but the contention that this "*must*" be unlimited or "*can*" only be limited by certain types of obligation is at best the assertion of a claim that states ought to be free of all other restraints, and at worst is an unreasoned dogma. For if in fact we find that there exists among states a given form of international authority, the sovereignty of states is to that extent limited, and it has just that extent which the rules allow. Hence we can only know which states are sovereign, and what the extent of their sovereignty is, when we know what the rules are; just as we can only know whether an Englishman or an American is free and the extent of his freedom when we know what English or American law is. The rules of international law are indeed vague and conflicting on many points, so that doubt about the area of independence left to states is far greater than that concerning the extent of a citizen's freedom under municipal law. None the less, these difficulties do not validate the *a priori* argument which attempts to deduce the general character of international law from an absolute sovereignty, which is assumed, without reference to international law, to belong to states.

. . .

Analogies of Form and Content.

To the innocent eye, the formal structure of international law lacking a legislature, courts with compulsory jurisdiction and officially organized sanctions, appears very different from that of municipal law. It resembles, as we have said, in form though not at all in content, a simple regime of primary or customary law. Yet some theorists, in their anxiety to defend against the sceptic the title of international law to be called "law," have succumbed to the temptation to minimize these formal differences, and to exaggerate the analogies which can be found in international law to legislation or other desirable formal features of municipal law. Thus, it has been claimed that war, ending with a treaty whereby the defeated power cedes territory, or assumes obligations, or accepts some diminished form of independence, is essentially a legislative act; for, like legislation, it is an imposed legal change. Few would now be impressed by this analogy, or think that it helped to show that international law had an equal title with municipal law to be called "law"; for one of the salient differences between municipal and international law is that the former usually does not, and the latter does, recognize the validity of agreements extorted by violence.

A variety of other, more respectable analogies have been stressed by those who consider the title of "law" to depend on them. The fact that in almost all cases the judgment of the International Court and its predecessor, the Permanent Court of International Justice [PCIJ], have been duly carried out by the parties, has often been emphasized as if this somehow offset the fact that, in contrast with municipal courts, no state can be brought before these international tribunals without its prior consent. Analogies have also been found between the use of force, legally regulated and officially administered, as a sanction in municipal law and "decentralized sanctions," i.e. the resort to war or forceful retaliation by a state which claims that its rights under international law have been violated by another. That there is some analogy is plain; but its significance must be assessed in the light of the equally plain fact that, whereas a municipal court has a compulsory jurisdiction to investigate the rights and wrongs of "self help," and to punish a wrongful resort to it, no international court has a similar jurisdiction.

Some of these dubious analogies may be considered to have been much strengthened by the obligations which states have assumed under the United Nations Charter. But, again, any assessment of their strength is worth little if it ignores the extent to which the law enforcement provisions of the Charter, admirable on paper, have been paralysed by the veto and the ideological divisions and alliances of the great powers. The reply, sometimes made, that the law-enforcement provisions of municipal law *might* also be paralysed by a general strike is scarcely convincing; for in our comparison between municipal law and international law we are concerned with what exists in fact, and here the facts are undeniably different.

There is, however, one suggested formal analogy between international and municipal law which deserves some scrutiny here. [Hans] Kelsen and many modern theorists insist that, like municipal law, international law possesses and indeed must possess a "basic norm," or what we have termed a rule of recognition, by reference to which the validity of the other rules of the system is assessed, and in virtue of which the rules constitute a single system. The opposed view is that this analogy of structure is false: international law simply consists of a *set* of separate primary rules of obligation which are not united in this manner. It is, in the usual terminology of international lawyers, a set of customary rules of which the rule giving binding force to treaties is one. It is notorious that those who have embarked on the task have found very great difficulties in formulating the "basic norm" of international law. Candidates for this position include the principle *pacta sunt servanda.* This has, however, been abandoned by most theorists, since it seems incompatible with the fact that not all obligations under international law arise from "pacta," however widely that term is construed. So it has been replaced by something less familiar: the so-called rule that "States should behave as they customarily behave."

We shall not discuss the merits of these and other rival formulations of the basic norm of international law; instead we shall question the assumption that it must contain such an element. Here the first and perhaps the last question to ask is: why should we make this *a priori* assumption (for that is what it is) and so prejudge the actual character of the rules of international law? For it is surely conceivable (and perhaps has often been the case) that a society may live by rules imposing obligations on its members as "binding," even though they are regarded simply as a set of separate rules, not unified by or deriving their validity from any more basic rule. It is plain that the mere existence of rules does not involve the existence of such a basic rule. In most modern societies there are rules of etiquette, and, though we do not think of them as imposing obligations, we may well talk of such rules as existing; yet we would not look for, nor could we find, a basic rule of etiquette from which the validity of the separate rules was derivable. Such rules do not form a system but a mere set, and, of course, the inconveniences of this form of social control, where matters more important than those of etiquette are at stake, are considerable.... Yet if rules are in fact accepted as standards of conduct, and supported with appropriate forms of social pressure distinctive of obligatory rules, nothing more is required to show that they are binding rules, even though, in this simple form of social structure, we have not something which we do have in municipal law: namely a way of demonstrating the validity of individual rules by reference to some ultimate rule of the system.

... It is ... a mistake to suppose that a basic rule or rule of recognition is a generally necessary condition of the existence of rules of obligation or "binding" rules. This is not a necessity, but a luxury, found in advanced social systems whose members not merely come to accept separate rules piecemeal, but are committed to the acceptance in advance of general classes of rule, marked out by general criteria of validity. In the simpler form of society we must wait and see whether a rule gets accepted as a rule or not; in a system with a basic rule of recognition we can say before a rule is actually made, that it *will* be valid *if* it conforms to the requirements of the rule of recognition.

... We may be persuaded to treat as a basic rule, something which is an empty repetition of the mere fact that the society concerned (whether of individuals or states) observes certain standards of conduct as obligatory rules. This is surely the status of the strange basic norm which has been suggested for international law: "States should behave as they have customarily behaved." For it says nothing more than that those who accept certain rules must also observe a rule that rules ought to be observed. This is a mere useless reduplication of the fact that a set of rules are accepted by states as binding rules.

Again once we emancipate ourselves from the assumption that international law *must* contain a basic rule, the question to be faced is one of fact. What is the actual character of the rules as they function in the relations between states? Different interpretations of the phenomena to be observed are of course possible; but it is submitted that there is no basic rule providing general criteria of validity for the rules of international law, and that the rules which are in fact operative constitute not a system but a set of rules, among which are the rules providing for the binding force of treaties. It is true that, on many important matters, the relations between states are regulated by multilateral treaties, and it is sometimes argued that these may bind states that are not parties. If this were generally recognized, such treaties would in fact be legislative enactments and international law would have distinct criteria of validity for its rules. A basic rule of recognition could then be formulated which would represent an actual feature of the system and would be more than an empty restatement of the fact that a set of rules are in fact observed by states. Perhaps international law is at present in a stage of transition towards acceptance of this and other forms which would bring it nearer in structure to a municipal system. If, and when, this transition is completed the formal analogies, which at present seem thin and even delusive, would acquire substance, and the sceptic's last doubts about the legal "quality" of international law may then be laid to rest. Till this stage is reached the analogies are surely those of function and content, not of form. Those of function emerge most clearly when we reflect on the ways in which international law differs from morality, some of which we examined in the last section. The analogies of content consist in the range of principles, concepts, and methods which are common to both municipal and international law, and make the lawyers' technique freely transferable from the one to the other. Bentham, the inventor of the expression "international law," defended it simply by saying that it was "sufficiently analogous" to municipal law. To this, two comments are perhaps worth adding. First, that the analogy is one of content not of form; secondly, that, in this analogy of content, no other social rules are so close to municipal law as those of international law.

Legitimacy and Authority in International Politics*

IAN HURD

What motivates states to follow international norms, rules, and commitments? All social systems must confront what we might call the problem of social control—that is, how to get actors to comply with society's rules—but the problem is particularly acute for international relations, because the international social system does not possess an overarching center of political power to enforce rules. Yet, taken in balance with other values, a measure of order is a valued good. Some

* Reprinted by permission from 53 INTERNATIONAL ORGANIZATION 379 (1999).

take this absence of centralized power to mean that the international system is like a Hobbesian state of nature, where only material power matters; others see it as evidence that international rules have force only when they are in the self-interest of each state. I show that these two conclusions are premature because of their shallow reading of international society and misinterpretation of the ways in which authority works in domestic society.

Consider three generic reasons why an actor might obey a rule: (1) because the actor fears the punishment of rule enforcers, (2) because the actor sees the rule as in its own self-interest, and (3) because the actor feels the rule is legitimate and ought to be obeyed. The trait distinguishing the superior from the subordinate is different in each case. In the first, it is asymmetry of physical capacity; in the second, a particular distribution of incentives; and in the third, a normative structure of status and legitimacy. In other words, the currency of power is not the same for all relations. Political theorists traditionally isolate three ideal-type mechanisms of social control that correspond to the three currencies of power, which I call coercion, self-interest, and legitimacy. These devices recur in combination across all social systems where rules exist to influence behavior, ranging from the governing of children in the classroom, to the internal structure of organized crime syndicates, to the international system of states. Where rules or norms exist, compliance with them may be achieved by one or a combination of these devices. Studies of domestic political sociology rotate around them, with scholars arguing variously for making one of the three devices foundational or combining them in assorted ways. It is generally seen as natural that a social system may exhibit each at different moments or locations.

In international relations studies, talking about compliance secured by either coercion or self-interest is uncontroversial, and well-developed bodies of literature—falling roughly into the neorealist and rationalist-neoliberal schools, respectively—elaborate each of these notions. However, the idea that states' compliance with international rules is a function of the legitimacy of the rules or of their source gets less attention; and when it is attended to, scholars generally fail to spell out the process by which it operates. In this article I address those who would ignore—for reasons of epistemology or methodology—the workings of legitimacy in international relations and those who make reference to legitimacy without spelling out what it is, how it works, and how it differs from other motivations for behavior. Only after we are clear on the conceptual differences among self-interest, legitimacy, and coercion can we look at the historic development and operation of each in specific institutions.

My primary goal in this article is to show that there is no obvious reason, either theoretical or empirical, why the study of the international system should be limited to only two of these three mechanisms and that to do so means missing significant features of the system. This should be a matter of empirical study, not assumption. . . .

Legitimacy, as I use it here, refers to the normative belief by an actor that a rule or institution ought to be obeyed. It is a subjective quality, relational between actor and institution, and defined by the actor's *perception* of the institution. The actor's perception may come from the substance of the rule or from the procedure or source by which it was constituted. Such a perception affects behavior because it is internalized by the actor and helps to define how the actor sees its interests. I make no moral claim about the universal legitimacy, or even less the moral worth, of any particular international rule; I am interested strictly in the subjective feeling by a particular actor or set of actors that some rule is legitimate. In this sense, saying a rule is accepted as legitimate by some actor says nothing about its justice in the eyes of an outside observer. Further, an actor's belief in the legitimacy of a norm, and thus its following of that norm, need not correlate to the actor being "law abiding" or submissive to authority. Often, precisely the opposite is true: a normative conviction about legitimacy might lead to *noncompliance* with laws when laws are considered in conflict with the conviction.

Significant issues are at stake in the question of whether there exist international rules and institutions that evoke this kind of feeling. First, since a legitimate institution contributes to the actor's definition of its interests, identifying legitimate institutions in international society would help unravel how states define their "national interests" and may shed light on the differing notions of interest that separate the realist, liberal, and constructivist accounts of international relations. In particular, it can augment rationalist approaches by providing a theory of the background material or "common knowledge" that actors bring to a "game." Second, the presence of legitimate institutions calls into question the notion of the system as an anarchy. To the extent that a state accepts some international rule or body as legitimate, that rule or body becomes an "authority"; and the characterization of the international system as an anarchy is unsustainable, as is the traditional distinction between domestic and international systems on the basis of the absence of international "authority." This does not mean the end of a distinction between domestic and international, only that we need to clarify the nature of the distinction.

. . .

Models of Social Control

The issue of social control is central to international relations and to all social life. This is so because some measure of order is a prerequisite to attaining most other human objectives and because attempts to create order involve imposing one set of values over others, which is a source of enormous conflict and violence. Consequently, it is worth asking where order comes from and how it is maintained in international society. All systems possess some rules governing the conduct of actors, be they laws, directives, or norms, and these rules vary in the degree to which they are followed and the reasons for compliance. Coercion, self-interest, and legitimacy constitute Weberian ideal types for modes of social control, and each generates compliance with society's rules by a different mechanism. Although each can be analytically separated from the others, in practice they are rarely found in pure isolation. In this section, I identify the conceptual features that make each distinctive.

Coercion

Coercion refers to a relation of asymmetrical physical power among agents, where this asymmetry is applied to changing the behavior of the weaker agent. The operative mechanism is fear or simple "compellance"; fear produces acquiescence. An actor who obeys a rule because of coercion is motivated by the fear of punishment from a stronger power. The rule itself is irrelevant except as a signal for what kinds of behavior will and will not incur the penalty. If a social system relies at base on coercion to motivate compliance with its rules, we would expect to see enormous resources devoted to enforcement and surveillance and low levels of compliance when the enforcing agent is not looking.

. . .

The importance of this model is its clear delineation of one pole in the triad of the mechanisms of social control. Its emphasis on threats and force in generating compliance comes at the expense of attention to either the normative content of rules or more complicated calculations of self-interest by actors. Coercion is a relatively simple form of social control, and it is inefficient from the point of view of the central power. It does not, in general, provoke voluntary compliance. A common lesson of studies of complex organizations is that coercion and repression tend to generate resentment and resistance, even as they produce compliance, because they operate against the normative impulses of the subordinate individual or group. As a result, each application of coercion involves an expenditure of limited social capital and reduces the likelihood that the subject will comply without coercion in the future. For this reason, few complex social orders are primarily based on coercion, although all likely resort to force at some point. Coercion and sanction are costly mechanisms of control, quite unsuited for regulating activities that require any measure of creativity or enthusiasm in subordinates. To anticipate, social orders based on coercion tend over time to either collapse from their own instability or reduce their coercive component by legitimating certain practices and creating stable expectations among actors. . . .

Self-Interest

A second possible motivation for compliance with rules is the belief that compliance in fact promotes one's self-interest. It is not uncommon in the social sciences to presume that such calculations of self-interest are the foundation of most social action. This view suggests that any rule following by individuals is the result of an instrumental and calculated assessment of the net benefits of compliance versus noncompliance, with an instrumental attitude toward social structures and other people. . . .

Self-interest needs to be carefully delineated if it is to be a useful (and potentially falsifiable) concept for social science. The bounds of a self-interest explanation need to be clearly drawn so as not to subsume all other categories. Self-interest is related to coercion in that both are forms of utilitarianism.... The key difference is that an application of coercion leaves the coerced actor worse off than it was beforehand (even if it accedes to the coercion out of a sense of self-interest), whereas a self-interest perspective sees the actor as better off then it would be taking any other available path (even if the menu of available paths has been coercively restricted by others). Put differently, self-interest involves *self-restraint* on the part of an actor (as does legitimacy), whereas coercion operates by *external* restraint....

The distinction between self-interest and legitimacy, on the other hand, can be seen through the distinction between interest and self-interest. All three models (coercion, self-interest, and legitimacy) assume actors are "interested" in the sense of pursing their interests, and so self-interest must add something more. Actors who are interested act rationally to pursue goals, but we know nothing a priori about what those goals are. Assuming *self*-interest involves adding a presumption about the egoistic attitude of the self toward others or to the rules.... [A] "self-interested" orientation in the strict sense ... implies a continuous reassessment of every rule and relationship from an instrumental point of view. Nothing is taken for granted or valued for its own sake, only for the payoff it brings to the self. This stance is fixed, not variable. Self-interest is necessarily amoral with respect to one's obligations toward others; others are mere objects to be used instrumentally, although, of course, this does not preclude cooperative behavior if done for instrumental reasons.

A society where compliance with rules is based principally on the self-interest of the members will exhibit several characteristic features. First, any loyalty by actors toward the system or its rules is contingent on the system providing a positive stream of benefits. Actors are constantly recalculating the expected payoff to remaining in the system and stand ready to abandon it immediately should some alternative promise greater utility. Such a system can be stable while the payoff structure is in equilibrium, but the actors are constantly assessing the costs and benefits of revisionism....

Therefore, we should avoid confusing the generic statement that individuals pursue "interests" in the sense of choosing means to achieve goals, with the particular assumption of "self-interestedness," referring to an instrumental attitude toward other actors and toward rules. Many diverse models of human behavior accept that actors pursue "interests," but they disagree on whether they are "self-interested" in this strong sense. The distinction is essential, because the controversy between self-interest and legitimacy comes in competing accounts of how interests are formed, not in whether actors pursue goals. Without this difference, there is no behavior that could possibly contradict the self-interest hypothesis.

Legitimacy

Finally, compliance with a rule may be motivated by a belief in the normative legitimacy of the rule (or in the legitimacy of the body that generated the rule). Legitimacy contributes to compliance by providing an internal reason for an actor to follow a rule. When an actor believes a rule is legitimate, compliance is no longer motivated by the simple fear of retribution, or by a calculation of self-interest, but instead by an internal sense of moral obligation: control is legitimate to the extent that it is approved or regarded as "right." Mark Suchman, an organizational sociologist, defines legitimacy as "a generalized perception or assumption that the actions of an entity are desirable, proper, or appropriate within some socially constructed system of norms, values, beliefs, and definitions." This definition nicely encompasses both the sense within the individual of the appropriateness of a body, and the contextual, cultural origin of the standards of appropriateness. When several individuals share a common definition of what is legitimate, we say they constitute a community.

The operative process in legitimation is the internalization by the actor of an external standard. Internalization takes place when the actor's sense of its own interests is partly constituted by a force outside itself, that is, by the standards, laws, rules, and norms present in the community, existing at the intersubjective level. A rule will become legitimate to a specific individual, and therefore become behaviorally significant, when the individual internalizes its content and reconceives his or her interests according to the rule. Compliance then becomes habitual, and it is noncompliance that requires of the individual special consideration and psychic costs. This is the kind of compliance that parents often try to instill in their children and governments socialize in their citizens: "it is right to do as I say, because I say so." One incidental consequence of internalization is the futility of statements structured in the form: "the power of legitimacy is shown when an actor complies with a legitimate rule that goes against its interests." This is internally inconsistent because the rule has affected the actor's own definition of its interests, not just the value of the payoffs of the different options. Thus the actor does not perceive a conflict between its interests and its obligations.

Legitimacy as a device of social control has long-run efficiency advantages over coercion in reducing some kinds of enforcement costs and increasing the apparent "freedom" of subordinates, although it is more expensive in the short run. Robert A. Dahl and Charles E. Lindblom observe that "legitimacy is not indispensable to all control. Nevertheless, lack of legitimacy imposes heavy costs on the controllers. For legitimacy facilitates the operation of organizations requiring enthusiasm, loyalty, discretion, decentralization, and careful judgment." The efficiency advantages of authority probably motivate the commonly observed impulse of the powerful to try to legitimate their power. Max Weber noted "the generally observable need of any power, or even advantage of life, to justify itself," and David Beetham sees "justification" (that is, legitimacy) as one response to the inherently contested nature of political power: "Because it is so problematical, societies will seek to subject it to justifiable rules, and the powerful themselves will seek to secure consent to their power from at least the most important among their subordinates." The internalization of external standards can also defuse Olsonian problems of collective action by causing actors to interpret the mutually cooperative option as also being the individually rational option. Thus legitimacy can be a powerful ordering tool. Michael Hechter summarizes Emile Durkheim and Talcott Parsons, saying that "the maintenance of social order depends on the existence of a set of overarching rules of the game, rules that are to some degree internalized, or considered to be legitimate, by most actors. Not only do these rules set goals, or preferences, for each member of society, but they also specify the appropriate means by which these goals can be pursued."

The relation of coercion, self-interest, and legitimacy to each other is complex, and each is rarely found in anything like its pure, isolated form. Further, they are probably related to each other in a patterned, systematic fashion, in that most social structures first emerge from relations of coercion or from individual self-interest; but once established they may come to develop supporting and independent bases of legitimacy. It is sometimes suggested that legitimacy is derivative of coercion because the social consensus on which legitimacy is premised can be created by coercion. Many governance relations that are today widely accepted as legitimate began as relations of coercion, including perhaps all modern liberal democratic states. Although I agree that the use of power in the pursuit of legitimacy is one of the more interesting aspects of legitimacy, this cannot mean that legitimacy and coercion are the same thing or that the former is reducible to the latter. Even if it began as coercion, legitimacy, as a product of internalization, operates differently than the power relation in which it originated. Precisely because something changes when a relation of coercion becomes legitimized is why studying legitimacy is worthwhile in the first place. Whatever its origins, a structure of legitimate relations operates in interestingly different ways than do structures of coercion or self-interest—they have different costs and consequences, different means of achieving compliance, and different modes of reproduction. . . .

Conclusion

. . .

The arguments presented here may be fairly read as an attempt to revive the domestic analogy in the study of international society. A proper application of the domestic analogy should begin with a recognition that the basis of social order in many domestic systems is legitimate authority and not coercion or self-interest. As critical as he was of most kinds of domestic analogy, Hedley Bull recognized the significance for international relations of the fact that "order in the modern state" is maintained "not by directly upholding or implementing the rules, but by shaping, molding, or managing the social environment in which the rules operate in such a way that they have the opportunity of continuing to do so." In some domains international order is maintained in the same way. Turning around the domestic analogy, the arguments presented in this article demonstrate once again the historically contingent nature of the state. There is nothing unique about the organization of authority into a territorial government. Authority can exist (and coexist) in many institutional arrangements, of which the legitimate international institution is one and the territorial state is another. An important question is "can our theories of the state accommodate a locus of authority outside the state?"

With this in mind, the search for the source of international order on the domestic model does not end at the obvious fact that no international government exists. Instead, it continues on to look for evidence of international community and of the norms and rules that such a community presses onto individual states. The advanced industrial states at the end of the twentieth century constitute an international community of unparalleled depth and breadth, and the norms they follow, from the fundamental rules of sovereignty to the complex rules of commerce and regulation, are evidence of the ordering power of that community. Sovereignty is thus one mode of international governance without an international government. This conclusion is, I believe, generalizable to many of the rules and regimes present in the international system today, including collective security and some liberal economic institutions. Defense of these generalizations cannot be made here, but stand as worthwhile further research into the topic of the bases of international order. Hints in this direction are provided by [John] Ruggie with respect to the liberal international economy, by [Alexander] Wendt with respect to the Western system of collective security in the Cold War, and by [Abram] Chayes and [Antonia Handler] Chayes on international regulation.

My argument about the existence of international rules that some states accept as legitimate may be wrong. However, any counterargument against this thesis must provide an explanation for why international society should have only two or one structure(s) of order (coercion and/or self-interest) while domestic societies can have three (coercion, self-interest, and legitimate authority). Such an account cannot be based on the absence of a centralized international government as the difference, since the presence of order in the absence of government is precisely the phenomenon we are trying to explain. Even if one disagrees with the thesis that the international system contains some institutions of legitimate authority, there remains the difficulty of justifying the present tendency of many scholars to reject a priori that such a thing is conceivable. To be compelling, that rejection must account for why the international social system should be incapable of developing structures and forms that hold such an important place in domestic social spheres systems.

Fairness in International Law and Institutions*

THOMAS M. FRANCK

Fairness and International Law: An Analytical Framework

Maturity and Complexity in International Law

... Like any maturing legal system, international law has entered its post-ontological era. Its lawyers need no longer defend the very existence of international law. Thus emancipated from the constraints of defensive ontology, international lawyers are now free to undertake a critical assessment of its content.

With new opportunities come new challenges! The questions to which the international lawyer must now be prepared to respond, in this post-ontological era, are different from the traditional inquiry: whether international law is law. Instead, we are now asked: is international law effective? Is it enforceable? Is it understood? And, the most important question: Is international law fair?

The Post–Ontological Search for Fairness

There are two reasons why the question—is international law fair?—should be asked and addressed: one procedural and the other substantive.

a. Legitimacy as Procedural Fairness

The pursuit of a perfect ordering of relationships characterizes the approach of the legal system to the international system. The quest is as admirable as its goal is unattainable, but a system's reach should exceed its grasp, or what's a heaven for? To be effective, the system must be *seen* to be effective. To be seen as effective, its decisions must be arrived at discursively in accordance with what is accepted by the parties as *right process*.

In procedural terms: humanity wants reassurance that the emerging legal system is capable of ensuring both stability and progressive change. There are certain consequential values by which institutions and processes are judged: do they provide the consequences which people expect, by means of an appropriate discursive and distributive process? For example, does the system ensure, through a justifiable distribution of sustenance, that people are fed? A system which does so will be seen as preference-sensitive and therefore more fair than a system which fails to provide for basic needs in a manner which satisfies reasonable expectations. However, people expect more than food. They also expect peace, good order, and security, and to be free of the stress of perpetual

* Reprinted by permission from THOMAS M. FRANCK, FAIRNESS IN INTERNATIONAL LAW AND INSTITUTIONS (1995).

revolution, even if that revolution has benevolent redistributive intent. They expect that decisions about distributive and other entitlements will be made by those duly authorized, in accordance with procedures which protect against corrupt, arbitrary, or idiosyncratic decision-making or decision-executing. The fairness of international law, as of any other legal system, will be judged, first by the degree to which the rules satisfy the participants' expectations of justifiable distribution of costs and benefits, and secondly by the extent to which the rules are made and applied in accordance with what the participants perceive as right process.

These two aspects of fairness—the substantive (distributive justice) and the procedural (right process)—may not always pull in the same direction, because the former favors change and the latter stability and order. The tension between stability and change, if not managed, can disorder the system. Fairness is the rubric under which this tension is discursively managed.

Legitimacy thus expresses the preference for order, which may or may not be conducive to change. Nevertheless, it is a key factor in fairness, for it accommodates a deeply felt popular belief that for a system of rules to be fair, it must be firmly rooted in a framework of formal requirements about how rules are made, interpreted, and applied. For example, a belief that many persons are cheating on their taxes will encourage others to do so, because it will appear unfair to them that they should have to abide by rules which are not enforced against everyone. The rule is seen as illegitimate. Conversely, a belief in the law's legitimacy re-enforces the perception of its fairness and encourages compliance.

b. Distributive Justice as Fairness

At a second, even more basic, level of inquiry, any analysis of fairness must include consideration of the consequential effects of the law: its distributive justice. I am more likely to pay my taxes without cheating if I believe that the law apportions the tax burden in accordance with a principle which I recognize as "just." For me (as for most persons and states) this is not the same as the perception that an allocation is "to my advantage." I can understand the need to provide everyone with basic health care even if my personal level of health care will be lowered to achieve that objective. The capacity to accept an allocational principle and the law which implements it, even though it is not to an individual's direct advantage, is the consequence of that individual's capacity for moral choice. An unfair law, that is: one that distributes burdens unfairly, is likely to provoke resistance, even from some of those who benefit. The large majority of Americans who have excellent health care have nevertheless concluded that the system, in denying decent care to a minority, is so unfair as to require reform, even though the outcome of such reform would probably result in their direct personal disadvantage.

Thus the perception that a rule or system of rules is distributively fair, like the perception of its legitimacy, also encourages voluntary compliance. Unlike legitimacy, however, distributive justice is rooted in the moral values of the community in which the legal system operates. The law promotes distributive justice not merely to secure greater compliance, but primarily because most people think it is *right* to act justly.

The moral pursuit of distributive justice should engage us because, like Socrates, our intellects should harbor an "all-engrossing eagerness for answers to moral questions, beginning with the most urgent of all: how should we live?" The question of fairness encompasses that moral issue because fairness supposes a moral compass, a sense of the just society. The law must create solutions and systems which take into account society's answers to these moral issues of distributive justice, for we are moral as well as social beings.

Legitimacy and distributive justice are two aspects of the concept of fairness. While one has a primarily procedural, and the other a primarily moral, perspective, they combine to answer the law-maker's version of the question posed by both Socrates and Jeremy Bentham: "What shall we do about sharing and conserving in order to maximize human well-being?" This, fortunately, has replaced "is international law, law?" as the question with which the international lawyer is most actively engaged. The answer to that question, or rather the starting point in the search for an answer, is misleadingly simple: "we must do that which is fair."

Two Preconditions of Fairness Discourse

Now is the time for international lawyers to focus on the issue of fairness in the law. The new maturity and complexity of the system calls out for a critique of law's content and consequences. Its extensive coverage and its audacious incursions into state sovereignty demand a new emphasis on the system's values, aims, and effects.

The argument for a critical assessment of the *corpus juris* is strengthened by the circumstances of the existential moment in which the preconditions for such a critique are present. Discussion about fairness, which is at the center of such a critique, is most likely to be productive when the allocation of rights and duties occurs in circumstances which make allocation both necessary and possible. This circumstance, which presents an optimal opportunity, John Rawls has aptly called a condition of "moderate scarcity."

a. Moderate Scarcity

If a particular mineral which was essential to a newly discovered cure for cancer were to exist only in one small area of an ocean floor, and in very limited quantities, the discourse over rights to seabed mineral resources would differ significantly from the tone of previous debate about an international regime for management of the resources of the ocean floor. Questions of "fair share" would tend to be dismissed as moral idealism on the part of the disadvantaged by hard-nosed states endowed with strategically situated coastlines and highly developed ocean-mining technology. Where allocations are made in zero-sum settings of resources which are valuable and scarce, fairness discourse is at its most difficult.

In a situation of moderate scarcity, on the other hand, discourse about the legal system's allocational fairness can rise to the top of the agenda. Manganese nodules which lie on the ocean floor are a finite, non-renewable resource requiring allocation and management, but the manganese, nickel, and cobalt elements in the nodules are not in particularly short global supply. It is primarily in circumstances such as these that lawyers can expect to be able to raise the issue of fairness in relation to those rules by which a society allocates its "goods": that is, things desired, ranging from material possessions to abstract "goods" such as peace, power, and liberty. When everyone can expect to have a share, but no one can expect to have all that is desired, the critical moment for considerations of fairness is met. It is only then that modes of allocation do not contend in the arena of the zero-sum game, one that pits the survival of each against the survival of all.

Fortunately, in most (but not all) allocational respects, the resources of the world generally are, for the moment, in such a situation of moderate scarcity, one which demands regulation but without, as yet, evoking the stridency which identifies a crisis as unmanageable. Through exploration, synthesis, and improved management, the pool of earthly goods and resources is, with some exceptions, expanding more rapidly than the population. Some "goods" are not only renewed but increased, "liberty" is an example, as they are shared.

b. Community

Moderate scarcity is thus the first of two structural preconditions for optimal fairness discourse and critique. The second is community. For rules to be subject to a meaningful scrutiny from the perspective of fairness, they must be seen to operate in the context of a community: a social system of continuing interaction and transaction. It is only in a community that the bedrock of shared values and developed principles necessary to any assessment of fairness is found.

A community is based, first, on a common, conscious system of reciprocity between its constituents and this system of reciprocity conduces to fairness dialogue. This is because a perception of the fairness of any particular rule depends, in major part, on its implicit promise to treat like with like. In order to achieve the expectation that the rule in any one instance will also be the rule in other comparable instances, there must be an underlying assumption of an ongoing, structured relationship between a set of actors: in other words, a community.

The element of reciprocity which underpins the emergence of community is not solely concerned with rights and rules, it is also about shared moral imperatives and values. To appreciate this aspect of the reciprocal nature of a community, it is necessary to understand that its members share a system not only of legal but also of moral obligations. The laws in a community thus evince not only the generally held belief that each must do what he or she is legally required to do, but also that each will discharge towards all others those obligations arising from the shared moral sense.

c. The Existential Moment: Moderate Scarcity and Community Now

As it happens, we are witnessing the dawn of a new era, defined both by moderate scarcity and by an emerging sense of global community. We have not arrived there yet, but that is where we seem to be heading as we turn the corner into the third millennium. Both moderate scarcity and a shared sense of community have become constant characteristics of our contemporary world. These economic, social, and political conditions have eventuated at the same time as the international legal system has reached a high level of maturity and complexity. This confluence of factors makes discussion of fairness both opportune and necessary.

. . .

The Gatekeepers of Fairness Discourse

Even if "everyone" were to agree, at least in theory, that fairness is a necessary condition of allocational rules, this unfortunately would not assure that everyone shared the same sense of fairness or agreed on a fixed meaning. Fairness it is not "out there" waiting to be discovered, it is a product of social context and history....

As we shall see, this does not mean that a fair allocational formula is the same as any agreed formula of sharing. Here one must return to the idea of an ascertainable "everyone." To constitute a sufficient community able to formulate and implement an enterprise of fair sharing there must be more than a mere shared sense of a common danger inherent in failure to allocate. It is not enough for "everyone" to agree that without sharing we might all die, or go without. There must also be some shared, irreducible core of beliefs as to what the search for fairness itself entails.

In practice, the search for fairness begins with a search for agreement on a few basic values which take the form of shared perceptions as to what is unconditionally unfair. In other words, there must be common accord that some formulas for allocation are simply outside the pale. A discourse on fairness must be preceded by a discourse about the discourse, leading to the erection of a few agreed conceptual barriers. "Everyone," in other words, must begin by agreeing on a set of minimal assumptions which will operate in the forthcoming discussion of fairness. These assumptions must be few, otherwise the community of "everyone" will be decimated by dissent before it begins its work. But these negative, or barrier, assumptions must be recognized not as immutable or divinely ordained, but as useful gatekeepers to the discourse, admitting those willing to participate in a common enterprise of fairness discourse and excluding only those who are not predisposed to participate seriously in it.

What validates such gatekeepers? First, agreement as to such a shared core of assumptions is minimal evidence of the existence of a community within which the bedrock of reciprocity already exists and on which a legal system can be constructed. Second, such a common core circumscribes the ambit of otherwise unlimited choice, and thereby facilitates the process by which a body of applied fairness may be derived by common consent. If there is no such core, if there is no agreement on any basic assumptions to govern discourse, if nothing is excluded, nothing "off the table" by reference to shared basic assumptions, then there can be little hope of real agreement. There may be agreement on texts, but they will be so vague, so evidently the result of a papering over of unresolved differences, that the resulting rule will be severely undermined by its indeterminacy. Being indeterminate, the resulting text will not be appreciated and supported by states and persons but, rather, scorned for its indeterminacy. The rule fabric will be seen to be full of holes. The rule will invite creative evasion. The result will be to undermine not only the legitimacy of that which has been negotiated, but further to undermine the legitimacy of other community norms, and even the communitarian discourse by which such norms are formulated.

To some extent, indeterminacy is inherent in all rule-creating discourse. In some instances, moreover, "papering over" disagreements can be useful, for example in negotiating a cease-fire. The "papering over" of a disagreement can have the advantage of creating a breathing space, suspending a crisis for long enough to think again, and rousing popular expectations of more precise agreements to follow. In the midst of a discourse on fairness, we must not forget that other societal values must be served besides fairness, and the need for short-term solutions to immediate crises may often require a suspension of doubts based on considerations of fairness. Papered-over short-term palliatives are, however, not the objective of a system for allocating "goods" nor of a critique of allocations already in place. Here, we are interested in the "long haul" towards objectives which are unlikely to be perceived, much less attained, in the absence of fairness discourse. The task in fairness discourse is not to achieve quick, temporary relief. We do not seek an amelioration or a palliative, but a grander objective. Step by step, slowly, we want to bring to the global agenda a heightened interest in making the expanding universe of international law fair.

An important first task, therefore, is to identify that irreducible core of shared assumptions about fairness—or, more exactly, as it happens: unfairness—which, once identified and agreed upon, will enable the community to embark on the fairness discourse proper, and to proceed with negotiations which address specific allocational problematics. Again, it should be stressed that these irreducible core principles are merely gatekeepers, intended to exclude from the discourse dissonant notions of fairness discourse itself which would, if admitted, preclude agreement on any specific rules for making actual allocations of real goods and resources.

a. No Trumping

A tribe may believe that fairness is an expression of God's will, revealed through the holy man who heads the tribe. This prophet is irrevocably appointed for life through the reading of portents by the tribe's hereditary council of seers. His people believe that the Holy Man's witness of God's word can tell them what is fair in general, and also in any particular circumstance. This tribe's notions of fairness, for example in allocating fish from a lake shared with other tribes, may happen to coincide with those of others. But while the various tribes might negotiate a fisheries sharing formula, the tribe headed by the Holy Man could not participate effectively in a fairness discourse. Its members would not be free to enter into meaningful discussions as to the fair allocation of anything. They would not be free negotiating agents but only envoys bound by the instructions of their infallible Holy Man, instructions which originate with God and are thus non-negotiable.

What this example suggests is that a global community of fairnesss could not include any group which believes in an "automatic trumping entitlement." Another tribe might believe that trumping answers to problematics of allocational fairness could be established definitively by reference to science: by reference to market value, the "unseen hand" of economics, for instance. Such a trumping entitlement does not preclude agreement, but does render impossible negotiated agreement among a putative community of states and persons. In other words, agreement could not arise from a discursive pursuit of intersecting beliefs and interests, but only from initial agreement between all the parties on the pre-emptive supremacy of whatever automatic trumping entitlement a party has proposed. Such agreement would make negotiations superfluous.

. . .

b. Maximin

In addition to this important no-trumping principle, there is at least one other which, despite disagreement by some on political and philosophical grounds, may be coming close to universal acceptance as a core principle of fairness. The "maximin" principle is this: that inequalities in the access to, or the distribution of, goods must be justifiable on the basis that the inequality has advantages not only for its beneficiaries but also to a proportionate or greater degree for everyone else. In other words, unequal distribution is justifiable only if it narrows, or does not widen, the existing inequality of persons' and/or states' entitlements. A scheme which allots $100 to every person who already has $100 but only $50 to persons with $10 proportionately narrows the gap between them and thus is not axiomatically excluded from fairness discourse. Although the parties might still agree that such a distribution was unfair, it would not be ruled out of contention by a gatekeeper principle.

"Maximin" is a neo-egalitarian principle of distributive fairness. It is not neutral, but rather manifests a moral preference, in the words of its principal champion, the philosopher John Rawls, for "equal liberty for all, including equality of opportunity, as well as equal distribution of income and wealth." However, Rawls cautions that "there is no reason why this acknowledgment should be final. If there are inequalities in the basic structure that work to make everyone better off in comparison to the benchmark of initial equality, why not permit them?" In a pragmatic community everyone would "concede the justice of these inequalities. Indeed, it would be shortsighted of him not to do so. He would hesitate to agree ... only if he would be dejected by the bare knowledge or perception that others were better situated...." Thus, "[in]equalities are permissible when they maximize, or at least contribute to, the long-term expectations of the least fortunate group in society." Rawls' notion is of relative equalization, with tolerance for inequalities that benefit the less advantaged.

...

A Caveat

It remains, in this introduction, to stress that legitimacy as process fairness and distributive justice as moral fairness are different aspects of fairness. In a critique of an existing or proposed rule, they may coincide or not. However, while a rule may be legitimate and yet distributively unjust (and thus only imperfectly or contingently fair) and vice versa, there is much overlap between legitimacy and justice. The Load Line Convention, for example, merely establishes legitimate technical uniformity. Yet technical uniformity has an element of distributive justice. As John Locke made clear, human beings organize themselves into a community primarily to establish a regime which will afford them mutual protection. A system of rules, when it is perceived as legitimate and secures compliance, distributes equally to all participants in that regime the benefits of conflict resolution and order, which in turn may conduce to secondary "goods" such as economic growth and psychological well-being. Legitimacy, the utilitarian aspect of fairness, thus has a distributive element, just as distributive justice has its utilities.

It is as easy to overstate as to overlook this caveat. Thomas Hobbes thought that legitimacy was justice, for example that when a covenant is duly made, justice requires that it be carried out; that justice is propriety in the making of rules or covenants backed by coercive power to compel compliance. More recently, Professor Oscar Schachter has written that a legal commitment such as a treaty or transnational contract "is itself a determinant of what is due and therefore of what is equitable...." However, Schachter does not argue that all contractual agreements are fair, merely that they may be evidence of what the parties thought to be fair at the time of contracting. Even this is not always true, since the parties in international transactions have historically often not been "at arm's length." The better view is that legitimacy may coincide with justice and thereby create a harmonious framework for fairness discourse. Or it may not. The fairness claim advanced from the perspective of legitimacy may clash with a fairness claim based on distributive justice. The two are independent variables in the concept of fairness.

It comes to this. The notion of "fairness" encompasses two different and potentially adversary components: legitimacy and distributive justice. These components are indicators of law's, and especially fair law's, primary objective: to achieve a negotiated balance between the need for order and the need for change. As Martti Koskenniemi has observed, the international legal system "derives ... both its intuitive plausibility and vulnerability from the tension between such notions." What matters is how this tension is managed discursively through what Koskenniemi calls "the social conception" of the legal system. This "social conception" manifests itself in the discursive pursuit of fairness.

...

Legitimacy and Fairness

The Indicators of Legitimacy

...

We shall now examine the legitimacy of the primary rules, the ordinary laws, whether made by legislatures, bureaucrats, judges, or plebiscites, which the rule-making process of the community generates. Obviously, rules made in violation of the community's secondary rules of reference, for example by a body or functionary not duly authorized to make such rules by the community's constitutive code, will be perceived as lacking legitimacy. However, a rule's conformity with associative secondary rules is only one of the determinants of that rule's legitimacy. Each rule, whether a law of the state or a customary law or treaty of the international community, is likely to be perceived as more or less legitimate in accordance with four variables. These four indicators of legitimacy are: *determinacy, symbolic validation, coherence,* and *adherence.* Measuring the legitimacy of a rule is not a purely theoretical exercise. The extent to which any rule exhibits these qualities will determine its legitimacy. The more plausible a community's perception of a rule's legitimacy, the more persuasive that rule's claim to fairness, the stronger its promotion of compliance, and the firmer its re-enforcement of the sense of community.

a. Determinacy

Textual determinacy is the ability of a text to convey a clear message, to appear transparent in the sense that one can see through the language of a law to its essential meaning. Rules which have a readily accessible meaning and which say what they expect of those who are addressed are more likely to have a real impact on conduct.

To illustrate the point, let us compare two textual formulations defining the boundary of the underwater continental shelf. The 1958 Convention places the shelf at "a depth of 200 meters or, beyond that limit, to where the depth of the superjacent waters admits of the exploitation of the natural resources of the said areas." The 1982 Convention on the Law of the Sea, on the other hand, is far more detailed and specific. It defines the shelf as "the natural prolongation of ... land territory to the outer edge of the continental margin, or to a distance of 200 nautical miles from the baselines from which the breadth of the territorial sea is measured," but takes into account such specific factors as "the thickness of sedimentary rocks" and imposes an upper limit: "not [to] exceed 100 nautical miles from the 2,500 metre isobath," which, in turn, is a line connecting the points where the waters are 2,500 meters deep. The 1982 standard, despite its complexity, is far more determinate than the elastic standard in the 1958 Convention, which, in a sense, established no rule at all. Back in 1958, the parties simply covered their differences and uncertainties with a formula whose content remained in abeyance pending further work by negotiators, courts, and administrators and by the evolution of customary state practice. The vagueness of the rule did permit a flexible response to further advances in technology, a benefit inherent in indeterminacy.

Indeterminacy ... has costs. Indeterminate normative standards make it harder to know what conformity is expected, which in turn makes it easier to justify noncompliance. Conversely, the more determinate the standard, the more difficult it is to resist the pull of the rule towards compliance and to justify noncompliance. Since few persons or states wish to be perceived as acting in obvious violation of a generally recognized rule of conduct, they may try to resolve conflicts between the demands of a rule and their desire not to be fettered by "interpreting" the rule permissively. A less elastic determinate rule is more resistant to such an evasive strategy than an indeterminate one.

...

b. Symbolic Validation

Determinacy communicates meaning. Symbolic validation communicates authority. Both affect the legitimacy of a rule or a rule-making or implementing process, its capacity to pull towards compliance. Both thereby also reinforce the sense of a "rule community."

A rule is symbolically validated when it has attributes, often in the form of cues, which signal its significant part in the overall system of social order. Ritual and pedigree are examples of cues which signal that a rule should be obeyed because otherwise the fabric of social order might be unraveled. Continuity signals stability of expectations, the aspect of fairness served by legitimacy.

Symbols also signal that authority is being exercised in accordance with right process, that it is institutionally recognized and validated. There are many examples of ritual and other symbolic reinforcement of legitimacy in the international system. Thus, the United Nations Organization is authorized to fly its own flag, not only at headquarters but over regional and local offices around the world. The flag has been used at the instigation of the Secretary–General to immunize such UN battle-front operations as clearing sunken ships from the Suez Canal in 1956, protecting members of the Palestine Liberation Organization being evacuated from Lebanon in 1983 and, more recently, bringing relief supplies to civilians in the former Yugoslavia and in Somalia. The United Nations also issues stamps which are not only accepted for mail delivery by member states, but also generate an annual independent income of approximately $10 million. Peacekeeping forces and truce observers under UN command and wearing UN symbols are stationed between hostile forces in Kashmir, the Golan Heights, Cyprus, Lebanon, Iran–Iraq, and Croatia. They are lightly armed, if at all, and palpably unable to defend themselves in the event of renewed hostilities; but, with their distinctive emblems, they have come to symbolize the world's interest in the continuance of an agreed truce or armistice. The blue and white helmets and arm bands also symbolize a growing body of rules applicable to peacekeeping operations, manifesting and emphasizing the authority of forces which are usually neither as numerous, nor as well armed, as those amon[g]st whom they must keep peace. Their role is purely, and effectively, symbolic of the desire of bitter enemies, and of the international community, for respite from combat. Yet their presence has a far more inhibitory effect on the behavior of states than can be explained by their minimal coercive power. It is these forces' perceived legitimacy, symbolically validated, which serves as their shield and which usually induces more powerful forces to defer to their intangible authority. However, when such forces are stationed between antagonists which have not yet resolved to stop fighting, that symbolic authority cannot readily be converted into actual military power to compel compliance. Rather, the symbolic currency tends to be devalued by those incidents in which a symbolic UN force suddenly finds itself a third-party combatant.

. . .

c. Coherence

The perceived legitimacy of rules depends also on the generality of the principles which the rules apply. At the lowest end of this generality spectrum is the bill of attainder, which is regarded as so illegitimate as to be prohibited by the United States Constitution. The negative perception of illegitimacy and unfairness derives from a rule's lack of generality; it is expressly made applicable only in one instance. Such laws are evidently unprincipled; they do not treat likes alike and they therefore lack coherence. They fail to connect with the skein of general legal principles which make up the body of the law.

Coherence is a key factor in explaining why rules compel. A rule is coherent when its application treats like cases alike and when the rule relates in a principled fashion to other rules of the same system. Consistency requires that a rule, whatever its content, be applied uniformly in every "similar" or "applicable" instance. This is the opposite of what [Ronald] Dworkin calls "checkerboarding," which, he asserts, gives rise to a greater sense of unfairness than a result which is manifestly uniform in its coverage even if unfavorable to one's interest. "Even if I thought strict liability [(liability without fault)] for accidents wrong in principle," he states, "I would prefer that manufacturers of both washing machines and automobiles be held to that standard rather than that only one of them be. I would rank the checkerboard solution not intermediate between the other two [no strict liability and universal strict liability] but third, below both, and so would many other people." Such "compromises are wrong, not merely impractical." They are lacking in legitimacy, and thus lack also fairness.

. . .

d. Adherence

"Adherence" is the vertical nexus between a single primary rule of obligation ("a state's territorial sea extends seaward to a distance of twelve miles") and a pyramid of secondary rules governing the creation, interpretation, and application of such rules by the community. The legitimacy of each primary rule depends in part on its relation (adherence) to these secondary rules of process. Primary rules unconnected to secondary rules tend to be mere *ad hoc* reciprocal arrangements. Often these prove perfectly capable of obligating the parties; they may even connect coherently to other rules. However, rules are better able to pull towards compliance if they are demonstrably supported by the procedural and institutional framework within which the community organizes itself, culminating in the community's ultimate rule, or canon of rules, of recognition.

In most national communities, a law draws support from its having been made in accordance with the process established by the constitution, which is the ultimate rule of recognition. Thus, an ultimate rule of recognition might prescribe the processes by which the constitution can be amended, laws are enacted, and courts are to function. Secondary rules of recognition elaborate this process, often by such maxims as *audi alterem partem* or "no taxation without representation." The legitimacy of each primary rule (a municipal tax code, for example) accrues as it can be shown that its adoption was not merely *ad hoc* but in conformity with the secondary and ultimate rules of recognition.

The international community also has such secondary rules of recognition. As well as legitimating the primary rules, secondary rules are the parametric sinews of the system, which manifest the normativity of interactions between states, providing evidence of a *community* which defines, empowers, and circumscribes statehood, and supporting a public perception of the law's fairness.

. . .

Equity as Fairness

Since the cold war, the role of international law has become both wider and more secure. As a result of this, lawyers have been able to take a greater interest in the *quality* of international law. Whereas it was once common for international lawyers to devote much effort to defending the "law-likeness" of their subject, that battle has long been won. The newly widespread application of legal principles in the conduct of global systemic relations has thus both allowed and obliged lawyers to turn their professional attention to the issue of the fairness of international law.

As noted in the preceding chapters, fairness is a composite of two independent variables: legitimacy and justice. We turn now to an examination of the role of justice. One (at present the most highly developed) approach to an inquiry into the justice of international law is to study the emerging role of *equity* in the jurisprudence of international tribunals.

In its international as in its domestic legal context, equity is sometimes derided as a "contentless" norm amounting to little more than a license for the exercise of judicial caprice. This criticism, while addressing a potential problem, ignores the very real "content" attributed to equity by scholars and international courts, arbitral proceedings, and organizations. In fairness discourse, the most restrained justice-based claims may be advanced in the form of equity, which embodies a set of principles designed to analyse the law critically without seeming to depart too radically from the traditional preference for normativity in the exercise of authority, nor to present too bold a challenge to the community's expectations of legitimacy in legal rules and processes. . . .

Equity as Law's Justice: Historic Origins

. . . Equity plays the same role in international law as in domestic jurisprudence, and seeks similarly to protect itself from direct confrontation with expectations of legitimacy by adopting many of the appurtenances of normativity. Thus, the ICJ has noted that:

> the justice of which equity is an emanation is not abstract justice but justice according to the rule of law: which is to say that its application should display consistency and a degree of predictability; even though it looks with particularity to the more peculiar circumstances in an instant case, it also looks beyond it to principles of more general application. This is precisely why courts have, from the beginning, elaborated equitable principles as being, at the same time, means to an equitable result in a particular case, yet also

having a more general validity and hence expressible in general terms.

This demanding attempt to make the element of justice more normative is seen in the development, primarily by the courts, of general principles of equity. It is likewise apparent in judges' efforts to locate those principles in the domestic jurisprudence common to members of the international community. That the effort has not been entirely convincing is made clear by Professor Rosalyn Higgins' powerful critique of equity's tendency to allow a court to achieve a "result [that] is nowhere articulated other than [by] the self-serving description of 'equitable.' "

a. "Unjust Enrichment"

"Unjust enrichment" advances the justice-based proposition that one party should not unfairly enrich itself at the expense of another. Courts and arbitral tribunals have invoked the principle chiefly in the context of the calculation of damages resulting from expropriation of the property of foreign nationals. The *Chorzow Factory* case is one example. After determining in 1926 that Poland's expropriation of a German-owned nitrate concern violated the terms of a convention on Upper Silesia, the PCIJ in 1928 applied the doctrine against unjust enrichment for guidance in calculating damages. Under general international law, the measure of damages in cases of expropriation would have been based on the book value of the property at the time of its dispossession, plus interest. The Court held that, while this standard might be appropriate to a legal expropriation, it did not adequately remedy an illegal one. Since the value of the property as a going concern could well have exceeded its book value, the general standard would have left Poland with a gain to which it was not entitled. The true measure of damages, the Court continued, should reflect not merely the value of the property at the time of dispossession, but the loss sustained because of the expropriation.

. . .

b. Estoppel or "Bon Fois" (Good Faith)

Equitable estoppel imposes on states a duty to refrain from engaging in inconsistent conduct *vis-a-vis* other states. This norm figured prominently in the *River Meuse* case. The Netherlands had complained that Belgium's construction of a lock to take water from the river violated a conventional regime governing access to the river's waters. A few years earlier, however, the Netherlands had constructed a lock remarkably similar to the one of which it complained. After concluding that the Belgian lock did not violate the terms of the convention, the Court suggested that, even if it had found the lock to be in violation, a principle closely akin to estoppel would have impelled it to reject the Dutch claim. "The court finds it difficult to admit," it wrote, "that the Netherlands are now warranted in complaining of the construction and operation of a lock of which they themselves set an example in the past."

. . .

c. Acquiescence

Acquiescence, or prescription, is another form of equitable estoppel recognized as a general principle of "law as justice." Thus, silence or absence of protest may preclude one state from later challenging the claim of another. To succeed in a defense of acquiescence, the defendant state must prove that the plaintiff state had knowledge of its claim. As the *1951 Fisheries* case demonstrates, this knowledge can usually be inferred from the circumstances. That case arose out of a dispute over the boundary of Norway's continental shelf. To erase the irregularities of its fjord-indented coast, Norway had for decades used straight base-lines to delimit its fisheries zone, rejecting the general practice of using a line based on a coastal low water mark. Holding in Norway's favor partly on grounds of acquiescence, the ICJ rejected Britain's argument that it had not known of this system of delimitation. Since Britain was a maritime power with a strong interest in Norwegian waters, the Court reasoned, it must have known of Norway's practice and could therefore not excuse its earlier failure to protest.

. . .

Equity as a Mode of Introducing Justice into Resource Allocation

Since World War I, "equity as justice" has become relevant to one of the most vexing problems confronting international courts: the allocation among states of scarce resources. This problem arises primarily from the failure of the earth's system of territorial boundaries satisfactorily to resolve the attribution of certain resources, such as the riches of the continental shelf. Equity lends important assistance in this task, affording judges a measure of discretion, within a flexible rule-structure, commensurate with the uniqueness of each dispute and the rapid evolution of new resource recovery and management technology.

International lawyers, however, are engaged in a debate as to the proper role of equity in this context. Professor Daniel Bardonnet sees the use of equity as an invitation to introduce elements both of "reasonableness" and of the international community's "common ethic." He notes its use in individualizing and particularizing a case: "the facts, the situations, especially the geographic situation (special physical characteristics, or special environmental ones), the [specific] interests or claims of the parties." Professor Higgins, however, cautions that these considerations need not be entered solely "through the door marked 'equity.' Further the invocation of the concept of equity provides no guidance in selecting among these various factors," which Professor Higgins argues, make the process un-lawyerlike because it is "subjective." Professor Alain Pellet responds by pointing out that the search for genuine objectivity in adjudication is an illusion, that all judge-made law is (to some extent) subjective. He notes that the juridical process is far from resting on "objectively verifiable" cognition.

All participants in this debate accept, however, that the case for introducing elements of distributive justice into the law of natural resource allocation has been made. Fairness discourse is no longer exceptional, whether before courts or in law-making diplomatic negotiations. In such fairness discourse, consideration of justice (equity, reasonableness, or ethics) are not out of order. However, much controversy remains as to which considerations should properly be taken into account and about how much weight should be assigned to them. There is also room for much disagreement about the facts actually in dispute, facts which are often crucial to justice discourse.

At least three approaches to equitable allocation have emerged. In the first model, which may be labeled "corrective equity," equity occupies the important but peripheral role of tempering the gross unfairness which sometimes results from the application of strict law. In the second model, "broadly conceived equity," equity displaces strict law but is still rule-based, evolving into a set of principles for the accomplishment of an equitable allocation. In the third model, "common heritage equity," equity serves a dual creative function, determining the conditions for exploitation and ensuring conservation of mankind's common patrimony. Both courts and norm-negotiating diplomats have, understandably, turned primarily to corrective equity. In law-making diplomatic forums, however, the second and third models have begun to be applied and incorporated into treaties. As this relatively recent practice matures, courts will increasingly be compelled to apply broader notions of distributive justice, which challenge head on some long-established practices and expectations.

. . .

Conclusions

Far from being contentless, equity is developing into an important, redeeming aspect of the international legal system. This system still pertains primarily to sovereign states, and tends therefore to be somewhat cautious in its recourse to notions of redistributive justice. The case for such caution is based on legitimacy, stressing the need for determinacy and coherence in the law. Nevertheless, there are good reasons for introducing elements of justice into legal discourse and process. Those reasons stem from two important current conditions of global society: the revolutionary pace of technological and scientific innovation and the great and widening chasm between rich and poor.

The rapidity of technological and scientific progress is such that the context in which human endeavors are undertaken is constantly redefined. Therefore any legal system which seeks to impose principles of general application on those endeavours must possess a corresponding degree of flexibility. The growing inequality in the distribution of desired goods indicates that the formal equality of states before the law must be made actual by recourse to notions of justice. Justice, as an augmentation of law, is also needed to protect those interests not ordinarily recognized by traditional law, such as the well-being of future generations and the "interests" of the biosphere. Finally, justice has a tempering role to play when the apportionment of goods (as in a continental shelf) occurs in the context of an almost infinite number of possible geographical, geological, topographical, economic, political, strategic, demographic, and scientific variables. In such cases "hard and fast" rules of apportionment can be applied only at the risk of achieving results which lead to moral outrage and law's *reductio ad absurdum.* In that sense, fairness discourse which aims to temper the imperative of legitimacy with that of justice serves not to undermine but to redeem the law.

. . .

Notes and Comments

1. Most modern international legal scholarship begins with the assumption that, as Columbia Law Professor Louis Henkin famously put it, "almost all nations observe almost all principles of international law and almost all of their obligations almost all of the time." LOUIS HENKIN, HOW NATIONS BEHAVE 47 (2d ed. 1979) (emphasis omitted). Its efforts to explain state behavior under international law therefore grow out of an almost diametrically opposed perspective from that found in much of political science scholarship. As Henkin eloquently explains:

> [T]o many an observer, governments seem largely free to decide whether to agree to new law, whether to accept another nation's view of existing law, whether to comply with agreed law. International law, then, is voluntary and only horatory. It must always yield to national interest. Surely, no nation will submit to law any questions involving its security or independence, even its power, prestige, influence....
>
> These depreciations of international law challenge much of what the international lawyer does. Indeed, some lawyers seem to despair for international law until there is world government or at least effective international organization. But most international lawyers are not dismayed. Unable to deny the limitations of international law, they insist that these are not critical, and they deny many of the alleged implications of these limitations. If they must admit that the cup of law is half-empty, they stress that it is half-full. They point to similar deficiencies in many domestic legal systems. They reject definitions (commonly associated with legal philosopher John Austin) that deny the title of law to any but the command of a sovereign, enforceable and enforced as such. They insist that despite inadequacies in legislative method, international law has grown and developed and changed. If international law is difficult to make, yet it is made; if its growth is slow, yet it grows. If there is no judiciary as effective as in some developed national systems, there is an International Court of Justice whose judgments

> and opinions, while few, are respected. The inadequacies of the judicial system are in some measure supplied by other bodies: international disputes are resolved and law is developed through a network of arbitrations by continuing or *ad hoc* tribunals. National courts help importantly to determine, clarify, develop international law. Political bodies like the Security Council and the General Assembly of the United Nations also apply law, their actions and resolutions interpret and develop the law, their judgments serve to deter violations. If there is no international executive to enforce international law, the United Nations has some enforcement powers and there is "horizontal enforcement" in the reactions of other nations. The gaps in substantive law are real and should be filled, but they do not vitiate the force and effect of the law that exists, in the international society that is.
>
> Above all, the lawyer will insist, critics of international law ask and answer the wrong question. What matters is not whether the international system has legislative, judicial, or executive branches, corresponding to those we have become accustomed to seek in a domestic society; what matters is whether international law is reflected in the policies of nations and in relations between nations. The question is not whether there is an effective legislature; it is whether there is law that responds and corresponds to the changing needs of a changing society. The question is not whether there is an effective judiciary, but whether disputes are solved in an orderly fashion in accordance with international law. Most important, the question is not whether law is enforceable or even effectively enforced; rather, the question is whether law is observed, whether it governs or influences behavior, whether international behavior reflects stability and order. The fact is, lawyers insist, that nations have accepted important limitations on their sovereignty, that they have observed these norms and undertakings, that the result has been substantial order in international relations.

HENKIN, *supra*, at 225–26. Note that among political realists, Morgenthau, for one, does not disagree with Henkin's empirical assertion. See Note 7 to Part II.A.1 above.

2. Do you agree that international law lacks a "basic rule providing general criteria of validity for the rules of international law"? Is that claim more or less true today than it was when Hart's book was first published (in 1961)? Do you agree with Hart that reliable sanctions for violations of international law are not necessary for international law to really be "law"? Does the theory articulated by Franck depend on clearly establishing that international law is "law"? Does the label of "law" carry any import? For a valuable contribution on the role of sanctions in international law compliance, see Lori Fisler Damrosch, *Enforcing International Law Through Non-Forcible Measures*, 269 RECUEIL DES COURS 13 (1997).

3. Legal scholar Phillip Trimble offers a strong defense of the power of international law to shape state behavior even in the absence of central enforcement. Like Franck, Trimble emphasizes the importance of law's legitimacy in engendering compliance with it (though he cautions that international law has frequently failed to meet this requirement):

> Most international law implementation . . . depends less on the prospect of formal enforcement and sanctions and more on a belief by decisionmakers in the rule of law and on the sense that the law is legitimate. In this regard it is important to understand international law as rhetoric, and to ask why it is or is not persuasive as such. Some writers characterize international law as a specialized language in which international relations are carried out. For example, if a government's military forces erroneously shoot down another's civilian airliner, a diplomat representing the families of the deceased passengers may say to the other government, "You owe compensation because you violated international law," rather than "You must pay compensation because you made a mistake," or "You must pay because you are weaker than we." This use of international law is common. The interesting question is why a claim expressed in legal terms is chosen over other types of claims.
>
> An international law claim carries some implicit messages. It appeals to the self-interest embodied in the legal norm that made it acceptable at some time in the past, and it contains the threat of retaliation or at least the prospect of embarrassment at having been exposed for acting unlawfully. These two messages are not likely to be overpowering in situations where an issue has arisen that will lead to an international dispute. In such a situation, the interests served by the legal norm at stake are likely to be outweighed or severely threatened by other short-term interests, or else the state would not be threatening to breach the norm. Moreover, legality is unlikely to be adjudicated by any regular process and retaliation is certainly not assured. Hence, the power of an international claim may come down to its ability to induce a favorable response just because "it is the law."
>
> The popular view disparages international law precisely because it seems to rest on "moral" suasion, voluntary compliance in the absence of formal enforcement, and the "court of world public opinion." But most people obey domestic law in part because of some notion that "it is the law." Part of that reaction no doubt depends on enforcement. The task of ascertaining a person's motivation for compliance with law is obviously complicated and difficult, if not impossible. There is nevertheless some evidence, and much anecdotal belief, that people obey law in part because they think it is right to do so. This kind of compliance depends on a sense of the law's legitimacy. Here is where international law tends to falter.

Phillip R. Trimble, *International Law, Work Order, and Critical Legal Studies*, 42 STANFORD LAW REVIEW 811, 838–39 (1990) (book review) (footnote omitted).

4. Franck's *Fairness in International Law and Politics* has been criticized by some scholars as ethnocentric. Professor John Tasioulas asks, "in a world characterized by radical diversity in moral and political practice and belief, how can 'fairness' be anything more than a name for a culture-specific value-construct that Franck is proposing arbitrarily to foist on adherents of other cultures through international law and institutions?" John Tasioulas, *International Law and the Limits of Fairness*, 13 European Journal of International Law 993 (2002). Phillip Trimble (a former U.S. ambassador to Nepal) makes a related critique, but argues that fairness can and should play an important role in international law even if a community with shared values does not exist. He writes:

> I find [Franck's] framework problematic because ... there is no global community of people.... Fortunately, ... this problem is not fatal, because there is no need to have a single, universal formula for assessing fairness in order to support the necessary work of international institutions. The important thing is that Ugandans, Americans, Chinese, Egyptians, and so on, each see the process and results of international law as fair from their different perspectives and using their own ways of thinking about fairness. The quest for a universal philosophical explanation of international law and its legitimacy is misplaced. It does not exist.

Phillip R. Trimble, *Globalization, International Institutions, and the Erosion of National Sovereignty and Democracy*, 95 Michigan Law Review 1944, 1952 (1997) (book review). Which perspective do you find more persuasive? Is Franck right to postulate that an international community with shared values is coming into existence? Is such a community a precondition for fairness discourse? Is there a mechanism for adjudicating between competing claims of fairness? And what kind of community does Franck see emerging? Is the community that Franck postulates a community of persons? A community of states? Where do other transnational actors, such as NGOs and corporations, fit into Franck's concept of an international community?

5. Franck's work has also been criticized by rationalists. A frequent critique is that the argument is circular and lacks a causal explanation. For example, Robert Keohane argues: "Franck describes a rule's compliance 'pull power' as 'its index of legitimacy.' Yet legitimacy is said to explain 'compliance pull' making the argument circular.... When we seek to establish causality, we are left with an incomplete argument and empirical ambiguity." Robert Keohane, *International Relations and International Law*, 38 Harvard International Law Journal 487, 493–94 (1997). How would Franck respond to this charge? Are political scientists more committed than international lawyers to proving causality?

6. Franck's elaboration of distributive justice, especially his maximin theory, is based explicitly on John Rawls' theory of social justice, articulated in Rawls' seminal work *A Theory of Justice*. The core of Rawls' theory is that in a society: "All social primary goods—liberty and opportunity, income and wealth, and the basis of self-respect—are to be distributed equally unless an unequal distribution of any or all of these goods is to the advantage of the least favored." JOHN RAWLS, A THEORY OF JUSTICE 303 (1971). Interestingly, Rawls himself has argued that his theory is not applicable to the international realm. JOHN RAWLS, THE LAW OF PEOPLES (1999). *See also* THOMAS FRANCK, THE POWER OF LEGITIMACY AMONG NATIONS (1990) 208–55. However, many international political philosophers disagree and have sought to extend Rawls' theory to the international arena. *See, e.g.*, CHARLES R. BEITZ, POLITICAL THEORY AND INTERNATIONAL RELATIONS (1979); THOMAS POGGE, REALIZING RAWLS (1989). For a good introduction to theories of international justice more generally, see Chris Brown, *Theories of International Justice*, 27 BRITISH JOURNAL OF POLITICAL SCIENCE 273 (1997). To the extent that Rawls' own theories owe much to Kant, is Franck's view Kantian? Is it Liberal?

7. Is Franck correct to limit fairness to distributive justice and legitimacy? Are there other substantive values which might exert a compliance pull? Some values that have been postulated include principles of retributive and corrective justice, humanitarian values of compassion and benevolence, liberty and autonomy, and the value inherent in preserving nature. See John Tasioulas, *International Law and the Limits of Fairness*, 13 EUROPEAN JOURNAL OF INTERNATIONAL LAW 993 (2002). *See also* Lea Brilmayer, *International Justice and International Law*, 98 WEST VIRGINIA LAW REVIEW 611 (1996) (contending that corrective justice is the most important form of justice in the international arena); OSCAR SCHACHTER, INTERNATIONAL LAW IN THEORY AND PRACTICE 61 (1991) (discussing the role of equity and distributive justice in international relations). Similarly, Franck's conception of legitimacy is only one of several found in the international literature. For instance, compare Franck's conception of legitimacy to that of political scientist Inis L. Claude: "The problem of legitimacy has a political dimension that goes beyond its legal and moral aspects.... [T]he process of legitimatization is ultimately a political phenomenon, a crystallization of judgment that may be influenced but is unlikely to be wholly determined by legal norms and moral principles." Inis L. Claude, Jr., *Collective Legitimization as a Political Function of the United Nations*, 20 INTERNATIONAL ORGANIZATION 367, 369 (1966). *See also* ERNEST HAAS, WHEN KNOWLEDGE IS POWER: THREE MODELS OF CHANGE IN INTERNATIONAL ORGANIZATION (1990) (presenting a theory of legitimacy from organizational theory). These and other theories of legitimacy are discussed in Jose E. Alvarez, *The Quest for Legitimacy*, 24 NEW YORK UNIVERSITY JOURNAL OF INTERNATIONAL LAW AND POLITICS 230 (1991). Franck's theory of legitimacy is largely grounded in the work of jurisprudence scholar Ronald Dworkin. RONALD DWORKIN, LAW'S EMPIRE (1986). Compare to this a conception of fairness offered by Louis Kaplow & Steven Shavell in their book *Fairness Versus Welfare* (2002), in which they equate fairness and efficiency and argue that social policies should be assessed entirely on their effects on individuals' well-being.

8. Two recent symposia provide detailed analyses of Franck's work: Conference, *International Law and Justice in the Twenty First Century: The Enduring Contributions of Thomas M. Franck,* 35 NEW YORK UNIVERSITY JOURNAL OF INTERNATIONAL LAW AND POLITICS 291 (2003); Symposium, 13 EUROPEAN JOURNAL OF INTERNATIONAL LAW 909 (2002).

C. Legal Process Theories

Several important normative approaches come under the broad heading of "legal process theories." These approaches, which arise from the Legal Process tradition in post-World War II American legal scholarship, share an emphasis on the role of legal interactions in securing and maintaining compliance. This section outlines two central strands of international legal process theory. The "managerial" school, represented most notably by Abram Chayes and Antonia Handler Chayes, can be characterized as "horizontal legal process" for its emphasis on intergovernmental coordination at the nation-state level. The "transnational legal process" school, as developed by Harold Hongju Koh, captures the managerial school in a broader framework that includes the interaction between horizontal legal process and "vertical legal process," or the process of norm diffusion from the international level down into the domestic law of individual states.

1. Managerial Theory ("Horizontal Legal Process")

The Managerial Theory of state behavior challenges the conventional wisdom of interest-based theory that stronger enforcement is the best way to obtain compliance with international law. In their book, *The New Sovereignty*, Abram Chayes and Antonia Handler Chayes assert that international cooperation and management are the keys to ensuring that states obey treaty obligations. In their view, the norm of *pacta sunt servanda* (treaties are to be obeyed) is an entrenched feature of state behavior, hence states have a "propensity to comply" with international law. Any noncompliance is a result primarily of lack of state capacity or insufficient information about treaty requirements.

This theory has evoked a strong response among interest-centered scholars, who maintain that deep legal compliance is impossible without strong enforcement—a feature that all agree is frequently missing from international law. In the article excerpted below, George Downs, David M. Rocke, and Peter N. Barsoom respond directly to the theory of international legal compliance put forward by Chayes and Chayes. Focusing on the often superficial nature of international treaties, they argue that any compliance with international law that is found in the absence of strong enforcement is merely coincidental or shallow. International law, they maintain, will not change state behavior in any significant way in the absence of strong enforcement.

The New Sovereignty*

ABRAM CHAYES and ANTONIA HANDLER CHAYES

A Theory of Compliance

. . .

If treaties are at the center of the cooperative regimes by which states and their citizens seek to regulate major common problems, there must be some means of assuring that the parties perform their obligations at an acceptable level. To provide this assurance, political leaders, academics, journalists, and ordinary citizens frequently seek treaties with "teeth"—that is, coercive enforcement measures. In part this reflects an easy but incorrect analogy to domestic legal systems, where the application of the coercive power of the state is thought to play an essential role in enforcing legal rules. Our first proposition is that, as a practical matter, coercive economic—let alone military—measures to sanction violations cannot be utilized for the routine enforcement of treaties in today's international system, or in any that is likely to emerge in the foreseeable future. The effort to devise and incorporate such sanctions in treaties is largely a waste of time.

The deficiencies of sanctions for treaty enforcement are related to their costs and legitimacy. The costs of military sanctions are measured in lives, a price contemporary publics seem disinclined to pay except for the most urgent objectives, clearly related to primary national interests. The costs of economic sanctions are also high, not only for the state against which they are directed, where sanctions fall mainly on the weakest and most vulnerable, but also for the sanctioning states. When economic sanctions are used, they tend to be leaky. Results are slow and not particularly conducive to changing behavior. The most important cost, however, is less obvious. It is the serious political investment required to mobilize and maintain a concerted military or economic effort over time in a system without any recognized or acknowledged hierarchically superior authority.

Because the political cost is high, efforts to impose sanctions will be intermittent and ad hoc, responding not to the need for reliable enforcement of treaty obligations, but to political exigencies in the sanctioning states. There is nothing inherently wrong with these characteristics. But an effort that is necessarily ad hoc cannot be systematic and evenhanded. Like cases are not treated alike. Such an effort to ensure compliance with treaty obligations is fatally deficient in legitimacy. Moreover, to have a chance of being effective, military and, especially, economic sanctions must have the support and participation of the most powerful states. In practice, active support if not direction by the United States is decisive for the success of any important sanctioning action. It is evident

* Reprinted by permission of the publisher from ABRAM CHAYES & ANTONIA HANDLER CHAYES, THE NEW SOVEREIGNTY: COMPLIANCE WITH INTERNATIONAL REGULATORY AGREEMENTS (1995). Harvard University Press, Copyright © 1995 by Abram Chayes and Antonia Handler Chayes.

that the United States neither could nor would nor should play such a universal policing role for ordinary treaty obligations. In any event, a system in which only the weak can be made to comply with their undertakings will not achieve the legitimacy needed for reliable enforcement of treaty obligations. . . .

As against this "enforcement model" of compliance, this book presents an alternative "managerial model," relying primarily on a cooperative, problem solving approach instead of a coercive one. . . .

The Propensity to Comply

We start with a somewhat novel conception of compliance and the compliance problem. The position of mainstream realist international-relations theory goes back to Machiavelli: "[A] prudent ruler cannot keep his word, nor should he, where such fidelity would damage him, and when the reasons that made him promise are no longer relevant." This rational-actor conception of compliance may be useful for theory or model building, but no calculus can supply rigorous, nontautological support for the proposition that states observe treaty obligations—or any particular treaty obligation—only when it is in their interest to do so.

By contrast, foreign policy practitioners operate on the assumption of a general propensity of states to comply with international obligations. Foreign ministers, diplomats, and government leaders devote enormous time and energy to preparing, drafting, negotiating, and monitoring treaty obligations. It is not conceivable that they could do so except on the assumption that entering into a treaty commitment ought to and does limit their own freedom of action, and in the expectation that the other parties to the agreement will feel similarly constrained. The meticulous attention devoted to fashioning treaty provisions no doubt reflects the desire to limit the state's own commitment as well as to secure the performance of others. But either way, the enterprise makes sense only if the participants accept (presumably on the basis of experience) that as a general rule, states acknowledge an obligation to comply with the agreements they have signed. For these officials, dealing with the occasional egregious violator is a distinct problem, but it is not the central issue of treaty compliance.

We identify three sorts of considerations that lend plausibility to the assumption off propensity to comply: efficiency, interests, and norms. Of course these factors, singly or in combination, will not lead to compliance in every case or even in any particular case. But they support the assumption of a general propensity for states to comply with their treaty obligations, and they will lead to a better understanding of the real problems of noncompliance and how they can be addressed.

Efficiency

Decisions are not a free good. Governmental resources for policy analysis and decision making are costly and in short supply. Individuals and organizations seek to conserve these resources for the most urgent and pressing matters. In these circumstances, standard economic analysis argues against the continuous recalculation of costs and benefits in the absence of convincing evidence that circumstances have changed since the original decision. The alternative to recalculation is to follow the established treaty rule. Compliance saves transaction costs. In a different formulation, students of bureaucracy tell us that bureaucratic organizations operate according to routines and standard operating procedures, often specified by authoritative rules and regulations. The adoption of a treaty, like the enactment of any other law, establishes an authoritative rule system. Compliance is the normal organizational presumption. A heavy burden of persuasion rests on the proponent of deviation.

Interests

A treaty is a consensual instrument. It has no force unless the state has agreed to it. It is therefore a fair assumption that the parties' interests, were served by entering into the treaty in the first place. Accordingly, the process by which international agreements are formulated and concluded is designed to ensure that the final result will represent, to some degree, an accommodation of the interests of the negotiating states. Modern treaty making, like legislation in a democratic polity, can be seen as a creative enterprise through which the parties not only weigh the benefits and burdens of commitment but also explore, redefine, and sometimes discover their interests. It is at its best a learning process in which not only national positions but also conceptions of national interest evolve and change.

. . .

Norms

Treaties are acknowledged to be legally binding on the states that ratify them. In common experience, people—whether as a result of socialization or otherwise—accept that they are obligated to obey the law. The existence of legal obligation, for most actors in most situations, translates into a presumption of compliance, in the absence of strong countervailing circumstances. So it is with states. It is often said that the fundamental norm[1] of international law is *pacta sunt servanda*—treaties are to be obeyed. In the United States and many other countries, they become a part of the law of the land. Thus, a provision contained in an agreement to which a state has formally assented entails a legal obligation to obey and is presumptively a guide to action.

It seems almost superfluous to adduce evidence or authority for a proposition that is so deeply ingrained in common understanding and so often reflected in the speech of national leaders. Yet the realist argument that national actions are governed entirely by a calculation of interests is

1. We use "norm" as a generic term that includes the concepts of principles, precepts, standards, rules, and the like. For our present purposes, it is adequate to think of legal norms as norms generated by processes recognized as authoritative by a legal system. Compare H.L.A. Hart, *The Concept of Law* . . . .

essentially a denial of the operation of normative obligation in international affairs. This position has held the field for some time in mainstream international relations theory (as have closely related postulates in other positivist social science disciplines). Nevertheless, it is increasingly being challenged by a growing body of empirical study and academic analysis.

. . .

The Sources of Noncompliance

If a state's decision whether or not to conform to a treaty is the result of a calculation of costs and benefits, as the realists assert, the implication is that noncompliance is a premeditated and deliberate violation of a treaty obligation. Clearly some of the most worrisome cases of noncompliance take that form: Iraq's invasion of Kuwait, and North Korea's refusal to permit International Atomic Energy Agency (IAEA) inspection in accordance with its obligation under the Nuclear Non–Proliferation Treaty (NPT), for example. On occasion a state may enter into a treaty to appease a domestic or international constituency, with little intention of carrying it out. This may have been the case when the Soviet Union and some other totalitarian states signed the international human rights covenants—although in the event, the undertakings did not prove to have been as empty as had been supposed.... A passing familiarity with foreign affairs, however, suggests that such cases are the exception rather than the rule. Only infrequently does a treaty violation fall into the category of a willful flouting of legal obligation.

Yet enough questions remain about noncompliance and incomplete compliance with significant treaty obligations to warrant analysis of the methods by which international systems can bring deviant behavior into conformity with treaty norms. The analysis must begin with a diagnosis of the reasons for observed noncompliance. If the violations are not deliberate, what explains this behavior? We identify three circumstances, infrequently recognized in discussions of compliance, that in our view often lie at the root of much of the behavior that may seem to violate treaty requirements: (1) ambiguity and indeterminacy of treaty language, (2) limitations on the capacity of parties to carry out their undertakings, and (3) the temporal dimension of the social, economic, and political changes contemplated by regulatory treaties.

In one sense, these factors might be considered "causes" of noncompliance. But from a lawyer's perspective, they might be thought of as defenses—matters put forth to excuse, justify, or extenuate a prima facie case of breach (subject, like all other issues of compliance, to the overriding obligation of good faith in the performance of treaty obligations). If the plea is accepted, the conduct is not a violation, strictly speaking. Of course, in the international sphere, these charges and defenses are rarely made or determined in a judicial tribunal, but diplomatic practice in other forums can be understood in terms of the same basic structure. Still a third perspective—the one that animates this book—is that of regime management. Where and how can resources and energy be most effectively committed to improve compliance with treaty obligations?

. . .

The New Sovereignty and the Management of Compliance

If we are correct that the principal source of noncompliance is not willful disobedience but the lack of capability or clarity or priority, then coercive enforcement is as misguided as it is costly. A more sophisticated strategy directly addressing these deficiencies is needed to deal with the large bulk of compliance problems. Elements of such a strategy can be discerned in the characteristic activities of regulatory regimes, although they are not always employed with a full consciousness of their implications, and they are seldom integrated into a unified and coherent whole.

At the simplest level, participating in the regime, attending meetings, responding to requests, and meeting deadlines may lead to a realignment of domestic priorities and agendas, setting policies in motion that will operate to improve performance over time. But an array of more pointed activities can reinforce this general effect.

Ensuring Transparency

Transparency—the generation and dissemination of information about the requirements of the regime and the parties' performance under it—is an almost universal element of management strategy. Transparency influences strategic interaction among parties to the treaty in the direction of compliance:

- It facilitates coordination converging on the treaty norms among actors making independent decisions.
- It provides reassurance to actors, whose compliance with the norms is contingent on similar action by other participants, that they are not being taken advantage of.
- It exercises deterrence against actors contemplating noncompliance.

In pure coordination problems, the parties have a common interest in achieving a common objective, and the potential for relative gains is small. The treaty, by establishing the rules, avoids the transaction costs of ad hoc coordination. Most international regulatory problems, however, are not pure coordination problems. The parties have incentives to compete as well as to cooperate. They need reassurance that the others are complying, if the cooperative incentives are to prevail. Elinor Ostrom's study, *Governing the Commons*, shows that in successfully managed common pool resources, the members pursue a "contingent strategy." They will follow the rules so long as most others similarly situated follow them also. Transparency is the key to reassurance, and thus to compliance.

. . .

The first step toward transparency is the development of data on the performance of the parties as to the principal treaty norms and on the general situations of concern to the regime. Self-reporting is the method of choice in most regimes. In fact, the incidence of reporting requirements is so high that they seem to be included almost pro forma in many agreements, with little concern about whether they will be taken seriously. The record of compliance with reporting requirements varies. It is excellent in the ILO [International Labor Organization], fair to poor in many environmental treaties, and seriously deficient in human rights treaties. Here as elsewhere, the level of compliance depends on what the parties as a group are prepared to live with. Experience shows that performance can be substantially improved by technical and financial assistance to build capacity, by clarifying and simplifying the requirements, and by giving greater emphasis and attention to the reporting function....

Verification, both to check the reliability of reported baseline data and to ensure compliance, was the most hotly contested issue in cold war arms control agreements, and U.S. insistence on stringent verification standards was a major limitation on the scope and number of arms control agreements. Although some aspects of the cold war paradigm have continuing value, especially in nonproliferation regimes, much of its elaboration and thoroughness reflects the extreme caution and low financial constraints of an earlier era.

Short of formal and costly verification systems, external checks are often available against which the reliability of national reports can be tested. Other states and nongovernmental scientific and interest groups make their own measurements of atmospheric conditions, ozone depletion, species populations, or, in the area of human rights, the condition of prisoners, minorities, and others who may face harsh treatment. National governments, business groups, and private organizations generate and publish a wide range of economic data for a variety of purposes. Nongovernmental organizations are playing an increasing role in providing information to treaty managers. These sources are generally sufficient to provide the necessary reassurance, if in fact the items or goals are measurable. Compliance problems that are exposed by verification and monitoring are then addressed in other phases of the process....

Dispute Settlement

Where ambiguity or vagueness in treaty language creates compliance problems, the traditional prescription is dispute settlement machinery. Despite the fixation of international lawyers on the virtues of binding adjudication (preferably in the International Court of Justice, but if not, then by a specialized tribunal or arbitral panel), most treaty regimes turn to a variety of relatively informal mediative processes if the disputants are unable to resolve the issues among themselves. Authoritative interpretation of controverted provisions, either by the plenary body of the regime, the secretariat, or a designated interpretative organ, is common, perhaps surprisingly so. It is less contentious than conventional dispute resolution procedures, and in many cases it has a preventive or anticipatory value. On the whole, it has not seemed to matter whether the dispute settlement procedure is legally required or the decision is legally binding, so long as the outcome is treated as authoritative.

Although formal international adjudication, like its domestic counterpart, is costly, contentious, cumbersome, and slow, there is a recent disposition on the part of some regimes to revert to compulsory and more binding forms of dispute settlement. The most important instance is the GATT, which, after almost two decades of incremental tinkering, adopted a new procedure in the Uruguay Round that is to all intents and purposes binding adjudication. . . .

A possible middle ground found in some recent agreements is compulsory conciliation resulting in a nonbinding recommendation from the conciliators on the issues in dispute. This ensures that the regime will be able to address the entire range of disputes. The reported views of the conciliators are likely to carry considerable weight both with the parties in general and with the disputants. Yet the niceties of sovereignty are observed, and the parties are not forced to accept the decision. . . .

Capacity Building

Deficits of technical and bureaucratic capability and financial resources have received increasing attention in the context of the difficulties of domestic enforcement of measures adopted in compliance with recent international environmental obligations. The current jargon is "capacity building," but technical assistance has been a major function of many treaty organizations for many years. In practice this aid has inevitably carried a certain tacit conditionality, but the Montreal Protocol,[2] for perhaps the first time, expressly provides for technical assistance as an affirmative device for enabling countries to comply with both the reporting and the control requirements of the treaty. . . .

The Uses of Persuasion

These disparate elements—transparency, dispute settlement, capacity building—all of which are to be found in some regimes, can be considered to be parts of a management strategy. They merge into a broader process of "jawboning"—the effort to *persuade* the miscreant to change its ways—that is the characteristic method by which international regimes seek to induce compliance. It is remarkable that lawyers and international relations scholars, whose everyday stock-in-trade is persuasion—including persuasion of decision makers—should pay so little attention and, by implication, attach so little significance to the role of argument, exposition, and persuasion in influencing state behavior. Our experience as well as our research indicates that, on the contrary, the

2. [Editors' Note: The 1987 Montreal Protocol on Substances That Deplete the Ozone Layer requires states that ratify to phase out the consumption and production of compounds that deplete ozone in the stratosphere. To facilitate this goal, it stipulates a mechanism for providing technical assistance to member states to enable them to comply with the control measures.]

fundamental instrument for maintaining compliance with treaties at an acceptable level is an iterative process of discourse among the parties, the treaty organization, and the wider public.

We propose that this process is usefully viewed as management, rather than enforcement. As in other managerial situations, the dominant atmosphere is one of actors engaged in a cooperative venture, in which performance that seems for some reason unsatisfactory represents a problem to be solved by mutual consultation and analysis, rather than an offense to be punished. States are under the practical necessity to give reasons and justifications for suspect conduct. These are reviewed and critiqued not only in formal dispute settlement processes but also in a variety of other venues, public and private, formal and informal, where they are addressed and evaluated. In the process, the circumstances advanced in mitigation or excuse of nonperformance are systematically addressed. Those that seem to have substance are dealt with; those that do not are exposed. Often the upshot is agreement on a narrower and more concrete definition of the required performance, adapted to the circumstances of the case. At all stages, the putative offender is given every opportunity to conform. Persuasion and argument are the principal engines of this process, but if a party persistently fails to respond, the possibility of diffuse manifestations of disapproval or pressures from other actors in the regime is present in the background.

In its most advanced form, this justificatory discourse is expressly recognized as a principal method of inducing compliance. The treaty itself or practices that have grown up under it require each member to report systematically and periodically on policies and programs relevant to the achievement of regime norms and objectives. After analysis by the secretariat (and sometimes by concerned nongovernmental organizations), these reports are reviewed and assessed at a general meeting of the members, where the reporting state presents and defends its report. The discussion and debate culminates in agreement on ever more narrowly specified undertakings and targets to be achieved by the reporting state in the next reporting periods. . . .

The process works because modern states are bound in a tightly woven fabric of international agreements, organizations, and institutions that shape their relations with each other and penetrate deeply into their internal economics and politics. The integrity and reliability of this system are of overriding importance for most states, most of the time. These considerations in turn reflect profound changes in the international system within which states must act and decide.

Traditionally, sovereignty has signified the complete autonomy of the state to act as it chooses, without legal limitation by any superior entity. The state realized and expressed its sovereignty through independent action to achieve its goals. If sovereignty in such terms ever existed outside books on international law and international relations, however, it no longer has any real world meaning. The largest and most powerful states can sometimes get their way through sheer exertion of will, but even they cannot achieve their principal purposes—security, economic well-being, and a decent level of amenity for their citizens—without the help and cooperation of many other participants in the system, including entities that are not states at all. Smaller and poorer states are almost entirely dependent on the international economic and political system for nearly everything they need to maintain themselves as functioning societies.

That the contemporary international system is interdependent and increasingly so is not news. Our argument goes further. It is that, for all but a few self-isolated nations, sovereignty no longer consists in the freedom of states to act independently, in their perceived self-interest, but in membership in reasonably good standing in the regimes that make up the substance of international life. To be a player, the state must submit to the pressures that international regulations impose. Its behavior in any single episode is likely to affect future relationships not only within the particular regime involved but in many others as well, and perhaps its position within the international system as a whole. When nations enter into an international agreement, therefore, they tend to alter their mutual expectations and actions over time in accordance with its terms. The need to be an accepted member in this complex web of international arrangements is itself the critical factor in ensuring acceptable compliance with regulatory agreements. Robert Putnam, in *Making Democracy Work,* traces the difference between low levels of effective cooperation in regional governments in southern Italy and the much higher levels in the north to the existence of a similarly thick network of associations, on the domestic plane, in the northern regions. As in the international arena, "The sanction for violating [the norms and expectations generated by this network] is not penal, but exclusion from the network of solidarity and cooperation."

Sovereignty, in the end, is status—the vindication of the state's existence as a member of the international system. In today's setting, the only way most states can realize and express their sovereignty is through participation in the various regimes that regulate and order the international system. Isolation from the pervasive and rich international context means that the state's potential for economic growth and political influence will not be realized. Connection to the rest of the world and the political ability to be an actor within it are more important than any tangible benefits in explaining compliance with international regulatory agreements.

The need to be a member in good standing of the international system ensures that most compliance problems will yield to the management process we describe. If they do not, the offending state is left with a stark choice, between conforming to the rule as defined and applied in the particular circumstances and openly flouting a concrete and precisely specified undertaking endorsed by the other members of the regime. This turns out to be a very uncomfortable position even for a powerful state to find itself in.... Not even the so-called hermit state of North Korea has been completely able to resist this kind of escalating pressure.

Indeed an important consequence of the process is the winnowing out of reasonably justifiable or unintended failures to fulfill commitments—those that might be consistent with a good faith compliance standard—and the identification and isolation of the few cases of egregious and willful violation. This in turn becomes part of the mobilization of consensus for harsher sanctions in the rare cases in which they may be necessary.

. . .

Is the Good News About Compliance Good News About Cooperation?*

GEORGE W. DOWNS, DAVID M. ROCKE, and PETER N. BARSOOM

. . .

The endogeneity and selection problems

It is not difficult to appreciate why the findings of the managerial school [such as those of Chayes and Chayes] suggest that both international institutions and even international law have a far brighter future than most international relations specialists have believed for the past fifty years. Apart from sharply contradicting the pessimistic expectations of many realists and neorealists about the inability of cooperation and self-regulation to flourish in an anarchic world, they also run counter to the claims of cooperation researchers in the rational-choice tradition. Such researchers emphasize the centrality of enforcement concerns in regulatory environments and characterize them as mixed-motive games, where the danger of self-interested exploitation is significant, as opposed to coordination games, where it is not. Such findings certainly add credibility to the frequent speculation that the rational-choice tradition's affection for the repeated prisoners' dilemma has led it to overemphasize enforcement and underemphasize the potential for voluntary compliance and noncoercive dispute resolution.

In trying to understand the prescriptive significance of the managerialists' compliance findings, it is useful to consider the following hypothetical story. An article has recently appeared in an education journal criticizing the state of musical education in an age of funding cutbacks. The author, a longtime music teacher, argues that such cutbacks inevitably have dire consequences for the quality of school music programs. A member of the school board who has aggressively supported the elimination of frivolous expenditures is skeptical of what she believes to be characteristically self-interested reasoning. In an effort to get to the bottom of the issue, she attends fifteen concerts in her district and fifteen concerts in a rival district that has not reduced its support of music education or extracurricular activities. She finds that the quality of the two orchestras as measured by the number of mistakes they made

* Reprinted by permission from 50 INTERNATIONAL ORGANIZATION 379 (1996).

to be pretty much the same and quite low in both cases. Noting that the orchestras in her district have achieved this high level of performance despite a 75 percent reduction in the number of rehearsals, she is delighted. Not only has she demonstrated that the cutbacks have had no effect on school orchestras but she believes that she has confirmed her long-held suspicion that rehearsals do not make school orchestras better, they simply line the pockets of music teachers eager to buy hot tubs and Steinway pianos.

These conclusions may, however, be invalid. It is likely that orchestras in her district may have adapted to the decrease in resources by playing less demanding pieces. No orchestra is eager to embarrass itself, and one of the most effective ways to avoid doing so is to play Haydn rather than Mahler or Stravinsky. Unless the school board member counting mistakes figures out a way to control for the difficulty of repertoire, we do not really know what her findings tell us about the impact of the budget cuts. A treaty, like the selection of an orchestra's repertoire, is also an endogenous strategy. States choose the treaties they make from an infinitely large set of possible treaties. If some treaties are more likely to be complied with than others or require more enforcement than others, this will almost certainly affect the choices states make. Just as orchestras will usually avoid music that they cannot play fairly well, states will rarely spend a great deal of time and effort negotiating agreements that will continually be violated. This inevitably places limitations on the inferences we can make from compliance data alone. As in the case of the orchestra's mistakes, we do not know what a high compliance rate really implies. Does it mean that even in the absence of enforcement states will comply with any agreement from the set of all possible agreements, or does it mean that states only make agreements that do not require much enforcement? If the latter is the case, what are the implications for the future of regulatory cooperation?

To even begin to overcome the problems that endogeneity poses for understanding the role of enforcement in regulatory compliance, we need to control for the basis of state selection; that is, those characteristics of international agreements that play the same role for states as musical difficulty does for the school orchestras. One likely candidate is what we have termed the depth of cooperation. International political economists define the depth of an agreement by the extent to which it requires behind-the-border integration with regard to social and environmental standards as well as with regard to the reduction of barriers to trade. Here, however, the depth of an agreement refers to the extent to which it captures the collective benefits that are available through perfect cooperation in one particular policy area. Given the difficulties involved in identifying the cooperative potential of an ideal treaty, it is most useful to think of a treaty's depth of cooperation as the extent to which it requires states to depart from what they would have done in its absence. If we are examining the critical subset of regulatory treaties that require states to reduce some collectively dysfunctional behavior like tariffs or pollution, a treaty's theoretical depth of cooperation would refer to the reduction it required relative to a counterfactual estimate of the tariff or pollution level that would exist in the absence of a treaty. Of course, the depth of cooperation that a treaty actually achieved might be quite different than this figure. Here we measure depth of cooperation by the treaty level because that is the figure which serves as the basis for judging the level of compliance. In the absence of a trustworthy theoretical estimate of this counterfactual, it could be based on the status quo at the time an agreement was signed or on a prediction derived from the year-to-year change rate prior to that time.

Either estimate of depth of cooperation is obviously quite crude. There are doubtless policy areas in which, for any number of reasons, the potential for cooperation is much smaller than others. In such cases our depth measure will make cooperation in these areas appear shallower than it really is. Yet if one is willing to concede, as both managerialists and more conventional institutionalists argue, that there are substantial cooperative benefits that are as yet unrealized in the areas of arms control, trade, and environmental regulation, this depth of cooperation measure provides a rough idea of what states have accomplished. We can in turn use it to interpret compliance data and help assess the role of enforcement. While this measure of depth is hardly perfect, there is no reason to expect that it is biased in such a way as to distort the relationship between the depth of cooperation represented by a given treaty, the nature of the game that underlies it, and the amount of enforcement needed to maintain it.

. . .

Discussion

This logical connection between the depth of cooperation represented by a given treaty and the amount of enforcement that is needed in mixed-motive games suggests that evaluating the importance of enforcement by examining how high compliance is when it is low or absent might be misleading. We need to worry about the possibility that both the high rate of compliance and relative absence of enforcement threats are due not so much to the irrelevance of enforcement as to the fact that states are avoiding deep cooperation—and the benefits it holds whenever a prisoners' dilemma situation exists—because they are unwilling or unable to pay the costs of enforcement. If this were true, prescribing that states ignore enforcement in favor of other compliance strategies would be equivalent to telling the school orchestras to avoid wasting their time rehearsing. Just as the latter would condemn the orchestras to a repertoire of simple compositions, the prescriptions of the managerial school would condemn states to making agreements that represent solutions to coordination games and shallow prisoners' dilemmas.

Of course, knowing that statistics about the role of enforcement might be misleading is hardly equivalent to establishing its importance as a compliance strategy. If members of the managerial school are correct in believing in their (usually implicit) assumption that mixed-motive games and prisoners' dilemmas play a much smaller role in critical regulatory arenas than game theorists assume, the argument fizzles. Unfortunately, settling this controversy is no easy matter. Utility functions are notoriously difficult to access directly and any attempt to cope with selection by estimating the character of the set of regulatory agreements that are potentially possible would be hopelessly circular.

Given the circumstances, it seems advisable to sidestep any attempt to inventory the nature of the underlying game and to evaluate some of the implications of the rival theories. We examine two. First, we will assess the depth of cooperation and the level of enforcement connected with prominent regulatory agreements that involve the reduction of behaviors that states have concluded are collectively counterproductive but that contain few enforcement provisions. Ideally, one would like to examine the correlation between enforcement and depth of cooperation, but as we noted above, we agree with the managerial school's observation that such strongly enforced regulatory agreements are relatively rare. If the managerial school is correct, the absence of strong enforcement provisions or the informal threat of enforcement should have no bearing on the depth of cooperation. There should be numerous examples of states agreeing to alter dramatically the trajectory that they were following at the time a treaty was signed while paying little attention to enforcement. If the game theorists are correct that most important regulatory agreements are mixed-motive games of some variety, any tendency of states to avoid committing themselves to punishing noncompliance is likely to be associated with either a world in which there are relatively few deeply cooperative agreements or in which violations run rampant. Since we agree that while regulatory violations exist they are not frequent, we expect the former to be true.

Second, we will examine the managerial school's claim that self-interest rarely plays a conspicuous role in the treaty violations that do take place and that violations are driven instead solely by a combination of the ambiguity of treaties, the capacity limitations of states, and uncontrollable social and economic changes. We are skeptical of this assertion because the set of violations should be less distorted by selection than the set of treaties. This is true because we expect that, ceteris paribus, the rate of violation connected with mixed-motive game treaties should in the absence of perfect information and appropriate enforcement be much higher than the rate of violation connected with coordination game treaties. Hence, even if there are fewer such treaties they would be overrepresented relative to coordination game based-treaties in any sample of violations.

. . .

Enforcement and the future of cooperation

. . . It is not appropriate to counter skepticism about the success of treaties that require steep cuts in nontariff barriers, arms, or air pollution but that contain no enforcement provision with statistics about the average rate of compliance with international agreements that require states to depart only slightly from what they would have done in the absence of an agreement. Techniques used to ensure compliance with an agreement covering interstate bank transfers cannot be counted on to ensure the success of the WTO's new rules governing intellectual property.

It is possible, of course, that deeper cooperation (e.g., stricter arms control or environmental regulation) can be ensured without much enforcement. This can occur whenever the underlying game changes in such a way that there is less incentive to defect from a given agreement. One of the points too rarely made by either the managerial or political economy (i.e., enforcement) school is that changes in technology, relative prices, domestic transitions, and ideas have inspired more international cooperation and regulatory compliance than have all efforts at dispute resolution and enforcement combined. This is particularly true in the area of trade liberalization. As Kenneth Oye recently has noted, "Over the long term, the diffusion of ideas, the impact of market-driven shifts in exchange rates, and fundamental concerns over productivity and growth are more consequential sources of pressure for reducing protection." Yet, while we agree that ideas and relative prices are important determinants of compliance, they are not well-specified strategies that instruct policymakers how they can increase the rate of compliance. We know relatively little about how to use ideas to change preferences about discount rates, consumption versus savings, or the environment and still less about the endogenous manipulation of relative prices for policy aims such as arms control. We know much more, as crude as our knowledge may be, about the impact of enforcement coupled with managerial variables such as transparency.

If the managerialists want to hope (like most of us) that ideas or relative prices will inspire states to value the environment more or to be more energetic in controlling arms, this is understandable. It is nevertheless different from the prescriptions that they are currently emphasizing and may also prove overly optimistic. While some regimes appear over the years to have been strengthened by the changes in relative prices, the dissemination of progressive ideas about the potential of cooperation, and the weakening of parochial domestic interests, others have shown signs of weakening because of these same factors. The nonproliferation regime, for example, has shown signs of fraying because the relative cost of nuclear weaponry has declined.

We do not mean to imply that the managerial model and the failure to embrace the idea that enforcement is often necessary are the only things preventing deeper cooperation. Obviously, states have reasons to refrain from vigorous enforcement. The question is whether it is better to cope with such reluctance by declaring that its importance has been vastly exaggerated or by trying to remedy matters.

We obviously prefer the second course of action, and we believe that the managerialists' vision of cooperation and compliance distracts political scientists from a host of problems that lie squarely within their area of expertise. For example, the vast majority of political economists would argue that the reason the GATT has encountered compliance problems and the reason why states have not obtained the cooperative benefits that would be possible through the use of more aggressive enforcement strategies involves an agency problem. Political leaders, if not the consumers who make up their constituencies, are left better off if they acquiesce to protectionist demands during those periods (e.g., recessions, following a technological breakthrough by foreign competition) when interest groups are likely to pay a premium that is greater than the electoral punishment they are likely to receive. Because the timing of such events is uncertain and most leaders are similarly vulnerable to such events, they deal with this situation by creating penalties for violations that are high enough to prevent constant defection but low enough to allow self-interested defection when circumstances demand it. Even leaders of states that are, for whatever reason, more committed to free trade are reluctant to increase the penalty for violations to a very high level because they suspect (probably correctly) that the "protectionist premium" is at times far greater than the cost of any credible punishment for violations. Thus, their hand is stayed not by any appreciation for the accidental nature of defection but by an appreciation for just how unaccidental it is.

This is a dimension of political capacity that the managerial school rarely discusses and that is unlikely to be exorcized by technical assistance. It is, however, intimately connected to the design of both domestic political institutions and international regimes. One possible strategy is to restrict regime membership to states that will not have to defect very often. The idea is that whatever benefit is lost by excluding such states from the regime will be more than made up by permitting those that are included to set and also enforce a deeper level of cooperation—in this case a higher standard of free trade. This may be a reason, quite different from the large-*n* coordination concerns of collective action theory, why many deeply cooperative regimes have a limited number of members and why regimes with a large number of members tend to engage in only shallow cooperation. Is this trade-off real? Must states sometimes choose between aggressively addressing an environmental or trade problem and trying to create a community of states? We do not know. What we do know is that to ignore the issue on the basis of high compliance rates and the relative absence of enforcement is dangerously premature.

Notes and Comments

1. One of the underlying assumptions of both Chayes and Chayes and Downs et al. is that states are the primary actors in international law. Does this assumption make sense, especially given that Chayes and Chayes themselves focus on international legal process? Harold Hongju Koh addresses the problems with this assumption in his article *Transna-*

tional Legal Process, 75 NEBRASKA LAW REVIEW 181 (1996), discussed in the Notes and Comments for the following section. Constructivists such as Martha Finnemore have also argued that states are by no means the only important actors in international relations, as discussed above. As will be seen in the following section, Koh also highlights the interplay among actors at not just at the intergovernmental level, but among the transnational, intergovernmental, and domestic levels.

2. In the excerpt above, Chayes and Chayes argue that "[t]he need to be an accepted member in this complex web of international arrangements is itself the critical factor in ensuring acceptable compliance with regulatory agreements." Compare this to Frank's argument in *The Power of Legitimacy Among Nations*, where he analogizes the international system to a social club:

> The rules of the international system obligate—to the extent they do—primarily because they are like the house rules of a club. Membership in the club confers a desirable status, with socially recognized privileges and duties and *it is the desire to be a member of the club, to benefit by the status of membership, that is the ultimate motivator of conformist behavior: that and the clarity by which the rules communicate, the integrity of the process by which the rules were made and are applied, their venerable pedigree and conceptual coherence. In short, it is the legitimacy of the rules which conduces to their being respected.* ... [O]bligations of states in the global community much more closely approximate the house rules of a club, or the social rule about keeping appointments, than they resemble the duty of citizens to cross intersections only on the green light.

THOMAS FRANCK, THE POWER OF LEGITIMACY AMONG NATIONS 38 (1990). What role does the concept of community play in each of these approaches? Is it possible that states might wish not to be a part of the community of nations? How would Franck and the Chayeses account for rogue nations? Are these the exceptions that prove the rule or does the existence of such states pose a challenge to Franck and the Chayeses?

3. What role does discourse play in Franck's and the Chayeses' approach to international law? In this regard, consider the work of scholars affiliated with Critical Legal Studies and "New Stream" schools, who view discourse as essential to international law. See generally, David Kennedy, *A New Stream of International Scholarship*, 7 WISCONSIN INTERNATIONAL LAW JOURNAL 1 (1988) ("I have sought to dislodge this resignation and rejuvenate the field as an area of meaningful intellectual inquiry in part by recapturing its history and substantive aspiration, and in part by heightening the move to process—by reimagining the field rhetorically."); MARTTI KOSHENNIEMI, FROM APOLOGY TO UTOPIA: THE STRUCTURE OF INTERNATIONAL LEGAL ARGUMENT (1989).

4. Which argument do you find more persuasive: the managerial approach or the rationalist approach? Are you presuaded by the critique of Downs, Rocke, and Barsoom? Whether or not Downs, Rocke and Barsoom are correct, is there a role for "shallow" treaties that do not require states to change their behavior significantly? Can a treaty that is not backed by sanctions nonetheless have an impact on state behavior? (For discussions of when and how treaties may shape state behavior in the absence of meaningful transnational sanctions, see Oona A. Hathaway, *Do Human Rights Treaties Make a Difference?*, 111 YALE LAW JOURNAL 1935 (2002); Oona A. Hathaway, *The Cost of Commitment*, 55 STANFORD LAW REVIEW 1821 (2003); and Oona A. Hathaway, *Between Power and Principle: A Political Theory of International Law*, 71 UNIVERSITY OF CHICAGO LAW REVIEW (forthcoming May 2005).)

5. In 1998, Downs responded to the Chayeses' invitation in their book to review their theories in light of empirical data and particular cases in George W. Downs, *Enforcement and the Evolution of Cooperation*, 19 MICHIGAN JOURNAL OF INTERNATIONAL LAW 319 (1988). In the article, Downs argues that formal enforcement provisions are "disproportionately present in regulatory agreements that require significant changes in behavior." *Id.* at 320. More specifically: "In a set of multilateral environmental agreements, the correlation between what is termed the depth of cooperation and the extent of enforcement is 0.74. [Furthermore, data indicates that] as multilaterals increase their level of cooperation over time (e.g., in the manner of the EU or WTO), they also increase their level of enforcement, a fact for which managerial theory provides little explanation." *Id.* Do these findings (assuming for the moment that they are correct) change your view as to which approach is more persuasive? Can the managerial theory be reconciled with Downs' findings?

6. How is the Legal Process approach similar to and different from the constructivist approach outlined in Part III.A.?

2. Transnational Legal Process ("Horizontal and Vertical Legal Process")

This section focuses on both vertical and horizontal legal process. This strand of legal process theory draws less on Chayes and Chayes' managerial approach than on what Abram Chayes had previously termed "international legal process," an approach he had pioneered in collaboration with Thomas Ehrlich and Andreas Lowenfeld in their casebook, INTERNATIONAL LEGAL PROCESS: MATERIALS FOR AN INTRODUCTORY COURSE (1968). Chayes had served as Legal Advisor of the U.S. State Department, and Ehrlich and Lowenfeld had served as his deputies, during the Kennedy Administration. After leaving the government, they assembled original documents about matters upon which they had worked in government into a new international law casebook. Throughout the cases they examine, Chayes, Ehrlich and Lowenfeld aim to understand "How—and how far—do law, lawyers, and legal institutions operate to affect the course of international affairs?"[3] Noting the growth of international organizations, they assert that "The ability of an international body to act without authorization or approval of national parliaments

3. CHAYES, EHRLICH AND LOWENFELD, INTERNATIONAL LEGAL PROCESS: MATERIALS FOR AN INTRODUCTORY COURSE (1968), at xi.

represents a far-reaching shift in the locus of power away from individual sovereign states. And that ability imposes restraints on the exercise of national power inconceivable a few generations ago."[4] Their work thus foreshadows the inclusion of nonstate actors into international legal scholarship.

Different commentators have applied the concept of international legal process to the modern day in different ways. In this section, Mary Ellen O'Connell summarizes what is essentially still a "horizontal" view, providing an intellectual history of the development of legal process theory and setting up the shift toward the more vertical approaches. The excerpts from Harold Koh's work develop the idea of transnational legal process, in which legal interactions provoke a process of norm-internalization that involves both the international and domestic levels. In doing so, he adds to the legal process view a vertical, as well as horizontal perspective. Koh describes the process of vertical norm-internalization as having three steps: *interaction* (a transaction instigated by a transnational actor) that leads to *interpretation* (the interpretation of an international legal norm by an interpretive body) that promotes the *internalization* of the international norm into the law of a domestic legal system.

New International Legal Process

MARY ELLEN O'CONNELL*

International legal process (ILP) emphasizes understanding how international law works. It concentrates not so much on the exposition of rules and their content as on how international legal rules are actually used by the makers of foreign policy.... ILP, as a study of international law in its actual operation and the consideration of how international law could work better, has had a significant influence on American international law scholarship.

. . .

Origins and Premises of International Legal Process

ILP began its existence with the Chayes, Ehrlich and Lowenfeld adaptation of American legal process to international legal studies in their 1968 casebook, International Legal Process. The book acknowledges the authors' debt to Professors [Henry] Hart and [Albert] Sacks of Harvard University, considered among the chief architects of the American legal process method (LP). LP became in the 1950s—and remains—a principal legal methodology in the United States. During the past two decades scholars have worked to reform legal process. The recent work of Harold Koh has indicated that this resulting "new legal process" has applications to international law. Professor Koh, encourages the view that a far more complete legal methodology for international law could

4. *Id.*, at xi.

* Reprinted with permission from 93 AMERICAN JOURNAL OF INTERNATIONAL LAW 334 (1999).

be built from the tenets of legal process, both new and old. This section examines American legal process, the teachings of LP that have been applied to date to international law, and recent developments in American legal process that could be applied to ILP to create "new international legal process."

American Legal Process

Hart, Sacks and the many other legal process scholars of their generation developed a method for answering the questions: What is law for? How does law operate? What is the relationship between law and society? It was not a theory of law such as positivism, Marxism, or natural law but, rather, a method for understanding, using and improving upon positivism. Positivism provided the theory of obligation, but these scholars wanted to modify the legal method they had learned as students, legal formalism, for applying positivism. They also wished to improve upon a method that had already developed to respond to legal formalism, namely Legal Realism.

With the rise of administrative agencies and the increased activity of courts and lawyers in the 1920s and 1930s in the United States, scholars sought to develop a more authentic account than existed in legal formalism of the role of institutions, formal and informal, in the legal system. Concentrating on courts, legal realists rejected the formalistic view that judges could mechanically apply legislation or common-law precedents. Judges must interpret laws and sometimes even make them; they do not simply apply them. LP parted company with Legal Realism, however, because, "once the realists demonstrated that inarticulate considerations of social policy inform judges' decisions, it naturally followed [for the realists] that legal decision-makers should explicitly consider social and economic consequences when developing or applying a rule." This did not naturally follow for LP. According to Hart, "A court in making law is bound to base its action not on free judgment of relative social advantage, but on a process of reasoned development of authoritative starting points (i.e., statutes, prior judicial decisions, etc. etc.)."

LP agreed with the realists that courts must from time to time make law, but LP sought to constrain that lawmaking. It should not be done with the view of realizing a judge's personal view of policy but, rather, that of the larger society. LP insisted "that law is accountable to reason and not just fiat." In addition, LP wished to provide a truer picture of what law actually was—legislation and judicial decisions, yes, but also agency decisions and the private agreements negotiated by lawyers. In urging understanding of law's institutions, Hart and Sacks also urged "consideration of legal doctrine in light of law's purposes and the polity's underlying principles." Law's purpose is to settle "by authority of the group various types of questions of concern to the group." The acceptable answers to such questions should be guided by society's values, which Hart and Sacks theorized in the United States to be democratic values. Ensuring reasoned decisions consistent with law's purpose and society's values could be done by establishing who the legally competent decision makers are and requiring those decision makers to provide "reasoned elaboration" of their decisions.

International Legal Process

International law also had its realists, but ILP developed not in response to them, but to realists from the discipline of international relations. By the beginning of the Cold War, international relations realists were arguing that international law played virtually no role in international affairs, especially in the area of the use of force. Chayes, Ehrlich and Lowenfeld, in the tradition of Hart and Sacks to whom their casebook is dedicated, embarked on the path of helping students to understand not American society and its law, but international society and international law, examining the role that law and lawyers actually play in international society. Chayes and his co-authors could not agree with the realists that law and lawyers played no role because they had themselves been part of the process of international law during the Kennedy administration.

While they found that "the whole field of international law is undergoing fundamental theoretical reexamination," their book, "by contrast, is addressed primarily to the study of the international legal process itself. How—and how far—do law, lawyers, and legal institutions operate to affect the course of international affairs?" They were not as interested in the content of rules as with four interrelated questions, very much derived from the Hart and Sacks perspective:

> First, the allocation of decision-making competence in international affairs.... Second, the reasons why a particular regulatory arrangement is adopted for a particular subject-matter area, rather than another mode of control or none at all. Third, the ways in which particular institutions and the system as a whole develop to restrain and organize national and individual behavior. And finally, the elements of the political, economic and cultural setting that predispose to success or failure in that development.

They concluded that, while law was not usually decisive, it was usually important to international affairs, and "like Hart and Sacks, [they] posited that legal issues mainly arise not before courts, but in the process of making policy decisions, with lawyers playing a more important role than judges, and consent playing a greater role than command." Chayes and Ehrlich followed up the casebook with examinations of the role of law in decisions on the use of force. Chayes looked at the Cuban missile crisis and Ehrlich examined the situation in Cyprus. Both concluded that law "constrained," "justified" and "organized" decision makers' actions, even if it did not dictate them.

These scholars were not, however, trying to develop a "school." They were interested in how law worked in international society and also in relating to students the actual role of international law and international lawyers in international relations. They did not go as far as Hart and Sacks in identifying the values of the legal system, focusing rather on describing the workings of international legal processes—especially the formal and informal institutional processes such as the way foreign offices incorporated international law in decision making. They also advocated consideration of how the processes of international law could be improved. Chayes turned to work on the compliance-attracting power of international treaty regimes. Ehrlich considered the body of rules governing the use of force and the role of institutions in applying and enforcing them in International Law and the Use of Force. Lowenfeld concentrated on the functioning of international trade institutions and international arbitration for the settlement of disputes. And along with them, a great number of American international lawyers concentrated on describing the actual workings of international law, explaining why the law works the way it does, and promoting ways to improve it.

New International Legal Process

At about the time Chayes, Ehrlich and Lowenfeld were applying LP to international society, American legal process fell on hard times within the United States. Democratic values were criticized as leaving out underrepresented minorities. The reliance of dispute settlement on precedent and deference to elected legislatures meant that courts and agencies were not correcting democracy's "pathologies." Legal process became the target of the critical legal studies movement, feminism, critical race theory, and others.

In the 1980s, however, scholars in the United States began to work on LP's normative deficit. New American legal process (NLP) or "new public law," which appears to be a different name for a related group of concepts, has a number of identifiable characteristics that update and enrich Hart and Sacks's legal process. Eskridge and Frickey have added to Hart and Sacks's democratic values, with insights from feminism, republicanism, hermeneutics, and so on. In addition to expanding LP's normative element, Eskridge and several co-authors describe NLP as continuing old legal process's faith in institutions and the need for institutional decision makers to be purposive in decision making. They now want this purposiveness to expand, however, to "dynamic" decision making. In looking at judicial interpretation of statutes, for example, more elements should be borne in mind than merely the statute's purpose, including the need to respond to change over time, to respond to legislative and agency pathologies, and to value new substantive norms beyond liberal democratic principles. "The mood is centrist, taking traditional formal authorities seriously but purposively. The agenda is to balance form and substance, to view the legal system as a purposive whole, and to explore both functionally and formally institutional competence and the role of process."

Professor Koh, writing about this movement, finds that these scholars "saw the law's legitimacy as resting not just on process but also on its normative content. They viewed lawmaking as not merely the rubber-stamping of a pluralistic political process, but as a process of value-creation in which courts, agencies, and the people engage in a process of democratic dialogue." Inspired by the work of new legal process, Koh has called on scholars to add the insights of the NLP and other new legal movements to international legal theory. He points to the importance of thinking beyond the functioning of a process to the normativity of that process. Koh's own work has both described the "dynamic," "non-traditional," and "non-statist" processes of international law and mentioned the normativity of these processes.

By pointing to normativity in international law, Koh's work indicates the normative deficit of earlier ILP. ILP did not develop an answer to the questions What is law for? and What is the relationship between law and society? So the values of the system were not revealed, nor were the procedures that decision makers should follow in reaching them. Koh does not himself elaborate on these questions beyond indicating their importance to a methodology.

Following the direction of his lead would suggest looking to feminism, liberalism, law and economics, republicanism, and other new international legal theories to supplement the values of positivism in developing the normative goals of the system. Human rights, peace and protection of the environment, for example, would be values for international society as understood by these contemporary perspectives on society. In addition to these new values, it seems appropriate for ILP to add the values of legal process that were not originally incorporated into ILP, but that remain even after the reform of LP. In particular, confidence in institutional settlement continues as a central NLP value.

The resulting new ILP, therefore, would advocate knowledge of the legal system and valuing institutional settlement in line with international society's values, to resolve society's rapidly expanding issues. Institutions for settlement should follow dynamic procedures, meaning that as society's values evolve, duly established decision makers should "have the authority to develop new legal standards and even to adapt otherwise clear . . . text to accommodate a changed societal and legal environment" through reasoned elaboration of their decisions.

Why Do Nations Obey International Law?

HAROLD HONGJU KOH*

Transnational Legal Process

Despite their methodological differences, both Franck and the Chayeses ultimately reach the same intuitive answer to why nations obey. If our goal is better enforcement of global rules, they reason, voluntary obedience, not coerced compliance, must be the preferred enforcement mechanism. If nations internally "perceive" a rule to be

* Reprinted by permission from 106 YALE LAW JOURNAL 2599 (1997).

fair, says Franck, they are more likely to obey it. If nations must regularly justify their actions to treaty partners in terms of treaty norms, suggest the Chayeses, it is more likely that those nations will "voluntarily" comply with those norms. Both analyses suggest that the key to better compliance is more *internalized* compliance, or what I have called *obedience*. But by what process does norm-internalization occur? How do we transform occasional or grudging compliance with global norms into habitual obedience?

... [S]uch a process can be viewed as having three phases. One or more transnational actors provokes an *interaction* (or series of interactions) with another, which forces an *interpretation* or enunciation of the global norm applicable to the situation. By so doing, the moving party seeks not simply to coerce the other party, but to *internalize* the new interpretation of the international norm into the other party's internal normative system. The aim is to "bind" that other party to obey the interpretation as part of its internal value set. Such a transnational legal process is normative, dynamic, and constitutive. The transaction generates a legal rule which will guide future transnational interactions between the parties; future transactions will further internalize those norms; and eventually, repeated participation in the process will help to reconstitute the interests and even the identities of the participants in the process.

... [T]he various theoretical explanations offered for compliance are complementary, not mutually exclusive. In his classic statement of neorealism, *Man, the State and War*, Kenneth Waltz posited three levels of analysis, or "images," at which international relations could be explained: the international system (systemic); the state (domestic politics); and the individuals and groups who make up the state (psychological/bureaucratic). These images are not mutually exclusive, but sit atop one another like a layer cake; thus, interest and international society theorists seek to explain compliance primarily at the level of the international system, while identity theorists seek to explain it at the level of domestic political structure. Transnational legal process analysts, by contrast, seek to supplement these explanations with reasons for compliance that are found at a *transactional* level: *interaction*, *interpretation*, and *internalization* of international norms into domestic legal structures. While the interest, identity, and international society approaches all provide useful insights, none, jointly or severally, provides a sufficiently thick explanation of compliance with international obligations.

Instrumentalist interest theories, by specifying variables such as payoffs and costs of compliance, discount rates, and transactions costs, seek to reduce complex habits and patterns of compliance into a large reiterated game-theoretic, in which all societies are the same and decisionmakers respond only to sanctions, not norms. The theory works best in such global issue areas as trade and arms control law, where nation-states remain the primary players, but essentially misses the transnational revolution. Not surprisingly, interest theory has thus far shown relatively little explanatory power in such areas as human rights, environmental law, debt restructuring, or international commercial transactions, where nonstate actors abound, pursue multiple goals in complex nonzero-sum games, and interact repeatedly within informal regimes.

Similarly, "liberal" identity theory, in my view, has missed the *neomonist* revolution represented by both human rights and international commercial law. Its essentialist analysis treats a state's identity as somehow exogenously or permanently given. Yet as constructivist scholars have long recognized, national identities, like national interests, are socially constructed products of learning, knowledge, cultural practices, and ideology. Nations such as South Africa, Poland, Argentina, Chile, and the Czech Republic are neither permanently liberal nor illiberal, but make transitions back and forth from dictatorship to democracy, prodded by norms and regimes of international law. Identity analysis leaves unanswered the critical, constructivist question: To what extent does compliance with international law itself help *constitute the identity* of a state as a law-abiding state, and hence, as a "liberal" state? Furthermore, the notion that "only liberal states do law with one another" can be empirically falsified, particularly in areas such as international commercial law, where states tend to abide fastidiously by international rules without regard to whether they are representative democracies. Moreover, like the discredited "cultural relativist" argument in human rights, the claim that nonliberal states somehow do not participate in a zone of law denies the universalism of international law and effectively condones the confinement of nonliberal states to a realist world of power politics.

A constructivist, international society approach at least recognizes the positive transformational effects of repeated participation in the legal process. But it does not isolate, much less fully account for, the importance of process factors that arise, not merely from the *existence* of international community, but from countless iterated transactions within it. As governmental and nongovernmental transnational actors repeatedly interact within the transnational legal process, they generate and interpret international norms and then seek to internalize those norms domestically. To the extent that those norms are successfully internalized, they become future determinants of why nations obey. The international society theorists seem to recognize that this process occurs, but have given little close study to the "transmission belt," whereby norms created by international society infiltrate into *domestic* society.

. . .

These institutional habits lead nations into default patterns of compliance. Thus, in Henkin's words, "almost all nations observe almost all principles of international law ... almost all of the time." When a nation deviates from that pattern of presumptive compliance, frictions are created. To avoid such frictions in a nation's continuing interactions, national leaders may shift over time from a policy of violation to one of compliance. It is through this transnational legal process, this repeated cycle of interaction, interpretation, and internalization, that international law acquires its "stickiness," that nation-states acquire their identity, and that nations come to "obey" international law out of perceived self-interest. In tracing the move from the external to the internal, from one-time grudging compliance with an external norm to habitual internalized obedience, the key factor is repeated participation in the transnational legal process. That participation helps to reconstitute national interests, to establish the identity of actors as ones who obey the law, and to develop the norms that become part of the fabric of emerging international society.

As I have described it, transnational legal process presents both a theoretical explanation of why nations obey and a plan of strategic action for prodding nations to obey. How, then, to study this process? Although a full account will require book-length interdisciplinary treatment, let me identify some basic inquiries, using international human rights as an example. In the human rights area, treaty regimes are notoriously weak, and national governments, for reasons of economics or *realpolitik*, are often hesitant to declare openly that another government engages in abuses. In such an area, where enforcement mechanisms are weak, but core customary norms are clearly defined and often peremptory (*jus cogens*), the best compliance strategies may not be "horizontal" regime management strategies, but rather, vertical strategies of interaction, interpretation, and internalization.

If transnational actors obey international law as a result of repeated *interaction* with other actors in the transnational legal process, a first step is to empower more actors to participate. It is here that expanding the role of intergovernmental organizations, nongovernmental organizations, private business entities, and "transnational moral entrepreneurs" deserves careful study. How, for example, do international human rights "issue networks" and epistemic communities form among international and regional intergovernmental organizations, international and domestic NGOs on human rights, and private foundations? How do these networks intersect with the "International Human Rights Regime," namely, the global system of rules and implementation procedures centered in and around the United Nations; regional regimes in Europe, the Americas, Africa, Asia, and the Middle East; single-issue human rights regimes regarding workers' rights, racial discrimination, women's rights; and "global prohibition regimes" against slavery, torture, and the like? Within national governments and intergovernmental organizations, what role do lawyers and legal advisers play in ensuring that the government's policies conform to international legal standards and in prompting governmental agencies to take proactive stances toward human rights abuses?

Second, if the goal of interaction is to produce *interpretation* of human rights norms, what fora are available for norm-enunciation and elaboration, both within and without existing human rights regimes? If dedicated fora do not already exist, how can existing fora be adapted for this purpose or new fora, such as the International Criminal Tribunal for Rwanda and the former Yugoslavia, be created?

Third, what are the best strategies for *internalization* of international human rights norms? One might distinguish among *social*, *political*, and *legal* internalization. Social internalization occurs when a norm acquires so much public legitimacy that there is widespread general obedience to it. Political internalization occurs when political elites accept an international norm, and adopt it as a matter of government policy. Legal internalization occurs when an international norm is incorporated into the domestic legal system through executive action, judicial interpretation, legislative action, or some combination of the three. The ABM Treaty controversy thus exemplified the incorporation of a norm (narrow treaty interpretation) into U.S. law and policy through the executive action of the President, acting through his delegate, the U.S. Arms Control and Disarmament Administration. Judicial internalization can occur when domestic litigation provokes judicial incorporation of human rights norms either implicitly, by construing existing statutes consistently with international human rights norms, or explicitly, through what I have elsewhere called "transnational public law litigation." Legislative internalization occurs when domestic lobbying embeds international law norms into binding domestic legislation or even constitutional law that officials of a noncomplying government must then obey as part of the domestic legal fabric.

The relationship among social, political, and legal internalization can be complex. In the Haitian refugee case, for example, U.S. human rights advocates failed to achieve judicial internalization of an international treaty norm, but in tandem with the growing social outrage about the treatment of Haitian refugees, eventually achieved political internalization: a reversal of the Clinton Administration's policy with respect to Haiti. Similarly, beginning with *Filartiga v. Pena-Irala*, U.S. human rights litigators began to promote domestic judicial incorporation of the norm against torture in a manner that eventually helped push President Bush to ratify the U.N. Convention against Torture and Congress to enact the Torture Victim Protection Act of 1991. In the United Kingdom, the issue of legislative internalization has similarly been brought to the fore by the first general election in five years, in which the opposition Labour party has promised, if elected, to incorporate the European Convention on Human Rights into U.K. law. This issue has been a major human rights issue in British politics since the Clement Attlee government first ratified the Convention in the early 1950s. Since then, the Convention has been internalized in part through judicial construction. Yet judicial refusal to recognize explicit incorporation has given new impetus to a political internalization movement that at this writing seems likely to bring about legal internalization of the European Convention into U.K. law by an act of Parliament.

Thus, the concept of transnational legal process has important implications, not just for international relations theorists, but also for activists and political leaders. For activists, the constructive role of international law in the post-Cold War era will be greatly enhanced if nongovernmental organizations seek self-consciously to participate in, influence, and ultimately enforce transnational legal process by promoting the internalization of international norms into domestic law. Nor can political leaders sensibly make foreign policy in a world bounded by global rules without understanding how legislative, judicial and executive branches can and should incorporate international legal rules into their decisionmaking.

Bringing International Law Home

HAROLD HONGJU KOH*

What Does "Obedience" Mean?

From Coincidence to Obedience

Let me begin with the *definitional* question: what does it mean for a nation to "obey" rules of international law or, for that matter, any kind of law? Let me distinguish among four kinds of relationships between stated norms and observed conduct, which for shorthand purposes I will call: coincidence, conformity, compliance, and obedience.

Suppose that after living all my life in the United States, I arrive in England on sabbatical and notice that both the law and the practice seem to be that everyone drives on the left-hand side of the road. One could imagine at least four possible relationships between the legal rule and the observed conduct.

The first is that no causal relationship exists: it is simply a massive *coincidence* that everyone appears to "follow" the same rule. Coincidence might explain, for example, why two or three consecutive cars driving off the ferry into England from France, where cars drive on the right side, might all choose to swerve to the left side of the road. But, coincidence cannot explain convincingly why millions of people disembarking should all choose to do the same.

This example suggests a second, alternative explanation: *conformity*. People might loosely conform their conduct to the left-hand drive rule when they find it convenient to do so, but feel little or no internal obligation—legal or moral—to follow the rule.

A third possibility is *compliance*, namely, that people are both aware of the rule *and* consciously accept its influence, but do so in order to gain specific rewards (*e.g.*, insurance benefits) or to avoid specific punishments (*e.g.*, traffic tickets).

The fourth possibility, *obedience*, occurs when a person or organization adopts rule-induced behavior because the party has *internalized* the norm and incorporated it into its own internal value system.

Notice that as we move down the scale from coincidence to conformity to compliance to obedience, three shifts occur. First, there is a shift from the external to the internal. We witness an increase in the degree of *norm-internalization*, or the actor's internal acceptance of the rule as a guide for behavior. As one moves from grudging, one-time acceptance

* Reprinted by permission from 35 HOUSTON LAW REVIEW 623 (1998).

to habitual obedience, the rule transforms from external sanction to internal imperative. We repeatedly observe this evolutionary process in everyday life—whenever we put on bicycle helmets, snap seat belts, recycle cans, or refrain from smoking. In each case, grudging compliance with an external rule gradually becomes habitual obedience. Over time, the norm becomes *internalized* into the regulated actor's value set.

A second shift is from the instrumental to the normative. As we move down the scale from coincidence to obedience, we see an increase in *normatively driven conduct*. When a car careening along the highway temporarily slows to sixty miles per hour to pass a parked police car, then speeds up again, we can conclude that the driver is complying, but not necessarily obeying. We think of compliance as a calculated, *instrumental* form of behavior that occurs in response to specific *external* factors, here to avoid the sanction of a ticket. But when we observe a driver routinely driving sixty miles per hour, without regard for the police, we can conclude that we are witnessing an *internalized normative form of behavior* deriving from norms of legitimacy, fairness, or obligation that have become integral to that person's value set.

A third shift is from the coercive to the constitutive. We intuitively understand that the best way to get people to worship, to stop smoking, to start jogging, or to pay their taxes is not to coerce them, but to convince them to think of themselves as religious, non-smokers, joggers, or taxpayers. The most effective legal regulation thus aims to be *constitutive*, in the sense of seeking to shape and *transform personal identity*. As my colleague Bob Ellickson has noted, self-enforcement is widely recognized as both more effective and more efficient than third-party controls. Thus, whether the slogan is "Just say no," "Let's recycle," "Don't be a litterbug," or "Don't drive drunk," we intuitively recognize that an internalized system of self-enforcement is a better way to ensure widespread compliance with the law than such external sanctions as "three strikes and you're out." So, as we move down the scale of internalization and normativity toward greater obedience, we observe not just increasing social conformity with declared rules, but also the gradual *transformation* and *reconstitution* of a person's identity from lawless to law-abiding.

Indeed, thinking in terms of obedience has significant policy implications for all legal regulators. For if our goal is more compliance with prescribed rules, our preferred regulatory strategy is not so much coerced compliance, as it is more *obedience*, or what may be thought of as *internalized compliance*....

Notes and Comments

1. Although O'Connell highlights the normative content of New International Legal Process, Koh takes the reconceptualization of international legal process much further, emphasizing the role of domestic factors. As he summarizes in his article on transnational legal process:

> Transnational legal process has four distinctive features. First, it is nontraditional: it breaks down two traditional dichotomies that have historically dominated the study of international law: between domestic and international, public and private. Second, it is nonstatist: the actors in this process are not just, or even primarily, nation-states, but include nonstate actors as well. Third, transnational legal process is dynamic, not static. Transnational law transforms, mutates, and percolates up and down, from the public to the private, from the domestic to the international level and back down again. Fourth and finally, it is normative. From this process of interaction, new rules of law emerge, which are interpreted, internalized, and enforced, thus beginning the process all over again. Thus, the concept embraces not just the descriptive workings of a process, but the normativity of that process. It focuses not simply upon how international interaction among transnational actors shapes law, but also on how law shapes and guides future interactions: in short, how law influences why nations obey.

Harold Hongju Koh, *Transnational Legal Process*, 75 Nebraska Law Review 181, 184 (1996).

2. Like the Liberal approach described earlier, a transnational legal process approach focuses on domestic constitutional and legal structure as an important factor in promoting compliance. Yet a transnational legal process approach is less focused on the structure of domestic systems, than upon the two-level game that transpires when actors pursue norm-enunciation in one forum with an eye toward promoting norm-compliance in another forum. For a parallel, international relations perspective on the interplay between domestic and international politics, see Robert Putnam's classic article, *Diplomacy and Domestic Politics: The Logic of Two–Level Games*, 42 International Organization 427 (1988).

3. How can we reconcile the "horizontal" and "transnational" approaches? How do interactions among nonstate actors influence states and their intergovernmental relations? How might the process of norm-internalization relate to the process of managing compliance at the intergovernmental level, through clarity and state capacity?

4. Within the American legal academy, the transnational legal process approach found important intellectual roots not just in the Harvard School of International Legal Process, but also in the Policy Science or New Haven School of International Law, pioneered at Yale by Myres McDougal, Harold Lasswell, and their associates. The Policy Science school had argued that transnational actors' compliance with transnational law could be explained by reference to the process by which these actors interact in a variety of public and private fora to translate claims of legal authority into national behavior. The New Haven School grew out of the American theory of legal realism, which focused on the interplay between rules and social process in enunciating the law. Laura Kalman, Legal Realism At Yale, 1927–1960 (1986). The New Haven School sought to develop "a functional critique of international law in terms of social ends . . . that shall conceive of the legal order as a process and not as a condition." ROSCOE POUND, PHILOSOPHICAL THEORY AND INTERNATIONAL LAW, quoted in Myres McDougal, INTERNATIONAL LAW, POWER AND POLICY: A CONTEMPORARY CONCEPTION 137 (1954) For a jurisprudential history of the New Haven School, see NEIL DUXBURY, PATTERNS OF AMERICAN JURISPRUDENCE 191–203 (1995).

"Within the decision-making process," McDougal and Lasswell wrote, "our chief interest is in the legal process, by which we mean the making of authoritative and controlling decisions." Myres S. McDougal & Harold D. Lasswell, *The Identification and Appraisal of Diverse Systems of Public Order*, 53 AMERICAN JOURNAL OF INTERNATIONAL LAW 1, 9 (2004). In its modern incarnation as the "World Public Order" school, New Haven School leaders Myres McDougal and W. Michael Reisman argue that international law is itself a "world constitutive process of authoritative decision," not merely a set of rules, whose goal is a world public order of human dignity, designed to serve particular ends and values by establishing regimes of effective control. While Myres McDougal and W. Michael Reisman elaborated the claims of policy science in various fields of public international law, they were joined in that effort by scholars of such diverse political orientation as Richard Falk, John Norton Moore, Rosalyn Higgins, Oscar Schachter, and Burns Weston, who share the School's process methodology without adopting its social ends or policy values. As one prominent member of the school, Dame Rosalyn Higgins (now British judge on the International Court of Justice), put it: "International law is a process, a system of authoritative decision-making. It is not just the neutral application of rules.... The role of international law is to assist in the choice between ... various alternatives [arguably prescribed by existing rules]. International law is a process for resolving problems." ROSALYN HIGGINS, PROBLEMS AND PROCESS 267 (1994). But over time, the New Haven School's overriding focus on value-orientation came to trouble even those who sympathized with its methodological ambitions. By connecting process and context with an overriding set of normative values, critics argued, "[i]f applied with a nationalist bias, [the New Haven approach] becomes an ideological instrument to override specific restraints of law ...[,] a unilateralist vision of policy jurisprudence in which law plays a secondary role and policy is determined by the perception of self-interest of a particular state." See Symposium, *McDougal's Jurisprudence: Utility, Influence, Controversy*, 79 AMERICAN SOCIETY OF INTERNATIONAL LAW PROCEEDINGS 266, 271 (1985) (remarks of Oscar Schachter).

5. Consider some more recent examples of transnational legal process at work after the terrorist attacks of September 11, 2001:

a. The efforts of human rights activists to bring about judicial review of the conditions and status of detainees at the U.S. naval base at Guantanamo Bay, Cuba through litigation in U.S. and British courts as well as the Inter–American Human Rights Commission. See *Rasul v. Bush*, 124 S. Ct. 2686 (2004).

b. Activity in the United States courts to clarify the status and due process rights of U.S. citizens, such as Yasser Hamdi and Jose

Padilla, being held in U.S. military facilities as suspected terrorists. See *Rumsfeld v. Padilla*, 124 S. Ct. 2711 (2004); *Hamdi v. Rumsfeld*, 124 S. Ct. 2633 (2004).

c. Efforts to limit the use of the death penalty in the United States in light of contrary international law norms. In the LaGrand Case (*F.R.G. v. U.S.*), 2001 I.C.J. 104 (June 27), Germany sued the United States in the World Court for threatening to execute two German nationals without according them rights pursuant to the Vienna Convention on Consular Relations. Although the ICJ issued provisional measures enjoining the execution of Karl LaGrand, American officials essentially ignored the orders, the United States Supreme Court declined to intervene, and LaGrand was executed. See generally Symposium, *Reflections on the ICJ's LaGrand Decision: Foreword*, 27 YALE JOURNAL OF INTERNATIONAL LAW 423, 424 (2002). In *Avena v. Other Mexican Nationals (Mexico v. United States)*, March 31, 2004, available at http://www.icj-cij.org/icjwww/idocket/imus/imusframe.htm, the International Court of Justice ruled that the United States had breached its obligations to Mexico and to 51 Mexican nationals by the failure of state officials to inform the detained foreign nationals of their right to contact consular officials for assistance under the Vienna Convention before sentencing them to death. The ICJ directed the United States to review and reconsider the convictions and sentences of the Mexican nationals in light of the treaty violation. At this writing, a number of cases pending before the U.S. Supreme Court again raise the question of whether the Court should pay some form of deference to the ruling of the International Court of Justice when reviewing the death sentence of a Mexican national who failed to receive the consular notifications required by the Vienna Convention. See, e.g., No. 04–5928, *Medellin v. Dretke, reviewing* 371 F.3d 270 (5th Cir. 2004).

d. For a discussion of these and other post–9/11 developments, see Harold Hongju Koh, *Transnational Legal Process After September 11th*, 22 BERKELEY JOURNAL OF INTERNATIONAL LAW 337 (2004).

6. Another intriguing development in U.S. courts has been the increasing willingness of the United States Supreme Court to consider international practice when construing provisions of the United States Constitution. This is a form of norm-internalization, inasmuch as international norms are shaping the way in which a domestic court construes its own fundamental law. For recent examples, see *Lawrence v. Texas,* 123 S. Ct. 2472 (2003) (construing constitutional right of privacy in light of European human rights understandings of privacy); *Atkins v. Virginia*, 536 U.S. 304 (2002) (striking down the practice of executing persons with mental retardation under the Eighth Amendment's "cruel and unusual punishments clause," and taking into account the view of the international community). For a discussion of these cases, see generally Harold Hongju Koh, *International Law as Part of Our Law*, 98 AMERICAN JOURNAL OF INTERNATIONAL LAW 43 (2004).

IV

Applications

Our examination of the scholarship of international law and politics has thus far focused on the various theoretical frameworks that have been used by scholars to understand state behavior. We now turn to the task of applying those theories in particular areas of global concern—human rights, trade, the environment, humanitarian intervention, international criminal law, and war. In each area we offer works that give contrasting perspectives on a set of issues that are important to modern global governance.

We can offer here only a small slice of the rich set of debates currently raging over how best to understand—and shape—states' actions and decisions. It is our hope that readers will take these readings as a starting point for debate, and consider how the different theoretical perspectives offered in the first part of the book might illuminate the issues raised herein. Is there an approach to explaining state conduct that serves as the best guide to understanding the actions of states outlined in all of the different contexts? Are some theories good at explaining what states do under some conditions but less successful at explaining what they do under others? We hope that, by considering the power of the theories to explain state action in these real world contexts, readers will begin to form a better understanding of how states behave and what role international law and politics can play in shaping what states do.

A. Human Rights

International human rights law is the ideal starting point for efforts to understand state behavior. Over the last half-century, human rights have moved from the periphery to the center of international global governance efforts. Nonetheless, states' decisions to join human rights treaties are difficult to explain. Unlike many other treaties, human rights treaties do not offer states any obvious material benefits. Why, for example, would a state want to join an agreement that requires it to provide fair trials (a potentially expensive and intrusive prospect) when all it receives in return is a reciprocal promise by other members to treat their own citizens with similar respect. Moreover, the major engines of compliance that exist in other areas of international law are for the most part absent in the area of human rights. Unlike the public international law of money, for example, there are no "competitive market forces" that press for compliance. And, unlike in the case of trade agreements, the costs of retaliatory noncompliance are low to nonexistent because a nation's actions against its own citizens do not directly threaten or harm other states. Human rights law thus stands out as an area of international law in which countries have little incentive to police noncompliance with treaties or norms.

At the heart of recent scholarship over international human rights are two interrelated questions: Why do states ratify international treaties on human rights and what influence do those treaties have on what states actually do? The excerpts below provide three contrasting perspectives on these issues. Andrew Moravcsik, writing from the republican liberal view, examines the origins of the European Convention for the Protection of Human Rights and Fundamental Freedoms and offers a counterintuitive explanation for the creation of the most successful human rights regime in existence. Next, Margaret Keck and Kathryn Sikkink offer a constructivist argument that sheds light on how non-state actors contribute to the adoption and enforcement of human rights norms by states. Finally, in a piece that seeks to expose and fill gaps in existing theoretical accounts of state behavior, Oona Hathaway examines why states ratify the Convention against Torture and the impact that decision has on those states' behavior.

The Origins of Human Rights Regimes: Democratic Delegation in Postwar Europe*

ANDREW MORAVCSIK

The fiftieth anniversary of the UN Universal Declaration on Human Rights marks an appropriate moment to reconsider the reasons why governments construct international regimes to adjudicate and enforce human rights. Such regimes include those established under the European Convention for the Protection of Human Rights and Fundamental Freedoms (ECHR), the Inter-American Convention on Human Rights, and the UN Covenant on Civil and Political Rights.

* Reprinted by permission from 54 INTERNATIONAL ORGANIZATION 217 (2000).

These arrangements differ from most other forms of institutionalized international cooperation in both their ends and their means. Unlike international institutions governing trade, monetary, environmental, or security policy, international human rights institutions are not designed primarily to regulate policy externalities arising from societal interactions across borders, but to hold governments accountable for purely internal activities. In contrast to most international regimes, moreover, human rights regimes are not generally enforced by interstate action. Although most arrangements formally empower governments to challenge one another, such challenges almost never occur. The distinctiveness of such regimes lies instead in their empowerment of individual citizens to bring suit to challenge the domestic activities of their own government. Independent courts and commissions attached to such regimes often respond to such individual claims by judging that the application of domestic rules or legislation violates international commitments, even where such legislation has been enacted and enforced through fully democratic procedures consistent with the domestic rule of law. Arrangements to adjudicate human rights internationally thus pose a fundamental challenge not just to the Westphalian ideal of state sovereignty that underlies realist international relations theory and classical international law but also—though less-frequently noted—to liberal ideals of direct democratic legitimacy and self-determination. The postwar emergence of these arrangements has rightly been characterized as the most "radical development in the whole history of international law."

. . .

There is a real theoretical puzzle here. Why would any government, democratic or dictatorial, favor establishing an effective independent international authority, the sole purpose of which is to constrain its domestic sovereignty in such an unprecedentedly invasive and overtly nonmajoritarian manner?

To answer questions such as this, political scientists tend to espouse either a realist or an ideational explanation for the emergence and expansion of formal human rights regimes.[1] Democratic governments and transnationally active members of democratic civil societies either coerce other governments to accept human rights norms (the realist view) or persuade other governments to do so (the ideational view). Some scholars espouse both positions at once, arguing that powerful democracies are persuaded for essentially idealistic reasons to coerce others to respect human rights norms.

. . .

Republican Liberalism: Democratic Peace and Domestic Commitment

If realist and ideational explanations view the motivations for establishing human rights regimes as involving international coercion or

1. [Editors' Note: Realism is discussed in greater depth in Part II.A. of this reader. Moreover, what Moravcsik labels "ideational" explanations are discussed herein under the heading "norm-based" theories in Part III.]

persuasion, a "republican liberal" explanation views them as resulting from instrumental calculations about domestic politics. In general, republican liberal theories stress the impact of varying domestic political institutions—in particular, the scope and bias of political representation—on foreign policy. The most prominent among such theories include institutional explanations of the "democratic peace," yet the family of republican liberal theories offers a far wider range of potential explanations, subsuming theories of the role of cartelized elites and independent militaries in provoking war, and of interest group capture (or the countervailing delegation of authority to strong executives) in foreign economic policy. In contrast to the idealist theories considered earlier, which assume that social actors are responsive to external socialization and often altruistically motivated, republican liberal theories assume that states are self-interested and rational in their pursuit of (varying) underlying national interests, which reflect in turn variation in the nature of domestic social pressures and representative institutions.

A useful republican liberal starting point for the problem at hand is to assume that international institutional commitments, like domestic institutional commitments, are self-interested means of "locking in" particular preferred domestic policies—at home and abroad—in the face of future political uncertainty. This presumption, which is not only consistent with republican liberalism but also draws on theories widely employed to explain domestic delegation to courts and regulatory authorities in American and comparative politics, treats domestic politics as a game in which politicians compete to exercise public authority. Terry Moe observes that "most political institutions . . . arise out of a politics of structural choice in which the winners use their temporary hold on public authority to design new structures and impose them on the polity as a whole. . . . [Institutions are] weapons of coercion and redistribution . . . the structural means by which political winners pursue their own interests, often at the great expense of political losers." Governments establish courts, administrative agencies, central banks, and other independent bodies as means by which the winners of political conflict seek to commit the polity to preferred policies. From this perspective, a rational decision to delegate to an independent body requires that a sitting government weigh two crosscutting considerations: *restricting government discretion* and *reducing domestic political uncertainty.*

Consider first the surrender of national discretion, which in the international context might be termed the *sovereignty cost* of delegation to an international authority. All other things equal, governments in power prefer to maintain short-term discretion to shape collective behavior or redistribute wealth as they see fit. They are therefore inherently skeptical of delegation to independent judges or officials, since there is always some "agency cost" to the operation of central banks, administrative agencies, courts, and other quasi-independent political authorities. Judges, in particular, may seek to negate government actions by nullifying them outright or by failing to enforce them effectively. Legal scholars William Landes and Richard Posner observe that "the outcomes of the struggle can readily be nullified by unsympathetic judges—and why should judges be sympathetic to a process that simply ratifies political power rather than expresses principle?" They point to the sixty years preceding the New Deal in the United States, during which the federal judiciary obstructed reforms favored by Congress.

In the international realm, the defense of governmental discretion translates into the defense of national sovereignty. All other things equal, the "sovereignty cost" of delegating to an international judge is likely to be even greater than that of delegating to a domestic judge. One reason is that cross national variation in the precise nature, scope, application, and enforcement of human rights is likely to be greater than domestic variation. Any common international list of human rights is therefore likely to diverge further from individual national traditions and practices. In the most extreme cases, for example, Great Britain, international human rights regimes introduce an explicitly enumerated bill of rights for the first time. Many international human rights regimes establish, moreover, single, centralized institutional mechanisms for interpreting, enforcing, and balancing various rights. For such bodies to develop a coherent jurisprudence, they must override local particularities. Whereas judicially imposed harmonization may seem attractive to those who draft international covenants, it clearly imposes inconvenient constraints on individual national governments. Particularly for nations without a constitutional court—again, Britain is a striking example—the procedure marks a significant innovation. These inconveniences may arise, moreover, not simply as a result of pressure from parochial special interests or unthinking adherence to tradition, but also through divergence in deeply rooted historical conceptions of the relationship between citizens and the state. From this perspective, the defense of "national sovereignty" is, in part, a legitimate defense of national ideals, political culture, and even democratic practices—a problem of which the framers of post–World War II human rights documents (and their academic advisers) were quite aware.

Why would a national government, democratic or not, ever accept such external normative and institutional constraints on its sovereignty? The answer lies in the second major consideration that enters into a government's decision whether to delegate to an independent political body: reducing political uncertainty. In the republican liberal view, politicians delegate power to human rights regimes, such as domestic courts and administrative agencies, to constrain the behavior of future national governments. As Moe explains, a politician must always calculate that "while the right to exercise public authority happens to be theirs today, other political actors with different and perhaps opposing interests may gain that right tomorrow." To limit the consequences of this eventuality, government authorities may thus seek to "lock in" favored policies in such a way, thereby insulating them from the actions of future governments.

From this perspective, human rights norms are expressions of the self-interest of democratic governments in "locking in" democratic rule through the enforcement of human rights. By placing interpretation in the hands of independent authorities managed in part by foreign governments—in other words, by alienating sovereignty to an international body—governments seek to establish reliable judicial constraints on future nondemocratic governments or on democratically elected governments that may seek (as in interwar Italy and Germany) to subvert democracy from within. In the language of international relations theory, this "two level" commitment "ties the hands" of future governments, thereby enhancing the credibility of current domestic policies and institutions. Salient and symbolic international constraints serve as signals to trigger domestic, and perhaps also transnational and international, opposition to any breach of the democratic order. Thus democratic regimes seek to prevent political retrogression or "backsliding" into tyranny.

The decision of any individual government whether to support a binding international human rights enforcement regime depends, in this view, on the relative importance of these two basic factors: Sovereignty costs are weighted against establishing human rights regimes, whereas greater political stability may be weighted in favor of it. If we assume that the inconvenience governments face is constant (or randomly distributed), it follows that a country is most likely to support a human rights regime when its government is firmly committed to democratic governance but faces strong internal challenges that may threaten it in the future. Its willingness to tolerate *sovereignty costs* increases insofar as the costs are outweighed by the benefits of reducing *domestic political uncertainty.*

If the republican liberal view is correct, *the strongest support for binding human rights regimes should come not from established democracies but from recently established and potentially unstable democracies.* Only where democracy is established but nondemocratic groups (military officers, communists, fascists, and religious fundamentalists, for example) pose real threats to its future is the reduction of political uncertainty likely to outweigh the inconvenience of supranational adjudication.

It is obvious that opposition will come in part from *dictatorships* (or transitional regimes), since such governments both lack any interest in democracy and suffer particularly large inconveniences from persistent challenges to their (nondemocratic) domestic order. (Governments striving to complete a transition to democracy through extralegal means are likely to be almost as skeptical.) Less obvious and in striking contrast to realist and idealist accounts, however, is the prediction that dictatorships will be joined in opposition to binding commitments by well-established liberal democracies. By accepting binding obligations, governments in established democracies incur an increased, if modest, risk of de facto nullification of domestic laws without a corresponding increase in the expected stability of domestic democracy, since the latter is already high. Such governments have good reason—indeed, a democratically legitimate reason—to reject any reciprocal imposition of international adjudication and enforcement of human rights claims.

This is not to say that established democracies never have an incentive to support international human rights instruments. According to republican liberal theory, established democracies have an incentive to promote such arrangements for others—which may involve some small risk of future pressure on established democracies to deepen their commitment—in order to bolster the "democratic peace" by fostering democracy in neighboring countries. This is most likely to occur when democratization is expected to pacify a potentially threatening neighbor or solidify opposition to a common nondemocratic enemy. In such cases, established democracies can be expected to support rhetorical declarations in favor of human rights and regimes with optional enforcement that bind newly established democracies but exempt themselves. Yet there is little reason to believe that this concern will outweigh domestic interests; thus they are likely to remain opposed to reciprocally enforceable rules. Further observable implications concerning national tactics and confidential discussions are developed in the next section.

Testing the Theories: The Negotiation of the ECHR

What light does the negotiating history of the ECHR cast on the power of these three competing theories? The negotiation of the ECHR took place between 1949 and 1953 under the auspices of the Council of Europe. At the first session of the Council of Europe's Consultative Assembly in September 1949, its legal committee under the chairmanship of the Frenchman Pierre–Henri Teitgen recommended that an organization be created to ensure adherence to human rights in Europe. Extended meetings of governmental committees and consultations with the assembly itself through the first half of 1950 led to the signing of the ECHR, which came into force three years later.

Realist, ideational, and liberal institutional theories all offer prima facie explanations for the general form and timing of the ECHR's establishment. For realists, this period marked the dawning of an "American century" and a moment in which the West became embroiled in a bipolar conflict with the Soviet Union. For ideational theorists, it immediately followed the Holocaust, a salient historical event of considerable moral force, and occurred immediately after the rise to salient Western leadership of two long-established democratic exemplars, the United States and the United Kingdom. During the immediate postwar period, republican liberals might observe, a wave of new liberal democracies emerged (or reemerged) across Western Europe. Nondemocratic institutions were widely viewed as a source of both World War II and the Cold War, and, accordingly, the democratization of Germany, Italy, and other West European nations was seen as a guarantee against both a revival of fascism and the spread of communism.

To assess the relative importance of these three plausible theories, we therefore require more fine-grained evidence than a simple coincidence of timing or the existence of occasional public rhetorical justification. I consider three types of evidence: the cross-national pattern of national positions, the process of international negotiation, and the direct documentary record of national motivations. What does the historical record reveal?

Cross-National Variation in National Preferences

We have seen that both realist and ideational theories predict that the most firmly established and committed democracies (or democratic great powers)—in short, the major Western powers led by the United States and the United Kingdom—would have been the primary supporters of binding international human rights norms. On the contrary, the historical record strongly supports the republican liberal theory, which predicts that newly established democracies will spearhead support for binding international human rights guarantees, whereas long-established democracies will support only rhetorical or optional commitments—and even these only where needed to bolster the "democratic peace." Dictatorships or governments that have not completed the transition to democracy will be opposed outright.

We can measure the willingness of governments to accept binding obligations by examining their position on two related elements of the institutional design of the ECHR—both essential to the future effectiveness of the regime.

- *Compulsory jurisdiction:* Should the regime mandate that member states recognize the jurisdiction of an independent international court, as opposed to a body of foreign ministers?
- *Individual petition:* Should the regime mandate that member states grant private individuals and groups standing to file cases?

Since both mandatory binding jurisdiction *and* individual petition are required to render a system of international human rights adjudication effective, a vote for both is defined as support for a reciprocally binding regime, whereas a vote against either marks opposition. Positions on these two issues generated parallel (if not precisely identical) coalitions among national governments, suggesting that they tap a single underlying dimension of state preference.

To investigate the relationship between democratic governance and support for binding regimes, we also require a measure of how stable a democracy is expected to be. European political systems involved in the negotiations can be divided into three categories. The first category, "established democracies," contains those systems that had been continuously under democratic rule since before 1920 and remained so thereafter: Belgium, Denmark, Luxembourg, Netherlands, Norway, Sweden, Netherlands, and the United Kingdom. (Occupation is not coded as a suspension of domestic democracy, but the establishment of a nondemocratic domestic regime is—for example, Vichy France.) The second category, "new democracies," contains those that were firmly established during the negotiations and remained so thereafter, but only since a point between 1920 and 1950: Austria, France, Italy, Iceland, Ireland, and West Germany. The third category, "semidemocracies and dictatorships," contains the two governments that were not fully democratic by 1950, because of civil war or internal repression (and did not remain so thereafter), namely Greece and Turkey. Spain and Portugal, though not involved in the negotiations, also belong in this category.

Turning to the findings, we see little evidence of the positive correlation between support for binding regimes and power or length of democratic rule predicted by realist and idealist theory. Instead, we observe the inverse-U-shaped relationship between the stability of democracy and support for binding human rights commitments predicted by republican liberal theory. Table 2 summarizes the findings. All six new democracies (plus one of the ten long established democracies, Belgium) support binding human rights guarantees. In contrast, six of the seven established democracies join the four transitional governments and nondemocracies in opposing one or both such guarantees (or, in the case of Luxembourg, abstaining). Even the sole exception, Belgium, is not fully disconfirming, since Belgian representatives originally sided with the other established democracies against binding guarantees, shifting their position only late in the negotiations. The correlation is so strong that even recategorization of borderline cases—France and Turkey, say—would not undermine the striking relationship.

. . .

TABLE 2. *Stability of democratic governance and national positions on the European Convention on Human Rights*

	Unstable or nondemocracies (stable democracy not yet clearly established by 1950)	*New democracies (continuous democracies only since a date between 1920 and 1950)*	*Established democracies (continuous democracy since a date before 1920)*
Supports enforcement (individual petition and compulsory jurisdiction mandatory)	—	Austria, France, Italy, Iceland, Ireland, Germany	Belgium
Opposes enforcement (individual petition and/or compulsory jurisdiction optional or absent)	Greece, Turkey (Portugal, Spain)	—	Denmark, Sweden, Netherlands, Norway, United Kingdom, Luxembourg

Republican liberal theory also seems to offer the most accurate account of the instrumental attitude governments adopted toward more detailed provisions of the ECHR. Should the convention create, governments asked themselves, an independent court, a quasi-judicial body of government representatives, or no central institution at all? Cleavages around this issue were similar to those around compulsory jurisdiction and individual petition, with opponents of effective enforcement opposing the court. Governments favorable to binding human rights adjudication proposed that the members of the intermediary Commission on Human Rights be nominated by the court—a clear effort to render international institutions more independent—whereas more skeptical governments favored granting power of nomination to the intergovernmental Committee of Ministers.

Similar cleavages formed around the enumeration of rights. Some skeptics considered delaying the proceedings, as well as limiting future uncertainty, by pressing for a precise enumeration of rights or transferring the issue to the less effective UN Commission on Human Rights. In the end, the precise enumeration of rights, which was considerably narrower than that granted by any member state with such a constitutional enumeration, resulted from a careful calculation of instrumental, self regarding considerations. Representatives of right and left wing parties were concerned about the status of particular laws favored by their constituencies. Social Democratic representatives assured that social welfare rights were not threatened and that property rights did not restrict state intervention. Christian Democratic representatives assured that rights of private familial, educational, and religious choice were maintained, while opposing any right to redistribution of property. The final document offended neither side, because it was constrained to include only the least controversial among basic political and civil rights.

. . .

Generalizing the Argument: Human Rights and Beyond

We have seen that the origins of the ECHR, the most successful international human rights adjudication and enforcement regime in the world today, lies not in coercive power politics or socialization to idealistic norms, as contemporary international relations theories predict. Instead its origins lie in self-interested efforts by newly established (or reestablished) democracies to employ international commitments to consolidate democracy—"locking in" the domestic political status quo against their nondemocratic opponents. This empirical finding has three broader implications for future research on domestic politics and international relations.

The Origin and Evolution of Human Rights Regimes

The first implication of the theoretical argument is that the tendency of states to enhance the credibility of domestic policies by binding themselves to international institutions may help explain the origins and evolution of human rights enforcement regimes more generally. In negotiations to create the Inter-American Convention on Human Rights, the UN Covenants, and the emergent African human rights system, we should expect to see a similar pattern of support from new democracies, suspicion from established democracies, and hostility from dictatorships.

. . .

Republican liberal theory also explains a troubling anomaly for scholars and activists alike, namely, the consistent unwillingness of the United States to accept multilateral constraints on its domestic human rights practices under the Inter–American and UN systems. This unwillingness is generally attributed to ad hoc, idiosyncratic factors: the United States' superpower status (as is often said of its opposition to binding UN obligations), its uniquely segregated southern states (as is often said of support for the Bricker Amendment in the early 1950s),[2] or its unique political institutions (federalism and supermajoritarian treaty ratification rules). From the republican liberal perspective, in contrast, U.S. skepticism is the norm, not the exception, among established democracies—a norm related to the relatively low level of offsetting domestic benefits in an established, self-confident democracy, not the nature of American objections per se.

. . .

Generalizing the Theory to Other Issue Areas

A second direction for future research is to extend the theory to cooperation in other issue-areas. Despite the "republican liberal" label, the theoretical distinctiveness of the explanation advanced here is only incidentally connected to the liberal content of the philosophy embodied in human rights regimes. In other words, the argument is *theoretically* rather than substantively liberal. Distinct to republican liberal theory is the decisive role of domestic political representation in world politics and, by extension, the possibility that international institutions, like their domestic counterparts, can enhance the credibility of domestic political commitments, thereby "locking in" current policies. Whether or not governments are "liberal," international institutions may "strengthen the state" domestically by expanding its domestic control over initiative, information, ideas, and institutions. Compared with more conventional "functional" theories of international regimes, which stress reciprocal commitments to manage transnational societal transactions, this analysis points to a more purely domestic or "two-level" motivation for establishing international institutions.

Under what general conditions should we expect to observe international commitments of this kind? Republican liberal theory suggests three conditions: (1) governments fear future domestic political uncertainty, (2) the position of the national government is supported by a consensus of foreign governments, and (3) international cooperation helps induce domestic actors to support the maintenance of current policies.

. . .

2. [Editors' Note: The Bricker Amendment, which was introduced into the Senate in February 1952 and which enjoyed strong support in the South, would have amended the Constitution to provide that any treaty that conflicts with the Constitution would have no force or effect and that treaties could only become effective in the United States through legislative enactment.]

Realism and Idealism in International Relations Theory

The third and broadest implication of this analysis is that it counsels caution about the uncritical acceptance of certain ideational explanations for the emergence of international norms. Recent scholarship has been quick to assume that if realist (or regime) theory fails to explain international cooperation—say, in areas like human rights and environmental policy—the motivation for cooperation must lie in ideational socialization to altruistic beliefs. This assumption, once termed "idealist" or "utopian," seems plausible at first glance. The realist explanation for the emergence of human rights norms is manifestly weak. In a modern world increasingly dominated by liberal democratic practice, human rights seem salient and attractive ideals. Political action to protect them, moreover, clearly requires mobilizing a diffuse constituency in favor of the provision of what is in fact a public good, which in turn often requires that political actors issue strong normative appeals. Ideational theorists have little trouble finding public professions of moral conviction to support their view.

Yet scholars should not jump too quickly to the conclusion—as many recent studies of foreign aid, arms control, slavery, racism, and human rights invite them to do—that altruism must motivate the establishment of morally attractive international norms. The tendency to jump to this conclusion demonstrates the danger of conducting debates about world politics around the simple dichotomy of realism versus idealism (or realism versus constructivism), as seems the current norm. Presumptive evidence for the importance of altruistic or "principled" motivations vis-à-vis a realist account may melt away, as we have seen, as soon as the underlying theory is tested against more sophisticated rationalist, yet nonrealist (in this case, liberal) theories of self-interested political behavior. Moreover, to establish methodologically the existence of altruistic motivations and socialization processes, rather than alternative liberal theories, one must do more than cite public professions of idealism, document the actions of moral entrepreneurs, or invoke the desirability of the ultimate end. Talk and even mobilization are often cheap and often redundant or futile; accordingly, such evidence is often misleading. Cross-national comparison and primary-source documentation of decision making are the critical tests.

In the case of the establishment of the ECHR, the proper theory and method reverses an idealist conclusion that might appear to offer a plausible alternative to realism. What seems at first to be a conversion to moral altruism is in fact an instrumental calculation of how best to lock in democratic governance against future opponents—a practice hardly distinct from similar practices in the most pecuniary areas of world politics, such as trade and monetary policy. I am not denying, of course, that ideas and ideals matter in foreign policy; I am challenging only a particular idealist argument. Surely some domestic support for democratic governance may be ideological, even idealistic, in origin. But if we can learn a single lesson from the formation of the world's most successful formal arrangement for international human rights enforcement, it is that in world politics pure idealism begets pure idealism—in the form of parliamentary assemblies and international declarations. To establish binding international commitments, much more is required.

Activists Beyond Borders*

MARGARET E. KECK and KATHRYN SIKKINK

World politics at the end of the twentieth century involves, alongside states, many nonstate actors that interact with each other, with states, and with international organizations. These interactions are structured in terms of networks, and transnational networks are increasingly visible in international politics. Some involve economic actors and firms. Some are networks of scientists and experts whose professional ties and shared causal ideas underpin their efforts to influence policy. Others are networks of activists, distinguishable largely by the centrality of principled ideas or values in motivating their formation. We will call these *transnational advocacy networks*.

Advocacy networks are significant transnationally and domestically. By building new links among actors in civil societies, states, and international organizations, they multiply the channels of access to the international system. In such issue areas as the environment and human rights, they also make international resources available to new actors in domestic political and social struggles. By thus blurring the boundaries between a state's relations with its own nationals and the recourse both citizens and states have to the international system, advocacy networks are helping to transform the practice of national sovereignty.

. . .

Scholars have been slow to recognize either the rationality or the significance of activist networks. Motivated by values rather than by material concerns or professional norms, these networks fall outside our accustomed categories. More than other kinds of transnational actors, advocacy networks often reach beyond policy change to advocate and instigate changes in the institutional and principled basis of international interactions. When they succeed, they are an important part of an explanation for changes in world politics. A transnational advocacy network includes those relevant actors working internationally on an issue, who are bound together by shared values, a common discourse, and dense exchanges of information and services. Such networks are most prevalent in issue areas characterized by high value content and informational uncertainty. At the core of the relationship is information exchange. What is novel in these networks is the ability of nontraditional international actors to mobilize information strategically to help create new issues and categories and to persuade, pressure, and gain leverage over much more powerful organizations and governments. Activists in networks try not only to influence policy outcomes, but to transform the terms and nature of the debate. They are not always successful in their efforts, but they are increasingly relevant players in policy debates.

Transnational advocacy networks are proliferating, and their goal is to change the behavior of states and of international organizations. Simultaneously principled and strategic actors, they "frame" issues to make them comprehensible to target audiences, to attract attention and encourage action, and to "fit" with favorable institutional venues. Network actors bring new ideas, norms, and discourses into policy debates, and serve as sources of information and testimony. Norms, here, follow the usage given by Peter Katzenstein,

> to describe collective expectations for the proper behavior of actors with a given identity. In some situations norms operate like rules that define the identity of an actor, thus having "constitutive effects" that specify what actions will cause relevant others to recognize a particular identity.

They also promote norm implementation, by pressuring target actors to adopt new policies, and by monitoring compliance with international standards. Insofar as is possible, they seek to maximize their influence or leverage over the target of their actions. In doing so they contribute to changing perceptions that both state and societal actors may have of their identities, interests, and preferences, to transforming their discursive positions, and ultimately to changing procedures, policies, and behavior.

Networks are communicative structures. To influence discourse, procedures, and policy, activists may engage and become part of larger policy communities that group actors working on an issue from a variety of institutional and value perspectives. Transnational advocacy networks must also be understood as political spaces, in which differently situated actors negotiate—formally or informally—the social, cultural, and political meanings of their joint enterprise.

We refer to transnational networks (rather than coalitions, movements, or civil society) to evoke the structured and structuring dimension in the actions of these complex agents, who not only participate in new areas of politics but also shape them. By importing the network concept from sociology and applying it transnationally, we bridge the increasingly artificial divide between international and national realms. Still, social science theories did not dictate our choice of "network" as the name to be given to the phenomena we are studying. The actors themselves did: over the last two decades, individuals and organizations have consciously formed and named transnational networks, developed and shared networking strategies and techniques, and assessed the advantages and limits of this kind of activity. Scholars have come late to the party.

Given our enterprise, it should be clear that we reject the separation common in our discipline between international relations and comparative politics. Moreover, even liberal theories of international relations that recognize that domestic interests shape states' actions internationally, and that states are embedded in an interdependent world where nonstate actors are consequential, cannot explain the phenomena we describe. Robert Putnam's "two-level game" metaphor has taken liberal theorists some distance toward seeing international relations as a two-way street, in which political entrepreneurs bring international influence to bear on domestic politics at the same time that domestic politics shapes their international positions. But however valuable its insights, even this two-way street is too narrow, implying a limited access to the international system that no longer holds true in many issue areas.

Instead, we draw upon sociological traditions that focus on complex interactions among actors, on the intersubjective construction of frames of meaning, and on the negotiation and malleability of identities and interests. These have been concerns of constructivists in international relations theory and of social movement theorists in comparative politics, and we draw from both traditions. The networks we describe in this book participate in domestic and international politics simultaneously, drawing upon a variety of resources, as if they were part of an international society. However, they use these resources strategically to affect a world of states and international organizations constructed by states. Both these dimensions are essential. Rationalists will recognize the language of incentives and constraints, strategies, institutions, and rules, whereas constructivists and social constructionists will be more comfortable with our stress on norms, social relations, and intersubjective understandings. We are convinced that both sets of concerns matter, and that recognizing that goals and interests are not exogenously given, we can think about the strategic activity of actors in an intersubjectively structured political universe. The key to doing so is remembering that the social and political contexts within which networks operate at any particular point contain contested understandings as well as stable and shared ones. Network activists can operate strategically within the more stable universe of shared understandings at the same time that they try to reshape certain contested meanings.

. . .

What is a Transnational Advocacy Network?

Networks are forms of organization characterized by voluntary reciprocal, and horizontal patterns of communication and exchange. The organizational theorist Walter Powell calls them a third mode of economic organization, distinctly different from markets and hierarchy (the firm). "Networks are 'lighter on their feet' than hierarchy" and are "particularly apt for circumstances in which there is a need for efficient, reliable information," and "for the exchange of commodities whose value is not easily measured." His insights about economic networks are extraordinarily suggestive for an understanding of political networks, which also form around issues where information plays a key role, and around issues where the value of the "commodity" is not easily measured.

In spite of the differences between domestic and international realms, the network concept travels well because it stresses fluid and open relations among committed and knowledgeable actors working in specialized issue areas. We call them advocacy networks because advocates plead the causes of others or defend a cause or proposition. Advocacy captures what is unique about these transnational networks: they are organized to promote causes, principled ideas, and norms, and they often involve individuals advocating policy changes that cannot be easily linked to a rationalist understanding of their "interests."

Some issue areas reproduce transnationally the webs of personal relationships that are crucial in the formation of domestic networks. Advocacy networks have been particularly important in value-laden debates over human rights, the environment, women, infant health, and indigenous peoples, where large numbers of differently situated individuals have become acquainted over a considerable period and developed similar world views. When the more visionary among them have proposed strategies for political action around apparently intractable problems, this potential has been transformed into an action network.

Major actors in advocacy networks may include the following: (1) international and domestic nongovernmental research and advocacy organizations; (2) local social movements; (3) foundations; (4) the media; (5) churches, trade unions, consumer organizations, and intellectuals; (6) parts of regional and international intergovernmental organizations; and (7) parts of the executive and/or parliamentary branches of governments. Not all these will be present in each advocacy network. Initial research suggests, however, that international and domestic NGOs [non-governmental organizations] play a central role in all advocacy networks, usually initiating actions and pressuring more powerful actors to take positions. NGOs introduce new ideas, provide information, and lobby for policy changes.

Groups in a network share values and frequently exchange information and services. The flow of information among actors in the network reveals a dense web of connections among these groups, both formal and informal. The movement of funds and services is especially notable between foundations and NGOs, and some NGOs provide services such as training for other NGOs in the same and sometimes other advocacy networks. Personnel also circulate within and among networks, as relevant players move from one to another in a version of the "revolving door."

Relationships among networks, both within and between issue areas, are similar to what scholars of social movements have found for domestic activism. Individuals and foundation funding have moved back and forth among them. Environmentalists and women's groups have looked at the history of human rights campaigns for models of effective international institution building. Refugee resettlement and indigenous people's rights are increasingly central components of international environmental activity, and vice versa; mainstream human rights organizations have joined the campaign for women's rights. Some activists consider themselves part of an "NGO community."

Besides sharing information, groups in networks create categories or frames within which to generate and organize information on which to base their campaigns. Their ability to generate information quickly and accurately, and deploy it effectively, is their most valuable currency; it is also central to their identity. Core campaign organizers must ensure that individuals and organizations with access to necessary information are incorporated into the network; different ways of framing an issue may require quite different kinds of information. Thus frame disputes can be a significant source of change within networks.

. . .

The Boomerang Pattern

It is no accident that so many advocacy networks address claims about rights in their campaigns. Governments are the primary "guarantors" of rights, but also their primary violators. When a government violates or refuses to recognize rights, individuals and domestic groups often have no recourse within domestic political or judicial arenas. They may seek international connections finally to express their concerns and even to protect their lives.

When channels between the state and its domestic actors are blocked, the boomerang pattern of influence characteristic of transnational networks may occur: domestic NGOs bypass their state and directly search out international allies to try to bring pressure on their states from outside. This is most obviously the case in human rights campaigns. Similarly, indigenous rights campaigns and environmental campaigns that support the demands of local peoples for participation in development projects that would affect them frequently involve this kind of triangulation. Linkages are important for both sides: for the less powerful third world actors, networks provide access, leverage, and information (and often money) they could not expect to have on their own; for northern groups, they make credible the assertion that they are struggling with, and not only for, their southern partners. Not surprisingly, such relationships can produce considerable tensions.

On other issues where governments are inaccessible or deaf to groups whose claims may nonetheless resonate elsewhere, international contacts can amplify the demands of domestic groups, pry open space for new issues, and then echo back these demands into the domestic arena. The cases of rubber tappers trying to stop encroachment by cattle ranchers in Brazil's western Amazon and of tribal populations threatened by the damming of the Narmada River in India are good examples of this.

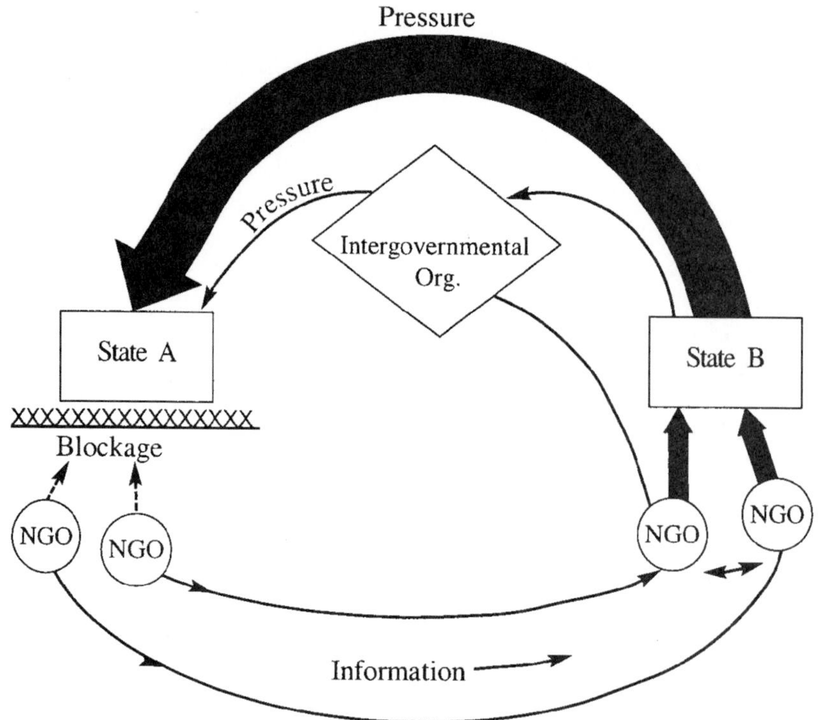

Figure 1 Boomerang pattern. State A blocks redress to organizations within it; they activate network, whose members pressure their own states and (if relevant) a third-party organization, which in turn pressure State A.

Political Entrepreneurs

Just as oppression and injustice do not themselves produce movements or revolutions, claims around issues amenable to international action do not produce transnational networks. Activists—"people who care enough about some issue that they are prepared to incur significant costs and act to achieve their goals"—do. They create them when they believe that transnational networking will further their organizational missions—by sharing information, attaining greater visibility, gaining access to wider publics, multiplying channels of institutional access, and so forth. For example, in the campaign to stop the promotion of infant formula to poor women in developing countries, organizers settled on a boycott of Nestlé, the largest producer, as its main tactic. Because Nestlé was a transnational actor, activists believed a transnational network was necessary to bring pressure on corporations and governments. Over time, in such issue areas, participation in transnational networks has become an essential component of the collective identities of the activists involved, and networking a part of their common repertoire. The political entrepreneurs who become the core networkers for a new campaign have often gained experience in earlier ones.

. . .

Human Rights Advocacy Networks in Latin America

. . . To demonstrate the impact of the network in practices, we need to look at the effectiveness of these pressures in specific cases.

Argentina

Even before the military coup of March 1976, international human rights pressures had influenced the Argentine military's decision to cause political opponents to "disappear," rather than imprisoning them or executing them publicly. (The technique led to the widespread use of the verb "to disappear" in a transitive sense.) The Argentine military believed they had "learned" from the international reaction to the human rights abuses after the Chilean coup. When the Chilean military executed and imprisoned large numbers of people, the ensuing uproar led to the international isolation of the regime of Augusto Pinochet. Hoping to maintain a moderate international image, the Argentine military decided to secretly kidnap, detain, and execute its victims, while denying any knowledge of their whereabouts.

Although this method did initially mute the international response to the coup, Amnesty International [AI] and groups staffed by Argentine political exiles eventually were able to document and condemn the new forms of repressive practices. To counteract the rising tide of criticism, the Argentina junta invited AI for an on-site visit in 1976, In March 1977, on the first anniversary of the military coup, AI published the report an on its visit, a well-documented denunciation of the abuses of the regime with emphasis on the problem of the disappeared. Amnesty estimated that the regime had taken six thousand political prisoners, most without specifying charges, and had abducted between two and ten thousand people. The report helped demonstrate that the disappearances were part of a deliberate government policy by which the military and the police kidnapped perceived opponents, took them to secret detention centers where they tortured, interrogated, and killed them, then secretly disposed of their bodies. Amnesty International's denunciations of the Argentine regime were legitimized when it won the Nobel Peace Prize later that year.

Such information led the Carter administration and the French, Italian, and Swedish governments to denounce rights violations by the junta. France, Italy, and Sweden each had citizens who had been victims of Argentine repression, but their concerns extended beyond their own citizens. Although the Argentine government claimed that such attacks constituted unacceptable intervention in their internal affairs and violated Argentine sovereignty, U.S. and European officials persisted. In 1977 the U.S. government reduced the planned level of military aid for Argentina because of human rights abuses, Congress later passed a bill eliminating all military assistance to Argentina, which went into effect on 30 September 1978. A number of high-level U.S. delegations met with junta members during this period to discuss human rights.

Early U.S. action on Argentina was based primarily on the human rights documentation provided by AI and other NGOs, not on information received through official channels at the embassy or the State Department. For example, during a 1977 visit, Secretary of State Cyrus Vance carried a list of disappeared people prepared by human rights NGOs to present to members of the junta. When Patricia Derian* met with junta member Admiral Emilio Massera during a visit in 1977, she brought up the navy's use of torture. In response to Massera's denial, Derian said she had seen a rudimentary map of a secret detention center in the Navy Mechanical School, where their meeting was being held, and asked whether perhaps under their feet someone was being tortured. Among Derian's key sources of information were NGOs and especially the families of the disappeared, with whom she met frequently during her visits to Buenos Aires.

Within a year of the coup, Argentine domestic human rights organizations began to develop significant external contacts. Their members traveled frequently to the United States and Europe, where they met with human rights organizations, talked to the press, and met with parliamentarians and government officials. These groups sought foreign contacts to publicize the human rights situation, to fund their activities, and to help protect themselves from further repression by their government, and they provided evidence to U.S. and European policymakers. Much of their funding came from European and U.S.-based foundations.

Two key events that served to keep the case of Argentine human rights in the minds of U.S. and European policymakers reflect the impact of transnational linkages on policy. In 1979 the Argentine authorities released Jacobo Timerman, whose memoir describing his disappearance and torture by the Argentine military helped human rights organizations, members of the U.S. Jewish community, and U.S. journalists to make his case a cause célèbre in U.S. policy circles. Then in 1980 the Nobel Peace Prize was awarded to an Argentine human rights activist, Adolfo Pérez Esquivel. Peace and human rights groups in the United States and Europe helped sponsor Pérez Esquivel's speaking tour to the United States exactly at the time that the OAS was considering the IACHR [Inter-American Commission on Human Rights] report on Ar-

* Patricia Derian was Assistant Secretary of State for Human Rights and Humanitarian Affairs in the Carter Administration.

gentina and Congress was debating the end of the arms embargo to Argentina.

The Argentine military government wanted to avoid international human rights censure. Scholars have long recognized that even authoritarian regimes depend on a combination of coercion and consent to stay in power. Without the legitimacy conferred by elections, they rely heavily on claims about their political efficacy and on nationalism. Although the Argentine military mobilized nationalist rhetoric against foreign criticism, a sticking point was that Argentines, especially the groups that most supported the military regime, thought of themselves as the most European of Latin American countries. The military junta claimed to be carrying out the repression in the name of "our Western and Christian civilization." But the military's intent to integrate Argentina more fully into the liberal global economic order was being jeopardized by deteriorating relations with countries most identified with that economic order, and with "Western and Christian civilization."

The junta adopted a sequence of responses to international pressures. From 1976 to 1978 the military pursued an initial strategy of denying the legitimacy of international concern over human rights in Argentina. At the same time it took actions that appear to have contradicted this strategy, such as permitting the visit of the Amnesty International mission to Argentina in 1976. The "failure" of the Amnesty visit, from the military point of view, appeared to reaffirm the junta's resistance to human rights pressures. This strategy was most obvious at the UN, where the Argentine government worked to silence international condemnation in the UN Commission on Human Rights. Ironically, the rabidly anticommunist Argentine regime found a diplomatic ally in the Soviet Union, an importer of Argentine wheat, and the two countries collaborated to block UN consideration of the Argentine human rights situation. Concerned states circumvented this blockage by creating the UN Working Group on Disappearances in 1980. Human rights NGOs provided information, lobbied government delegations, and pursued joint strategies with sympathetic UN delegations.

By 1978 the Argentine government recognized that something had to be done to improve its international image in the United States and Europe, and to restore the flow of military and economic aid. To these ends the junta invited the Inter-American Commission on Human Rights for an on-site visit, in exchange for a U.S. commitment to release Export–Import Bank funds and otherwise improve U.S.-Argentine relations. During 1978 the human rights situation in Argentina improved significantly. Figure 3 shows that the practice of disappearance as a tool of state policy was curtailed only after 1978, when the government began to take the "international variable" seriously.

The value of the network perspective in the Argentine case is in highlighting the fact that international pressures did not work independently, but rather in coordination with national actors. Rapid change occurred because strong domestic human rights organizations documented abuses and protested against repression, and international pressures helped protect domestic monitors and open spaces for their protest. International groups amplified both information and symbolic politics of domestic groups and projected them onto an international stage, from which they echoed back into Argentina. This classic boomerang process was executed nowhere more skillfully than in Argentina, in large part due to the courage and ability of domestic human rights organizations.

Some argue that repression stopped because the military had finally killed all the people that they thought they needed to kill. This argument disregards disagreements within the regime about the size and nature of the "enemy." International pressures affected particular factions within the military regime that had differing ideas about how much repression was "necessary." Although by the military's admission 90 percent of the *armed* opposition had been eliminated by April 1977, this did not lead to an immediate change in human rights practices. By 1978 there were splits within the military about what it should do in the future. One faction was led by Admiral Massera, a right-wing populist, another by Generals Carlos Suarez Mason and Luciano Menéndez, who supported indefinite military dictatorship and unrelenting war against the left, and a third by Generals Jorge Videla and Roberto Viola, who hoped for eventual political liberalization under a military president. Over time, the Videla–Viola faction won out, and by late 1978 Videla had gained increased control over the Ministry of Foreign Affairs, previously under the influence of the navy. Videla's ascendancy in the fall of 1978, combined with U.S. pressure, helps explain his ability to deliver on his promise to allow the Inter–American Commission on Human Rights visit in December.

The Argentine military government thus moved from initial refusal to accept international human rights interventions, to cosmetic cooperation with the human rights network, and eventually to concrete improvements in response to increased international pressures. Once it had invited IACHR and discovered that the commission could not be co-opted or confused, the government ended the practice of disappearance, released political prisoners, and restored some semblance of political participation. Full restoration of human rights in Argentina did not come until after the Malvinas War and the transition to democracy in 1983, but after 1980 the worst abuses had been curtailed.

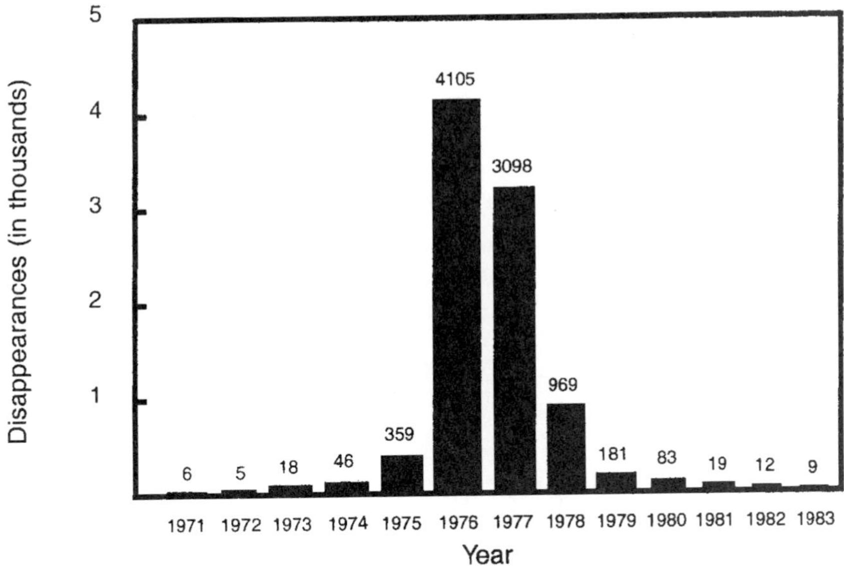

Figure 3. Disappearances in Argentina, 1973–1983. *Source:* Annex to the report of Nunca Mas (Never Again), published by the National Commission on Disappeared People, 1984.

In 1985, after democratization, Argentina tried the top military leaders of the juntas for human rights abuses, and a number of key network members testified: Theo Van Boven and Patricia Derian spoke about international awareness of the Argentine human rights situation, and a member of the IACHR delegation to Argentina discussed the OAS report. Clyde Snow and Eric Stover provided information about the exhumation of cadavers from mass graves. Snow's testimony, corroborated by witnesses, was a key part of the prosecutor's success in establishing that top military officers were guilty of murder. A public opinion poll taken during the trials showed that 92 percent of Argentines were in favor of the trials of the military juntas: The tribunal convicted five of the nine defendants, though only two—ex-president Videla, and Admiral Massera were given life sentences. The trials were the first of their kind in Latin America, and among the very few in the world ever to try former leaders for human rights abuses during their rule. In 1990 President Carlos Menem pardoned the former officers. By the mid–1990s, however, democratic rule in Argentina was firmly entrenched, civilian authority over the military was well established, and the military had been weakened by internal disputes and severe cuts in funding.

The Argentine case set important precedents for other international and regional human rights action, and shows the intricate interactions of groups and individuals within the network and the repercussions of these interactions. The story of the Grandmothers of the Plaza de Mayo is an exemplar of network interaction and unanticipated effects.[3] The persistence of the Grandmothers helped create a new profession—what one might call "human rights forensic science." (The scientific skills existed before, but they had never been put to the service of human rights.) Once the Argentine case had demonstrated that forensic science could illuminate mass murder and lead to convictions, these skills were diffused and legitimized. Eric Stover, Clyde Snow, and the Argentine forensic anthropology team they helped create were the prime agents of international diffusion. The team later carried out exhumations and training in Chile, Bolivia, Brazil, Venezuela, and Guatemala. Forensic science is being used to prosecute mass murderers in El Salvador, Honduras, Rwanda, and Bosnia. By 1996 the UN International Criminal Tribunal for the former Yugoslavia had contracted with two veterans of the Argentine forensic experiment, Stover and Dr. Robert Kirschner, to do forensic investigations for its war crimes tribunal. " 'A war crime creates a crime scene,' said Dr. Kirschner, 'That's how we treat it. We recover forensic evidence for prosecution and create a record which cannot be successfully challenged in court.' "

The Promise and Limits of the International Law of Torture*

OONA A. HATHAWAY

The Convention against Torture and Other Cruel, Inhuman or Degrading Treatment or Punishment is regularly celebrated as one of the most successful international human rights treaties. Its adoption by the United Nations in 1984 culminated an effort to outlaw torture that began in the aftermath of atrocities of World War II. Nations that ratified the Convention consented not to intentionally inflict "severe pain or suffering, whether physical or mental," on any person to obtain information or a confession, to punish that person, or to intimidate or

3. [Editors' Note: The *Abuelas de Plaza de Mayo*, Grandmothers of Plaza de Mayo, are a group of women in Argentina whose children and grandchildren "disappeared." Founded in 1977, it has searched for over 200 "disappeared" grandchildren, who were born in clandestine detention centers where there mothers were held by the government or who were captured along with their parents. The Grandmothers of Plaza de Mayo have succeeded in raising awareness of the plight of the "disappeared" and in locating 56 of the missing children, whose parents had been killed and who were raised under false identities by adoptive families.]

* Reprinted by permission from TORTURE: PHILOSOPHICAL, POLITICAL, AND LEGAL PERSPECTIVES (Sanford Levinson ed., Oxford University Press 2004).

coerce him or a third person. Today, with a membership of over 130 countries, the Convention stands as a symbol of the triumph of international order over disorder, of human rights over sovereign privilege.

Yet while the Convention and its regional counterparts are indisputably remarkable achievements, events of the post-September 11 era have given reason for pause. Torture, we have learned, is not just a practice of the past. As the United States prepared to go to war in Afghanistan, the Bush administration repeatedly drew attention to the Taliban's use of torture to maintain a semblance of control. And no one who followed the news during the following year could not be aware that Saddam Hussein's regime survived for so long in no small part by instilling a paralyzing fear in the population through the widespread use of torture and killing of those it deemed a threat.

Even more troubling, it has become apparent that our enemies in the war on terrorism are not the only ones who have made use of what had previously been seen as unthinkable practices. As noted in Sanford Levinson's introduction, it is an open secret that many of the suspects caught by the United States in the course of the war on terrorism have been turned over to Saudi, Egyptian, Syrian, and Jordanian officials, who are suspected of using torture in the course of their subsequent questioning. Indeed, even before the scandal over the treatment of prisoners held by the United States at the Abu Ghraib prison in Iraq erupted, it was well known that the United States has itself used "stress and duress" techniques that skirt and perhaps sometimes cross the line dividing legal interrogation from torture.

These revelations pose not only a moral challenge, which the earlier chapters in this book have explored, but also a challenge to those who believe in the power of international law to impose global order. All of the nations mentioned earlier, except Iraq and Syria, have ratified the Convention against Torture and thereby made an international legal commitment not to use torture. Yet they are known to have continued, if not expanded, its use. Recent events thus leave exposed the dark underbelly of the international legal regime against torture: it is not so clear that it really works.

In this chapter, I explore the place of international law in efforts to bring an end to the practice of torture. The debate over whether international law "works" has until now been highly polarized. On the one hand, skeptics of international law claim that international law is mere window dressing. States don't give up the right to engage in torture unless they have no intention of using it anyway. And once they join treaties like the Convention against Torture, states will act no differently from if they had not done so.

On the other side of the debate are those who reject this dismissive view of international law. They argue that states do not simply join treaties that are in their material interests. Rather, states will join a treaty if they are committed to the ideas and goals it embodies, even if doing so may be costly. And once states join, believers in international law argue, they will abide by their international legal commitments "most of the time."

I, by contrast, argue that international law has a real effect, but not one that either friends or foes of international law would expect. In short, neither advocates nor skeptics of international law examine the whole picture. Both fail to consider the role of internal enforcement of international treaties on countries' willingness to join and abide by them. Moreover, both ignore almost completely the indirect effects of treaties on countries' decisions to accept international legal limits on their behavior and then to violate or abide by them. Recognizing these dynamics creates a broader perspective on the role that international law plays in shaping how states actually behave and hence provides a more accurate picture of both the potential and the limits of international law.

Who Joins the Treaties Prohibiting Torture and What Effect Do They Have?

Let us begin by examining the facts. Which states commit to the Convention against Torture and thereby agree not to take advantage of this possibly useful (if horrific) tool? Do states that do so actually improve their practices as a result?

My examination of the practices of over 160 nations over the course of forty years provides some answers to these questions. The evidence supports several key findings. First, countries that ratify treaties outlawing torture do not always have better torture practices than those that do not. Second, democratic countries are more likely overall to make the legal commitment not to use torture than nondemocratic countries. Third, democratic nations that use torture more frequently are less likely to join the Convention against Torture than those that engage in less. Fourth, nondemocratic nations that use more torture are more likely to join the Convention against Torture than those that use it less. Finally, and perhaps most surprising, not only does it appear that the Convention does not always have the intended effect of reducing torture in countries that ratify, but, in some cases, the opposite might even be true.

I begin by examining which nations make the legal commitment not to engage in torture. Do countries that sign and ratify treaties that outlaw torture have better torture practices than do those that do not? Contrary to the predictions of both critics and advocates of international law, the answer is no. Indeed, countries with worse torture ratings are slightly *more likely* to ratify the Convention against Torture than those with better ratings. Even more striking, states that have ratified the regional conventions prohibiting torture have *worse* practices on average than those that have not, or that did so only after letting several years pass. On the other hand, the opposite is true of articles 21 and 22 of the Convention against Torture (which have stronger enforcement provisions that countries can separately agree to accept). Countries with better torture ratings have committed to articles 21 and 22 at four times the rate of those that have worse torture ratings.

Table 11.1: Who Accepts Limits on Torture?

	Countries that Torture Less	Countries that Torture More
Convention against Torture	41% *	47% *
Articles 21 and 22	22% *	6% *

*Indicates pairs for which the difference is statistically significant at the 95% level or higher.

The story becomes even more interesting when we compare the willingness of democratic and nondemocratic nations to accept international legal limits on their torture practices, as revealed in tables 11.2 and 11.3. First, it is apparent that democratic nations are more likely, on the whole, to join the Convention against Torture. That, perhaps, is not all that surprising, particularly given that democratic nations are less likely to torture than nondemocratic nations. What is surprising, however, is that nondemocratic nations that reportedly use torture frequently are *more* likely to join the Convention than nondemocratic nations that reportedly use torture infrequently. For example, Afghanistan, Cameroon, and Egypt—all of which have well-documented histories of using torture—ratified the treaty almost immediately after it opened for signature, whereas Oman and the United Arab Emirates, with their comparatively good records, have yet to ratify. These patterns are found across the board. As table 11.3 demonstrates, as democracies' torture ratings grow worse, they are increasingly less likely to make legal commitments that prohibit them from engaging in torture. Again, the opposite is *true* of dictatorships: those with worse reported torture practices are *more* likely to join the Torture Convention than those with better reported practices.

Table 11.2: Comparing Democracies and Nondemocracies

		Better Torture Ratings	Worse Torture Ratings
Nondemocratic	Ratified Convention:	24% * (776)	40 * (383)
	Signed Convention:	35% * (776)	50% * (383)
Democratic	Joined articles 21 and 22:	4% (776)	6% (383)

Ratified Convention:	57% (790)	62% (201)
Signed Convention:	76% (790)	74% (201)
Joined articles 21 and 22:	40%* (790)	6%* (201)

* Indicates pairs for which the difference is statistically significant at the 99% level.

Table 11.3: Comparing Democracies and Dictatorships

Torture Rating:		1 (No Verified Allegations of Torture)	2	3	4	5 (Torture Is "Prevalent" or "Widespread")
	Ratified Convention:	7% (73)	14% (218)	35% (410)	41% (218)	43% (109)
Dictatorship	Signed Convention:	7% (94)	22% (259)	40% (487)	47% (247)	53% (125)
	Joined Article 22:	1% (94)	1% (259)	5% (487)	2% (247)	6% (123)
	Ratified Convention:	69% (221)	76% (279)	53% (223)	50% (115)	60% (43)
Democracy	Signed Convention:	85% (264)	83% (300)	67% (236)	64% (121)	68% (47)
	Joined Article 22:	49% (264)	34% (600)	20% (236)	10% (121)	11% (47)

Note: The number of observations appears in parentheses.

All of these results hold up in a more sophisticated statistical analysis that holds states' economic and political characteristics constant. Looking at the group of states as a whole (grouping together democratic and nondemocratic states), I find that states that reportedly engage in more torture are no less likely to commit to the Convention against Torture or to articles 21 and 22 than states that reportedly engage in less torture. But again, if we look at democratic regimes alone, we find that they differ from the nondemocratic states in two interesting ways. First, they are simply more likely to join the Convention against Torture and articles 21 and 22. Second, even though they are more likely on the whole to join the Convention and articles, the more torture they use, the less likely they are to join—a pattern exactly opposite of that seen among nondemocratic regimes.

We now know something about which states join the Convention against Torture. But whether states will actually abide by international legal commitments once they are made is, of course, another issue altogether. Again, the empirical evidence holds some surprises for traditional accounts. My research indicates that human rights treaties do not always have the effects their proponents intend. A state's ratification of the Convention against Torture provides no guarantee that its actions will improve. Egypt, Cameroon, and Mexico were among the earliest to ratify the Convention against Torture, yet they continued to have some of the worse torture practices well into the 1990s. Indeed, if one compares states that share otherwise similar economic and political characteristics, it turns out that—if anything—those that ratify the Convention against Torture are reported to engage in *more* torture than those that have not ratified.

Accounting for the Evidence

As the foregoing evidence amply demonstrates, traditional accounts of international law that see it as either almost wholly effective or almost wholly ineffective are simply wrong. States do not only agree to the Convention against Torture if it requires them to do what they are already doing, as critics contend. They actually join it even it commits them to do something more. Yet, at the same time, states that ratify the Convention might sometimes have practices that are actually worse than those of states that have not *ratified.* Advocates of international law are *equally* at a loss to explain the empirical results. States with poor torture records commit so readily to the Convention against Torture that it would not be unreasonable *to* conclude that they do so only because they do not take the commitment seriously. More troubling for advocates of international law, however, is the evidence suggesting that countries that ratify the Convention against Torture and articles 21 and 22 do not engage in less torture as a result. In fact, some countries that ratify might possibly torture their citizens more!

Hence neither side of the existing debate provides a convincing account of the facts. In what follows, I argue that their failure to do so is due to their common oversight of important parts of the broad landscape that defines the role and effect of international law in modern society. More specifically, both fail to consider the role that domestic institutions play in shaping states' willingness to join and to comply with international legal rules. Both also ignore almost completely the role that concern about reputation plays in states' decisions to commit to and abide by international legal rules. These two dynamics have long been overlooked in international law scholarship; yet both, I will show, are central to understanding state choices to commit to and abide by international law.

Domestic Institutions and Self-Enforcement

Often ignored in the celebrations of the Convention against Torture is the fact that while it is quite strong in substance, it is remarkably weak in enforcement. The central enforcement procedure in the treaty is a requirement that states submit reports to the Committee against Torture, an international body created by the treaty to oversee the Convention. But failure to abide by even this minimal commitment is frequently ignored. Stronger enforcement procedures are available but wholly optional: countries can agree to allow states and individuals to file complaints against them with the Committee against Torture, but they are not required to do so in order to join the treaty. Consequently, only about 30 percent of those who have joined the Convention have accepted these additional procedures. According to the skeptical view of international law, these weak enforcement provisions mean that states will never change their behavior to obey the Convention.

Unquestionably, it is true that fear of enforcement is an important reason that states follow international rules. Thus the absence of significant enforcement provisions in the Convention against Torture (and, indeed, in much of international law) certainly means that the Convention is less likely to be closely observed. Yet it does not mean, as some skeptics would argue, that the Convention will have no effect. Indeed, if enforcement were the only reason people followed the law, the world would be a much messier place. Individuals abide by the law for a complex mix of reasons, including, among others, fear of enforcement by private parties or of retribution by the wronged party, internalization of the legal rule, and concerns about the impact on their reputation if others learn of their wrongdoing. Hence, even if there is no chance that individuals will be punished for a legal transgression, there are still many reasons why they might abide by the law.

As advocates of international law are quick to point out, the same is true of states. There are many reasons other than enforcement that states can be expected to follow international law. Yet when it comes to specifying what those reasons are, the advocates of international law tend to fall short. They often fall back on the relatively imprecise claim that *pacta sunt servanda* is the central proposition of international law. Or they argue that norms of international law are "internalized" by states, without giving much guidance as to when and why certain rules or propositions will be internalized and others will not.

The notion of "self-enforcement"—the use of domestic institutions by domestic actors against the government to uphold international rules—provides more precise guidance. International law is not obeyed only when states fear that an international organization or other state actor will levy sanctions against those who disobey the law, as many skeptics assume. Much of international law is instead obeyed primarily because domestic institutions create mechanisms for ensuring that a state abides by its international legal commitments, whether or not particular governmental actors wish it to do so. In democratic nations, in particular, actors outside government can use litigation, media exposure, and political challenges to compel governments to abide by their international legal commitments. In states lacking these institutions, however, it is more difficult for domestic actors to pressure the government to live up to the commitments it has made. For this reason, the extent to which domestic institutions permit domestic actors to pressure the state to abide by international law can have an important influence on a state's record of compliance.

However, a perverse prediction arises from these claims. The more likely a state is to engage in self-enforcement, the more likely it is to expect to be required to change its practices to abide by an international treaty. And the more likely a state expects to change its practices to abide by a treaty, the more costly and hence less attractive membership will appear. States that are more likely to engage in self-enforcement of the terms of a treaty are therefore less likely to commit to the treaty in the first place. Put another way, the more likely the treaty is to lead to an improvement in a state's practices, the less likely the state will be to join it.

This is, of course, exactly what the evidence outlined earlier shows. This approach thus helps explain why the democratic nations that are reported to engage in more torture are less likely to ratify the Convention against Torture than those that reportedly engage in less (even though, on the whole, nations that reportedly engage in more torture are no less likely to ratify the Convention than those that reportedly engage in less). It also helps account for why nondemocratic nations actually appear to be substantially more likely to ratify the Convention if they have worse torture records than they are if they have better torture records.

The dynamic of self-enforcement described here enriches both skeptical and sanguine accounts of the role of international law. For skeptics, it has the effect of broadening the notion of enforcement to include internal enforcement efforts. For advocates, it gives a more detailed and precise mechanism to account for the process of internalization. To determine when and why some international rules will be internalized and some will not one can simply look to the treaty terms (is it self-executing?) and the domestic institutions of member states (can actors independent of the government compel it to abide by its international legal commitments?).

The Role of Reputation

Traditional accounts of international law not only tend to ignore the role of domestic institutions in enforcing international law. They have also, for the most part, turned a blind eye to the effects of states' concerns about their reputations. This is a serious oversight, for in many areas—particularly the international law of torture—reputational concerns often play a more significant role than do the much-studied sanctions imposed by a treaty in states' decisions to commit to international legal limits on their torture practices and then abide by or shirk them.

Simply put, states join treaties like the Convention against Torture in no small part to make themselves look good. In doing so, they may hope to attract more foreign investment, aid donations, international trade, and other tangible benefits. The consistent result is that those that do not engage in prohibited practices will be less likely to join treaties because they have little to gain (their reputation is already good) and something to lose. Conversely, those who are reported to engage in prohibited practices will *be more* likely as a result to join treaties because *they* stand to gain something and put very little at risk.

Concerns about reputation at home and abroad can also provide states with a powerful motivation to abide by their international legal commitments once they are made. Where violations are likely to be discovered (as is often true, for example, of international trade laws), states will be likely to follow international rules in order to foster a good impression among other members of the international community. But where violations of international commitments are difficult to detect—for example, torture—violations will probably be more common. Moreover, states that already possess good reputations are more likely to abide by their commitment under treaties than are those with poor reputations—again because they have more to lose. This, in turn, further reinforces the counterintuitive dynamic noted earlier: to the extent that those with good reputations expect to expend time and energy ensuring that their treaty commitment will be followed (thus protecting their strong reputations), the prospect of making a treaty commitment will be viewed as more costly, and hence the state will be more reluctant to commit in the first place. Thus, once again, states that are more likely to comply with a treaty's requirements will be less likely to *agree to* them in the first place as a consequence.

Once again, reference to the actions of states in the real world confirms these claims, some of which are deeply counterintuitive. To begin with, states that have better torture records (and better reputations) are *less,* not more, likely to join the Convention against Torture than states that have worse torture records (and worse reputations). This is particularly true among dictatorships (who do not face the countervailing pressure of self-enforcement discussed earlier). Dictatorships are not only more likely on the whole to join the Convention against Torture if their practices are worse than if they are better but also their likelihood of joining the Convention against Torture grows with each successive increment of worsening torture ratings. Moreover, it appears that the calculated risk that states with poor torture records (and reputations) take in joining the Convention may in fact pay off. The empirical evidence suggests that, if anything, states that join the Convention have *worse* practices than they would be expected to have had they not joined the Convention. This puzzling result may arise because states that ratify receive a boost in their reputations and consequently feel less incentive to make real improvements in their actual torture practices (improvements that would undoubtedly be more difficult and more expensive to achieve than the highly visible but potentially costless act of ratifying a treaty).

Lessons for the Future

What lessons can be drawn from the successes and shortcomings of the Convention against Torture? I will highlight three in particular here. First, while enforcement of international law by international actors is not essential to effective international law, it is far from irrelevant. Where international institutions do not put in place effective enforcement mechanisms, there is of necessity greater reliance on other methods of maintaining compliance, such as domestic enforcement and reputational incentives. But these other methods do not, as I have shown, always have the effects that are intended. In particular, the reliance on domestic enforcement to fill the gap left by weak international enforcement can produce a regime that is shunned by precisely those states who would be the best members. There is, therefore, a tradeoff between widespread participation in the regime and its effectiveness: the more effective the regime would be at changing a state's behavior, the more reluctant the state is to join it in the first place. Any modifications to the international legal torture regime must be made with an awareness of this tradeoff.

Second, the evidence presented here makes clear that strong domestic institutions are essential not only to domestic rule of law but also to international rule of law. Where international bodies are less active in enforcement of treaty commitments, it falls to domestic institutions to fill the gap. In some states, this reliance on domestic institutions is effective. In others, however, it is less so. Because the international torture regime relies so heavily on domestic rule of law institutions, strengthening those institutions could have a profound impact on compliance with the international legal torture regime.

Third, and finally, state reputation plays a central role in state decisions to participate in and comply with the international torture regime. This, again, sometimes produces unintended consequences. At present, membership in the Convention against Torture can confer a boost to a state's reputation, regardless of whether it actually abides by the Convention's requirements. This is possible because the international community does little to police the treaty requirements, leaving member states facing little risk of external exposure if they fail to abide by the Convention's requirements. As a consequence, states that engage in torture and have weak domestic rule of law institutions have every reason to join the Convention. However, simply monitoring the activities of treaty members could substantially improve the situation. If states' violations of the terms of the treaty were likely to be made public, states that do not intend to abide by the treaty would be substantially less likely to join.

The Convention against Torture has not brought an end to states' horrific abuse of their own citizens. Far from it. Each day we learn of new violations, even by states that joined the Convention in its earliest days. Violations of both the letter and spirit of the law are rampant. Yet while the Convention is not a panacea, neither is the problem of torture beyond the reach of international law. Although the Convention has not achieved its lofty goals, it has contributed to the now almost universal view that torture is an unacceptable practice. By facing up to the Convention's successes and its failures, we can begin to learn how to harness the real but limited power of international law to continue to change the world for the better.

Notes and Comments

1. Would the various theorists studied in the earlier parts of this book agree or disagree with the perspectives offered in the pieces above? For example, how might the republican liberal view offered by Moravcsik compare to a realist explanation of the emergence of the European Convention on Human Rights?

2. Feminist scholarship has in the last decade revealed the failure of much of international law and international relations scholarship on human rights to take account of women. One particularly effective essay on the topic is Hilary Charlesworth, *What are "Women's International Human Rights"?*, *in* HUMAN RIGHTS OF WOMEN: NATIONAL AND INTERNATIONAL PERSPECTIVES (Rebecca J. Cook ed., 1994). She writes:

> ... [T]he development of international human rights law generally has been partial and androcentric, privileging a masculine worldview. Non-governmental organizations have recently begun to document abuse of women that falls within the traditional scope of human rights law. But the very structure of this law has been built on the silence of women. The fundamental problem women face worldwide is not discriminatory treatment compared with men, although this is a manifestation of the larger problem. Women are in an inferior position because they have no real power in either the public or private worlds, and international human rights law, like most economic, social, cultural, and legal constructs, reinforces this powerlessness.
>
> ... [A]ll international human rights law rests on and reinforces a distinction between public and private worlds, and this distinction operates to muffle, and often completely silence, the voices of women.... The dichotomy is central to liberalism—the dominant political, and legal, philosophy of the west. It assumes a public sphere of rationality, order, and political authority in which political and legal activity take place, and a private "subjective" sphere in which regulation is not appropriate.

Id. at 58. For more on the feminist critique of international human rights law, see Kathleen Mahoney, *Theoretical Perspectives on Women's Human Rights and Strategies for their Implementation*, 21 BROOKLYN JOURNAL OF INTERNATIONAL LAW 799 (1996); Berta E. Hernandez–Truyol, *Women's Rights as Human Rights—Rules, Realities, and the Role of Culture: A Formula for Reform*, 21 BROOKLYN JOURNAL OF INTERNATIONAL LAW 605 (1996); Eva Brems, *Protecting the Human Rights of Women*, *in*

International Human Rights in the Twenty-First Century (Gene Lyons & James Mayall eds., 2003); Gayle Binion, *Human Rights: A Feminist Perspective*, 17 Human Rights Quarterly 509 (1995), and the excellent collection of work found in Human Rights of Women, *supra*. For more general critiques of legal and political science scholarship from a feminist perspective, see, e.g., Hillary Charlesworth et al., *Feminist Approaches to International Law*, 85 American Journal of International Law 613 (1991); Catherine MacKinnon, Towards a Feminist Theory of the State (1989); Carol Smart, Feminism and the Power of Law (1989).

3. There has also been a more general debate over the universality of the human rights principles that have formed the center of the post-World War II human rights movement. See, e.g., Jack Donnelly, Universal Human Rights in Theory and Practice (2003) (discussing the international human rights regime in "regime theory" terms); Negotiating Culture and Human Rights (Lynda S. Bell et al. eds., 2001); Human Rights and Global Diversity (Simon Caney & Peter Jones eds., 2001).

4. Over the last decade, a debate has also emerged over the role and responsibility of multinational corporations in the area of human rights. Human rights organizations have increasingly worked to hold multinational corporations responsible for human rights violations to which they can be said to have contributed, either directly (by providing inhumane working conditions) or indirectly (by supporting governments that suppress their populations). See, e.g., Steven R. Ratner, *Corporations and Human Rights: A Theory of Legal Responsibility*, 111 Yale Law Journal 443 (2001) (arguing that international law can and should place duties on corporations to respect human rights); Peter T. Muchlinski, *Human Rights and Multinationals: Is There a Problem?*, 77 International Affairs 31 (2001) (examining the debate over extending human rights obligations into the private sphere). What responsibility, if any, do private actors have to ensure human rights? Do any of the theories discussed in Parts II–III of the reader provide any guidance for thinking about the role and responsibility of private actors in pursuing human rights?

5. Consider what role nonstate actors play in shaping states' human rights practices. Are there certain conditions that must be in place for them to have an impact? (What would a constructivist scholar or legal process scholar have to say about this?) How does this influence your view of how best to improve human rights practices?

6. There is an ongoing debate over not only the explanations of empirical findings on compliance with and commitment to human rights treaties, but also over the proper methods for studying the effectiveness of human rights treaties. Responding to the article, Oona A. Hathaway, *Do Human Rights Treaties Make a Difference?*, 111 Yale Law Journal 1035 (2002), which provides a quantitative empirical analysis of over 160 nations' commitment and compliance records under several universal and regional human rights treaties, Ryan Goodman and Derek Jinks argue:

> Public international law desperately needs work like Hathaway's—studies that connect the law to events on the ground. There is a real danger that, absent such efforts, international lawyers will act in ways that have negligible or perverse effects on the injustices they seek to combat. But because the stakes are so high, it is important that we make accurate connections between what the law does and what happens on the ground. Those connections cannot be ascertained through the research design that Hathaway employed. Perhaps the answer is to discard this type of statistical modeling and adopt a softer kind of empiricism, something more sociological than economic. Perhaps it's something else. We certainly have not given up hope for statistical approaches in this area, as there are many devices that can be employed to help conduct such studies. In any event, this much is clear: we still do not satisfactorily know the full effects of human rights treaties. Absent such knowledge, the best assumption remains the conventional one: human rights treaties advance the cause they seek to promote, not the other way around.

Ryan Goodman & Derek Jinks, *Measuring the Effects of Human Rights Treaties*, 14 European Journal of International Law (2003). Hathaway responds to Goodman and Jinks in Oona A. Hathaway, *Testing Conventional Wisdom*, 13 European Journal of International Law 185 (2003). Compare the methodological approaches of the three excerpts above. Is one significantly more effective than the others? Are these approaches competitors with or complements to one another?

7. Harold Hongju Koh provides a transnational legal process perspective on enforcement of human rights law. He writes:

> "What do we mean when we say that any laws are enforced?" Are any laws perfectly enforced? Even here in Bloomington, Indiana, the height of civilization, are the parking laws or burglary laws perfectly enforced? Of course, you would concede, parking violations occur here in Bloomington, and burglaries occur, perhaps even daily; sometimes egregiously. But those facts alone hardly mean that there is no enforcement of laws against parking violations or burglary. Here in Indiana, the laws against burglary may be underenforced, they may be imperfectly enforced, but they are enforced, through a well-understood domestic legal process of legislation, adjudication, and executive action. That process involves prosecutors, statutes, judges, police officers, and penalties that interact, interpret legal norms, and work to internalize those norms into the value sets of citizens like ourselves.
>
> But if we are willing to give that answer to the question "how is domestic law enforced?," why not similarly answer the question whether international human rights law is enforced? . . . I . . . argue that in much the same way, these international norms of international human rights law are underenforced, imperfectly enforced; but they are enforced through a complex, little-understood legal process that I call transnational legal process[:] . . . the institutional

interaction whereby global norms of international human rights law are debated, interpreted, and ultimately internalized by domestic legal systems. To claim that this complex transnational legal process of enforcing international human rights law via interaction, interpretation, and internalization exists is not to say that it always works or even that it works very well. As I will be the first to concede, this process works sporadically, and that we often most clearly see its spectacular failures, as in Cambodia, Bosnia, and Rwanda. But the process of enforcing international human rights law also sometimes has its successes, which gives us reason not to ignore that process, but to try to develop and nurture it....

What does this have to do with international human rights law? I would argue that in the international arena, we are seeing the exact same process at work; a process by which norms and rules are generated and internalized and become internal rules, normative rules, and rules that constitute new nations. The best example we have is South Africa; a country which for many years was an outlaw, was subjected to tremendous external pressure and coercive mechanisms over a long period of time. Through a gradual process, South Africa has converted itself into a country that has undergone a fundamental political transformation. It has now reconstituted itself as a law-abiding country that through its constitutional processes has internalized new norms of international human rights law as domestic law.

In the same way, if the United States is attempting to encourage China to follow norms of international human rights law, the analysis above suggests the need to act at all five levels: at the level of power and coercion, to apply external and political sanctions; at the level of self-interest, to develop carrots that can be offered to China in terms of trade benefits or other kinds of economic incentives; at the level of liberal theory, to encourage Hong Kong's liberal legal identity to bubble up to the Beijing government; at the level of communitarian values, to seek to encourage China to ratify the International Covenant on Civil and Political Rights and other multilateral communities of international human rights observance; and finally, from a legal process perspective, to seek to engage the Chinese people and groups in civil society in a variety of international interactions that will cause them to internalize norms of international human rights law.

As with the seat belt example, our goal is not simply to coerce conduct. More fundamentally, we seek to encourage a change in the nature of the Chinese political identity to reconstitute China as a nation that abides by core norms of international human rights law. In short, a theory of transnational legal process seeks to enforce international norms by motivating nation-states to obey international human rights law—out of a sense of internal acceptance of international law—as opposed to merely conforming to or complying with specific international legal rules when the state finds it convenient.

Harold Hongju Koh, *How is International Human Rights Law Enforced?*, INDIANA LAW JOURNAL 1397 (1999). What are similarities and differences between the constructivist "boomerang model" of Margaret Keck and Kathryn Sikkink and the transnational legal process perspective of Harold Hongju Koh?

8. The argument offered by Moravcsik centers on the origins of the European human rights regime. Is the argument applicable outside that context? Does it provide a convincing explanation, for example, of states' decisions to create and commit to the Convention against Torture? What, if any, implications does Moravcsik's argument about the origins of human rights regimes have for states' compliance with those regimes once they are committed to them? How might one begin thinking about conceptualizing a human rights regime in a region of the world, such as the Mideast, where the generations-old ethnic and religious conflict has interfered with the development of shared region-wide human rights norms?

9. Keck and Sikkink do not explicitly discuss the role of international law in the excerpt provided above, but might international law play a role in Keck and Sikkink's model? If so, how? What is the relationship between international law and international norms?

10. In September 2004, U.S. Secretary of State Colin Powell pronounced actions of the Khartoum government and the Janjaweed militias in Darfur, Sudan to constitute "genocide." Article I of the Convention on the Prevention and Punishment of the Crime of Genocide confirms "that genocide, whether committed in time of peace or in time of war, is a crime under international law which [the Contracting States] undertake to *prevent and to punish*" (emphasis added). What steps could and should the international human rights regime or regional human rights regimes take to give content to that duty? Are different international law norms emerging about the duty to prevent, as opposed to the duty to punish, gross human rights violations?

B. Environment

Over the last several decades, international environmental law has gradually moved to the center of the world stage. This has occurred even in the face of what appeared to be important structural hurdles to its creation and effectiveness. Like human rights law, environmental law offers states few tangible benefits and in return asks them to bear substantial costs. Moreover, environmental law poses a particular challenge to states in that it requires them to regulate the actions of private parties. It is, after all, most often not the state itself that produces the environmental pollution that it is supposed to restrain, but the industries and individuals within it that do so. Yet despite these challenges—or perhaps in some cases because of them—efforts to regulate environmental pollution on an international scale have proliferated. As is to be expected in an area of law that poses such challenges, many of the international legal limitations on state environmental practices are largely symbolic and carry little or no consequences for the states that join them. One agreement, however, stands out as an acknowledged success: the Montreal Protocol on Substances That Deplete the Ozone Layer.

Enacted in 1987, the Montreal Protocol places limits on states' use of chlorofluorocarbons. How did it arise and how effective has it been? These are the questions that form the central focus of this section. Working from a constructivist perspective, Peter Haas's article examines the role of what he calls an ecological "epistemic community" in identifying the problem of global warming and in creating pressure for a global legal solution. Detlef Sprinz and Tapani Vaahtoranta take a contrasting interest-based perspective. They argue that states' positions on the Protocol can be explained by looking at two variables: the state's ecological vulnerability and the costs of abatement. Finally, Daniel Bodansky examines the role of legitimacy in the growth of international environmental law.

Banning Chlorofluorocarbons: Epistemic Community Efforts to Protect Stratospheric Ozone*

PETER HAAS

The protection of the stratospheric ozone layer is a striking instance of international cooperation. Governments adopted regulations for a $100 billion global industry in the Montreal Protocol on Substances That Deplete the Ozone Layer of September 1987. The protocol imposes severe limits on the global use of chlorofluorocarbons (CFCs), which were suspected of decreasing stratospheric ozone, even though scientists and industry representatives agreed that in 1987 "there was not enough data to provide definitive answers about the cause of the decreases." A British journalist puzzled, "Why, when professionals cannot make up their minds even about what is happening in the Antarctic, should the world's diplomats be locked in negotiations?"

The successful coordination of national policies to protect the ozone layer was strongly influenced by the activities of an ecological "epistemic community," a knowledge-based network of specialists who shared beliefs in cause-and-effect relations, validity tests, and underlying principled values and pursued common policy goals. Their orientation is perhaps best expressed in the words of one member, who voiced his willingness to accept the "plausibility of a causal link without certainty."

In the face of foreign policy decision makers' uncertainty about the causes of the problem and the possible consequences of action, the epistemic community was largely responsible for identifying and calling attention to the existence of a threat to the stratospheric ozone layer and

* Reprinted by permission from 46 INTERNATIONAL ORGANIZATIONS 187 (1992).

for selecting policy choices for its protection. The community channeled discussions toward a strong ozone treaty by spreading information that suggested the need for stringent international CFC controls. Its viewpoint prevailed in policy disputes within the U.S. administration and led the United States to pressure other countries to adopt a stringent treaty. Moreover, by directly influencing the major CFC producer, DuPont, the epistemic community enhanced the prospects of enforcement of the treaty by creating market incentives for smaller actors to gradually eliminate CFCs. The community framed the range of alternatives that actors considered, advocated strong controls within those parameters, and pushed for speedy implementation of controls in the countries in which it had consolidated bureaucratic power. Thus, it directly affected outcomes through the activities of its members within their own governments and organizations, and it indirectly affected outcomes as well by altering the market conditions from which smaller actors formulated their interests and strategies.

A focus on the role of the epistemic community analytically supplements more traditional studies of international leadership that are based on the international distribution of power. Contrary to the more limited expectations of neoliberal institutionalists, who would predict that the extensive uncertainties about costs and time frames would lead to the adoption of an insurance regime, the Montreal protocol is in fact a strong regulatory regime. While the outcomes roughly correlate with the international distribution of power, the ends to which U.S. power was directed elude the systemic explanations offered by structural neorealists. Although the United States played a leadership role throughout the treaty negotiations, dissension within the Reagan administration made it extremely unclear until the very last minute whether the U.S. delegation would be able to uphold its initial commitment to stringent controls. The final choice ran contrary to U.S. domestic particularistic interests, which opposed regulation, and also differed from a contemporary assessment of the aggregate national interest.

Until late in the negotiations, the U.S. "interest" as perceived by the foreign policy community was not clearly expressed, and the "interest" that was finally identified was seriously at odds with previous U.S. behavior in the area of international environmental politics. As Lynton Caldwell noted, "Three considerations, essentially domestic in origins, appear to have influenced Reagan's environmental policies abroad. [They were the] desire to obtain advantage wherever possible for American economic interests ... [the] ideological bias against any increases in U.S. financial contributions to intergovernmental agencies ... [and the] preference for reliance upon market forces as a corrective to environmentally harmful practices." Conversely, U.S. behavior in the ozone case was characterized by a willingness to forgo advantages for U.S. producers and by a strong interest in regulation. Although a nominal interest in preserving market rules as a guide to international behavior was preserved, the U.S. position was modified in that market signals would now be used to pursue a new principled objective. As argued below, this new objective was instilled by the ecological epistemic community as its members were consulted by their own national administrations.

Repeated environmental crises precipitated action for controlling CFCs and set the pace for international activities. These crises alerted governments to the urgent need for collective action. They revealed the extent of scientific understanding and uncertainty about the nature of the problem and identified the group of actors to whom governments felt they must turn to explicate the variety of possible policies.

The ecological epistemic community

The ozone negotiations were framed by an ecological epistemic community composed of atmospheric scientists and of policymakers who were sympathetic to the scientists' common set of values, which stressed preserving the quality of the environment, and accepted their causal analysis. The common causal beliefs lay in an acceptance of the 1974 Rowland–Molina hypothesis that the chlorine in CFC emissions upsets the natural ozone balance by reacting with and breaking down ozone molecules and hence depleting the thin layer of stratospheric ozone. Their policy enterprise consisted of preserving this ozone layer, which prevents harmful ultraviolet rays from reaching the earth.

The epistemic community was transnational, consisting of officials of the United Nations Environment Programme (UNEP), the U.S. Environmental Protection Agency (EPA), and the U.S. State Department's Bureau of Oceans and International Environmental and Scientific Affairs (OES) as well as atmospheric scientists in the international scientific community. The officials seldom had training in atmospheric science but were eager to accept the scientists' advice because of a shared interest in conserving environmental quality. The scientists were in frequent, informal contact, whereas the government officials interacted less often.

. . . Through their contacts, the scientists shared and diffused information, making it difficult for government agencies to monopolize and control information if they had wanted to do so.

While atmospheric research was predominantly an American activity both in terms of federal support for investigations (NASA's ozone budget was about $100 million per year) and in terms of the number of active researchers, atmospheric scientists conducted vigorous studies in Belgium, Britain, France, Japan, Norway, Sweden, West Germany, and the Soviet Union. . . .

The epistemic community's most potent political resource was its ability to articulate what scientific developments implied for policy, an ability based on its reputation for expertise in atmospheric chemistry. Although the scientific evidence was not clear-cut and did not gain wide consensus until after the ozone treaty was concluded, the scientists were responsible for briefing their political colleagues on where the uncertainties lay and on whether the scientific evidence was approaching closure. As the science improved, the credibility of the epistemic community was enhanced. [Richard] Benedick[1] acknowledged that CFC regulation "couldn't have occurred without modern science, without atmostpheric chemistry, computer models, and projections. It couldn't have happened as recently as 1982."

Origins of Concern

CFCs as a class of chemicals were discovered by General Motors in 1931 and soon became widely used for refrigeration, air conditioning, and insulation. Hailed as perfect chemicals because of their inert, nontoxic, noncarcinogenic, and nonflammable properties, CFCs underwent a steady increase in production, with global manufacturing quadrupling in the 1960s alone....

At the time of the ozone treaty negotiations, CFCs were being produced by only seventeen companies with operations in sixteen countries. Within this oligopolistic market, DuPont was the world leader. With its headquarters in the United States and with subsidiaries and joint ventures in six other countries, DuPont held 50 percent of the U.S. market, was responsible for over 25 percent of global production, and was the only company to produce CFCs for all three major world markets: North America, Europe, and Japan. Given the size of DuPont's market and the fact that the United States was the largest CFC-producing and CFC-consuming country, it is not surprising that the United States became the most powerful actor involved in ozone research and negotiations.

International concern about the depletion of the ozone layer first emerged in the United States in 1970, when scientists on the President's Science Advisory Council voiced fears that supersonic transports could destroy up to 50 percent of the earth's ozone layer. Although this particular concern died along with the demise of widespread supersonic transport use, the problem of ozone depletion continued to be studied. In 1974, Sherwood Rowland and Mario Molina, two chemists at the University of California at Irvine, argued that the chlorine in CFC emissions reacts with and breaks down ozone molecules in the thin layer of stratospheric ozone and thus hinders the ozone layer's ability to prevent harmful ultraviolet rays from reaching the earth....

Policy Responses

Although the Rowland–Molina hypothesis remained unconfirmed and contested after its appearance, it did seize popular attention and gave rise to an initial spasm of international regulation. The governments of nine countries, including the United States, banned the use of

1. [Editors' Note: Ambassador Richard Benedick was the chief U.S. negotiator and a principal architect of the Montreal Protocol. He authored the book, Ozone Diplomacy: New Directions in Safeguarding the Planet (1991), on the negotiations leading to the Protocol.]

CFCs as aerosol propellants, and many others passed voluntary limits on aerosol use. . . .

In 1985, there was broad consensus that the ozone layer had to be protected, but delegations were soon polarized about what measures should be taken. Governments suggested international efforts consistent with the measures they had already adopted nationally. . . .

. . . On 22 March 1985, a framework agreement called the Vienna Convention for the Protection of the Ozone Layer was signed by twenty countries, but it lacked specific control measures. It merely called for research cooperation and the development of means for controlling activities that might modify the ozone layer. [Mostafa] Tolba [an Egyptian microbiologist serving as UNEP's executive director] recommended a cooling off period during which the scientific evidence could be reappraised. He also called for a number of workshops to precede a resumption of negotiations on a detailed protocol stipulating actual control measures, which he hoped could be adopted in April 1987.

Negotiations were galvanized by the unanticipated discovery that a dramatic thinning of the ozone layer over Antarctica occurred every autumn. In 1985, Joseph Farman and his colleagues reported that during the 1977–85 period, they had observed a 40 percent seasonal decrease in the Antarctic ozone layer and had concluded that possible chemical causes must be considered. . . . The discovery of the ozone hole, combined with the unexpected increases in CFC use, alarmed the public and added a sense of urgency to the international discussions. . . .

During 1986, the EPA convened two symposiums on risk assessment and health effects from ozone depletion, UNEP sponsored two workshops on economic issues related to CFC control, and the organizations jointly sponsored an international conference involving over three hundred participants and focusing on ozone depletion and climate change. The well-attended conference led to a four-volume report which concluded that accelerated rates of CFC use posed real threats to the environment and public health. . . .

The EPA–UNEP atmospheric ozone study served as the scientific basis for the ensuing international negotiations because, as an EPA administrator pointed out, it "established a common understanding of the fundamental scientific issues among all participating nations." However, its implications were immediately interpreted differently in different quarters. The risk averse ecological epistemic community concluded that immediate cuts in CFC emissions were required. The industry group and the European governments believed that the findings merely counseled a possible freeze at current CFC levels and an increase in research efforts, since even a 2 percent reduction in global ozone would be indistinguishable from naturally occurring depletion and there were still no actual observations of ozone depletion outside Antarctica. As the chairman of the industry group's Alliance for a Responsible CFC Policy stated, "We do not believe the scientific information demonstrates any actual risk from current CFC use or emissions." The industry group also emphasized that if a freeze were to take place, it must be multilateral. Since the United States accounted for less than a third of the global use of CFCs, unilateral control efforts would have little total impact on the ozone layer but would make American companies producing and using CFCs less competitive in the international market.

This controversy was abruptly truncated in September 1986, when DuPont issued a statement that undercut much of the industry position. In light of recent findings, DuPont administrators now favored a protocol to "limit" CFC emissions:

> All the models now predict that high sustained CFC growth rates [rates leading to emissions from 3 to 5 times the current levels] would result in significant ozone depletion.... The wisdom of permitting continued growth must be weighed against the existing ability of science to specify a safe longterm growth rate. Resolution of this and other key scientific uncertainties about the ozone issue and greenhouse effects could take decades; therefore, we conclude that it now would be prudent to limit worldwide emissions of CFCs while science continues to provide better guidance to policymakers.

DuPont also urged government provision of incentives to develop alternatives to CFCs in order to speed their economic replacement. By announcing acceptance of the need for at least a freeze, DuPont undermined the other companies' argument that the scientific evidence did not justify any action and at the same time bolstered the ecological epistemic community's claim that strong CFC control measures were necessary. The community's position thus gained support and eventually prevailed not because of any improved explanatory power but because the alternative position was undercut.

...

The biggest push toward compromise came from the epistemic community. In an effort to reduce scientific disagreements, Tolba, on his own authority, organized a multi-national meeting of atmospheric scientists to compare their models and assessments of ozone depletion. The meeting which included members of the epistemic community was convened in April 1987 in Wiirzburg, West Germany.... [The] scientists unambiguously concluded that seven substances—CFCs 11, 12, 113, 114, and 115 and halons 1211 and 1301—should be covered in the protocol.[2] Methyl chloroform and carbon tetrachloride were found to have less ozone-depleting potential and were therefore omitted from immediate plans for coverage....

In September 1987, the Montreal Protocol on Substances That Deplete the Ozone Layer was finally adopted and bore the epistemic community's imprint. The protocol covered the five CFCs and two halons identified at Wurzburg and called for two staggered cuts in consumption

2. [Editors' Note: Halons are manufactured substances containing chlorine and bromine. Once widely used as fire extinguishants, halons destroy many hundreds of times their own weight in atmospheric ozone. Halons 1211 and 1301 were commonly used in fire protection systems and extinguishers.]

that would lead to a 50 percent total reduction from 1986 levels. The first cut of 20 percent was to take effect in 1993, while the second cut of 30 percent would follow in 1998. The protocol also reflected a number of compromises, many of which were worded awkwardly during the negotiations and were not submitted to the UNEP legal office for editing lest the subtle compromises be upset before the protocol could be signed.

Included in the protocol were side payments to encourage compliance from various parties. To ensure future supplies of the chemicals for LDCs, production was reduced by only 40 percent. Rather than dictating that production and consumption of each of the chemicals be reduced by specific amounts, the protocol merely specified the total percentage of cuts, thereby allowing Japan to concentrate on using CFC 113 for computer chip manufacture while reducing the use of the other chemicals. The Soviet Union was granted permission to include in its 1986 baseline the capacity of two plants that were currently under construction. The EC "rationalization" plans were accommodated by a special provision indicating that once all twelve EC states ratified the treaty, the EC would be treated as a single entity. This would allow companies to redistribute production among plants in different countries to achieve the most efficient production.

In the media coverage of the agreement, one reporter noted that "the actual numbers included in the protocol specifying percentages are recognized as politically rather than scientifically based." While it is true that the actual controls, which still allow for a 2 percent long term depletion in ozone, were reached by political compromise and U.S. leverage, it is important to emphasize that the ecological epistemic community was responsible for determining the range of chemicals that were covered, the stringency of controls, and the time frame for implementing reductions. In essence, the epistemic community was in the position of satisfying competing claims to the pie by saying "I cut; you choose." By specifying the parameters of choice and using the Wurzburg consensus to bolster their efforts, members of this community were able to move negotiations in the direction of strong international CFC controls.

Environmental Bandwagoning

The terms of the Montreal protocol were accepted in September 1987, and the protocol was subsequently ratified by thirty-one countries, including the United States, the members of the EC [European Community], the Soviet Union, Japan, Egypt, and Nigeria. By the time the protocol went into force, on 1 January 1989, many of the participating governments had decided that it did not go far enough and were calling for accelerated implementation and an expansion of the list of substances covered. . . .

In early 1989, evidence from the most recent Antarctic expedition demonstrated that the ozone layer was being depleted more rapidly than originally predicted. The EC states and 123 other countries were now advocating full elimination of CFCs by the end of the century. . . .

Factors Influencing Responses to the Environmental Threat

While the overall speed with which CFCs were regulated internationally was quite dramatic, individual countries responded to the ozone threat at different rates. The pacing of national responses can be explained largely in terms of the extent of the epistemic community's influence on various governments and its ability to help them interpret the emerging scientific consensus and articulate appropriate policies.

The first countries to actively encourage global controls were those in which the epistemic community and the tradition of proenvironmental sentiment were the strongest: the United States, Canada, Finland, Norway, and Sweden. In general, the EC and other countries followed suit once channels had been established between individual epistemic community members and their own national administrations.

. . .

Decision Making Within the CFC Industry

The ecological epistemic community played a switchboard role, communicating with policymakers and CFC manufacturers alike, accelerating their endorsement of the ozone research findings, and encouraging corporate decision makers to hasten their search for new products that would enable the Montreal protocol cuts to be achieved. Among CFC manufacturers, DuPont assumed the leadership role, both in its 1986 acceptance of the need for CFC controls and in its 1988 announcement of its intention to phase out the production of CFCs.

While each of DuPont's key decisions was made by higher-level executives for diverse corporate reasons, the epistemic community was responsible for rapidly introducing new policy ideas to the company through the research wing of the Freon products division. . . .

Conclusions and Alternate Explanations

Suspecting a possible link between CFC emissions and the depletion of the stratospheric ozone layer, the ecological epistemic community played a primary role in gathering information, forming a consensus regarding the available scientific evidence, disseminating information to government and corporate decision makers, and helping them formulate policies regarding CFC consumption and production. Community members were effective in persuading the two major actors of the need for strong CFC controls: the United States, which was the largest CFC-producing and CFC-consuming nation, and DuPont, which was the world leader in CFC production. The United States in turn compelled other nations to accept its view, while DuPont's eventual decision to phase out CFC production changed the international market and compelled its competitors to follow.

Without the epistemic community, international controls would have been weaker and taken much longer to adopt and implement, and domestic controls would have been more disparate. In this regard, we can consider two counterfactuals. In the absence of a group of professionals with the ability to interpret the technical and scientific evidence, there would have been little incentive for the United States or other countries to try to move beyond the weak 1985 Vienna convention. Without U.S. leadership, traditional interest based negotiations among equals would have yielded at most an international protocol reflecting the lowest common denominator By helping U.S. negotiators formulate their position and by framing the broader context in which international negotiations occurred, the epistemic community added focus to the negotiations and moved them in the direction of strong CFC controls. Similarly, in the absence of a transnationally active epistemic community, national policy choices would have been influenced almost entirely by domestic politics: countries without CFC producers or with highly influential environmental groups would have been more likely to enact strong domestic controls, while countries with large and influential CFC producers would have adopted weak controls. . . .

The fact that the epistemic community was able to gain and exercise influence at both the national and international levels explains the rapid adoption of convergent policies to control CFCs. While the United States exercised hegemonic leadership, a deductive, structural focus on the distribution of power alone does not provide an accurate specification of U.S. interests or resources in the case of ozone protection. . . .

In summary, members of the epistemic community contributed to the timing and stringency of CFC regulations through a combination of strategies ranging from the persuasion of individuals and groups to the capture of various decision-making channels. Most important, by capturing the United States and DuPont and by limiting the range of alternatives that decision makers considered, the epistemic community changed the external environment in which policies were made by other governments and firms.

The interest-based explanation of international environmental policy*

DETLEF SPRINZ and TAPANI VAAHTORANTA

Despite growing international environmental interdependence, the international system lacks a central authority to foster environmental protection. As a consequence, countries have adopted different policies to reduce international environmental problems. More specifically, costly regulations are not universally supported. In order to explain the success and failure of international environmental regulation, it is necessary to systematically focus on the factors that shape the environmental foreign

* Reprinted by permission from 48 INTERNATIONAL ORGANIZATION 1 (1994).

policy of sovereign states. Since such an approach is missing from the literature, we develop an interest-based explanation of support for international environmental regulation and postulate what impact it should have on state preferences for international environmental regulation. Specifically we apply our framework to ... efforts to protect the stratospheric ozone layer....

The Interest-Based Explanation

The interest-based explanation of the international politics of environmental management focuses on those domestic factors that shape a country's position in international environmental negotiations. In other words, the interest-based explanation is a unit-level explanation of international relations. Unit-level explanations refer to elements located at the national or subnational levels, whereas systemic explanations suggest that differences at the unit level produce less variation in outcomes than one would expect in the absence of systemic constraints. While unit-level explanations emphasize the varying characteristics of countries, systemic theories suggest that countries with different internal characteristics tend to behave in the same way if they are similarly positioned in the international system.

The interest-based perspective on international environmental regulation offers a partial but parsimonious view of how a country's preferences for international regulations are shaped. It focuses on a few unit-level factors that shape a country's behavior toward controlling international ecological problems. These preferences may change during international negotiations if the domestic characteristics of a country change. In addition, the bargaining process itself is a potential source of change. However, including a bargaining theory of international negotiations is beyond the scope of this article. The aim of this article is to present a parsimonious explanation by concentrating on two unit-level factors of major importance, namely, a country's ecological vulnerability toward pollution and the economic costs of pollution abatement.

In our analysis we assume that each country is a self-interested actor that rationally seeks wealth and power by comparing the costs and benefits of alternative courses of action. To assert that countries pursue their national interest or seek wealth and power does not tell us what their specific preferences might be in a given situation. Thus, it is assumed for the issue-areas of ozone depletion and trans-boundary acidification that states are pursuing two main goals with the help of their environmental foreign policies. First, each country seeks to avoid vulnerability to air pollutants. Each state is concerned in the first place with its own territory and pays only lip service to the idea of "spaceship Earth." In particular, countries pursue policies that minimize adverse environmental effects on their own citizens and ecosystems ("ecological vulnerability"). Second, states are more inclined to participate in environmental protection when the costs of compliance are relatively minor. In addition a country may promote regulations that would benefit it by increasing international demand for its pollution abatement technology and its substitute compounds.

If all states pursue these goals, why do some promote international regulations vigorously while other countries do not? What makes some countries strive for tight international emission controls? Why do other countries try to prevent or slow internationally coordinated action toward environmental protection?

In most cases environmental policy is a reaction to environmental problems. Without actual or anticipated environmental degradation, there would be no need for environmental protection. Conversely, we hypothesize that the worse the state of the environment, the greater the incentives to reduce the ecological vulnerability of a state. National environmental policies, however, do not depend only on the degree of ecological vulnerability. There are several examples of countries that have not taken effective measures to address serious environmental problems in their territories. This holds because environmental policies are also shaped by socioeconomic and institutional capacities to protect the environment. We wish to emphasize the role that economic capacity plays in determining the ability of the state to strive for tight emission controls. We furthermore suggest that different degrees of ecological vulnerability and of economic capacity explain much of the cross-national variance found in support for international environmental regulation.

States are not equally affected by atmospheric pollution. A state can be a source of international pollution, its victim, or both. A victim country A, that is, a country that is ecologically vulnerable to emissions emanating from country B, should try to improve the state of its environment by asking country B to reduce its emissions. Therefore, we expect victim countries to favor international environmental protection. If the environment of a country is affected by domestic emissions, it is expected to favor international harmonization of environmental policies in order to avoid disadvantages in international competitiveness. Thus, there are two major reasons for a vulnerable country to push for international regulations. First, a country's unilateral abatement activities may be insufficient to substantively improve the state of its environment; and second, it would like to avoid putting its polluting industries at a comparative disadvantage in international markets. Conversely, if a country is in a position where foreign or domestic emissions do not much degrade its environment, it should be less eager to promote international environmental regulation.

Our understanding of the role of knowledge in environmental policymaking is somewhat different from that of the proponents of the theory of epistemic community. According to this theory, the role of knowledge-based experts is significant in shaping a country's environmental policy. For example, Peter Haas suggests that those countries where policymakers turn to experts for advice are likely to become "pushers" for stringent international controls: "The pacing of national response [to the ozone threat] can be explained largely in terms of the extent of the epistemic community's influence on various governments and its ability to help them interpret the emerging scientific consensus and articulate appropriate policies."

We do not deny the influence of the knowledge of experts on policy but emphasize the contents of knowledge rather than its mere existence. Since countries are often unequally affected by environmental problems, we expect that epistemic communities in ecologically vulnerable countries will exert stronger effects on governmental elites to seek international regulations as opposed to their impact in less ecologically vulnerable countries.

In addition, a country's capacity to abate pollution influences its propensity to seek international environmental regulation. In general we expect that the greater the abatement costs of emission reductions, the more reluctant a country should be to support international regulations (other factors being equal). If, on the other hand, international environmental protection is relatively inexpensive, a country should be more inclined to subscribe to international environmental regulations. In particular abatement cost functions are influenced by the state of abatement (or prevention) technology, behavior modification (which can lead to price changes), and other factors. New and cost-reducing abatement technologies may reduce the (actual or anticipated) socioeconomic effort needed to support substantive regulations of the environment.

By combining indicators of a country's ecological vulnerability (low and high) with abatement costs (low and high), countries can be classified into four categories: "pushers," "intermediates," "draggers," and "bystanders" (see Figure 1). It is hypothesized that countries in cell 2 of Figure 1 (i.e., those expected to act as pushers in international negotiations) strive for stringent international regulation, while countries in cell 3 (i.e., draggers) oppose international environmental regulation. The countries falling in cell 4, namely, intermediate countries, find themselves in a particularly precarious situation. On the one hand they have ecological incentives to participate in international environmental regulation, while on the other hand they may not be willing to shoulder the substantial costs involved. Finally, countries falling into cell 1 (bystanders) should have little ecological interests in international regulations, but they are likely to take more ambitious positions than draggers because of the low costs associated with their negotiation position.

Ecological Vulnerability

		Low	***High***
Abatement	***Low***	(1) Bystanders	(2) Pushers
Costs	***High***	(3) Draggers	(4) Intermediates

Figure 1: Classification of a country's support for international environmental regulation

Besides typifying the anticipated behavior of states, we also suggest an ordinal ordering of intensity of support for substantive (rather than purely declaratory) environmental regulation. We expect that pusher countries take more stringent environmental positions than intermediate countries do, while the latter group is expected to favor environmental protection more often than draggers. The likelihood of bystanders' supporting environmental protection should fall between those for pushers and draggers; however, no direct comparison with the intermediate group seems to be appropriate on theoretical grounds.

The purpose of the remainder of this article is to assess the extent to which state policies toward controlling air pollution conform to the interest-based hypothesis outlined above. The empirical analysis of state policies is based on the negotiations leading to the signing of the 1987 Montreal Protocol on Substances That Deplete the Ozone Layer (control of stratospheric ozone-depleting substances) ... [one of] the first ... major multilateral agreement [to] oblige national governments to reduce harmful air pollutants.

The Montreal Protocol

Because of the depletion of the stratospheric ozone layer, increased ultraviolet radiation may pose significant threats to human health (especially skin cancer, eye damage, and adverse impact on the immune response system) as well as to aquatic and terrestrial ecosystems. In order to limit these effects, international cooperation was sought to control the emission of substances that are believed to deplete the stratospheric ozone layer. As a first step, the Vienna Convention for the Protection of the Ozone Layer was signed in 1985. It places emphasis on cooperation in research and exchange of scientific information. Building on the Vienna Convention, the 1987 Montreal Protocol contains specific obligations to reduce the production and consumption of five CFCs by 50 percent between 1989 and 1999, using 1986 as a base year, and to freeze the production and consumption of three halons at their 1986 levels by 1994. The regulations were tightened in 1990 in London, where states agreed to a total phase-out of fifteen CFCs, three halons, carbon tetrachloride, and methyl chloroform during the next ten to fifteen years. Furthermore, in late 1992 it was decided in Copenhagen that current restrictions shall be implemented faster than envisioned in London; in addition, the new Copenhagen regulations are more inclusive than those agreed upon in Montreal or London. Given the optimism stemming from the London agreement, Joseph Glas concluded that "through efforts to address the ozone depletion issue, we appear finally to have found a way to behave as a global community and make a commitment to reduce the overall risks to society in the future." However, it is assumed by the interest-based explanation pursued in this article that national interests shape state policies toward protecting the stratospheric ozone layer. Despite the growing interest of social scientists in the politics of global environmental pollution, relatively little work has been done on explaining the policies undertaken by countries to protect the stratospheric ozone layer.

In general, six factors have been emphasized in the literature as having been conducive to the process of negotiating the Montreal Protocol: (1) the role of scientific understanding of ozone depletion, (2) the impact of public pressure on decision makers, (3) the role of technological developments, (4) the leadership role played by the United States, (5) the role of the epistemic community, and (6) the role of international institutions.

The writings of Glas, Peter Morrisette, and Richard Benedick emphasize the crucial role that the evolving scientific understanding of the causes, extent, and consequences of ozone depletion has played for the conclusion of the Montreal Protocol. By the mid–1980s, a strong scientific consensus had developed demonstrating that anthropogenic emissions pose a threat to the stratospheric ozone layer. The knowledge of ozone depletion caused concern among the mass publics and put pressure on decision makers to protect the ozone layer. Furthermore, it is assumed that the ability of industry to produce CFC substitutes made it easier for governments to reduce the production and consumption of CFCs. Benedick, the chief U.S. negotiator of the Montreal Protocol, emphasizes the role of political leadership. According to him, the U.S. government played a crucial role in persuading hesitant governments to agree to international regulations. Approaching the issue from a different perspective, Haas focuses on the role of the epistemic community in shaping attitudes of states toward protecting the stratospheric ozone layer. Furthermore Edward Parson emphasizes that international institutions—and the United Nations Environment Program (UNEP) in particular—were increasing the willingness of countries to agree to CFC controls. While scientific knowledge, expert opinion, public concern, bargaining process, and technological development undoubtedly contributed to the signing of the Montreal Protocol, the analyses do not sufficiently explain why some governments had stronger preferences to regulate ozone-depleting substances than other countries. Whereas Benedick refers to several potentially influential factors, Haas concentrates on a monistic explanation. In explaining why the United States began pushing for stringent international controls on ozone-depleting substances earlier than the European Community (EC), Haas refers to the different strengths of the epistemic community, the tradition of proenvironmental sentiment, and the differences in the relations between the scientific community and the governments on both continents. One would expect that these differences also have an impact on policies in other issue-areas. However, this does not seem to be the case. For example, the EC is more eager to control the emissions of carbon dioxide than is the United States. Thus we suggest that besides the impact of scientific knowledge and epistemic communities, policies are mainly shaped by a country's ecological vulnerability and economic capacity to control environmental degradation.

. . .

Policies Toward Stratospheric Ozone

In the case of stratospheric ozone depletion, we hypothesize that a country's preference for international controls is determined by the vulnerability of its population to increased ultraviolet radiation and the economic cost of reducing CFCs.

UNEP played a major role in making ozone protection a top priority by funding research on the issue and sponsoring international meetings. In 1978 a scientific committee established by UNEP issued an assessment of the scientific evidence of ozone depletion and noted "the consistency in model predictions" but also recognized the continued existence of "large uncertainties in both the predicted ozone depletions and the understanding of their consequences." In the mid–1980s, major difficulties concerning processes and observation of ozone depletion were not yet resolved. For example, it was difficult to quantify future ozone depletion: the estimates varied from 3 to 20 percent. This problem notwithstanding, all models predicted that the continued release of CFCs would damage the ozone layer. The general conclusions drawn by observers were incorporated in a report by UNEP in 1985 that summarized the contemporary understanding of stratospheric ozone depletion in the following way: "Nothing has been discovered to disturb the basic premise, identified some two decades ago, that the ozone layer is likely to be depleted if concentrations of trace gases, particularly chlorine containing substances, continue to increase.... Refinement of chemical theory points unwaveringly toward the existence of a problem of ozone layer modification and impacts for man and his environment that are universally bad."

By the mid–1980s, sufficient consensus among natural scientists existed to start formal negotiations on the ozone regime, but governments could still point to the lack of hard evidence regarding the theory of stratospheric ozone depletion.

Increased ultraviolet radiation is believed to have several adverse effects, but we concentrate here on a direct human health effect, skin cancer. During the early 1980s more was known about human health effects than other consequences, and state representatives had been predominantly concerned with skin cancer. It was known that ultraviolet light can produce considerable mortality and morbidity through the induction of skin cancer in white populations who live close to the equator and are therefore more exposed to ultraviolet radiation. Dark-skinned populations as well as populations living farther away from the equator were considered to be less affected by ultraviolet radiation. The threat of the effect of evenly spread global ozone depletion would have amplified the occurrence of skin cancer and exposed larger populations to the conditions found in equatorial regions. In order to determine the vulnerability of a country to global ozone depletion, one would ideally combine its latitude and the skin type of its population. Since no data were found for the latter indicator, the ecological vulnerability of states is determined on the basis of the incidence of skin cancer among their populations in the mid–1970s. No assumption was made regarding the relationship between the local variation in the degree of ozone depletion and skin cancer incidence because of lack of adequate data during the early 1980s. The analysis that follows assumes that the division of populations into categories of high and low skin cancer incidence as observed in the mid–1970s remained unchanged until the mid–1980s. During the negotiations the incidence of skin cancer was linked to policies toward ozone depletion. A representative of Australia mentioned the high incidence in his country to explain Australia's interest in having the ozone layer protected. In the words of a delegate from Malaysia, "Skin cancer doesn't seem to occur in tropical countries, which have been by and large bystanders" in the negotiations.

Besides ecological vulnerability, the economic costs of reducing harmful emissions is assumed to shape a country's preferences and to affect its environmental foreign policy. Specifically we hypothesize that the higher the consumption of CFCs is per unit of gross national product (GNP), the higher the abatement costs should be and vice versa.

. . .

On the basis of the data, we hypothesize that the ecological vulnerability of Australia, North America, and Northern Europe had been particularly high, and we expect the countries of these regions to favor strict environmental regulations. If the threshold of three cases of skin cancer per 100,000 inhabitants is employed to classify environmental vulnerability, ozone depletion should not have been regarded as a particularly serious problem in the Federal Republic of Germany (FRG), France, Italy, Japan, and the UK. Of the fourteen countries [surveyed], the former Soviet Union and the United States stand out because of their particularly high CFC intensity. Using a threshold of 3 metric tons per U.S. dollar of CFCs, the costs of reducing CFCs should also be relatively high in France, the FRG, Italy, Japan, and the UK. In the 1980s, these states should have had a strong economic interest in opposing significant reductions of CFC production and consumption.

. . .

Evaluation of the Interest-Based Explanation

The negotiations on the protection of the stratospheric ozone layer began when an ad hoc working group established by UNEP met for the first time in Stockholm in 1982. It held four sessions before the conclusion of the Vienna Convention on the Protection of the Ozone Layer three years later. Following this agreement, a new working group for the preparation of a protocol on emission reductions met three times in 1986–87 so that the Montreal Protocol could be signed in 1987. In order to assess the positions taken by countries during the negotiations, we rely mainly on written documentation. A time series of policy positions of all countries is unfortunately not available from accessible documentation. Country positions ranged from "no reductions" to virtual elimination of commercial use of CFCs.

Ecological Vulnerability

		Low	*High*
Abatement Costs	*Low*		Australia, Canada, Denmark, Finland, Norway, Sweden, Switzerland
	High	France, Federal Republic of Germany, Italy, Japan, former Soviet Union, U.K.	United States

Figure 2: Predicted positions of countries: stratospheric ozone depletion

The Nordic countries, namely, Denmark, Finland, Norway, and Sweden, strove for stringent internationally binding regulations from the very beginning of the negotiation process. Only the Netherlands clearly supported the Nordic initiative at the first session. In addition, Australia, Canada, and Switzerland were believed to be particularly interested in 1982 in bringing about an internationally binding treaty. Before 1983 the United States had regarded further scientific evidence as a prerequisite for international regulations because of the socioeconomic consequences of emission controls. By 1983 U.S. representatives pointed to the potentially serious impact of CFCs on the ozone layer and regarded it as prudent to take specific steps to control CFC emissions. However, while having banned all aerosol uses of CFCs in 1978, the U.S. government considered restrictions put on nonaerosol uses of CFCs as "inappropriate at this point in time."

In 1984 Canada invited the most active states pushing for international regulations to Toronto to add momentum to the diplomatic process. Seven states besides Canada attended the meeting: Austria, Denmark, Finland, Norway, Sweden, Switzerland, and the United States. While the goal of the "Toronto Group" was to offer an agreement on reducing the use of (aerosol) CFCs in spray cans and to sign the Vienna framework convention, besides the Toronto Group, only the Netherlands was willing to support a control protocol in 1984. During the negotiations in 1986–87, the members of the Toronto Group began to demand that virtually all CFC emissions should be stopped. The United States in particular was active in pushing for significant reductions of ozone-depleting emissions. In 1987 it proposed that the production of CFCs and halons first be frozen at 1986 levels and later eliminated step by step except for uses for which substitutes were not commercially available. Furthermore Canada, the Netherlands, and the Nordic countries were also pushing for large reductions in CFC production. The policy of the FRG also had changed by that time. As late as 1984 it had belonged to the group of dragger states. But the FRG acknowledged in 1987 that sufficient proof of CFC involvement in ozone layer modification had been accumulated to "justify immediate and world-wide action to restrict severely all CFC emissions."

France, Italy, Japan, and the UK tried most consistently to prevent the adoption of drastic reductions in CFC production and consumption. Since three of these countries belonged to the EC, the EC views reflected their interests. In the beginning these states were reluctant even to discuss a control protocol, since they either did not regard it as necessary or thought that any regulation concerning CFCs should be decided on after opening the framework convention for signature. A recommendation put forward in 1984 by six countries, including France, the FRG, Italy, and the UK, was typical of the dragger states' attitude. It contained two modest measures. First, it recommended that the effects of potentially harmful substances on the ozone layer be investigated within three or five years before any decisions on regulations were to be taken. Second, the recommendation encouraged the establishment of a code of conduct for enterprises producing CFCs.

The controversy between the actual (versus the predicted) pusher states (Canada, the Nordic countries, and the United States) and some dragger states (the EC and Japan) characterized the negotiations on the Montreal Protocol. During 1985–86 the EC was willing to limit only the production capacity of CFCs. The proposed ceiling was higher than the then-current production levels within the EC. However by 1987 the EC was convinced that more stringent international action was necessary to control emissions. The new policy of the EC included, besides the freeze on the production of CFCs, an automatic reduction in CFC production and imports of 20 percent, based on 1986 levels. In particular, Denmark, the FRG, and the Netherlands were pushing the EC to accept significant reductions in CFC production, while France and the UK still opposed tighter regulations. The Japanese policy also began to change by the end of the decade. In 1987 a representative of Japan considered it "realistic to establish immediate measures such as regulations on CFC–11 and CFC–12 and to consider to control other substances."

The arguments used by the former Soviet Union during the negotiations resembled those of the dragger states, but the overall policy of the Soviet Union was cautious. Although Winfried Lang, who chaired the sessions that prepared the Montreal Protocol, described the Soviet stand in 1986–87 as "friendly to reductions" ("*eine reduktionsfreundliche Haltung*"), and the press reported in 1987 that the Soviet Union favored big reductions, analysts of the negotiations tend to place the Soviet Union together with the EC and Japan as opponents of international regulations.

Building on this summary of the negotiation process, we assess the validity of the impact of ecological vulnerability and abatement costs on a country's position in international environmental negotiations. The states in the upper right-hand cell of Figure 2 correspond well with our hypotheses. These states acted as the most consistent pushers in the negotiations. In addition, Austria and the Netherlands (with low CFC production intensities of 0.5 and 1.0, respectively) were supportive of the position of the predicted pushers.

As expected on the basis of ecological and economic constraints, France, Italy, Japan, and the UK were the most visible dragger states in the negotiations. And the behavior of the former Soviet government is not necessarily surprising.

While the policies of the foregoing countries seem to support the interest-based explanation of support for international environmental regulation, the categorization of the FRG as a dragger state and of the United States as an intermediate is more problematic. Despite their domestic characteristics, both states began to support large reductions by the end of the negotiations. The United States unilaterally banned the aerosol use of CFCs as early as 1978, joined the Nordic countries in 1983 by calling for an international ban on the use of CFC–11 and CFC–12 in aerosol cans, and began to demand an end to all uses in 1986–87. The FRG opposed international regulations, though it reduced the use of aerosol CFC in the early 1980s. Its policy changed significantly in 1987 when the German representatives sought large international reductions in all CFC emissions and announced that they would aim to end production and consumption by the end of the century.

The Impact of Technology on Reducing Abatement Costs

Improvements of the state of technology seem to have played a major role in persuading the FRG and the United States to accept deep cuts in the production and consumption of CFCs. It appears that the environmental foreign policy of these countries toward ozone depletion changed as a result of the success of their industries in substituting new compounds for CFCs. In general the ability to produce substitutes reduces abatement costs and allows countries to favor more stringent regulations.

The covariation between the development of alternative compounds and policy is particularly evident in the United States. As mentioned above, the United States unilaterally banned the manufacture and shipment of CFC-propelled aerosols in 1978. The industry's response was muted, since technically feasible and economically acceptable alternatives existed for most propellant uses of CFCs. Another reason for the relatively low cost of the ban was that, from an economic perspective, aerosol use was not as important as were other uses of CFCs, such as for refrigeration and for air-conditioning.

With respect to international controls on CFCs, the United States had concluded by the early 1980s that it would not profit from being the only country to invoke stringent domestic standards on the use of CFCs. Accordingly the U.S. government continued to oppose international regulations with the exception of controls on the aerosol use of CFCs. In 1986–87 however the U.S. government began to strive for ending all uses for CFCs. It is noteworthy that the first reports about the development of new substitutes for CFCs appeared in the press at this point in time.

It was generally believed that the new position of the United States was bolstered by success in developing new forms of chemical compounds.

Industrial representatives originally opposed controls on CFCs, but by 1986 their opposition had softened considerably. In 1986 the Alliance for Responsible CFC Policy, an industry lobby group, announced that its members were prepared to support a global limit on the growth of CFC production. DuPont, a company based in the United States and the largest single producer of CFCs, took an even stronger position by calling for a worldwide limit on emissions of the chemicals. This new attitude toward CFC regulation was preceded by extensive industry research on substitutes for CFC–11 and CFC–12. DuPont, for example, initiated a large research effort as early as the mid–1970s. It ceased this line of research in the beginning of the 1980s, but by 1986 the company had reactivated its research program and announced that suitable alternatives could be available within five years. Two years later DuPont announced plans to build the world's first commercial-scale plant to produce a substitute for CFC–1249 and supported "an orderly transition to a total phaseout" of the most harmful CFCs. "It was later specified that the target was to complete the phaseout by no later than the end of the century."

Availability of substitutes for specific CFCs could also explain why the policy of the FRG toward regulating CFCs changed. Its government asked the chemical industry in 1987 for a near-total elimination of CFC production and consumption by the year 2000. The government announced that the reduction would begin by concentrating on the aerosol industry, and industry was willing to comply with the plan since it had already gone a long way toward the elimination of all but essential aerosol uses of CFCs.

The significance of the change in positions of the FRG and the United States is even more evident if compared with the situation in the main dragger states. Before the policies of the EC and Japan began to change, their representatives expressed concern during the negotiations that U.S. companies, with their successful development of substitutes, might enjoy a significant competitive advantage if drastic international regulations were adopted. Although the aerosol use of CFCs had declined steadily in the EC as a result of increased substitution by less-expensive propellants, EC representatives complained in 1987 that U.S. companies would benefit from a control protocol with drastic regulations, since they were ahead in the search for substitutes. In the words of a Japanese representative to the ozone negotiations, it was "very important that contracting parties to the protocol should have common access to technological information on substitute chemicals." He also proposed that "a system of international cooperation should be established with a view to making technological information available to all contracting states, thus avoiding the monopoly of that information by specific countries."

Given the positive covariation between the development of CFC substitutes and the more pro-regulatory preferences of national governments, two causal chains might be suggested. First, technological advances led to more ambitious preferences for environmental regulation. Second, public policy can force the development of more efficient environmental technologies. The latter causal chain is emphasized by Benedick, who suggests that changing scientific knowledge and public perceptions of environmental problems are needed to persuade industries to prepare themselves for more stringent environmental regulations. Similarly Alan Miller believes that without anticipation of a regulatory intervention, industry has little incentive to search for alternatives for existing products or production methods. These hypotheses are compatible with the interest-based explanation of international environmental regulation: a growing public perception of the severity of adverse ecological effects puts pressure on governments and creates expectations about regulatory policy. As a result, industry starts preparing itself for more stringent environmental controls by improving the state of abatement technology. As a consequence, lowered abatement costs enhance the likelihood of substantive international environmental regulation.

In conclusion, as a result of a growing perception of the vulnerability to ozone depletion in combination with advances in developing substitutes for CFCs, all states began gradually to perceive common interests in protecting the stratospheric ozone layer by phasing out harmful chemicals.

The Legitimacy of International Governance: A Coming Challenge for International Environmental Law?*

DANIEL BODANSKY

This article is about a problem only just becoming visible: the legitimacy of international environmental law, and more specifically, the perception that the international environmental process is insufficiently democratic. Until now, international lawyers have tended to focus on what environmental standards are needed and how those standards can be made effective. But as decision-making authority gravitates from the national to the international level, the question of legitimacy will likely emerge from the shadows and become a central issue in international environmental law....

Why hasn't the legitimacy of international institutions been a bigger issue heretofore?

The answer has two parts. First, until recently international institutions have generally been so weak—they have exercised so little authority—that the issue of their legitimacy has barely arisen. Indeed, many political scientists have questioned whether international institutions

* Reprinted with permission from 93 AMERICAN JOURNAL OF INTERNATIONAL LAW 596 (1999).

have any significant influence at all. Hence, international relations scholars have traditionally focused on the causal role—if any—of international institutions, rather than on their legitimacy.

Second, to the extent that international institutions do influence the behavior of states—to the extent that we can speak of "international governance"—this authority has generally been self-imposed, it rests on the consent of the very states to which it applies. . . .

As international institutions gain greater authority, however, and their consensual underpinnings erode, questions about their legitimacy are beginning to be voiced. . . .

These kinds of concerns will become louder and more widespread if, as appears likely, environmental decision-making authority continues to shift from the national to the international level—particularly if international institutions are compelled to depart from purely consensual modes of decision making in order to avoid gridlock and least-common-denominator outcomes. Already, the Montreal Protocol allows some of its regulations to be "adjusted" by qualified majority vote. Concern about global environmental problems has prompted calls for more such legislative mechanisms—calls emanating not just from environmental groups but from political leaders as well. In 1989, seventeen heads of state endorsed the Hague Declaration, which called for "new institutional authority" that involves non-unanimous decision making, in order to combat global climate change. It is hard to imagine how problems such as global climate change will be successfully addressed, without the eventual establishment of more authoritative international institutions to set standards and oversee compliance.

. . .

The article's provisional message is cautionary. It proposes no compelling basis of legitimacy. Democracy—at least as we usually use the term—does not seem to be an option, given the lack of a global "demos," a lack that makes suggestions to establish a global parliament or to hold global referenda not only utopian but unwise. Principles of procedural fairness—transparency, public access, and so forth—are important, but do not answer the crucial question of who should make decisions and how they should do so. Finally, expertise can play an important role in legitimizing international environmental decision making, but ultimately many of the most important questions will require value judgments, not simply technical solutions. Unless some other source of legitimacy can be found, international environmental law must continue to rely on its traditional foundations: self-interest, reciprocity, and consent. In the long run, this is likely to represent a limiting factor on efforts to develop stronger and more effective international regimes.

. . .

Legitimacy in Contemporary International Environmental Law

Legitimacy concerns the justification of authority; it provides grounds for deferring to another's decision, even in the absence of coercion or rational persuasion. Thus far, international environmental law has developed on a different basis, through a consensual rather than an authoritative process. States have negotiated and adopted international rules that they believe are in their self-interest, rather than recognize the rulemaking authority of international institutions. They realize that they cannot solve some transnational or global environmental problem through individual action, so they agree to collective action by means of a reciprocal exchange of promises—they agree, for example, to limit their use of ozone-depleting substances or to impose restrictions on the import and export of endangered species.

Even in this consensualist, state-oriented model of international law, however, the phenomenon of authority plays an ancillary role—and thus the issue of legitimacy plays a role as well. To begin with, there is the continuing authority of norms, once states have consented to them. Why should a state continue to be bound by a norm, once its interests change and it no longer consents? To answer this question, we need some notion that states can bind themselves through promises—that consent is a legitimate basis of obligation, and that obligations persist over time.

In considering the legitimating role of state consent, two types of consent should be distinguished: (1) *specific consent* to particular obligations or decisions—for example, by ratifying a treaty, joining consensus on a UN resolution, or accepting a court's jurisdiction in a particular case; and (2) *general consent* to an ongoing system of governance—for example, by ratifying a treaty such as the UN Charter, which creates institutions with quasi-legislative and adjudicatory authority. A constitution confers general consent; a contract, specific consent. Thus far, specific consent has played the predominant role in the formation of international environmental law. States have specifically consented to the vast majority of international obligations that bind them. They usually do so expressly—for example, by becoming a party to an agreement establishing particular obligations or by engaging in state practice that contributes to the formation of customary international law; in some cases, they do so tacitly—for example, by failing to object to a new norm as it comes into existence. By contrast, few existing international environmental obligations are the product of general consent. Among the exceptions are the "adjustments" adopted pursuant to the Montreal Protocol on Substances that Deplete the Ozone Layer, which allows a qualified majority of parties to tighten ("adjust") the controls on regulated substances.

. . .

The Emerging Problem of Legitimacy in International Environmental Law

. . . [S]tate consent and legality have until now provided a relatively firm foundation for international environmental law. But two developments are likely to undermine their ability to do so in the future. First, the coming generation of environmental problems will probably require more expeditious and flexible lawmaking approaches, which do not depend on consensus among states. Second, to the extent that international environmental law is beginning to have significant implications for non- or substate actors (who have not consented to it directly), rather than just for the relations among states, state consent may for them have little legitimating effect. As international environmental law continues to grow more like domestic environmental law, it will be held to the same standards of legitimacy, and its lack of transparency and accountability will become increasingly problematic.

Non-Consensus Decision-making Mechanisms

As noted earlier, international environmental law has developed primarily through the negotiation of treaties that bind consenting states to rules rather than governance structures. In practice, this has usually meant an effort to find consensus, since states are reluctant to take action against global problems such as climate change or ozone depletion unless everyone (or nearly everyone) is required to do so; unilateral action simply raises a country's costs, thereby injuring its competitiveness, without necessarily solving the problem, if others continue to pollute.

Consensus decision making, however, involves numerous, by now familiar, problems. Attempting to achieve consensus is time-consuming and difficult. Agreements tend to be inflexible, given the difficulties of gaining agreement on any changes. Moreover, agreements must either represent the least-common-denominator, and thus be weak, or must create different obligations for different states. In many cases, reaching agreement at all is impossible, so a consensus requirement in effect precludes collective action. For these reasons, among others, within domestic society, "the unanimity rule is recognized as incompatible with effective government."

International environmental law has employed a variety of mechanisms to circumvent the "slowest boat" phenomenon associated with consensus decision making and thereby make possible more robust international standard-setting. But, despite some successes, most notably the ozone regime, the consensus requirement puts international environmental law under a serious handicap. It is difficult enough to enact domestic legislation to control water or air pollution in a system of simple majority rule, particularly when decisions impose significant costs on identifiable segments of society. But imagine trying to adopt such rules through a consensus mechanism. Consensus decision making is even less likely to be able to address international problems such as climate change, where states have (or at least think they have) very different interests, where the costs may be extremely high, and where the regime may need to change rapidly as scientific understanding of the problem improves. Instead, successful international action will depend on the ability to require common action even in the absence of consensus among states—it will depend, that is, on some form of supranational authority.

Consider, for example, the ozone regime. Compared to climate change, the ozone problem is simple—the science is much better understood and, in most cases, replacement technologies exist at a reasonable cost. But even the ozone regime has found it desirable to provide for non-consensus decision making. The Montreal Protocol on Substances that Deplete the Ozone Layer states that, once a chemical is subject to control measures, those controls may be tightened ("adjusted") by a qualified majority vote. This decision-making rule does not simply prevent a minority from blocking action; it subjects the minority to the majority's will. Adjustments bind all parties to the Montreal Protocol, not just those that give specific consent. In this regard, the Montreal Protocol's adjustment procedure constitutes an embryonic legislative mechanism, rather than merely a contractual mechanism by which states voluntarily assume obligations.

. . .

To some degree, general consent could provide a basis of legitimacy for non-consensus decision-making mechanisms. States could agree to such a mechanism in a treaty, as they have done in the Montreal Protocol.... From the perspective of social contract theory, this general consent should give these regimes a strong claim to legitimacy—indeed, a stronger claim than many national governments, since these regimes are based on actual contracts to which each member state gave its express consent, rather than on a merely hypothetical social contract. So long as a regime stays within its constitutional limits (i.e., has legal legitimacy), then states that freely consented to a non-consensus decision-making process should be bound by the results.

The persisting questions about the legitimacy of the European Union and the Security Council, however, suggest that general consent may not be sufficient, in itself, to legitimate a general system of governance or its resulting rules. General consent involves a much more significant surrender of autonomy than specific consent—and thereby raises more serious concerns about legitimacy—since, in giving consent, a state does not know what particular constraints may be imposed on it in the future.... Although general consent may be sufficient to legitimate a relatively limited decision-making mechanism such as the Montreal Protocol adjustment procedure, where the range of possible decisions is narrowly circumscribed and the issues have a significant technical component, when an institution must be able to respond to changing problems in changing ways, "any concept of consent is unlikely to have any significant application ... unless we conceive it as a process, as a relationship ... that must be constantly renewed and maintained." That is why the consent of EU member states to the EU treaties, or of UN member states to the UN Charter, has not laid to rest questions about the legitimacy of the European Council or the Security Council respectively. By the same token, general consent i[s] unlikely to be sufficient to legitimate environmental institutions with broad decision-making powers, of the kind envisioned by the Hague Declaration.

. . .

Conclusion

The process of globalization has put mounting strains on the state system. Environmental problems are increasingly escaping the control of individual states and international institutions have often been too weak to step into the breach. The result has been a "decision-making deficit," an erosion in the ability of government to address environmental problems effectively. In the long run, overcoming this deficit will require stronger international institutions and decision-making mechanisms. But . . . the stronger the institution, the greater the concern about its legitimacy. Unless the issue of legitimacy is addressed, it is likely to act as a drag on the development and effectiveness of international environmental regimes.

Many factors can contribute to or detract from a regime's legitimacy. Legitimacy is a matter not of all or nothing, but of more or less. Authority should be exercised in accordance with law and principle (legal legitimacy). The decision-making mechanisms should be transparent and give people an opportunity to participate (participatory legitimacy). Furthermore, decisions should be based on the best scientific expertise (expert legitimacy). But these are minimum conditions. They contribute to legitimacy (and their absence undermines it), but by themselves do not provide a firm basis for legitimacy. They do not address the central problem, which is how decisions should be made when consensus cannot be reached—by whom, using what voting rule, and with what safeguards.

Calls for global environmental institutions with binding decision-making powers are usually criticized as utopian. This is perhaps too mild a criticism. The term "utopian" carries the connotation of desirable; the criticism suggests that global institution with real power would be a good thing, if only states would agree. But this is by no means clear, given the lack of a strong theory of legitimacy. In the absence of a global community, the one compelling candidate, democracy, does not provide an answer. And, at the moment, we lack any persuasive alternative.

. . .

Unless some other basis of legitimacy can be found, the continuing centrality of state consent (which remains, by default, the principal source of legitimacy for international environmental law) is likely to limit the possibilities of international governance. When states have common interests, and the issues involved are relatively technical, states might agree to establish institutions with flexible, non-consensus decision-making procedures, as they have done in the ozone regime. In such cases, general consent confers legitimacy initially, and technical expertise helps maintain this legitimacy on a continuing basis. But this approach is unlikely to work for problems such as climate change, where states have a much wider range of interests, and the issues involved are highly political. This is a sobering conclusion, but one that clarifies the challenges that lie ahead for international environmental law.

Notes and Comments

1. Nearly ten years after the formulation of the Montreal Protocol, some observers have concluded that, rather than changing state behavior, the agreement did no more than codify a pre-existing move away from CFC production. In *The Voluntary Provision of a Pure Public Good*, 63 Journal of Public Economics 331 (1997), James C. Murdoch & Todd Sandler contend that:

> [T]he Montreal Protocol was initially enacted because it codified reductions in CFC emissions that polluters were voluntarily prepared to accomplish as the scientific case against CFCs grew.... Our findings suggest that the Montreal Protocol may be more symbolic than a true instance of cooperat[ion]. By examining [data] ... we provide ... evidence that CFC cutbacks were voluntary, because these reductions characterized both ratifiers and nonratifiers [and] were at levels greater than the initial mandate [of the Protocol]....
>
> [After examining empirical data,] nations are seen as reducing emissions beyond treaty-mandated levels even prior to the Montreal Protocol taking effect. On average, 61 nations in our sample set reduced CFC emissions by 41.6% from 1986 to 1989, which is well in excess of the 20% cutback mandated by the Protocol from the year commencing on 1 July 1993. This finding suggests that the initial provisions of the Montreal Protocol are largely consistent with voluntary subscription cutbacks in CFC emissions....
>
> A number of policy conclusions follow. First, the Montreal Protocol may be a poor blueprint for other global agreements. Each global commons problem has its own pattern of payoffs based on publicness. Currently, ozone depletion is associated with more-certain and more-costly consequences than problems like global warming. Second, the wealthiest CFC emitters may be expected to adhere to the Montreal Protocol without the need of an enforcement mechanism, because the net benefits from doing so are apparently positive. Self-interests motivate compliance. Third, an increase in the number of democratic countries is apt to increase the number of nations that will take steps to curb transboundary emissions.

Id. at 332, 347.[3] As outlined in Haas's article above, the Montreal Protocol built on a framework agreement called the Vienna Convention for the Protection of the Ozone Layer, which went into effect in 1985. In light of this and in light of the readings above, do you find Murdoch and Sandler's claims convincing? What would Abram Chayes and Antonia

3. Reprinted from James C. Murdoch & Todd Sandler, *The Voluntary Provision of a Pure Public Good*, 63 Journal of Public Economics 331 (1997), with permission from Elsevier.

Chayes or George Downs, David M. Rocke, and Peter N. Barsoom (in Part III.C.) say?

2. Like Murdoch and Sandler, Carsten Helm and Detlef F. Sprinz followed Sprinz and Vaahtoranta's article (see above) with an effort to measure the effect of international treaties on the environment. See Carsten Helm and Detlef F. Sprinz, *Measuring the Effectiveness of International Treaty Regimes*, 45 JOURNAL OF CONFLICT RESOLUTION 630 (2000). This prompted a lively scholarly exchange on the effort to measure environmental treaty effectiveness. See Oran R. Young, *Determining Regime Effectiveness: A Commentary on the Oslo–Potsdam Solution*, 3 GLOBAL ENVIRONMENTAL POLITICS 97 (2003); Jon Hovi, Detlef F. Sprinz, and Arild Underdal, *The Oslo–Potsdam Solution to Measuring Regime Effectiveness: Critique, Response, and Extensions*, 3 GLOBAL ENVIRONMENTAL POLITICS 74 (2003); Oran R. Young, *Inferences and Indices: Evaluating the Effectiveness of International Environmental Regimes*, 1 GLOBAL ENVIRONMENTAL POLITICS 99 (2001); Jon Hovi, Detlef F. Sprinz, and Arild Underdal, *Regime Effectiveness and the Oslo–Potsdam Solution: A Rejoinder to Oran Young*, 3 GLOBAL ENVIRONMENTAL POLITICS 105 (2003). Why is there so much debate over the issue of treaty effectiveness? If the treaties were found to be ineffective in reducing pollution among ratifying nations, would this mean the treaties are necessarily not worthwhile? Are there other ways of measuring the success of a treaty regime? What might a constructivist or other norm-based scholar say?

3. There has been a great deal of debate in recent years about the connection of environmental regulations to international trade. Enviromental activists, in particular, have raised concerns that environmental protections might be diluted or reversed by the World Trade Organization. These fears were brought to the fore by a recent dispute filed with the General Agreement on Tariffs and Trade (GATT) (since superseded by the World Trade Organization), popularly known as the "tuna-dolphin case." The case arose after Mexican exports of tuna to the United States were banned under the United States Marine Mammal Protection Act, which provided that only countries that could certify that its tuna was caught using certain methods for protecting dolphins could export tuna to the Untied States. Mexico originally filed a complaint with the GATT against the United States in 1991 arguing that the United States had violated trade laws by banning its exports of tuna. The panel, in a report that was never formally adopted, concluded that the United States could not embargo the tuna simply because Mexican regulations on the way the tuna was produced differed from those of the United States. The GATT rules, it noted, do not allow a country to use trade restrictions to enforce its domestic laws abroad. A subsequent case involving similar issues filed by the European Union a few years later came to similar conclusions, though unlike the first ruling it did not rule out measures to protect resources outside a state's domestic jurisdiction. See GATT Dispute Settlement Panel Report on U.S.—Restrictions on Imports of Tuna, DS21/R, submitted to parties Aug. 16, 1991, not adopted, 30 I.L.M. 1594 (1991); GATT Dispute Panel Report on U.S.—

Restrictions on Imports of Tuna, DS29/R, circulated June 16, 1994, not adopted, 33 I.L.M. 839 (1994). Was the resolution of these cases correct? Putting the panel decisions to one side (the decisions, after all, were never adopted), can or should trade be used to enforce environmental regulations? Environmentalists have argued that because WTO panels are chosen from the world trade community, a population that tends to be unfamiliar with environmental concerns, continuing litigation of these issues before trade panels will lead to systematic undervaluing of environmental concerns. For one proposal on how better to link trade and environmental protection, see Daniel C. Esty, Greening the Gatt: Trade, Environment, and the Future (1993).

4. The United Nations Framework Convention on Climate Change (UNFCCC), which entered into force in 1994, aims directly at regulating practices that contribute to global warming. In 1998, a Protocol, popularly known as the "Kyoto Protocol" to the UNFCCC, opened for signature. The Protocol would commit industrialized countries that agree to it to reduce emissions of six greenhouse gases by 5% by 2012. The Protocol only goes into effect, however, once 55 parties to the UNFCCC, accounting in total for at least 55% of the total carbon dioxide emissions for 1990 among industrialized nations, have ratified the Protocol. As of mid-2004, 122 state parties had ratified or acceded to the Kyoto Protocol, yet the 55% requirement had not been met. The United States and Russia together produced more than 45% of the 1990 carbon dioxide emissions, hence the Protocol cannot go into effect unless one of the two ratifies the Protocol, which they have not yet done. (Russia announced in June 2004 that it intended finally to ratify the Protocol; if and when that happens, the Protocol will come into effect.) Under President Clinton, the United States signed the Protocol (though it was never submitted to the Senate for ratification), but President George Bush withdrew the United States signature soon after taking office, much to the dismay of environmental advocates. Why might the Kyoto Protocol have been structured in this way? How could you explain the decision of the United States to refuse to ratify the treaty and Russia's decision to delay ratification for several years? Relatedly, why have the states that have already ratified done so? And finally, does the experience with the Montreal Protocol give reason to think that the Kyoto Protocol will or will not be a success?

5. Haas focuses on a particular set of nongovernmental actors, especially scientists and policymakers who are a part of the epistemic community he identifies. Kal Raustiala takes a somewhat broader approach in his work on the role of NGOs in international environmental law. He argues that "NGOs are now major actors in the formulation, implementation, and enforcement of international environmental law" and that their participation "yields political, technical, and informational benefits for states ... without granting undue power to non-state actors." Kal Raustiala, *The Participatory Revolution in International Environmental Law*, 21 Harvard Environmental Law Review 537, 537–38 (1997); see also Kal Raustiala, *States, NGOs, and International Environmental Institutions*, 41 International Studies Quarterly 719 (1997). Which nongovernmental organizations participate in environmental lawmaking? Are the groups that participate in environmental lawmaking qualitatively different than those that participate in other areas of international lawmaking? How much power do NGOs have to shape international law? How much power should they have? How well do these groups reflect the public interest? As you weigh these questions, consider Daniel Bodansky's observation (in a portion of his article not included in the excerpt above) that when scholars speak of participation of "the public" in environmental lawmaking, "[w]hat is meant more precisely is participation by non-governmental groups such as Greenpeace, the Sierra Club and the Global Climate Coalition, which often have opposing positions and may or may not reflect the 'public interest'—if such a thing exists at all." Bodansky, *supra*, at 619.

6. Bodansky's article focuses on the legitimacy of international environmental law. What is the connection, according to Bodansky, between legitimacy of international environmental law and its effectiveness? Do you agree? When Bodansky speaks of "legitimacy," how much does his argument owe to the "Fairness School" described in Part III.B. above?

C. Trade

International trade has long been considered a central focus—some might say *the* central focus—of international law. Indeed, if there is one area in which international law is widely regarded as having played a vital role, it is international trade. Yet efforts to regulate international trade have not been without their critics. International trade law has been a subject of debate for centuries, with the foundations of modern debates running back over two hundred years to Adam Smith's 1776 classic, *The Wealth of Nations*, and David Ricardo's *The Principles of Political Economy and Taxation*, which both made the case that all nations could profit from engaging in free international trade.

The current legal framework for the international trade system emerged in the aftermath of the chaos and devastation of World War II, when several states joined together to form the 1947 General Agreement on Tariffs and Trade (GATT). The agreement created an international forum that encouraged free trade between member nations. Its central functions were to regulate and reduce tariffs on certain traded goods and to provide a mechanism for resolving trade disputes—functions that it is generally considered to have served effectively. Yet after several decades of largely successful operation of the GATT, a consensus began to emerge that a stronger set of legal and institutional arrangements was needed. In negotiations concluded in 1994 (commonly referred to as the "Uruguay Round"), the members of the GATT voted to expand and strengthen the international trade system by creating the World Trade Organization (WTO) Agreement. The agreement established the WTO as "the common institutional framework for the conduct of trade relations among its Members in matters related to the" WTO Agreement.

The readings in this chapter focus on the WTO—its creation, its operation, and its methods of enforcement. The first several pieces examine the WTO dispute settlement system from a largely norm-based perspective. We begin with a brief outline of the central structures and functions of the WTO and its dispute resolution process by Jeffrey Michael Smith. We then turn to Susan Esserman's and Robert Howse's review and assessment of the vehement criticism that the WTO's legal dispute settlement system has at times provoked. While they find some of the criticisms unfounded, they note that others point to areas in which the system can and should be refined. Next, Joost Pauwelyn's piece focuses on the enforcement provisions of the WTO's dispute settlement system, pointing out some of their weaknesses and proposing reforms. The last piece, by law-and-economics scholars Warren F. Schwartz and Alan O. Sykes, takes an interest-based perspective, and argues that the WTO enforcement mechanisms can best be understood using the economic theory of contract remedies.

The World Trade Organization*

JEFFREY MICHAEL SMITH

The World Trade Organization was formed in large part to further the goals of "raising standards of living, ensuring full employment and a large and steadily growing volume of real income and effective demand, and expanding the production of and trade in goods and services." The more than 140 WTO members have agreed to abide by certain international trade agreements covering goods, services, and intellectual property rights. Many members also adhere to so-called "plurilateral" trade agreements relating to civil aircraft, government procurement, dairy, and "bovine meat." . . .

The principal political institutions of the WTO are the Ministerial Conference, the General Council, and the Director–General. The Ministerial Conference brings together, at least once every two years, high level trade representatives. The Ministerial Conference has the power "to make decisions on all matters" pursuant to the various trade agreements that bind the WTO members. Between meetings of the Ministerial Conference, the functions of the WTO are conducted by the General Council, which also consists of one representative from each member nation. In addition to wielding these administrative powers, the General Council also doubles both as the Dispute Settlement Body (the titular head of the WTO's judicial functions) and as the Trade Policy Review Body. The Ministerial Conference appoints the Director–General of the WTO, and is empowered to adopt regulations governing his powers, duties, conditions of service, and length of term in office.

* Reprinted by permission from *Three Models of Judicial Institutions in International Organizations: The European Union, the United Nations, and the World Trade Organization* 10 Tulsa Journal of Comparative and International Law 115 (2002).

The WTO Dispute Resolution Process

The Dispute Settlement Body (DSB), an alter ego of the General Council, is nominally in charge of the WTO's dispute resolution functions, but, in actuality, it plays a very limited role in the dispute resolution process.

The complicated WTO dispute resolution process begins with a mandatory "consultations" phase. A WTO member that believes that another member is violating a WTO trade agreement requests that member to enter consultations aimed at reaching a settlement of the dispute. If the respondent party refuses consultations or if the consultations fail to settle the dispute, the complaining party may request that a dispute resolution panel be convened.

When a dispute reaches the (first) litigation stage, a panel is established to try the dispute.... This panel, appointed specifically for the dispute at hand, serves as the trier of fact and (in the first instance) of law. The panel, after receiving submissions from the parties, as well as other information it deems necessary, hands down its decision in the form of a panel report. The panel report is then adopted by the DSB in what is essentially a pro forma exercise. At this point, the losing party can either acquiesce to the decision, or appeal to the WTO's standing Appellate Body.... The appellate panel reviews the panel report, but its review is limited to "issues of law" and "legal interpretations." Thus, the appellate panel must take the initial panel's factual findings as given.

While the DSB and its panels can "clarify the existing provisions" of trade agreements, they cannot "add to or diminish the rights and obligations provided in the covered agreements." As such, WTO panels lack the powers of common law courts to shape and create new law or interpret a "living constitution." The panels are not empowered to seek amorphous ideals such as justice; rather, they are to provide "security and predictability." ...

The current WTO dispute resolution procedure is a relatively recent innovation. Prior to 1995, when the results of the Uruguay Round of negotiations took effect, the DSB's predecessor, the GATT Council, could adopt a panel decision only by consensus. As a result, any single member had a de facto veto over any decision. Thus ... the former dispute resolution process had no teeth.

...

The WTO dispute resolution process ensures respect for sovereignty through a variety of measures. First, the WTO panels are limited to interpretation of the treaties. They are explicitly forbidden from increasing or diminishing the rights and obligations in the written documents.... Second, the panels and the DSB lack the ability to directly coerce WTO members into obeying an order or judgment. Unlike the ECJ [European Court of Justice], the WTO panels cannot directly strike down or enact law in a member country. Nor can they order a member to pay money or to act in any other way. Rather, the WTO dispute resolution identifies treaty noncompliance, measures the cost of the noncompliance to the complaining member, and authorizes the complaining member to take proportionate action against the violator. Rather than acting as a super-sovereign, the WTO dispute resolution process channels the pre-existing power of the complaining member in a way that pushes the violator toward compliance with its obligations, while avoiding a full-scale trade war that would threaten the international trading system....

The WTO on Trial*

SUSAN ESSERMAN and ROBERT HOWSE

[In Fall 2002], a judicial panel of the World Trade Organization (WTO) issued a controversial ruling in a high-stakes corporate tax dispute between the United States and the European Union. Paying scant attention to the complexities of the case, the panel authorized Brussels to implement retaliatory sanctions of $4 billion—an unprecedented sum—against Washington. Notably, around the same time the United States and its European allies were also making headlines with another fierce legal battle: that over the authority of the International Criminal Court to prosecute American soldiers for alleged misdeeds committed abroad.

In the nineteenth century, Clausewitz famously wrote that war is politics conducted by other means; today, as these examples illustrate, the same could be said for the law. Many disputes that used to be settled by negotiation or even by force of arms now end up before a proliferating range of international courts, tribunals, and arbitral panels. Legal briefs are replacing diplomatic notes, and judicial decrees are displacing political compromises.

Less often considered is whether this ascendant legalism is good or bad for global prosperity and stability. In most cases, it turns out, it is still too early to say. There is one exception, however: the WTO. Nowhere else has international conflict resolution by judges emerged more forcefully or developed more rapidly. As in a domestic court—but unlike in most international bodies—WTO dispute settlement is both compulsory and binding. Member states have no choice but to submit to it and must accept the consequences of the WTO's ruling.

But what, exactly, does the WTO's record reveal about how it has used its unprecedented powers? ... Will the dramatic judicialization of international trade be reversed? So far, trade experts have revealed deep ambivalence about the WTO's experiment with binding adjudication, and there is little clear sense of where the system should go from here.

At the WTO's inception in 1995, the organization's provisions for legal dispute settlement were touted as state of the art and the crown

* Reprinted by permission from 82 Foreign Affairs 130 (2003).

jewels of the WTO system. Today, however, even some of the organization's original architects and supporters complain that the process has gotten out of hand. Critics accuse the WTO's appellate tribunal of improper judicial activism, much as conservative American jurists lambasted the U.S. Supreme Court in the 1960s and 1970s. Developing countries, meanwhile, complain that not all states are equal in their ability to use the WTO's laws to advance their own interests. Litigation, they argue, draws on different skills, resources, and even cultural attitudes than does diplomacy, placing certain nations at a real disadvantage.

An accurate assessment of the WTO's judicial record finds that the system has indeed reduced the role of international diplomacy, while strengthening the rule of law. At the same time, a number of measures, described below, should be implemented to strengthen the rule of law still further while also providing incentives for resolving trade disputes through negotiated solutions—a more prudent approach when the rules are unsettled and political and cultural differences are a large part of the problem.

On the Record

When the WTO was established in the mid–1990s at the end of the Uruguay Round of global trade negotiations, the fact that it included a new and improved dispute settlement system was regarded as a signal achievement. Under the preceding regime, the General Agreement on Tariffs and Trade (GATT), dispute resolution worked only if the countries involved voluntarily accepted both the jurisdiction of the arbitral panel and its ultimate ruling. Such rulings could take years to obtain, and the defending party could block the process from moving forward.

In the WTO system, however, parties can no longer block the process at any point. Panels must render their decisions within established time frames, and an Appellate Body has been established to review the initial decisions of the arbitral panels. Rulings by this higher court are final and automatically binding.

The institution of the Appellate Body is the most radical aspect of the new WTO system, and a most remarkable aspect of the Appellate Body is the independence of the jurists who compose it. Members of the Appellate Body do not act as advocates for the national interests of their home countries; in fact, the judges have displayed levels of integrity and independence that rival those found in the best domestic court systems.

As a result, disputes at the WTO are now settled largely on the basis of the rule of law rather than simple power politics. Each member country has equal rights within the system, and each also has an equal obligation to accept the results. Although developing countries have not yet fully reaped the benefits of the system, using the dispute settlement mechanism is crucial to full participation in the WTO. Binding adjudication, moreover, has increased the certainty that trade agreements, once negotiated, will be adhered to and enforced.

In fact, in a majority of cases over the last seven years where the complaining country won a WTO dispute, the losing state removed or revised the offending trade barriers. This positive track record may be surprising to some observers, since the cases that have attracted the most media attention were those few, difficult instances in which the losing party was either unable or unwilling to comply with the ruling.

Despite this largely positive record, WTO dispute settlement has attracted strident criticism. Some of the critiques have been ill-founded and self-serving, reflecting vested interests in specific issues or results. Other arguments, however, point to legitimate problems with the WTO system and highlight the need to refine it.

Making the Law?

The sharpest and most pervasive critique leveled at the WTO's Appellate Body has been the charge of judicial activism. Ironically, this accusation has come from two usually antagonistic camps: antiglobalization advocates and doctrinaire free traders. Each side has found evidence of judicial activism in those rulings with which it disagrees. But an open-minded look at the record shows that, in most areas, the Appellate Body has acted with due respect for state sovereignty and the letter of the law.

Take, for example, the beef hormones case, a favorite target of the antiglobalization movement. In that dispute, the Appellate Body upheld a panel ruling against an EU ban on U.S. and Canadian beef injected with growth hormones. Antiglobalization activists attacked the decision, claiming that the ban was a response to genuine consumer anxiety and should have been upheld. Given the scientific uncertainty that remains about the safety of hormones, the advocates argued, the Appellate Body should have deferred to the will of the EU's citizens.

The EU's own lawyers, however, refused to invoke the WTO rule that allows for temporary precautions (including import bans) in situations where scientific evidence of a risk has yet to be confirmed. Instead, the Europeans preferred to go for broke, pushing for a permanent ban. The Appellate Body therefore had little choice but to strike down Brussels' restriction, since it lacked the scientific justification required by WTO rules. But far from being a case of judicial activism as critics have charged, the ruling actually reflected respect for Europe's sovereignty, emphasizing as it did that the requirement of scientific evidence could be flexible and admit "non-mainstream" science.

Hard-core free traders, meanwhile, have taken aim at a different ruling, known as shrimp-turtle. In that case, Washington had banned the import of shrimp from countries that did not mandate the use of fishing techniques that were safe for endangered sea turtles. The Appellate Body found that the ban could have been justified under an environmental provision in the WTO agreement—except that in this case it had been applied in a discriminatory manner. The United States subsequently made changes to address these concerns, and the WTO tribunal approved the new measures in a later decision.

Critics have charged that this ruling, like the beef hormones case, was an instance of judicial activism, in part because it was inconsistent with an older GATT decision condemning a ban on tuna imports from countries that did not protect dolphins. The critics' complaint, however, reflects a belief that the WTO should not sanction any trade measures that are meant to address environmental concerns. But the problem with this argument is that the WTO treaty does not actually prohibit conservation-minded trade measures, so long as such measures are not merely a pretext for protectionism or unjustifiably discriminatory. Nor is there any rule in international law that prohibits the use of economic pressure on other countries for environmental ends. In fact, the preamble to the WTO agreement actually promotes the objective of sustainable development. Thus the Appellate Body's ruling was hardly radical, as its critics have charged; noting the commitment to sustainable development and the absence of any law banning measures such as the one at hand, the Appellate Body simply deferred to the sovereignty of the United States.

Another issue that has attracted charges of judicial activism is the Appellate Body's willingness to accept amicus curiae briefs from nongovernmental actors. Critics complain that the Appellate Body made this decision despite the fact that it has no explicit authorization in the WTO agreement to do so. But the WTO agreement is also not explicit about the right of governments to provide submissions in their own cases. Clearly, the drafters of the agreement left certain procedural matters to be resolved by the judges and their own sense of due process.

Other critics have suggested that the decision to accept amicus curiae briefs reflected a developed-country agenda hostile to the interests and legal culture of the developing world. Yet this argument is similarly flawed. The judges of the Inter–American Court of Human Rights—all of whom hail from developing countries—also allow amicus curiae briefs in their court, as do other international tribunals as diverse as the African Human Rights Commission and the World Bank's inspection panel. It was also sometimes objected that accepting briefs from nongovernmental actors would give them more rights than WTO member governments that weren't party to the dispute—but the Appellate Body has recently ruled that, in addition to private persons and groups, such states may also submit amicus briefs.

More of a Good Thing

The sweeping criticisms of judicial activism leveled at the WTO do not, therefore, withstand scrutiny. The Appellate Body can, however, learn a lesson from these attacks: namely, that a measure of judicial caution is essential in all international dispute settlement. This is true especially in contexts such as the WTO, where rulings are automatically binding. Moreover, international courts offer little room for redress. The rulings of domestic courts on most matters can be corrected by a single domestic legislature. But practically speaking, the decisions of the Appellate Body of the WTO can be corrected only by a consensus decision of the organization's 144 members.

For this and other reasons, international law principles, which the Appellate Body is directed to follow, incorporate judicial caution: when a treaty text is ambiguous and the negotiating history is nonexistent or unhelpful, judges should adopt the interpretation most deferential to state sovereignty. Generally speaking, the Appellate Body has followed this cautious approach.

There is one exception, however. In cases that involve domestic trade laws such as antidumping rules, the Appellate Body has tended to be intrusive in its interpretations of the WTO's rules, even when the treaty is ambiguous. This tendency is especially troubling in the antidumping context, where judges have failed to apply the deferential standard of review negotiated into the Uruguay Round agreement. Free traders have not objected to most of these rulings, since they believe that the domestic measures in question have often smacked of protectionism. But the fact is that trade remedies remain legal under the WTO and can be important safety valves that release political and economic pressures—pressures that might otherwise threaten WTO members' basic commitment to free trade.

Part of the problem is that the Appellate Body has too often made it difficult for domestic agencies to administer trade remedies in an expeditious and cost-effective fashion. National decisions on technical and procedural matters were not meant to be micromanaged by WTO panels. Doing so will ultimately have an inequitable effect on developing countries, which are newcomers to the use of trade remedies, have the least experience with them, and have the fewest resources to respond to WTO demands.

The WTO's rules are often unclear on their face—another reason for the Appellate Body to exercise restraint. Compiling a more comprehensive history of WTO negotiations would therefore be a useful way to guide the Appellate Body's approach to ambiguous treaty texts.

In addition, there are a number of other important systemic problems in the WTO regime that need to be addressed. Careful analysis of the past seven years suggests that several changes could safeguard and even enhance the judicial character of WTO dispute resolution while improving and augmenting alternatives to litigation. Such alternatives are important because in every legal system, whether domestic or international, there are cases that cannot be solved simply through applying the law as it is written. The facts may raise novel issues, or the political questions that are raised may be too sensitive for governments to leave to judges. In these situations, the use of judicial dispute settlement is neither constructive nor likely to promote a country's goals.

Although the WTO system makes it easy to litigate a dispute and secure a legal ruling, it unfortunately does not provide a structured way to achieve negotiated settlements. Such an alternative is sorely needed, and the WTO negotiations now under way provide an ideal opportunity to make such midcourse corrections.

The WTO's rules currently require consultations before litigation, with the objective of encouraging settlement. These consultations, however, have all too often proven perfunctory and ineffectual. Negotiations would become far more meaningful if the parties were assisted by an independent, professionally trained facilitator. Mediation already exists as a concept in the WTO, but only in the form of ad hoc intervention by the secretariat. It does not exist as a prehearing process conducted by independent experts schooled in alternative dispute resolution. The current rules should thus be amended to require mediation before a matter goes to full dispute settlement. Should the talks fail, the results of the mediation would remain confidential and not be provided to the WTO dispute settlement panel. Further, the panel could require a return to mediation at any stage of the dispute, provided that this did not lengthen the litigation.

When the panel does render decisions, its standard remedy is to recommend that the losing country change its laws or practices. A losing state, however, might have understandable domestic political reasons why it is not able, for example, to overhaul a complex scheme of legislation in the short or medium term. A distinctive feature of the WTO's system is that if the loser fails to comply with a ruling, an arbitral panel may award the winner the right to retaliate through trade restrictions.

Addressing noncompliance through retaliation, however, can be both ineffective and inequitable. Such trade restrictions may not be enough to induce powerful WTO members such as the United States or the EU to get into line. On the other hand, for smaller or poorer countries, such sanctions can be unfairly devastating. Retaliation also has the perverse effect of creating further distortions of trade through the reimposition of import barriers and thus may actually do harm to the interests of the winning party. Consider the recent $4 billion ruling against the United States; had the EU imposed the full measure of sanctions (as it was entitled to), it could not easily have avoided damaging its own industries, which have extensive commercial ties with the United States and may import many of the same American products targeted for retaliation.

Alternatives to retaliation should be available in cases where the losing party does not comply with a panel ruling. In a recent dispute between the EU and the United States over music copyrights, monetary payments were used to resolve the matter. This precedent should be generalized by explicitly amending the WTO treaty to allow the winner in a dispute to request monetary damages or increased trade concessions from the losing party as an alternative to retaliation. Although retaliation should remain available as a right of last resort, the winning party should have the flexibility to request less restrictive alternative penalties.

Meanwhile, although some developing countries, such as India and Brazil, have the capacity to participate fully in the WTO's dispute settlement proceedings, many others lack the resources. The WTO's Law

Advisory Center is meant to deal with this problem, but with only a handful of lawyers, most of whom are quite junior, it provides minimal assistance. Additional measures should therefore be considered. One possibility would be to implement cost rules—that is, to require that when a developed country loses a case against one of the least-developed ones, it is required to pay at least a portion of the winner's legal costs.

Although legal aid for poor developing countries is important, it is not a long-term solution to the current imbalance in power and resources. Legal education and training in WTO law and dispute settlement must therefore be improved within developing countries. These measures should be undertaken in partnership with universities and aid agencies. At present, despite the plentiful rhetoric about the need for "capacity building," meaningful support for such efforts is still scarce. For example, the World Trade Institute in Switzerland, which offers an advanced degree in WTO law and economics, may lose applicants because it is unable to provide scholarships.

The WTO's arbitral system also needs to improve its transparency and due process. The rulings of WTO judges affect the public interest in the broadest sense, as is especially evident in cases related to health and the environment. Yet the WTO's hearings and submissions remain secret, an unacceptable vestige of the old days of cloak-and-dagger diplomacy. Conducting hearings and appeals in secret undermines the legitimacy of the WTO and gives rise to unwarranted suspicions. Moreover, such secrecy is unnecessary; there is no good reason why WTO hearings should not be open to the public. Public input would also be enhanced by reaffirming the Appellate Body's decision to permit amicus curiae submissions.

The manner in which the WTO's panelists are chosen also needs to change. At present, selection is ad hoc and often not based on expertise in trade law. As long as that remains the norm, the Appellate Body will continue to revise extensively the rulings of the lower panels, all but ensuring that the Appellate Body continues to be accused of inappropriate activism. The WTO therefore should create a professional corps of judicial panelists, as the European Commission has proposed. Using full-time panelists who are experts in the law and properly compensated would enhance the quality of their decisions and reduce the tendency of the Appellate Body to substantially revise them. Reliance on a professional corps of panelists also might help prevent rulings that disregard international law and WTO precedent.

Finally, although in most cases the WTO's panels focus on treaty wording when interpreting the law—as they should—and read the treaties as part of international law as a whole, certain situations still arise when WTO judges end up ruling on ambiguous provisions. Such situations create a real risk that the resulting decision will exceed the limited consensus that framed the original agreement. Some WTO provisions on delicate matters, for example, such as the rules on dumping and subsidies, represent compromises that were heavily bargained and carefully scrutinized by domestic legislators. General international law permits adjudicators to examine the negotiating history of treaties when otherwise unable to resolve ambiguities. But to properly interpret these documents, a detailed public record of the negotiating process is needed. And yet, during the last round of WTO negotiations, such a detailed record was not kept. This oversight must be corrected so that future panels are not deprived of this important interpretive aid.

Role Model, Rule Model

The WTO's seven years of judicial dispute settlement have been a success overall, notwithstanding the objections of the system's critics. The very range of issues that have been submitted to the WTO's panels shows how much confidence member states now have in the system, and the experience has taught the world a great deal about the challenges inherent in judicializing an international organization.

As other international forums move in a similar direction, they should draw a number of lessons from the WTO's experience. First, the WTO's panels have shown that international tribunals can indeed function independently, with judges basing their rulings on the principled interpretation of the law—not on national affiliation. Second, the WTO has shown that when rulings directly affect the interests of citizens, the legitimacy of those rulings and the system as a whole depends on the transparency of the judicial process; secrecy and insulation from public input will no longer be tolerated. Third, the WTO's experience shows that once created, an effective international judicial system based on compulsory jurisdiction is likely to be used extensively and intensively. As the $4 billion award in the EU–U.S. tax case illustrates, the stakes in such disputes can be very high indeed. Ensuring adequate resources, equitable access, and the fair treatment of politically sensitive cases is therefore essential and must be thought through early on, ideally when the tribunal and its procedure are first being designed. Of course, no judicial system, no matter how well run, can avoid the inevitable messiness of politics, and no system will ever replace diplomacy. Nor should it. States must avoid the temptation to go to court in situations where political or diplomatic channels would offer a better, more equitable solution. The WTO must therefore also figure out how to improve its mechanisms for negotiated solutions, and not automatically resort to its judges.

Enforcement and Countermeasures in the WTO: Rules Are Rules—Toward a More Collective Approach*

JOOST PAUWELYN

In the thirty cases that have led to the adoption of dispute settlement reports in the World Trade Organization (WTO), the enforcement

* Reprinted by permission from 94 AMERICAN JOURNAL OF INTERNATIONAL LAW 335 (2000).

tool of last resort—countermeasures—has been invoked five times. This number is more—in five years—than in the forty-seven-year history of the General Agreement on Tariffs and Trade (GATT), the WTO's predecessor. In addition, on six occasions WTO members have invoked the expedited procedure to solve disagreements concerning compliance with dispute settlement reports, a procedure newly introduced with the establishment of the WTO. In another case, compliance procedures are looming.

This relatively frequent recourse to countermeasures and compliance procedures suggests that the practical enforcement of WTO rules through dispute settlement may be too arduous. The time is ripe for a critical review of the WTO dispute settlement system, especially its enforcement mechanism and the remedies it provides.

The first section of this Note summarizes how WTO rules and dispute settlement reports are enforced. The second section critically examines from a more general perspective the WTO regime of countermeasures and enforcement. The argument is that WTO rules should be considered as creating international legal obligations that are part of public international law, and that a more collective and effective enforcement mechanism, one aimed at inducing compliance, is required. The third section sets forth further suggestions for improving the practical enforcement of WTO rules. The Note ends on a word of caution.

How Are WTO Rules and Dispute Settlement Reports Enforced?

WTO rules are enforced through a WTO-specific dispute settlement system [DSU].... The adoption of the DSU brought about a legal revolution. Moving from one step to the next in the process no longer requires—unlike the GATT—the consensus of all WTO members. The establishment of a panel, the adoption of panel and Appellate Body reports, and the authorization to retaliate occur automatically *unless there is a consensus against it.* The DSU transformed the GATT's positive-consensus rule into a negative one. As a result, the WTO dispute settlement process is not only compulsory, but also virtually automatic. This novelty should be applauded. It allows politically sensitive cases to be pursued, and it protects the weaker WTO members that previously were either unable or insufficiently daring to muster a consensus in support of their complaints.

In the event a breach of WTO rules is found, the DSB recommends that the member concerned "bring the measure into conformity" with the WTO agreement that has been violated. "Withdrawal" of the measure concerned is usually required. In addition, the panel and Appellate Body may "suggest ways in which the Member concerned could implement the recommendations." Prompt compliance with the recommendations and rulings of the DSB is explicitly called for. If it is "impracticable to comply immediately," however, the losing member is given a "reasonable period of time" within which to comply, which is determined either by agreement or by binding arbitration.

If compliance is not achieved within the time period thus specified, the defaulting member can offer "compensation." It is generally understood, morever [sic], that compensation is to be offered not only to the winning party, but to all WTO members. Rather than being pecuniary in character, compensation involves the *lifting* of trade barriers—such as tariff reductions or increases in import quotas—by the losing party. Arrangements for compensation thereby work to support free trade principles. Nevertheless, since the prevailing member has to agree not only to be compensated, but with the specific amount thereof, compensation is a rare event.

If no satisfactory compensation can be agreed upon, the prevailing member can request authorization from the DSB to take countermeasures (in WTO jargon, "to suspend concessions or other obligations under the covered agreements"). DSB authorization of the countermeasures is virtually automatic; it can be withheld only if there is a consensus against them. DSU countermeasures need to be "equivalent to the level of the nullification or impairment" caused by the measure that was found to be in breach. Countermeasures in the WTO are of a bilateral nature. They can taken only by members that were complaining parties—not by third parties or, *a fortiori*, by members not involved in the dispute. As opposed to compensation, retaliation implies the *raising* of trade barriers by the winning member vis-à-vis the losing member, a move detrimental to free trade principles.

Three additional tools are available for the purpose of bringing about compliance. First, the DSB continuously monitors the implementation process, which is an important political inducement to comply. Second, in the event of disagreement on whether compliance occurred, the original panel can be called in to decide. Third, if parties disagree on the level of countermeasures or on certain other related matters, this dispute is sent to arbitration.

To make an analogy with the traditional international law remedies of "cessation" and "reparation," the first and last objective of compliance in the WTO—usually, the withdrawal of the inconsistent measure—can be seen as the equivalent of the international law obligation of cessation of wrongful conduct. With few exceptions, however, GATT, as well as WTO, recommendations and rulings have not required the member in breach of GATT/WTO rules to make reparation for the damage caused in the past. So far, WTO remedies have offered only prospective relief—in the best circumstances, an immediate withdrawal of the inconsistent measure upon the adoption of DSB recommendations and rulings. More probably, however, and strictly within legal bounds, the measure will be withdrawn only by the end of the "reasonable period of time." If not so withdrawn, "reparation" is provided in the form of compensation for damages, but typically counting only from the date of expiration of the "reasonable period of time." If compensation cannot be agreed upon, *member-to-member* countermeasures can be taken. There are currently no *collective* remedies or sanctions by the WTO membership as a whole.

Critical Examination of the WTO Regime of Countermeasure and Enforcement

The proliferation of substantive WTO rules, coupled with a quasi-automatic, rules-based dispute settlement system, led to an exponentially growing number of disputes being brought to the WTO, including the politically sensitive ones. This obvious success of the DSU is testimony to the high expectations that were raised by the new system. Regrettably, however, it seems that the proliferation of rules and the associated "legalization" of dispute settlement have not been paired with a strong enough enforcement mechanism. As a result, although many disputes under the GATT either did not achieve or would not have achieved a consensus for submission to a panel and for adoption of the panel's report, many such disputes have now been successfully brought to the WTO but been stranded against the wall of noncompliance. This enforcement problem may result, in part, from the move from a power-based to a rules-based system while leaving the domain of remedies largely untouched. The "legalization" of disputes under the WTO stops, in effect, roughly where noncompliance starts.

For members disputing a case at arm's length—in practice, mostly the developed members—the resurgence of economic and political power as factors in achieving compliance may be manageable. In those instances countermeasures may, indeed, gradually induce compliance. In the contrasting case where a weaker member is faced with noncompliance by a disproportionately stronger member, the reactivation of power politics—which are at play in negotiations on compensation and the possible imposition of countermeasures—may make compliance very hard to achieve. Such negotiations highlight and effectively uphold the inevitable economic and political inequality between WTO members (as equal as they may be in the eye of the law). Would it not be difficult in practice—indeed, even counter-productive—for say, Burkina Faso or Estonia to take countermeasures against, for example, the United States or the European Community? Difficult because retaliation may, in turn, provoke counterretaliation in non-WTO-related fields such as development aid, and counterproductive because fencing off Burkina Faso's or Estonia's market from much needed U.S. or EC imports would mostly harm the former, not induce compliance by the latter.

In addition to the disadvantages related to bilateral state-to-state countermeasures, the WTO enforcement regime lacks the remedy of reparation—at least in the traditional sense of compensation for damages in the past. By way of contrast, when the International Court of Justice (ICJ) issues a judgment and finds that a state has breached a rule of international law, the state held in breach will be responsible, first, to stop the breach if it is one of a continuing character and, second, to make reparation for it. In this sense, the WTO offers less than the ICJ.

In another respect, the WTO—in particular, the elaborate enforcement provisions of the DSU—is a step ahead of the ICJ and other international enforcement mechanisms, and provides one of the most developed enforcement regimes in international law. This comparative advantage is not merely the product of DSU's offering compulsory jurisdiction and a virtually automatic process. For example, although the ICJ calls for cessation, implicitly or explicitly, that is where its efforts normally end. There remains no doubt that the state in breach is under a legal obligation to stop the wrongful conduct, but the ICJ has no mechanism to enforce this so-called secondary legal obligation. Rules applicable to the ICJ do not foresee or address the problem of what to do in case of noncompliance. As a result, the wrongful conduct often continues, or the prevailing state may decide to take unilateral countermeasures without being subject to any further monitoring (contrary to DSU countermeasures, which are multilaterally approved and monitored). In this sense, the WTO's forward-looking approach towards enforcement—not only of primary WTO rules, but also of secondary WTO rules—can be seen as a major step ahead in international law. The same can be said about the mandate granted to WTO panels and the Appellate Body not only to decide whether or not a breach occurred, but also to make suggestions on how to bring measures into conformity with WTO rules—a powerful tool that should be used more often. In sum, rather than simply avoiding the problem of noncompliance by legally prohibiting it, the WTO enforcement regime faces the problem directly and tries to induce compliance through a set of detailed procedures. Although those procedures could be improved and might favor the strong, the WTO's enforcement regime is a distinctive and important advance within the international arena.

Both the weaknesses and the strengths of the WTO enforcement regime need to be understood and interpreted in light of the original GATT framework; that is, as a balance of negotiated concessions, not primarily as a set of legal rules. The WTO, like the GATT, is not an international agreement that can be invoked by mere acceptance. A state or independent customs territory does not become a WTO member simply in virtue of having signed myriad WTO agreements. An additional "entry fee" is required to become part of the WTO club. This "entry fee" consists of a series of trade concessions—tariff reductions, market-access commitments in respect of foreign services, and so on—that have to be granted to existing WTO members. These concessions are in addition to the multilateral obligations set out in the WTO agreements. Membership is secured only after these concessions are accepted by existing members as balancing the concessions that they will be giving to the newcomer through WTO membership. Consequently, at the foundation of a member-member relationship lies a delicately negotiated balance not only of rights and obligations explicitly enshrined in WTO agreements, but also of trade concessions exchanged at entrance and through a series of subsequent trade rounds.

As a result, instead of tackling breaches of international law obligations, the WTO's dispute settlement system, like that of the GATT, focuses on the "nullification or impairment" of benefits. By the same token, the WTO's remedy of last resort is to "suspend concessions or other obligations." In other words, what is actionable under the WTO is not so much the breach of obligations, but the upsetting of the negotiated balance of benefits consisting of rights, obligations, and additional trade concessions. This approach directly parallels that of the GATT, in which there were basically two possible remedies of more or less equal value to restore the negotiated balance of benefits—in much the same way that there are two possible ways to equalize unbalanced scales. Either the party being challenged *removes* the upsetting, trade restricting act—that is, some weight is *taken out* on one side of the scales—or the party challenging enacts its own trade restriction by removing an earlier trade concession—that is, some weight is *added* on the other side. The resulting enforcement regime was, however—and somewhat paradoxically—both lenient and strict. On the one hand, the system was lenient: the customary consequences linked to a breach of an international law obligation—in legal terms, cessation and reparation, and in political terms, the shunning linked to a non-law-abiding party—were avoided. On the other hand, however, the system was uniquely strict: parties were held "responsible" not only for breaches of GATT obligations, but also for "nullification or impairment" caused by conduct that did *not* conflict with any specific GATT provision—the so-called "non-violation nullification or impairment."

Even though, as explained earlier, rebalancing the scales is, within the WTO, stated to be only a temporary solution (the ultimate goal being compliance), these historical origins in the GATT are, unfortunately, still haunting the WTO legal system today. To quote one prominent author:

> Like the GATT that preceded them, the WTO rules are simply not "binding" in the traditional sense.... The only sacred, inviolable aspect of the GATT was the overall balance of rights and obligations, of benefits and burdens, achieved among members through negotiations.... The WTO substantially improved the GATT rules for settling disputes but did not alter the fundamental nature of the negotiated bargain among sovereign member states.

... Put in simple terms, a WTO member may be called to justice when and because it upsets the balance negotiated with another member, not because it violates multilaterally agreed rules in place for the benefit of all WTO members and their economic operators. To make a comparison with national law, this old line of thought sees the relationship between WTO members as purely contractual, within the sphere of private law. The WTO legal system is not considered to be an entity rooted in public law where public goods are at stake.

It is this background that must frame any discussion of enforcement in the WTO. If one holds the old GATT view and transposes it into the WTO, the current regime of countermeasures and enforcement might be justified as a logical element in the upholding of mainly bilateral equilibria. Nevertheless, with the advent of the WTO—its legal refinement, quasi-judicial dispute settlement system, and, in particular, major expansion into new fields that *directly affect individuals*—it may be time to move away from the idea of the GATT/WTO only as a package of bilateral balances between governments. Has time not come to introduce the WTO as a truly multilateral construct providing legal rules as public goods that merit collective enforcement for the good of governments *and* economic operators?

Two steps in this direction need to be considered: First, WTO rules can and should be considered to be normal international legal obligations that are part of public international law. Second, the enforcement of WTO rules can and should be seen as a collective rather than a mainly bilateral exercise.

WTO Rules As International Legal Obligations

WTO rules, as well as DSB recommendations, should be considered binding legal obligations. That is, if the DSB finds a breach of WTO rules, the member concerned should be considered to be violating its obligations under international law, as a consequence of which the member would be obligated, in turn, to stop the violation by bringing the inconsistent measure into conformity with WTO rules. This approach accords with the DSU's unambiguously providing that compensation and retaliation are only "temporary measures" that are not to be preferred to full compliance. The approach also accords with the WTO's very first report, in which the Appellate Body made it clear that the WTO legal system is no longer to be seen—as some saw the GATT—as a self-contained regime. Referring to DSU Article 3.2, which calls for WTO provisions to be clarified "in accordance with customary rules of interpretation of public international law," the Appellate Body made the following point: "That direction [in DSU Article 3.2] reflects a measure of recognition that the [GATT] is not to be read in clinical isolation from public international law." It is true that the DSU has to be considered as *lex specialis* and that it can—and in certain areas, does—deviate from general international law. If any ambiguity were to persist in the DSU, however, as to whether a breach of WTO rules activates the secondary obligation of cessation, recourse should be made to residual international law rules. These rules make clear beyond doubt that in case wrongful conduct is found, the state concerned has to stop that conduct. The DSU determines, in turn, the means by which the prevailing WTO member is authorized to obtain fulfillment of that secondary legal obligation of cessation.

The changing character of WTO rules and the parties they affect also provides some reason to move toward seeing WTO obligations as ones of international law. Ever more precise and expanding WTO rules increasingly affect not only members as governments, but also individuals, consumers, and other economic operators in domestic and global marketplaces. Whereas a balancing act may be acceptable to governments, legal rules affecting individuals call for greater predictability and stability. Such rules therefore need to be respected as international obligations, not as some political promise that can be withdrawn or exchanged for another. Moreover, with the entry into force of WTO agreements that are unrelated to the idea of balancing trade concessions that are additional to the rules set out in the agreement itself—such as the Agreements on Trade-Related Aspects of Intellectual Property Rights (TRIPS) and Sanitary and Phytosanitary Measures (SPS)—the customary rationale for enforcement, which is based on the adjustment of the bilateral-contractual balance of concessions between members, became less relevant. The fact that negotiating WTO agreements continues to be a balancing exercise of give and take—in which, for example, developing countries accepted the TRIPS Agreement in exchange of agreements on agriculture and textiles—does not, in and of itself, warrant a continued and exclusive focus on bilateral balances. Is not each and every international treaty the result of compromise and of give and take? Can there be no decision that a *binding* international treaty has been breached, just because the injured party can, in response to such breach, suspend the treaty (equalize the balance), in whole or in part? Obviously not.

In the context of reinterpreting WTO rules as creating international legal obligations, it would be opportune to revisit the WTO's unique rubric of the "nullification or impairment of benefits" through perfectly legal conduct. Instead of providing this cause of action against lawful conduct in very broad terms under almost all WTO agreements, it could, for example, be provided only in specific circumstances under certain WTO rules—when there is a clear justification for creating such a cause of action. In the end, what would then be actionable under WTO law would be conduct inconsistent with WTO rules, nothing more, nothing less.

Towards a More Collective Enforcement Mechanism in the WTO

Insofar as WTO rules are interpreted as international legal obligations to the benefit of all members and economic operators in domestic and global market places, the target of the DSU should be to eradicate WTO-wrongful conduct in pursuit of public goods. The idea of challenging a WTO-inconsistent measure as conduct beneficial to the collective membership has already left its first mark. In *EC—Bananas*, the Appellate Body decided that the United States could bring a case under GATT even though it hardly produces bananas and has not yet exported any. The Appellate Body found that in order to bring a case under the DSU, no legal interest is required. It quoted with approval the following remark from the panel report: "with the increased interdependence of the global economy.... Members have a greater stake in enforcing WTO rules than in the past since any deviation from the negotiated balance of rights and obligations is more likely than ever to affect them, directly or indirectly."

An interesting consequence of the *EC—Bananas* decision is that a member could win a case all the way through the Appellate Body without having a tangible trade interest in the WTO-inconsistent measure. When that member was faced with noncompliance, however, it would not be able to claim compensation or, arguably, retaliation; retaliation is explicitly linked to "nullification and impairment" of benefits, that is, to trade effects. This situation is representative of the growing tension within the WTO legal system between protecting bilateral-contractual balances and enforcing multilateral rules.

One means of easing this tension could be to make WTO remedies—and not only the legal standing to bring a case—more collective in character. Compensation, for example, already has that multilateral character, and, as noted earlier, it is generally understood that compensation is to be offered not only to the winning party, but to all WTO members. Countermeasures could also be made more collective. In this context it would be helpful to reconsider not only the actual effect of DSU countermeasures and the way they are calculated, but the specification of who is allowed to retaliate and what form such retaliation can take.

It should be recalled that DSU countermeasures are basically trade restrictions that a winning member is allowed to impose against goods coming from a losing member. They imply a rebalancing of the scales, referred to earlier, a solution that under the GATT could have been final, closing the case. Upon closer consideration, however, DSU countermeasures represent the epitome of mercantilism. The assumption is that protecting your market will bring you gains, offset the "nullification or impairment" caused by the measure found to be WTO inconsistent, and force the losing member to remove the inconsistency. It is worth noting the irony that the world body preaching the liberalization of trade depicts trade protectionism—countermeasures—as offering some kind of favor or benefit that should neutralize the effect and even force the disappearance of illegal trade restrictions imposed by others. Nevertheless, as conceded by the arbitrators in *EC—Bananas*, "the suspension of concessions is not in the economic interest of either [party]."

Independent of the actual effects that countermeasures have, arbitration panels have ruled (and in my view, correctly) that "the *purpose* of [DSU] countermeasures [is to] *induce compliance*." If you combine the above-mentioned economic inefficiency of countermeasures with the current *level* of DSU countermeasures, which has to be "equivalent" to the actual damage caused by the WTO inconsistent measure, however, it is difficult to see how this purpose of inducing compliance can be achieved (except when countermeasures are imposed by a member disproportionately stronger than the target of the countermeasures). Looking at the way the *level* of countermeasures is established—as equivalent to the nullification or impairment—countermeasures under the DSU seem to *aim* primarily (but, in my view, unsuccessfully) at "compensating" the winning party for the delay in implementation. Contrary to their stated purpose, the *effect* of DSU countermeasures does not seem to be that of inducing compliance—as in general international law, where countermeasures are retaliatory in character and put pressure on the losing party *on top of* and *distinct from* the obligation to compensate. In general international law, countermeasures exert pressure that is proportional to the original violation and serve as means to an end. Countermeasures—unlike compensation, for example—are not ends in themselves. Simply equalizing the score, as in compensation under the WTO, not only runs the risk that the lawbreaker is better off having broken the rules than it would have been had it complied with them (since no damages for the past are currently awarded). It also means that, apart from compensation, no further incentive is provided to remove the inconsistency. The WTO enforcement system thereby neglects the remedy of cessation—a remedy that is more important from the collective WTO membership's point of view.

It could therefore be suggested that even during the period that countermeasures are imposed, the legal obligation to compensate should continue to exist. Indeed, coupled with countermeasures, a broad scheme of compensation—additional market access offered by the losing party to WTO members—would provide genuine leverage to induce compliance, a move beneficial to all WTO members, and not just "compensation" to the one or few that brought the case. By thus distinguishing (as in general international law) between countermeasures, on the one hand, and compensation and trade damage, on the other, effective countermeasures—not necessarily linked to trade damage—would become available for the purpose of enforcing WTO rules.

To highlight the risks and inefficiencies of a bilateral enforcement mechanism for multilateral rules, consider this scenario. Imagine two WTO members that are involved in two separate trade disputes between each other, with each of them being a complainant in one case and a defendant in the other. Both cases are won by the complainant. Both members refuse to comply. Both obtain authorization to suspend concessions. The two WTO-inconsistent measures have a negative trade effect that is equivalent. Can one inconsistent measure be labeled as the countermeasure against the other inconsistent measure? In other words, can one measure be "compensated" by the other and, as a result, can both members agree to continue their mutually inconsistent relationship unchanged? On the face of it, this situation would seem to be a possibility, which highlights the absence of a genuine inducement to comply. Though satisfactory from the perspective of the two parties, this outcome would be an unfortunate one from the perspective of other WTO members, especially insofar as they were committed to seeing compliance with WTO rules as a collective good.

Another problem with the current regime of DSU countermeasures is that only the complaining party that prevailed in a dispute—and not other WTO members—can impose such countermeasures. A member prevailing in WTO dispute settlement therefore has to bear by itself not only the cost of legal proceedings, but that of taking economically inefficient countermeasures. This cost could be made multilateral if some kind of collective action were possible through or by the DSB. In that case it would be the WTO as an organization, not one specific member, that attempts to enforce WTO rules. Any member could, for example, be authorized to suspend concessions equivalent to the damage it has suffered, even if that member did not bring the case. Moving away from the inefficient suspension of market-access concessions, the DSB could also suspend the operation of other WTO obligations. It could, for example, suspend one or more WTO rules or agreements (for example, the DSU or the TRIPS Agreement) to the extent that they benefit the losing member, and create obligations owed to any other WTO member, not just to the winning member. (Even under current DSU rules, countermeasures can take the form of a suspension of "concessions *or other obligations*.") Through such collective enforcement, weaker members prevailing in a dispute, but economically unable to take member-to-member countermeasures, could then have access to an effective remedy. Moreover, these weaker members could, under such an approach, also reap the benefits of cases brought and won by other members with more resources.

Further Suggestions to Improve the Practical Enforcement of WTO Rules

Compensation under the DSU—which requires the losing party to *lower* its trade barriers—is difficult to obtain because it is subject to the agreement of the lawbreaker. It is, however, beneficial in the long term not only to the winning member, but also to the losing member and the entire WTO membership. Why not, therefore, make compensation compulsory and automatic the way that countermeasures currently are? Without requiring the approval of both parties, the DSB could then automatically approve a request for compensation of a certain amount, in the form of increased market access to be granted by the loser. If a dispute arises over the amount of compensation requested, binding arbitration along the lines of the arbitration now available for countermeasures could be employed. In addition, the current regime of countermeasures, which is aimed at inducing compliance rather than compensation, could be maintained (though perhaps also strengthened as suggested in the preceding section).

To ensure that the sector or industry that suffers the damage caused by a WTO-inconsistent measure actually benefits from the compensation, one could, alternatively, force the losing member to pay an amount of money equivalent to the damage caused. Following GATT/WTO practice, such pecuniary compensation would not need to work retroactively, that is, compensate for past damage. Pecuniary compensation would not only make more economic sense than both the suspension of concessions and a compensatory lifting of trade barriers in mostly unrelated sectors, it would also be easier to monitor and more accessible for weaker WTO members.

Finally, although (as mentioned earlier) the GATT/WTO legal system now offers only prospective remedies and not remedies to make good past damage, new consideration should be given to the possibility of granting WTO members the remedy that is so obvious in general international law: reparation, including reparation for past damage. Techniques could be used to limit such reparation in time (for example, not before January 1, 1995, the date of entry into force of the WTO) and scope (for example, by requiring a strict causal link between the WTO inconsistency and the damage for which reparation is claimed). As noted earlier, the WTO legal system is unique in its detailed focus on cessation and the consequences linked to its failure, a prospective remedy rarely addressed in general international law. To complement this uniqueness with some form of reparation would not only bring WTO law closer to public international law, however, but considerably strengthen the predictability and stability of the multilateral trading system. Nothing under the current rules or in any of the WTO disputes decided so far explicitly precludes reparation for the past. In the few cases where the issue was raised, it has not been decided.

Conclusion

The political reality today indicates that acceptance of many of these suggestions to strengthen the WTO enforcement mechanism and the remedies it provides—for example, *ex tunc* reparation for breaches of WTO law—is still far away. It would therefore be wrong to take these important steps precipitously and without extensive discussion; doing so could threaten the political support and legitimacy of the WTO, in general, and of its dispute settlement decisions, in particular. Nevertheless, one of the objectives of legal research is to prepare the ground for change. Further work is needed to examine and assess the different alternatives that are available at the intersection of WTO and general international law. Once WTO rules have been accepted as international legal obligations that affect individuals and merit collective enforcement for the public good, however, and once this new perception has come to be accepted and entrenched, it will be increasingly difficult to justify both the absence of certain traditional remedies, including reparation, and the lack of a more effective system to induce compliance with WTO rules. As Robert Hudec noted in respect of the more general GATT/WTO history of legal enforcement: "The process of creating any legal system, where none existed before, can only come about slowly and incrementally. The ideas and institutions that make a legal system 'effective' have to grind themselves into the political attitudes of the society—here, the society of governments—over time."

The Economic Structure of Renegotiation and Dispute Resolution in the World Trade Organization*

WARREN F. SCHWARTZ and ALAN O. SYKES

This paper . . . focuses on three central features of the WTO system that we believe have not been assigned sufficient importance or adequately explained by traditional international law scholars. The first can be found in the rules structuring the renegotiation and modification of WTO commitments. A prominent aspect of these provisions is that a

* Reprinted by permission from 31 JOURNAL OF LEGAL STUDIES 179 (2002).

member nation that wishes to deviate from its commitments may do so even if it is unable to secure permission from other nations by offers of compensatory trade concessions. If negotiations over compensation reach impasse, the nation wishing to deviate may proceed, and adversely affected nations may then withdraw "substantially equivalent" concessions in response. The second feature on which we focus involves the sanctions for breach of obligations. After a country is adjudged to be in violation of a WTO agreement, sanctions are limited to the withdrawal of substantially equivalent concessions previously granted to the country committing the violation by the country (or countries) harmed by the violation. More severe sanctions, which might at times be necessary if the violator is to be coerced into complying with its obligations, are not permitted. The third, related feature on which we focus concerns the measurement of substantially equivalent concessions. After a party has been found to be in violation of its obligations, it has a "reasonable time" to correct the problem. Only if it fails to do so within that time are sanctions allowed at all, and even then the sanctions are limited to measures substantially equivalent to the ongoing harm caused by the violation after the reasonable time for cure has elapsed. No sanctions are allowed for harm caused prior to that point in time.

We believe that these features can be understood using the economic theory of contract remedies. Economic theory teaches that a key objective of an enforcement system is to induce a party to comply with its obligations whenever compliance will yield greater benefits to the promisee than costs to the promisor, while allowing the promisor to depart from its obligations whenever the costs of compliance to the promisor exceed the benefits to the promisee. In the parlance of contact theory, the objective is to deter inefficient breaches but to encourage efficient ones. In the sections that follow, we will argue that the WTO provisions respecting renegotiation and the settlement of disputes over breach of obligations are carefully designed to facilitate efficient adjustments to unanticipated circumstances. We also conclude that formal sanctions in the WTO system are relatively unimportant to the other goal of contract remedies—the deterrence of inefficient breach.

. . .

Renegotiation and Modification of Concessions

Public choice teaches that the objectives that individual countries pursue through international agreements are determined by an interaction among organized interest groups.

. . .

[P]arties to trade agreements, like the parties to private contracts, enter the bargain under conditions of uncertainty. Economic conditions may change, the strength of interest group organization may change, and so on. Accordingly, officials cannot be certain that the bargain they strike will benefit them in all of its details. Likewise, even where the bargain on a particular issue is initially beneficial, changing circumstances may make it politically unappealing. For these reasons, the drafters of trade agreements may be expected to include devices for adjusting the bargain when it proves mutually disadvantageous.

. . .

[T]he parties to any kind of contract can facilitate efficient adjustment of obligations in three ways. First, they can specify in the contract itself the conditions under which performance will not be required or the price for a party to buy out of a particular obligation.... Second, when their contract is incomplete as to certain contingencies that may arise, they can agree on (or embrace a legal system that provides them with) a liability rule that encourages efficient nonperformance.... Third, the parties can embrace a property rule and simply renegotiate when performance becomes inefficient. The promisor can buy its way out of the obligation to perform by paying the promisee(s) an amount that makes it whole and still leaves the promisor better off than with performance of the original obligation.

The provisions of the WTO agreements pertaining to renegotiation exhibit aspects of the first two approaches but stop short of creating a property rule. Consider first the Article XIX escape clause, which authorizes temporary measures that would otherwise violate WTO commitments for the protection of industries that are experiencing severe dislocation due to increased import competition. Such industries are likely to have rates of return well below the competitive level and, as a result, to be losing quasi rents on fixed investments. On average, they will lobby more vigorously for protection than other industries because the benefits of protection are less dissipated (if at all) by new entry; to the extent that protection merely raises the rate of return toward the competitive level, no new domestic competitors will be induced to enter the industry. Industries that are profitable and growing are likely to have returns above the competitive level in many cases, which will eventually be dissipated by entry regardless of government policy at home or abroad. Hence, they have less incentive to lobby for domestic protection and less incentive to punish their political leaders for failing to maintain access to foreign markets at historical levels. Accordingly, it will be politically efficient, from the perspective of parties to trade agreements, to afford transitory protection, at the expense of growing and prosperous foreign competitors, to import-competing industries that suffer severe dislocation. The escape clause permits such measures and may thus be viewed as an example of the first option above for facilitating efficient nonperformance, a provision written into the contract that excuses performance under specified contingencies.

To be sure, the concern arises that a nation may abuse its right to use the escape clause, imposing protection when it creates more political detriment abroad than can be justified by the benefits it creates at home. A compensation requirement can help to deter such inefficient behavior and was included in the escape clause system until the Uruguay Round. The new, partial exemption from the compensation requirement for the first 3 years of an escape clause measure suggests a judgment by the WTO membership that oversight by the strengthened dispute resolution process can adequately police abuse of such measures and that a compensation requirement is no longer essential to keep the member nations "honest."

A more comprehensive provision for adjustment of the bargain is Article XXVIII of GATT 1994.... Unlike Article XIX, Article XXVIII does not set out specific contingencies under which deviation from obligations is permissible but instead establishes a procedure under which, subject to certain constraints, any tariff concession can be withdrawn for any reason for an indefinite period of time. It requires as part of this process that nations seeking to withdraw concessions offer compensatory concessions to affected trading partners. But it is noteworthy that Article XXVIII does not require the member who is withdrawing a concession to secure the permission of affected trading partners—it does not create a property rule. Instead, although members are asked to negotiate mutually satisfactory compensation with other members if possible, Article XXVIII provides that a member may proceed to withdraw concessions in cases where negotiations over compensation break down and further provides that adversely affected trading partners may at that point unilaterally withdraw substantially equivalent concessions or other obligations. Ultimately, then, concessions are protected by a liability rule. And the magnitude of "liability" is clearly specified—concessions substantially equivalent to those withdrawn by the member that proceeds under Article XXVIII.

We believe that the explanation for these provisions lies in the desire of signatories to facilitate efficient breach and in the relative superiority of a liability rule approach to that task. At first blush, this claim may seem surprising because the harm done to political officials by a breach of promise in the WTO is no doubt difficult to measure precisely, and when damages are hard to calculate, that fact is usually thought to be a heavy thumb on the scale favoring a property rule over a liability rule. But there is a countervailing consideration here that is compelling. Under the most-favored-nation principle of the WTO, trade concessions must extend equally to all WTO members (WTO membership includes 144 countries at this writing). Hence, under a property rule, a nation seeking to depart from a prior concession would have to secure the permission of potentially dozens of other nations. It would then face an acute holdout problem as each of the many promisees tried to capture as much as possible of the gain that the promisor could realize from avoiding the concession. Such strategic behavior might prevent agreement from being reached at all, or at least delay it uneconomically while negotiation and posturing dragged along. The liability rule approach of Article XXVIII averts this problem.

Further, by limiting the retaliatory withdrawal of concessions to those substantially equivalent, the system seeks to ensure that the price for nonperformance under the liability rule is not too high. Although the phrasing is somewhat vague, a withdrawal of substantially equivalent concessions may be understood as allowing members adversely affected by a withdrawal of concessions under Article XXVIII to raise their level of political welfare by reimposing protection for the benefit of domestic constituencies that will reward them for it, but only up to the point that their level of political welfare is restored to its original level. . . .

The Liability Rule Remedy . . .

The most intriguing use of a liability rule in the WTO system is pursuant to the DSU, which governs claims by one member nation that another has violated its obligations. Article 21(3) of the DSU provides that a member has a reasonable period of time to bring its policies into conformity with its obligations after it has been found to have violated them. Article 22(1) then states that compensation or a suspension of concessions may result if compliance has not been achieved within a reasonable period of time. The first step in the process is a negotiation over compensation, in effect to determine whether the case can be "settled." Should those negotiations fail, the aggrieved party (or parties) can propose a suspension of concessions, which must be substantially equivalent to the ongoing harm that they suffer from the violation. An arbitration procedure exists to examine the substantial equivalence question if the member faced with such a suspension of concessions objects that the suspension is excessive.

Plainly, as with Article XXVIII discussed above, this system is best seen as one embracing a liability rule rather than a property rule. A party found to be in violation of its obligations can, if it so chooses, continue to violate them. The ultimate price to be paid, if the case is not settled, is the withdrawal of substantially equivalent concessions. This structure must, we submit, reflect a collective judgment that a property rule (for example, a threat to expel the recalcitrant violator if it does not cease and desist) would be inferior. The reasons why relate to the considerations discussed above—the large transaction costs and opportunities for strategic behavior that would arise if a member trying to adjust its obligations had to secure the permission of all of the affected members.

Recent WTO decisions make clear that our interpretation of WTO law is correct, even if they do not clearly acknowledge the liability rule nature of the system. In the "bananas" dispute between the United States and the European Union (EU), the EU declined to comply with a panel ruling because it found that its tariff preferences for bananas from certain nations violated WTO law. The United States then invoked its retaliation rights and proposed substantial sanctions that the EU challenged before an arbitration panel as excessive. In defending its proposed sanctions, the United States argued that its "suspension (of trade concessions) is an incentive for prompt compliance. . . . Precision in measuring trade damage is not required." The United States thus suggested, in effect, that the purpose of the sanction was to enforce a property rule and that careful calibration of sanctions was unnecessary. The arbitrators rejected this position: "We agree with the United States

. . . that it is the purpose of countermeasures to induce compliance. But, this purpose does not mean that the DSB should grant authorization to suspend concessions beyond what is equivalent to the level of nullification or impairment. In our view there is nothing in [the relevant provisions of the DSU] that could be read as a justification for countermeasures of a punitive nature."

By refusing to permit the imposition of "punitive" sanctions, the arbitrators impliedly acknowledged that the sanction is more in the nature of compensation than punishment. They set a price for the EU's persistence in its violation of WTO law equal to the harm caused to its trading partners. The system thus allows violations to persist as long as the violator is willing to pay that price, which is the essence of a liability rule approach.

. . . Because circumstances change and the proper calibration of the substantially equivalent concessions may change as well, it is perhaps not surprising that the DSB should exercise some continuing oversight in these cases much as a conventional court might retain jurisdiction over a case where damages are payable over time (such as child support payments under family law or medical monitoring costs in tort). Likewise, ongoing violations may have an impact on parties other than the original disputants. Continued publicity and oversight may thus serve to alert other members who might suffer redressable harm. Finally, and related perhaps to the third-party effects just mentioned, we do not dispute that a "preference" for compliance seems implicit in the system. Ongoing oversight thus serves to check periodically on whether the impasse that led to compensation or retaliation may have lifted. In effect, the violating country is required to persuade the international community that persisting in the violation is desirable. Hence, the existence of continued oversight by no means excludes the possibility that members have the legal right to opt for paying damages in the form of a loss of trade concessions from other parties.

. . . We [also] note that the provisions of the DSU, taken as a whole, allow a violator to continue a violation in perpetuity, as long as it compensates or is willing to bear the costs of the retaliatory suspension of concessions. If WTO members really wanted to make compliance with dispute resolution findings mandatory, they would have imposed some greater penalty for noncompliance to induce it.

. . . It would seem then that, at least for some temporary period of time, a violation coupled with the withdrawal of concessions is acknowledged to be potentially superior to immediate compliance. Indeed, the fact that violators are given a reasonable period of time to conform their policies before sanctions or compensation become possible further supports the proposition that some period of deviation is seen as potentially valuable.

The reason why is not difficult to divine. World Trade Organization violations are typically the result of domestic laws and regulations enacted by the violating country. Thus, curing the violation requires a new law or regulation that repeals the one that constitutes the violation. For a number of reasons it may be politically difficult, conceivably impossible, to enact such a change. The legislative and regulatory processes are, of course, elaborate and costly. Proposed changes must compete for a place on the agenda. Interest groups who gain from the violation will oppose repeal and be able to exploit differences among supporters of repeal as to what compensating benefits, if any, should be granted to the industries who will lose the benefits of the law.

If these factors make some delay in compliance inevitable, as the system apparently acknowledges and tolerates, there is no reason to think that they may not at times make compliance politically infeasible for an extended period of time. And rather than expel the member who faces such political difficulty or impose some other draconian penalty, the system instead acknowledges that the joint interests of the parties may be better served by compensation or retaliation that restores the benefits of the bargain to aggrieved parties while allowing officials in the violator nation to continue doing what must be done out of political necessity.

Indeed, if one is to claim that the purposes of the WTO members would be better served by compliance in all circumstances, it seems that one must believe that at the time the WTO rules were devised, the drafters were able to anticipate every situation in which the costs of compliance would exceed the benefits of compliance and include provisions to excuse compliance in all of these circumstances. In the parlance of contract theory, the parties would have had to be able to write a complete contract expressly specifying what would be required in all circumstances that might arise. We think it plainly unrealistic to think that the many parties to the WTO agreement, covering as it does matters of great complexity, could have done so successfully. Knowing that, they framed a dispute resolution system designed to facilitate efficient breach by using a sensible liability rule for that purpose. . . .

In short, it seems clear to us that the WTO system contemplates departures from specified obligations when the costs of compliance exceed the associated benefits, whether those obligations are tariffs or nontariff issues. We can see no other purpose to the provisions that allow departure from obligations when agreement is not reached and confer on the promisee only the right to withdraw substantially equivalent concessions. Such a provision can only represent an institutional means for setting an appropriate price for violating commitments when the price cannot be determined through negotiations.

The Limited Scope of Sanctions in the World Trade Organization System

We have focused thus far on the role of a liability rule in the WTO system in facilitating efficient deviations from commitments following a change in circumstances. We now consider the second role of a liability rule—to deter violations when the benefits of compliance are greater than the costs of compliance.

The Absence of Sanctions Prior to the World Trade Organization

What is remarkable about the WTO/GATT system is how unimportant formal sanctions have been in encouraging compliance with trade commitments throughout its history. As noted, the WTO succeeded the GATT, which began in 1947. Until 1995, when the WTO agreements superseded the GATT, it was effectively impossible for a nation that was found to have violated the GATT to become subject to formal sanctions. The reason was the consensus rule, which held that any nation could block the authority for the imposition of sanctions, including the nation that had violated the GATT and was threatened with them! Indeed, until 1989, a potential disputant could even block the formation of a dispute resolution panel to hear the merits of a complaint. As a result, GATT dispute resolution was limited to system that would often (but not always) hear the merits of a complaint and render a decision about the existence of a violation but would never proceed to the point of imposing penalties when a violation was found.

Nevertheless, the GATT system held together rather well. Tariffs in the developed world fell from an average of nearly 50 percent in 1947 to an average of about 5 percent by the end of the GATT. To be sure, some cheating on obligations occurred, but the level of cheating was modest. We are unaware, for example, of any allegation in the history of the system that a nation flagrantly refused to comply with one of its tariff commitments by raising a tariff rate above an agreed tariff limit. Further, where cheating might be said to exist by some, it was often an efficient, tacit amendment of the bargain. When such tacit modifications are put to one side, the incidence of flagrant cheating under the GATT system was indeed quite low.

Our explanation for this state of affairs emphasizes that there are strong forces that induce countries to comply with their obligations, although no costs would be formally imposed on them by the GATT if they deviated. Three considerations explain why the system worked as well as it did: the domestic costs of violations, reputational sanctions for noncompliance, and unilateral retaliation against violators.

1. Domestic Costs of Violations

It will often be true that domestic political considerations encourage a country to comply with its commitments under trade agreements. This is true for two sets of reasons.

The first relates to the way the balance of political forces that favor trade protection and trade liberalization will change following the advent of a market-opening trade agreement. As a preliminary, protectionism induces inefficient investments in the domestic production of certain goods and services by importing nations. Those investments commonly entail sunk costs in the form of physical capital that cannot readily transfer to other uses and specific human capital with the same property. The owners of these sunk investments will lose quasi rents on them if protection is removed and will thus devote resources to the political process to protect those rents. These efforts by import-competing firms and workers may prove insufficient to prevent the lowering of trade barriers, however, because the exporters who benefit from reciprocal trade liberalization may be willing to pay more to their officials to secure access to foreign markets than import-competing interests will pay to keep their market protected. If so, a trade agreement will be struck. . . .

[P]olitical pressure to resist renewed protection may grow with time. In particular, where the imports in question are utilized by producing industries, which tend to be better organized than ordinary consumers, a constituency may develop whose returns on their own fixed investments would be impaired by a significant increase in the price of imports. . . .

A second domestic political reason why nations may be inclined to comply with their trade commitments relates to the fact that it may be more costly for interest groups to seek protection than to resist its abolition. In the United States, for example, trade agreements are followed by implementing legislation that conforms federal law (including tariff rates) to the new agreement. A constituency favoring renewed protection, then, must incur the costs of changing a federal statute. Prior to the agreement, by contrast, those favoring trade liberalization must incur the costs of changing the federal statute (as well as of encouraging the international negotiation). It is likely easier to defend an existing statute than to change it for a variety of reasons. Time on the legislative agenda is scarce. Also, individual members of Congress (such as key committee chairs) may have the effective power to veto change, yet they will lack the power by themselves to effect change. Thus, parties resisting change may need fewer political figures to support them than parties seeking change. . . .

As a result, once a trade-liberalizing agreement is reached and implemented, the balance of political power may shift importantly and immediately against those who were previously the beneficiaries of protection. . . .

2. Reputation

Nations that renege on their commitments may be expected to face some reputational cost in the form of having to deal with other nations on less favorable terms in the future. This cost will be borne not only in future dealings with the nation aggrieved by a breach of promise, but also in dealings with all other nations that are aware of the breach.

The skeptic might question whether such reputational penalties will be of much importance in the trading system, however, because their costs might seem to be widely diffused. . . .

This skeptical view is wrong for three reasons. First, in the WTO/GATT system, negotiations are ongoing more or less in perpetuity. Of late, for example, negotiations over commitments in various service sectors remain very much on the table, as do a number of other topics....

Second, it would be a mistake to suppose that reputation is cabined to the trade area. Nations are engaged in a never-ending series of diplomatic initiatives on matters ranging from trade to national security to human rights and so on....

Third, even if reputational costs in the form of forgone opportunities for future trade liberalization would be borne by a fairly diffuse group of exporters, it does not follow that they will be ineffective at organizing today to protect themselves. Exporting interests [for example] can form associations with the mission of overcoming such collective-action difficulties....

One difficulty with reputational penalties, of course, is that they depend on the quality of information in the trading community about the behavior of violators....

This concern highlights the value of a central dispute authority to hear the merits of complaints, even if that authority has no power to authorize sanctions. By serving as a vehicle for transmitting information about violations throughout the trading system, central dispute resolution enhances the reputational costs of cheating. We think that under the consensus-based system of the old GATT, this was the primary function of the dispute system. Further, the fact that a disputant could block the formation of a panel to hear the merits until 1989 did not destroy the efficacy of the system, for in most cases, the refusal of a disputant to allow the formation of a dispute panel would suffice for an adverse inference by other nations....

3. Unilateral Sanctions

When a nation breaches a trade commitment and the harm done is material and noticeable to the foreign exporters that benefit from the promise, those interest groups may be expected to complain to their political representatives and to reward those officials for taking action to correct the problem. Regardless of the nature of third-party dispute resolution at the international level, therefore, nations will have an incentive to punish breach of promise by other nations....

The prospect of unilateral sanctions is not merely hypothetical. In the United States, Section 301 of the Trade Act of 1974 has long authorized the executive branch to retaliate for breach of trade agreements by other nations. The EU has a similar statute on the books, and both statutes have been used. In other nations, statutory enactments that authorize retaliation may be absent, but the inherent powers of political authorities to take action often make formal authority unnecessary.

...

For the reasons given here, the level of compliance with trade commitments is quite high even if there is no credible threat of sanctions for misbehavior. The GATT system ... worked quite well without sanctions, and were it not for the recent innovations in the DSU we could end here. But the drafters of the WTO agreements decided to replace the old GATT dispute resolution system with a meaningful prospect of formal sanctions for violations that are not corrected after a reasonable period of time. We now offer an explanation for those changes in the system.

The New Prospect of Sanctions for Violations That Are Not Cured Within a Reasonable Time

The DSU changes the rules and embraces a "reverse consensus" principle, under which sanctions will be authorized after the dispute process has determined that a violation exists and a reasonable time for cure has elapsed, unless a consensus exists against sanctions (which would have to include the party (or parties) that filed the complaint and prevailed). Consequently, sanctions are a real threat to the recalcitrant violator and have already been employed a number of times. What has not been assigned sufficient importance, however, is that although the DSU made sanctions a real possibility, it did not change another feature of the system that greatly restricts the value of sanctions in inducing nations to comply with their obligations. As we have noted, a sanction cannot be imposed until a dispute panel finds that a violation has occurred, the appellate body affirms the panel's finding if an appeal is filed, and the violation continues although a reasonable period of time to cure it has elapsed. Thus, the sanction operates only prospectively. As a result, a country can commit a violation and continue it for a considerable time without incurring any formal penalty.

What is the logic of this new system? Does its adoption put the lie to our claim that formal sanctions are not necessary to achieve a high level of compliance? And if formal sanctions are indeed important to deter violations, why limit them to violators who have been caught and continue to cause harm after they have been given a chance to reform their behavior? Does that not invite cheating in hopes of avoiding detection, followed by delay when caught to exploit the reasonable time for cure?

...

Our answer is to suggest that the innovation of the DSU was intended not so much to deter violations of most substantive rules, for such violations, if clear, were already fairly well deterred.... What the new system really adds is the opportunity for the losing disputant to "buy out" of the violation at a price set by an arbitrator who has examined carefully the question of what sanctions are substantially equivalent to the harm done by the violation.

By contrast, the situation immediately prior to the entry into force of the WTO was one in which unilateral retaliation was becoming more and more common. Cases under Section 301 of the U.S. Trade Act of 1974, in particular, were becoming more frequent. And the 1988 amendments to that statute created a timetable for retaliatory action by the United States that could require it to sanction an alleged violator even before the GATT panel process had run its course. The distinct possibility thus arose that the United States would impose a sanction based on a unilateral determination that another party was in breach of the GATT, even if a dispute panel would find that the U.S. complaint lacked merit....

Under the new DSU ... a binding arbitration system is established to consider the magnitude of the sanctions. No sanctions can be imposed until the arbitration process has run its course if the violator nation insists on it. The new system thus does a better job of protecting violators from the actual or threatened imposition of excessive sanctions. In turn, it ought to perform better than the old system at ensuring that opportunities for efficient breach are not undermined.

Conclusion

Treaties are contracts of a sort, and the lessons developed by law and economics scholars regarding the way that private contracting parties structure their bargains accordingly have much to teach us about the structure of treaties. In this paper, we have argued that the WTO system prefers a liability rule to a property rule—roughly, expectation damages to a rule of specific performance—primarily because of the transaction costs and holdup problems that would arise under a property rule in a system with 144 players. We have further advanced a theory as to how formal sanctions are not needed to induce a high level of compliance with most WTO obligations, owing to the domestic pressures for compliance that often exist and to the reputational penalties and unilateral sanctions that further pressure parties to respect their commitments even absent formal sanctions. The value of dispute resolution cases, therefore, may lie more in clarifying the rules and filling in missing terms of the bargain than in detecting and punishing cheaters. It is for this reason that the losing party in a dispute proceeding pays no penalty if it obeys the recommendations of the dispute process. Last, we argue that the recent advent of formal sanctions for parties that lose a dispute proceeding and refuse to conform their policies within a reasonable time is a response not so much to the undercompliance with substantive obligations that arises absent these sanctions, but to the danger of excessive unilateral sanctions that exists in the absence of centralized oversight regarding the magnitude of sanctions. This problem arises because the harm done by a violation is not easily observable absent a careful examination by an arbitrator, and thus a party that imposes an excessive unilateral sanction will be hard to detect and so will not suffer the usual penalties associated with misbehavior. The new arbitral process substitutes an unbiased determination as to the proper magnitude of the sanction for a unilateral judgment about it by the aggrieved party and thus better ensures that the price for deviating from WTO obligations is not set inefficiently high.

Notes and Comments

1. The articles in this chapter have focused on the role of international law and institutions in promoting trade between nations. Is there a relationship between a state's domestic political structure and its international trade policy? In *Free to Trade: Democracies, Autocracies, and International Trade*, 94 AMERICAN POLITICAL SCIENCE REVIEW 305 (2000), Edward Mansfield, Helen Milner, and Peter Rosendorff suggest that democracies are more likely to have open trade relations with each other than with less liberal regimes.

> It is frequently argued that the foreign policies of democracies are distinctive, but few studies have focused on the trade policy choices made by such states.... The model we developed highlights the legislature's role in making trade policies in democracies. Having a legislature that ratifies the chief executive's trade proposals may create a credible threat that allows executives in democracies to arrive at freer trade outcomes than would otherwise occur. The possible veto of a trade deal by one or both legislatures ... may lead the executives to search for lower mutually acceptable levels of trade barriers.
>
> ...
>
> Our theoretical model generates two central predictions. First, aggregate trade barriers will be lower between democracies than between a democracy and an autocracy. Since a trade war between two protectionist legislatures is worse than a trade war involving just one such legislature, two democratic executives will choose significant trade liberalization. Our empirical results accord with this proposition.... By the 1990s ... the average volume of trade between a democracy and an autocracy was 40% less than that [between two democracies].
>
> ...
>
> Second, whether the level of aggregate trade barriers will be higher within autocratic pairs than within either democractic or mixed pairs depends on the relative trade preferences of the actors involved.... By and large, no significant differences exists between the volume of trade conducted within autocratic pairs and within democratic pairs, which suggests that both domestic institutions and the preferences of decision makers help shape trade policy.

Id. at 318. Do these predictions or their rationale surprise you? Do these readings confirm the assumptions of Liberal theory described in Part II.C. above? Many of the theories you have read attribute distinctive behavior by democracies to particular liberal norms or to the relatively greater power of interest groups to affect policy, not to the relations between branches of a democratic government itself. Which approach is more persuasive? For another domestic political perspective that differs from Mansfield, Milner, and Rosendorff, see Daniel Verdier, *Democratic Convergence and Free Trade*, 42 INTERNATIONAL STUDIES QUARTERLY 1 (1998). Verdier argues that because the democratization process empowers the same classes of individuals across nations, liberalization leads to increased competition over scarcer and scarcer opportunities, potentially resulting in more, not less, protectionism.

2. There has been a great deal of political and scholarly debate over the relationship between trade regimes like the GATT and WTO and environmental regulations. The recently closed Cartagena Protocol on Biosafety offers an example: The Protocol addressed, among other things, the trade of genetically modified goods. In order to curb dangers believed to be associated with genetically modified plants and animals, the Protocol's signatories developed a consent-based regime that requires nations seeking to export genetically modified goods to obtain permission from importers before beginning trade. Recognizing the potential for conflict between this new authorization system and existing WTO agreements, the signatories created a "savings clause" that allowed relief from new obligations to preserve rights under the WTO. Why do you think the conflict was resolved in this way? Is this the correct resolution? In general, when there are conflicting agreements on trade and the environment, which would you expect to prevail? Which should prevail? Is there a way to make trade agreements and environmental agreements more compatible with one another? For more on the Biosafety Protocol, see Sabrina Safin, *Treaties in Collision? The Biosafety Protocol and the World Trade Organization Agreements*, 96 AMERICAN JOURNAL OF INTERNATIONAL LAW 606 (2002).

3. Some political scientists have puzzled over why powerful states would join a trade agreement that might occasionally lead to unfavorable results. In response, Judith Goldstein argues that states often join trade agreements not to benefit from the arrangements themselves, but instead for other domestic political reasons. Judith Goldstein, *International Law and Domestic Institutions: Reconciling North American "Unfair" Trade Laws*, 50 INTERNATIONAL ORGANIZATION 541 (1996). Why have so many states joined the GATT and agreed to bind themselves to the WTO's strong dispute resolution procedures? And why, in particular, do extremely powerful states commit to the dispute resolution procedures and obey unfavorable decisions? Which of the theories from Parts II and III provide the most helpful insights into these questions?

4. Why do we find such a strong dispute settlement mechanism in the trade area and no similar provision (outside of the regional context) in the areas of human rights or the environment? Is it simply historical coincidence, inherent differences in the subject areas, or something else? Is the WTO dispute settlement system unique or can it be replicated in other contexts?

5. In the excerpts above, Pauwelyn writes that the time has "come to introduce the WTO as a truly multilateral construct providing legal rules as public goods that merit collective enforcement for the good of governments *and* economic operators." He goes on to propose that WTO rules be considered to be "normal international legal obligations that are part of public international law" and that the enforcement of WTO rules should be seen as a collective exercise. Would these proposals improve the WTO system? Would you expect states to agree to them? Why or why not?

6. How does the view of the WTO dispute resolution system offered by Schwartz and Sykes differ from those offered in the other pieces in this section? How would you characterize the readings in this chapter? How do their arguments compare to those you would expect from the various interest-based and norm-based traditions covered in Parts II and III of this book?

7. Which set of reforms would you expect to be more successful: those based on the law-centered approach put forward by Pauwelyn or the reforms suggested by the contract-based view of Schwartz and Sykes? What should be the goal of the WTO dispute resolution system? Should it deter all violations or only those that are "inefficient," as Schwartz and Sykes argue? In addition to Schwartz and Sykes' law and economics approach to international trade, see the following rationalist piece, which compares international trade law to the prisoner's dilemma: Kenneth W. Abbott, *The Trading Nation's Dilemma: The Functions of the Law of International Trade*, 26 Harvard International Law Journal 501 (1985). How does this debate over the proper goal and design of international law map onto the theoretical debates outlined in Parts II and III of this book?

8. Regardless of what you think about the merits of the various critiques and reform proposals offered in the readings above, which do you believe are most likely to be adopted? Under what circumstances is this sort of treaty change likely to happen? Which actors are most likely to advocate change? Are they likely to have influence over the treaty revision process?

9. Various authors have noted that the WTO dispute resolution process can and does put developing countries at a disadvantage relative to their developed counterparts. Do you think that enough has been done to protect the interests of developing countries? What additional protections, if any, should be afforded to these states?

10. Should nongovernmental organizations have a right of participation in WTO proceedings? See the Bodansky reading in Part IV.B., above. What would legal process theories predict about how NGO participation might influence the evolution and internalization of environmental and labor norms into domestic trade law?

D. Humanitarian Intervention

In the last decade, the law of humanitarian intervention has come to be understood as a separate and important subject in international law.

That it has become so central to international law indicates how much has changed in the field during the post-World War II period. No longer does state sovereignty act as a shield against international scrutiny of a state's treatment of its citizens. The international community has acknowledged (though it has not always acted upon) a shared commitment to protect human beings from the most extreme abuses, no matter the source. This area of law thus pits two central principles of international law and politics against one another: the duty to protect human beings from extreme abuse and the sovereign integrity of the nation state. How can the international community create a system that encourages interventions that ought to occur while preventing those that should not? Who should decide when interventions are appropriate and how? These are only a few of the challenging questions posed in debates over humanitarian intervention.

This chapter focuses on the decision of the North American Treaty Organization (NATO) to intervene in Kosovo to stop the acts of ethnic cleansing that erupted there in the aftermath of the disintegration of Yugoslavia. The 1999 NATO action marked a turning point in international humanitarian intervention and has thus become a focal point for scholarly and policy discussions. Was the NATO action legal? Was it morally required? And if it was morally required but not legal, how might the legal regime be reformed to accommodate the moral requirements? These are the questions with which we begin. Louis Henkin approaches them from a legal norm-based perspective. His answers lead him to a perplexing dilemma: How can the international community carry out necessary interventions when the only legitimating body is unwilling to act? Jules Lobel, taking a Realist-influenced perspective, views the Kosovo intervention not as a benign development to be replicated, but instead as a threat to the rule of law. Kosovo, he argues, is simply the latest effort by the United States to undermine UN control over the legitimate use of force. In the final excerpt, Kenneth Abbott takes a step back and examines how several different schools of thought would explain what he calls the modern "atrocities regime." He emphasizes that the different visions of state behavior have important implications for the future of the "regime," and focuses attention on the role that legal institutions play in its functioning and evolution.

Kosovo and the Law of "Humanitarian Intervention"*

LOUIS HENKIN

I.

Kosovo has compelled us to revisit the troubled law of "humanitarian intervention." The terrible facts in and relating to Kosovo in 1998–

* Reprinted by permission from 93 American Journal of International Law 824 (1999).

1999 are known and little disputed. The need to halt horrendous crimes against humanity, massive expulsions and war crimes, was widely recognized. NATO intervention by military force was widely welcomed, but it was also sharply criticized. And it inspired much searching of soul by students of international law.

Now that the *fait* of the NATO bombing is *accompli*, and has been assimilated into a political resolution blessed by the Security Council, the legal issues of humanitarian intervention can be addressed in comparative tranquility, and the legal lessons pursued with less urgency, and with greater wisdom.

Was military intervention by NATO justified, lawful, under the UN Charter and international law? Does Kosovo suggest the need for reaffirmation, or clarification, or modification, of the law as to humanitarian intervention? What should the law be, and can the law be construed or modified to be what it ought to be?

II.

Before the Second World War, international law prohibited "intervention" by any state within the territory of another without that state's consent: international law prohibited unilateral intervention in internal wars; international law prohibited intervention even for agreed, urgent humanitarian purposes. In 1945 the UN Charter reaffirmed those prohibitions as part of a general prohibition on the use of force.

Article 2(4) of the Charter prohibits "the threat or use of force against the territorial integrity or political independence of any state" (subject only to the right of self-defense, Article 51). Article 2(4), it has been accepted, prohibits intervention by a state in internal war in another state by military support for either side. It has been commonly accepted, too, that the prohibition on intervention applies regardless of the political (democratic or less-than-democratic) ideology or the moral virtue of the government of the target state or of either side in the internal war. War apart, there was general agreement, too, that the Charter prohibits intervention by any state for humanitarian purposes.

III.

In my view, unilateral intervention, even for what the intervening state deems to be important humanitarian ends, is and should remain unlawful. But the principles of law, and the interpretations of the Charter, that prohibit unilateral humanitarian intervention do not reflect a conclusion that the "sovereignty" of the target state stands higher in the scale of values of contemporary international society than the human rights of its inhabitants to be protected from genocide and massive crimes against humanity. The law that prohibits unilateral humanitarian intervention rather reflects the judgment of the community that the justification for humanitarian intervention is often ambiguous, involving uncertainties of fact and motive, and difficult questions of degree and "balancing" of need and costs. The law against unilateral intervention may reflect, above all, the moral-political conclusion that no individual state can be trusted with authority to judge and determine wisely.

But, as Professor Richard Falk wrote long ago: "The renunciation of [unilateral] intervention does not substitute a policy of nonintervention; it involves the development of some form of collective intervention." The need for intervention may sometimes be compelling, and the safeguard against the dangers of unilateral intervention lies in developing bona fide, responsible, collective intervention.

Serious efforts to develop "some form of collective intervention" began soon after the end of the Cold War, when it ceased to be hopeless to pursue collective intervention by authority of the UN Security Council. In 1991 and 1992, the Security Council authorized military intervention for humanitarian purposes in Iraq and Somalia. In principle, those interventions were not justified as "humanitarian" (a term that does not appear in the UN Charter); the theory supporting such actions was that some internal wars, at least when accompanied by war crimes, and massive human rights violations and other crimes against humanity even if unrelated to war, may threaten international peace and security and therefore were within the jurisdiction and were the responsibility of the Security Council under Chapters VI and VII of the Charter. Of course, under Article 27(3) of the Charter, a Security Council resolution to authorize intervention, like other "nonprocedural" matters, was subject to veto by any permanent member. Thus, by the sum (or product) of law and politics, humanitarian intervention by any state was prohibited; humanitarian intervention was permissible if authorized by the Security Council, but a single permanent member could prevent such authorization.

Kosovo surely threatened international peace and security, as the Security Council had held in several prior resolutions. And, in 1998–1999, when negotiation and political-economic pressures appeared futile, for many Kosovo begged for intervention by any states that could do so, and by any means necessary. NATO heeded the call. It did not ask leave or authorization from the Security Council.

The reason why NATO did not seek explicit authorization from the Security Council is not difficult to fathom. Even after the Cold War, geography and politics rendered unanimity by the permanent members in support of military action (especially in the Balkans) highly unlikely. Evidently, NATO decided that not asking for authorization was preferable to having it frustrated by veto, which might have complicated diplomatic efforts to address the crisis, and would have rendered consequent military action politically more difficult.

Subsequent events confirmed that fear of the veto had not been unfounded. After the NATO action was begun, the representative of the Russian Federation proposed a resolution in the Security Council to declare the NATO action unlawful and to direct that it be terminated. In the vote, the proposed resolution was supported by three states, including Russia and China, two of the permanent members. It was not implausible for NATO to have assumed that Russia, or China, would have vetoed a resolution authorizing military intervention by NATO.

IV.

Was the NATO action unlawful?

The Charter prohibition on intervention, even for humanitarian ends, is addressed to individual states, but what the Charter prohibits to a single state does not become permissible to several states acting together. Intervention by several states is "unilateral," i.e., "on their own authority," if not authorized by the Security Council. Was NATO intervention in Kosovo authorized? Was it a justifiable exception?

The argument for NATO might go something like this.

Human rights violations in Kosovo were horrendous; something had to be done. The Security Council was not in fact "available" to authorize intervention because of the veto. Faced with a grave threat to international peace and security within its region, and with rampant crimes reeking of genocide, NATO had to act.

NATO intervention was not "unilateral"; it was "collective," pursuant to a decision by a responsible body, including three of the five permanent members entrusted by the UN Charter with special responsibility to respond to threats to international peace and security. NATO did not pursue narrow parochial interests, either of the organization or of any of its members; it pursued recognized, clearly compelling humanitarian purposes. Intervention by NATO at Kosovo was a "collective" humanitarian intervention "in the common interest," carrying out the responsibility of the world community to address threats to international peace and security resulting from genocide and other crimes against humanity. The collective character of the organization provided safeguards against abuse by single powerful states pursuing egoistic national interests. And action by NATO could be monitored by the Security Council and ordered to be terminated. The NATO action in Kosovo had the support of the Security Council. Twelve (out of fifteen) members of the Council voted to reject the Russian resolution of March 26, thereby agreeing in effect that the NATO intervention had been called for and should continue. And on June 10, the Security Council, in Resolution 1244 approving the Kosovo settlement, effectively ratified the NATO action and gave it the Council's support.

V.

In my view, the law is, and ought to be, that unilateral intervention by military force by a state or group of states is unlawful unless authorized by the Security Council. Some—governments and scholars—thought that NATO too needed, but had not had, such authorization, at least ab initio. But many—governments and scholars—thought that something had to be done to end the horrors of Kosovo, that NATO was the appropriate body to do it, and perhaps the only body that could do it, and that the law should not, did not, stand in the way.

In 1991 Professor Oscar Schachter wrote:

> Even in the absence of such prior approval [by the Security Council], a State or group of States using force to put an end to atrocities when the necessity is evident and the humanitarian intention is clear is likely to have its action pardoned. But, I believe it is highly undesirable to have a new rule allowing humanitarian intervention, for that could provide a pretext for abusive intervention. It would be better to acquiesce in a violation that is considered necessary and desirable in the particular circumstances than to adopt a principle that would open a wide gap in the barrier against unilateral use of force.

Does that apply to Kosovo? Is it better to leave the law alone, while turning a blind eye (and a deaf ear) to violations that had compelling moral justification? Or should Kosovo move us to push the law along, to bring it closer to what the law ought to be?

Humanitarian intervention on the authority of the Security Council recognizes that the Charter prohibition on the use of force does not apply to the use of force "in the common interest"; it also recognizes that intervention authorized by the Security Council affords the strongest safeguard against abuse of humanitarian intervention that the contemporary political system provides. But, as Kosovo illustrated, the Council, as presently constituted and under prevailing procedures, remains seriously defective and may sometimes be unavailable for that awesome responsibility.

NATO did not seek the Council's mantle, presumably because of the fear of the veto. We are not about to see a major restructuring in the composition of the Security Council, and we are not likely soon to see an end to the veto generally. But might we pursue an exception to the veto, as regards humanitarian intervention, in practice if not in principle?

That may be what Kosovo in fact achieved, in some measure. For Kosovo, Council ratification after the fact in Resolution 1244—formal ratification by an affirmative vote of the Council—effectively ratified what earlier might have constituted unilateral action questionable as a matter of law. Unless a decision to authorize intervention in advance can be liberated from the veto, the likely lesson of Kosovo is that states, or collectivities, confident that the Security Council will acquiesce in their decision to intervene, will shift the burden of the veto: instead of seeking authorization in advance by resolution subject to veto, states or collectivities will act, and challenge the Council to terminate the action. And a permanent member favoring the intervention could frustrate the adoption of such a resolution.

VI.

Neither one state nor a collectivity of states should be encouraged to intervene on its own authority in expectation, even plausible expectation, of subsequent ratification or acquiescence by the Security Council. But that is likely to happen, as it did as regards Kosovo, unless the Security Council and the permanent members in particular are prepared to agree to adapt their procedures to permit the Council's consideration in advance, with the understanding that the veto would not be operative.

Changes in the law and in UN procedures and understandings to that end might begin with Chapter VIII of the Charter.

Article 52(1) provides:

> Nothing in the present Charter precludes the existence of regional arrangements or agencies for dealing with such matters relating to the maintenance of international peace and security as are appropriate for regional action, provided that such arrangements or agencies and their activities are consistent with the Purposes and Principles of the United Nations.

Article 53(1) adds: "The Security Council shall, where appropriate, utilize such regional arrangements or agencies for enforcement action under its authority."

Article 52 readily lends itself to using NATO and similar regional bodies, for pacific settlement of disputes within their region. Article 53 also contemplates that the Security Council might use regional arrangements for "enforcement action under its authority." It is unrealistic, and perhaps undesirable, to ask the Security Council to give general approval in advance for regional groupings to engage in military humanitarian intervention. But should the law and practice be that a recognized, responsible regional collective body may intervene for bona fide humanitarian purposes unless the Security Council orders it to cease and desist—by a vote not subject to the veto? Or, better, might there be agreement that recognized regional bodies may intervene if authorized in advance by vote of the Security Council not subject to veto?

Kosovo demonstrates yet again a compelling need to address the deficiencies in the law and practice of the UN Charter. The sometimes-compelling need for humanitarian intervention (as at Kosovo), like the compelling need for responding to interstate aggression (as against Iraq over Kuwait), brings home again the need for responsible reaction to gross violations of the Charter, or to massive violations of human rights, by responsible forces acting in the common interest. We need Article 43 agreements for standby forces responsible to the Security Council, but neither action by the Security Council under Article 42, nor collective intervention as by NATO at Kosovo, can serve without some modification in the law and the practice of the veto. The NATO action in Kosovo, and the proceedings in the Security Council, may reflect a step toward a change in the law, part of the quest for developing "a form of collective intervention" beyond a veto-bound Security Council. That may be a desirable change, perhaps even an inevitable change. And it might be achieved without formal amendment of the Charter (which is virtually impossible to effect), by a "gentlemen's agreement" among the permanent members, or by wise self-restraint and acquiescence. That, some might suggest, is what the law ought to be, and proponents of a "living Charter" would support an interpretation of the law and an adaptation of UN procedures that rendered them what they ought to be. That might be the lesson of Kosovo.

Benign Hegemony? Kosovo and Article 2(4) of the U.N. Charter*

JULES LOBEL

Introduction

The 1999 U.S.-led, NATO-assisted air strike against Yugoslavia has been extolled by some as leading to the creation of a new rule of international law permitting nations to undertake forceful humanitarian intervention where the Security Council cannot act. This view posits the United States as a benevolent hegemon militarily intervening in certain circumstances in defense of such universal values as the protection of human rights.

This article challenges that view. NATO's Kosovo intervention does not represent a benign hegemon introducing a new rule of international law. Rather, the United States, freed from Cold War competition with a rival superpower, is both less restrained by the Charter's norms and more compelled to rely on different rationales to justify military action. Particularly in light of the Afghanistan, Sudan, and Iraq military interventions, the Kosovo operation does not portend a new rule of international law. Rather, it poses a serious threat to the rule of law.

Post-World War II international relations can be roughly divided into three periods. The first, stretching throughout the Cold War, was one in which the competing superpowers maintained a formal deference towards the Charter's prohibitions on non-defensive uses of force, but attempted to stretch the concept of self-defense to justify what in reality were violations of the Charter. The second was a brief unipolar yet multilateral moment between the Cold War's end and the late 1990s. During this time a United States-led U.N. authorized various military actions by the United States and other nations. The third and current era is characterized by the recent United States use of force outside of the U.N. framework against Iraq, Afghanistan, Sudan, and Yugoslavia. This era presents the grave danger that U.S. hegemony will further undermine the post-World War II quest to place the use of force under the control of a truly international organization.

* Reprinted by permission from 1 CHICAGO JOURNAL OF INTERNATIONAL LAW 19 (1999).

I. The U.N. Charter in a Bipolar World

The drafters of the U.N. Charter attempted to create a bright-line rule limiting the use of force. The use of force by individual states was prohibited, except in self-defense, to respond to an armed attack by one country against another. The Charter required that the Security Council authorize all other uses of force.

The clear rules of the Charter were premised on a set of assumptions that proved faulty. The Charter's framers sought to prevent a recurrence of the traumatic World War II experience from which they had just emerged. They assumed that interstate violence would dominate the second half of the twentieth century as it had the first. In fact, however, intrastate conflict constituted the predominant form of warfare during the next five decades. Moreover, the framers assumed that the Security Council would intervene to stop warfare, at least where one of the five permanent members was not directly involved. This assumption also proved inaccurate, as the Security Council remained deadlocked for almost half a century during the Cold War.

Nonetheless, the bipolar Cold War struggle between the two superpowers strained, but did not break Article 2(4)'s restrictions on the use of force. While both the Soviet Union and the United States violated the Charter's prohibitions where their perceived national interest required—the Soviet invasions of Hungary, Czechoslovakia, and Afghanistan, and the U.S. military incursions against Cuba, the Dominican Republic, Nicaragua, Grenada, Libya, and Panama—both superpowers maintained a formal fealty to the principle that force not be used except in self-defense.

Neither the Soviet Union nor the United States and its allies chose to openly challenge the Charter's norms for several reasons. First, both had an interest in the stability of the formal rules stemming from World War II; neither desired the destabilizing effects that openly challenging the recently adopted Charter's scheme would bring. Second, United States foreign policy was premised on the concept of containment, which was ideologically closely attuned to the legal norm of self-defense. The policy of containment and the normative prohibition on the use of force, except to counter an armed attack, were designed to resist changes to the status quo. Both superpowers foreswore using armed force to change the status quo in Europe, a policy which avoided world war and dovetailed with the Charter. The Charter's norms coincided with the political reality that both blocs sought to avoid direct armed confrontation with each other. Therefore, when Kennedy and Kruschev resolved the Cuban Missile Crisis in 1963, the core agreement—Soviet withdrawal of missiles for a U.S. pledge not to invade Cuba—reflected Article 2(4)'s norms.

Third, the rise of scores of newly independent states in Africa and Asia also favored the rhetorical maintenance of the Charter's norms. Both superpowers sought legitimacy for their foreign policies: to openly attack the notion of sovereignty that lay behind the Charter's structure would have delegitimated the rule-breaker in the eyes of many states whose support both blocs sought. Finally, since the superpower conflict was not primarily fought militarily between states, but within the internal politics of the less industrialized states, it was possible for the two superpowers to generally foreswear the offensive use of force against other states, yet nonetheless to achieve their policy aims by covertly intervening in the target states.

. . .

The world's major powers ... rejected any broad exception to the Charter for humanitarian intervention. Despite occasional rhetoric to the contrary, U.S. policy officially eschewed any legal reliance on employing armed force for democracy, or for broad humanitarian goals. The U.S. supported the overwhelming majority in the U.N. that voted to condemn the Vietnamese invasion of Cambodia, despite the widely-recognized ongoing genocide of the Cambodian government. The British Foreign Office in 1986 gave three reasons that the overwhelming majority of legal opinion refused to recognize the existence of a right to use force on behalf of humanitarian intervention:

(1) The UN Charter and corpus of modern international law do not seem to specifically to [sic] incorporate such a right.

(2) State practice in the past two centuries, and especially since 1945, at best provides only a handful of genuine cases of humanitarian intervention, and, on most assessments, none at all; and

(3) on prudential grounds, that the scope for abusing such a right argues strongly against its creation.

The bipolar Cold War world therefore produced a situation where the two major hegemonic powers and their allies, as well as the weaker states of Asia, Africa, and Latin America, strongly supported maintaining the Charter's restraints on the use of force. The Charter regime served the dominant states' interests by legitimating containment and detente, and by precluding weaker states from resorting to force to change the status quo. It served weaker states' interests by installing state sovereignty and independence as a central norm of the international order. It also provided them with at least ideological, if not military, leverage to defend that independence. Nonetheless, despite the formal widespread agreement as to the governing formal law, both superpowers and regional powers used force to assert their national interests, and many observers noted the diminishing role of the Charter as a restraint on state conduct. A divergence emerged between the formal law and the practice of the more powerful states. Those states used force in violation of the Charter, but sought to justify such uses by fitting their actions uncomfortably within the Charter's norms. The resulting dissonance between formal law and practice could only be resolved either by a revitalization of the Security Council—a possibility precluded by the Cold War—or a formal renunciation of the Charter's norms.

II. The Unipolar and Multilateral Moment

The collapse of the Soviet Union left the United States as the uncontested superpower, yet also removed the central, guiding purpose of its post-World War II foreign policy. The search for a new foreign policy to replace the containment of communism led in two complementary directions. The 1990s witnessed a rebirth of Wilsonian international liberalism trumpeting a new world order, the international rule of law, and the extension of American values of democracy, market economy, and human rights throughout the world. The Bush and Clinton presidencies also sought to make combating new threats to national security more central to American policy—terrorists, drug dealers, rogue states, weapons of mass destruction, ethnic conflict, and disintegrating states. These new threats replaced the overarching Communist menace as a critical engine of U.S. foreign policy.

. . .

In the first half of the decade, the expansion of authority to use force beyond self-defense was generally legitimated by United Nations Security Council authorization. In Somalia, Rwanda, Haiti, and Bosnia, the Council explicitly authorized the use of force by Western powers as a humanitarian measure not occasioned by a claim of self-defense. The protection of the Kurds in Iraq in the immediate aftermath of the Gulf War might also fall within this category, although the U.N. authorization in that case was more ambiguous and somewhat contested. While some questioned the Security Council's authority to sanction military intervention into the internal affairs of other states, most states and scholars accepted the Council's characterization of grave human rights and humanitarian crises as threats to international peace and security and therefore within its purview. Indeed, the most common critique of the Council and its permanent members was their inability to forcibly intervene in a timely fashion in crises of genocidal proportions, such as the Rwandan and Bosnian tragedies.

. . . [E]arly post-Cold War euphoria unraveled quickly. The Cold War's end sharply escalated ethnic tensions and demands for self-determination that threatened to engulf the U.N. with pressure to intervene to protect human rights. The United Nations could not possibly accommodate these demands, which led to increased charges of inconsistency and favoritism. Moreover the operational difficulties attendant upon such U.N. interventions led to increasing caution on the part of the Clinton Administration in authorizing such actions, and a refusal to place U.S. troops under U.N. command. Finally, by the latter part of the 1990s, America's unipolar moment had passed, at least in the political, if not the military and economic, spheres. As Samuel Huntington has persuasively argued, global politics have now entered what he terms a transitional uni-multipolar period, characterized by one great superpower preferring unipolar hegemony, and several major regional powers who would prefer a multipolar system wherein they could restrain the superpower. While American military and economic power reflect a unipolar world where the United States spends more on military spending than the next six major powers combined, the political dynamic in the U.N. Security Council suggests a multipolar world polity. The tensions inherent in the uni-multipolar system described by Huntington have led the United States to turn away from reliance on United Nations to authorize the use of force. The key turning point was the Iraqi crisis of 1998, when France, Russia, and China opposed the use of force to compel Iraqi compliance with the inspections regime, and the United States and Britain acted alone. Similarly, the threatened veto by Russia and China of authorization of military action against the Serbs in Kosovo forced the United States to rely on NATO alone.

The Kosovo air campaign propelled, at least temporarily, humanitarian intervention to center stage in American and European foreign policy, but now shorn of the legitimacy derived from Security Council authorization. The question for the twenty-first century is: will the Charter's restraint on force survive this new interventionism?

III. Benign Hegemony?

The Spring 1999 NATO air campaign against Yugoslavia has been trumpeted as ushering in a new era of international relations, in which the U.S. and its Western allies are abandoning the old U.N. Charter rules that prohibited nations from attacking others for strictly humanitarian reasons. One prominent American international law scholar terms the Kosovo air assault a "critical moment and a basic change in international legal practice." In this view, international law is moving toward a new rule permitting nations to undertake forceful humanitarian intervention in certain circumstances, even without Security Council authorization.

The potential emergence of a new norm permitting non-U.N.-sponsored humanitarian intervention stems from several converging factors. The flowering and flourishing of the human rights movement in public consciousness, in nongovernmental organizations, in the media, and among elites is one critical factor. The breakdown of state sovereignty over much of the globe with the resulting ethnic warfare and slaughter is another. The final, and critical, factor is the demise of the bipolar world in which superpower competition restrained overt intervention on behalf of "universally" held values. During the Cold War, those "universal" values themselves were in dispute, and therefore, neither superpower was willing to permit the other to legally intervene to promote its values. The development of a new norm permitting humanitarian intervention would thus reflect not only the prominence of the human rights movement, but also the preeminence of the United States, mirroring in law the United States dominance in the political, economic, military, cultural, and ideological realms of global society.

What is new about the "new humanitarian intervention" in Kosovo is not that the United States asserted humanitarian reasons to justify its military actions, but rather, that it did not also rely on traditional self-defense reasons that would legitimate such action under the Charter. That it felt no obligation to do so is a product of the contemporary international order in which the United States is unchallenged politically, militarily, and economically, but faces a Security Council that still rests on a multipolar structure. With no competing superpower to either justify a broad invocation of self-defense nor to assert "humanitarian interventions" of its own, the United States apparently felt both freer and more compelled to rely primarily on humanitarian interests and not traditional national security reasons to justify its actions.

The new proposed rule permitting non-U.N.-sponsored humanitarian intervention where the Security Council cannot act is premised on a projected world order in which a benignly hegemonic United States, in conjunction with other Western democracies, act as protectors of human rights throughout the globe. The assumption underlying this view is that these democratic powers would intervene in cases where serious human rights abuses are occurring for primarily humanistic reasons, and not simply to promote their narrow self-interests.

The history of humanitarian military intervention suggests, however, that such a new world order would be easily subject to abuse, where "humanitarian interventions" functioned as a new rationale for the assertion of hegemonic power. That history is replete with examples of powerful states or coalitions invoking the doctrine to conceal their own geopolitical interests. A comprehensive analysis of the historical record of such interventions written in 1973 concluded that "in very few, if any instances has the right [to humanitarian intervention] been asserted under circumstances that appear more humanitarian than self-seeking and power-seeking." The Charter's reliance on an armed attack to trigger a right to use force in self-defense was therefore an attempt to curb the historical, pretextual uses of force, by relying on an objective, verifiable standard to trigger a legal right to use force.

The United States has not been immune from asserting humanitarian reasons to justify military interventions that have served its own geopolitical interests. President McKinley justified military intervention against Spain in the cause of humanity; President Johnson claimed that U.S. intervention in Vietnam and the Dominican Republic were undertaken for humanitarian reasons; President Reagan asserted that the interventions against Nicaragua and Grenada were designed to restore freedom and human rights for those people; and President Bush articulated the restoration of human rights and democracy as a rationale for the Panama invasion.

Moreover, humanitarian intervention has been and continues to be highly selective, based on the national interests of the hegemonic state. For example, the United States used force in Kosovo, but still sells arms to Turkey despite that country's brutal repression of the Kurds. The U.S. military also sells weapons to Columbia, whose military has committed widescale human rights violations in fighting guerrillas. Such selectivity both furthers doubts about the motives of the intervening states, and also highlights the difficulty of establishing a rule of law based on the humanitarian intervention model. The rule of law is inconsistent with a police force that intervenes to protect only certain people from particular thugs and not others.

Those scholars who view the Kosovo conflict as portending a new rule of international law permitting non-U.N.-authorized humanitarian intervention have therefore sought to articulate a rule that avoids the historical abuses associated with such intervention. The insurmountable problems associated with any broad rule permitting humanitarian intervention have led scholars to search for a narrower construct. Such narrow constructs invariably set forth various conditions that must be met to render a humanitarian intervention lawful. For example, one could argue that NATO's Kosovo action supports a rule permitting armed humanitarian intervention where:

(1) a nation's human rights abuses have been condemned by the Security Council as presenting a threat to peace under Chapter 7 of the Charter;

(2) the Security Council is paralyzed by a veto threat and the military action is undertaken by a regional organization which asserts that it is intervening to protect human rights;

(3) the Security Council subsequently is either silent or refuses to condemn the military intervention; and

(4) peaceful, non-forcible diplomatic options for ending the human rights violations have been exhausted.

This narrowly tailored norm arguably ameliorates the most problematic aspects of humanitarian intervention. Security Council condemnation of the human rights abuses under Chapter 7 provides an objective, verifiable standard that serious human rights abuses do exist in the target nation. The second prong—a requirement of a regional organization's intervention—seeks to mute the potential for abuse that exists where one country intervenes unilaterally. The Security Council's subsequent silence, or refusal to condemn the military intervention is proffered as evidence of implicit Council approval or ratification of the action. The last condition seeks to ensure that force is only used as a last resort.

. . .

The question . . . is who decides that the human rights violations are so gross and massive as to warrant armed intervention. The Kosovo case illustrates the problem. While very few would dispute that the Serbs were committing serious human rights violations prior to the NATO bombing, sharp disagreement exists as to whether those violations were sufficiently widespread and massive to justify a use of force. During the year prior to the bombings, approximately 2000 civilians had died in Kosovo's civil war between the Serbs and the KLA [Kosovo Liberation Army], and in the months immediately preceding the bombing, one mass killing of civilians by Serb forces, in which forty-five persons were killed in the town of Racak, has been documented. The OSCE [Organization for Security and Co-operation in Europe] observer force established by the Security Council had effectively prevented the commission of massive atrocities. Massive ethnic cleansing only commenced after the bombing began. NATO therefore argued that Milosevic planned all along to evict forcibly all the Albanians from Kosovo, even had NATO not commenced bombing, a charge that cannot be objectively verified and about which independent observers express skepticism. Irrespective of the accuracy of this charge, accepting such speculation as a legal basis for humanitarian intervention would permit the very type of abuses and pretextual military interventions that Article 2(4) was designed to prevent. Moreover, a rule that permits nations to use force once the Security Council condemns human rights violations could well have a perverse effect. Nations such as China may well be reluctant to vote to condemn such violations for fear that they are opening the door to armed intervention.

The second proposed narrowing principle—a requirement that the intervention be undertaken by a regional organization—is also problematic. While clearly preferable to unilateral action, such multilateral action still contains the inherent problem of hegemonic interest masquerading under humanitarian goals....

... Was the United States attempting to orchestrate a new post-Cold War expanded role for NATO, as a means of exerting its influence through a more malleable instrument than the U.N.? Did Western Europe have a strategic interest in further reducing Russian and Serb interest in the Western Balkans? Was this a case of the dominant world power enforcing its will against a recalcitrant gangster to teach him and others the costs of disobedience? In June 1998, why was the United States the only NATO nation to argue that NATO did not need explicit Security Council authorization to use force in Kosovo, yet only eight months later NATO nations unanimously, albeit in some cases reluctantly, lined up behind the United States' argument to circumvent the Council? Why did the Bush Administration, at a time when human rights did not purport to displace national interest as the motivating factor for military intervention, warn the Serbs in 1992 that it would use military force against Serbia itself if it escalated the conflict in Kosovo? Such a warning must have been based on U.S. strategic interests, not human rights, in that the U.S. at that very moment was allowing the slaughter in Bosnia to proceed without outside military intervention. The answers to these questions are undoubtedly complex. The fact that the intervention was a NATO/U.S. one does not, however, remove these concerns.

That the Security Council subsequently refuses to condemn the intervention is also a weak argument for implicit authorization. Security Council members might acquiesce in an unlawful action, yet not vote to approve it if given such an opportunity prior to its initiation. Moreover, another problem with a rule that recognizes after the fact, de facto ratification of unauthorized military actions is that it encourages member states to take illegal action with the expectation that the Security

Council will later acquiesce. Acquiescence ought not to constitute authorization.

Finally, the requirement that all non-forcible and diplomatic means for resolving the dispute be exhausted is essentially meaningless because whether peaceful means have in fact been exhausted will typically be disputed. Thus, the key question is who decides whether that constraint has been met—the regional grouping or the Security Council? The Charter assumes that where a country is attacked, it has a right to immediately defend itself. In other situations presenting threats to world peace, the Security Council is to determine whether peaceful means of resolving the dispute have been exhausted. To eviscerate that rule essentially leaves the exhaustion requirement meaningless. Every grouping that takes such action will argue that it has met the requirement and that assertion will be unreviewable.

NATO's Kosovo campaign illustrates the dilemma. While Secretary of State Madeline Albright claimed that "before resorting to force, NATO went the extra mile to find a peaceful resolution," other observers disagree. The Rambouillet agreement,[1] presented to the Serbs as a take-it or leave-it proposition, contained provisions that any nation would find difficult to accept. These included allowing NATO troops unimpeded access to all of Yugoslavia, not just Kosovo, and placing Yugoslav sovereignty over Kosovo in doubt. Neither the Russians nor the U.N. was involved in the negotiating process or proposed implementation of the Rambouillet agreement. That the final agreement that ended the bombing differed significantly from that offered at Rambouillet—the objectionable provisions were dropped, the U.N. received ultimate authority for Kosovo, and Russian troops were included as peacemakers—at least suggests that the "extra mile" was not regulation length. Whether more flexible diplomacy would have resolved the conflict prior to the bombing will never be known; what is ascertainable is that the U.S. diplomacy seemed unwilling to budge an inch towards the Serbs.

A final and overriding difficulty with the proposed narrow humanitarian intervention norm is its limited applicability. The occasions in which the suggested conditions will be met are rare, and certainly do not apply to most of the ethnic conflicts and slaughters occurring throughout the world. The doctrine's applicability and effectiveness is further limited by the U.S. and European disinclination to intervene where there is a risk of significant casualties to their military personnel, or where allied nations are committing those abuses. If the impetus behind amending or revising the Charter is the search for an effective solution to the problem of gross human rights violations where the Security Council is deadlocked, forcible humanitarian intervention is likely to be of little use for most cases. Indeed, by distracting the world from more long-term solu-

1. [Editors' Note: The Rambouillet agreement would have provided for an agreed end to hostilities between the warring parties in Kosovo and a framework for a three-year interim regime. Slobodan Milosevic's rejection of the agreement led to NATO bombing aimed at Serb forces.]

tions to these problems, such "humanitarian" intervention may play a counterproductive role.

Despite these scholarly efforts to construct a viable rule, I do not believe that the world is on the cusp of accepting a change in the Charter paradigm. The difficulty of articulating a principled and effective doctrine of humanitarian intervention makes it unlikely that the Kosovo campaign will usher in a new norm of international law to replace or supplement the Charter paradigm. Two other factors militate against the development of a new rule permitting unilateral or regional humanitarian intervention. First, not only do the majority of nations oppose such a rule, but even the NATO countries appear unsupportive of a change in the Charter's regime. Second, the United States' recent military attacks on Iraq, Sudan, and Afghanistan suggest that the Kosovo action reflects its unwillingness to be restrained by international law, not a desire to change it.

The first reason why a new world order permitting individual nations to use force to protect human rights is not in the offing is because the major powers, including the U.S. and Western Europe, do not support it. Neither NATO nor the United States offered any legal justification for their action during the Kosovo crisis. In the proceeding before the International Court of Justice on Yugoslavia's complaint, only Belgium, of the ten NATO countries, mentioned humanitarian intervention as a possible legal justification. Even Belgium later stated its "hope that resorting to force without the approval of the Security Council will not constitute a precedent." Others, such as the United States, referred to violations of human rights in Kosovo and the need to avoid a humanitarian catastrophe, yet did not argue for a rule of international law that would justify NATO's action.

NATO's failure to articulate and defend a legal justification for its actions based on humanitarian intervention did not stem from a paucity of legal talent available to NATO governments. Rather, it undoubtedly reflects those governments' political reluctance to support such a developing norm. NATO members do not support giving any regional group, such as the Russian-dominated Commonwealth of Independent States, the power to intervene in other nations to prevent human rights abuses from occurring. Nor do the United States or other NATO allies want to create the hydraulic pressure for intervention that would come from formally articulating and promoting a new norm that provides for humanitarian intervention. In most such cases, the United States and other NATO nations' interest is to avoid a military commitment, and not to be forced into one. Therefore, the United States and its NATO allies are likely to continue to support ad hoc intervention that allows them to pick and choose in which situations to selectively intervene, and not propound any new rules of international law.

. . .

Following shortly after the Sudan, Afghanistan, and Iraq bombings,[2] the U.S. and NATO's clear violation of Article 2(4) in Kosovo cannot be viewed as groping toward a new international law doctrine of humanitarian intervention, but rather, as a retreat to great power unilateralism. A common element of all three military operations was their disregard of both international law and the United Nations. Indeed, Secretary of State Albright has stated that multilateralism, and presumably international law, are means not ends, to be discarded when United States national interest warrants. For example, when in February 1998 U.N. Secretary General Annan negotiated an agreement regarding weapons inspections with Iraq, Albright stated that if "we don't like" Annan's agreement "we will pursue our national interests" and presumably use force anyway.

The United States' unlawful use of force over the past several years is reflective of a broader failure to accept international legal restrains on its conduct. The refusal to agree to an International Criminal Court or the Land Mines Treaty, the Senate's failure to ratify the Test Ban Treaty, the ratification of International Human Rights Agreements with reservations ensuring that the United States accepts no obligations not already found in domestic law, and the continuation and extension of the Cuban embargo, all bespeak an American policy unwilling to bow to normative international legal restraints.

The major legal disputes over the use of force for the first decade of the twenty-first century are therefore unlikely to revolve around whether a humanitarian exception to the U.N. Charter ought to be recognized. It is more probable that those disputes will more fundamentally involve questions of whether, in general, the use of force will be made subservient to international organization. For, the real test of the twenty-first century will be to find ways to strengthen international institutions and to subject all nations, even hegemonic ones, to the rule of law. On that issue the U.S. is likely to find itself, in Harvard Professor Samuel Huntington's words, as the lonely superpower.

International Relations Theory, International Law, and the Regime Governing Atrocities in Internal Conflicts*

KENNETH W. ABBOTT

Introduction: IR Theory and International Law

Over the last ten years, international relations (IR) theory, a branch of political science, has animated some of the most exciting scholarship

2. [Editors' Note: The article refers in a previous section to bombings by the United States on Al Qaeda training camps in Afghanistan, on a factory suspected of manufacturing chemical weapons in the Sudan, and in Iraq during the early 1990s.]

* Reprinted by permission from 93 AMERICAN JOURNAL OF INTERNATIONAL LAW 361 (1999).

in international law. If a true joint discipline has not yet emerged, scholars in both fields have clearly established the value of interdisciplinary cross-fertilization. Yet IR—like international law—comprises several distinct theoretical approaches or "methods." While this complexity makes interactions between the disciplines especially rich, it also makes them difficult to explore concisely. This essay ... [applies] the four principal schools of IR theory—conventionally identified as "realist," "institutionalist," "liberal" and "constructivist" ... to the norms and institutions governing serious violations of human dignity during internal conflicts (the "atrocities regime").

...

This essay suggests two important lessons for IR. First, IR scholarship has overlooked many issue areas in which international norms and institutions carry important consequences for individuals and states.... Second, most of these regimes are at least partially legalized, with legal rules, institutions, procedures and discourse that modify ordinary politics. The legal character of international cooperation is itself a significant political phenomenon.

...

Understanding the Atrocities Regime

This section explores how different schools of IR theory might explain three central features of the atrocities regime: the distinction between international and internal armed conflicts, the emergence of norms governing certain abuses outside of armed conflict, and the increasing reliance on criminal responsibility and criminal tribunals.... [T]he explanations IR theory offers—emphasizing political function, origin and meaning—shape and deepen our current understanding of legal rules and institutions, influence our predictions of future developments, and provide bases for reform.

To illustrate, assume we understood an international criminal tribunal functionally, as a means of deterring violations of agreed rules. We might then expect its evolution to depend on changing needs for deterrence, and might focus reform efforts on clarifying the rules, increasing the certainty of prosecution, and the like. If, however, we understood the tribunal in terms of its origins in the efforts of human rights organizations in countries experiencing atrocities, we might tie its evolution to the fortunes of those groups, and might focus reform on allowing them and the individuals they represent to appear before the tribunal. Finally, if we understood the tribunal subjectively, as embodying shared beliefs about appropriate conduct, we might link its future to the evolution of those beliefs, and might focus reform on facilitating dialogue between its judges and the community at large. If we treated these understandings as cumulative rather than alternative, we would have a rich menu of institutional improvements.

Humanitarian Law in International and Internal Conflicts

Two contrasting accounts of humanitarian law illustrate the range of explanatory approaches within IR. The first (like the first example in the preceding paragraph) is functional, state-centered and largely static; it aims at generalization. The second (combining the last two examples) encompasses private actors and normative beliefs, and is dynamic; it aims at describing the origins of a particular regime. These accounts represent very different intellectual "styles," and will appeal to different readers. Neither focuses explicitly on the international-internal distinction, but each sheds light on it.

First, James Morrow is developing a decentralized institutionalist account of the laws of war, informed by game theory.[3] For Morrow, international institutions allow states experiencing suboptimal outcomes in strategic interactions to improve their "payoffs" by establishing superior equilibria. For such an equilibrium to be stable, an institution must create common expectations about behavior: each actor must expect that all others will comply with a rule or agreement before it can be confident that its own compliance will be beneficial. To create such a "common conjecture" in situations characterized by unreliable information or "noise," agreed rules must be highly precise. Similarly, an equilibrium in international relations will only be stable if it is self-enforcing: the risk that a breach will lead others to defect must create sufficient incentives to comply.

In this view, humanitarian law reflects a welfare-enhancing equilibrium: states obligate themselves to behave in specified ways, e.g., to protect prisoners of war, so that others will make the same commitments. The formality and legal character of the Geneva Conventions allow states unambiguously to signal their intentions and engage their reputations, making commitments more credible in a fundamentally anarchic setting. States revise the Conventions after major wars—and before new conflicts skew negotiating positions—to incorporate recent experience. The precision of the Conventions creates common conjectures that limit mistakes and misperceptions. The Red Cross monitors compliance—forestalling both violations and erroneous retaliation—while aiding victims. For all this, Morrow views the Conventions as having little independent effect on behavior; they merely coordinate relations among states with preexisting cooperative interests. He would presumably view efforts to modify state interests through humanitarian law as misguided.

States comply with humanitarian law primarily because of expectations of reciprocity, though other considerations, including concern for their international reputation and domestic political support, also come into play. Even if national policy supports compliance, however, individu-

3. [Editors' Note: Abbott is referring to James D. Morrow, *The Laws of War as an International Institution*, paper presented at Program on International Politics, Economics and Security, University of Chicago (Feb. 1997); and James D. Morrow, *The Institutional Features of the Prisoners of War Treaties*, paper presented at Rational International Institutions conference, University of Chicago (Apr. 1998).]

al soldiers can violate the rules. Here it is dangerous to rely on reciprocity, which can easily get out of hand. Hence, the Conventions require parties to educate and supervise their own soldiers; that commitment is maintained by reciprocity. The "grave breaches" regime is a useful supplement.[4] It applies mainly to high-level violators, who are unlikely to discipline themselves but highly likely to flee. The threat of prosecuting such individuals helps deter serious violations.

Rough empirical data support elements of this account. During World War II, for example, where pairs of warring states had ratified the 1929 POW [Prisoners of War] treaty, both sides generally lived up to their commitments (e.g., Germany and the Allies). Where one or both parties had not ratified, however, treatment of POWs was abysmal—on both sides (e.g., Germany and the Soviet Union). (Other factors could explain some of these observations. For example, German troops may have mistreated Russian soldiers because of ethnic prejudice, though the reverse is less likely.) Symmetry in retaliatory capacity was also significant. Once Germany lost the ability to bomb British cities, Morrow asserts, the Allies ignored prewar pledges not to bomb civilians.

Symmetry and reciprocity help illuminate the legal distinction between international armed conflicts and other violent situations. In international conflicts, states can anticipate reasonable symmetry between opposing forces, facilitating tit-for-tat enforcement. Here the regime is strongest: the Geneva Conventions, Protocol I and their grave breaches regimes all apply. In internal conflicts, symmetry is less likely. Since insurrectionist groups cannot ratify the Conventions, they cannot clearly signal their intentions or formally engage their reputations. Such groups often operate anonymously, hampering verification and reciprocity. They may be unable to control their own fighters, creating noise. They may favor "dirty" tactics to counter superior forces. In these situations, states have been less willing to restrict their own operations, agreeing only to common Article 3 and Protocol II, with no grave breaches regime.[5] (Apart from symmetry, governments may perceive internal conflicts as direct threats to survival, requiring maximum flexibility of response.) Finally, civil disturbances and terrorist actions are even more asymmetrical, and thus are not considered "armed conflicts" at all; even common Article 3 and Protocol II do not apply. Indeed, with low-level violence increasing worldwide, Protocol II actually

4. [Editors' Note: Grave breaches of the Geneva Conventions of 1949 and the Additional Protocol of 1977 (also known as "Protocol I"), which can only occur in international armed conflicts, are defined within the treaties and include the "willful killing, torture or inhuman treatment" of civilians. Every state that has ratified the Geneva Conventions is legally obligated to search for and prosecute those in their territory suspected of having committed grave breaches.]

5. [Editors' Note: Article 3, which is repeated in all four Geneva Conventions, is the only part of the conventions that applies explicitly to internal armed conflicts. It sets forth the minimum protections and standards of conduct to which a state must adhere. Additional Protocol II of 1977, the "Protocol Additional to the Geneva Conventions of 12 August 1949, and Relating to the Protection of Victims of Non-International Armed Conflicts" also covers internal armed conflicts. As Abbott notes, neither includes a grave breaches regime.]

narrowed the definition of "armed conflict" to situations involving organized dissident forces under "responsible command," where the logic of reciprocity can operate. These examples illustrate how IR theory can help lawyers predict the success of legal rules and design them to maximize effectiveness.

Martha Finnemore has adumbrated a contrasting liberal-constructivist account that sees humanitarian law as a product of private political action and an expression of social values. Finnemore traces the origins of humanitarian law to the efforts of committed private individuals, notably the "political entrepreneur" Henry Dunant. Dunant's 1859 battlefield experiences and religious convictions led him to create what became the International Committee of the Red Cross. Within ten years, Dunant and his associates persuaded most major states to sign the first Geneva Convention, requiring aid for wounded combatants and granting protected status to medical and relief workers.

In this view, humanitarian law did not originate with states at all, but with a network of elite individuals who persuaded governments to accept it. Dunant's appeals, moreover, were based not on strategic considerations, but on morality and duty, even identity: what was appropriate for a modern "Christian nation." The rhetoric of participating governments, too, was moralistic, not strategic. More concretely, Finnemore argues that the early history of the Convention supports a value-based interpretation. First, contrary to liberal predictions, Prussia and other authoritarian states strongly supported the Convention; Britain opposed it. Furthermore, in early conflicts, contrary to a realist view, Prussia, Japan and other states applied the new rules unilaterally. Finally, during the Balkan Wars of the 1870s, the Red Cross decided that the Convention should apply to internal conflicts because of its humanitarian character.

Finnemore's optimistic (even idealistic) account has important implications for international lawyers. Finnemore suggests that national interests and preferences can be modified through persuasion, a conclusion relevant to institutional design as well as political action. Her analysis predicts widespread compliance even by nondemocratic states, and provides support for extending humanitarian law to internal conflicts.

International lawyers have a considerable stake in the accuracy of these accounts, but the evidence adduced to support them leaves many questions unanswered. If the Red Cross applied the first Geneva Convention to internal conflicts, how did the sharp international-internal distinction emerge? If some states applied that Convention unilaterally, what explains the contrary evidence from World War II? Have states with different domestic governance structures applied the rules differently in more recent times? Morrow suggests another empirical test: Do countries nearing victory disregard the rules, as his analysis implies? Or do they continue to comply, as Finnemore's suggests? Further research could elucidate these points.

The Law of Peacetime Atrocities

Why have states criminalized certain atrocities—including genocide, crimes against humanity, torture and disappearances—even outside of armed conflict? Why are these norms so inconsistent, with genocide clearly defined as an international crime, torture subject to a prosecute-or-extradite treaty regime but considered a customary international crime, crimes against humanity also considered a customary crime but defined only (and inconsistently) in the charters of international tribunals, and disappearances criminalized only in the Americas? And why are other atrocities—e.g., small-scale political executions—treated more lightly?

Realism has limited explanatory power here. Some human rights institutions undoubtedly benefit powerful states. The Nuremberg and Tokyo trials have been criticized as victors' justice, condemning Axis leaders for atrocities Allied forces also committed. Those proceedings, like other early actions on human rights, allowed Allied governments to distinguish themselves from the Axis for domestic political purposes. More recently, the interests of powerful states have produced an inconsistent pattern of institutionalization. The ICTY [International Criminal Tribunal for the Former Yugoslavia] reflects big-power concern for Balkan stability—while deflecting attention from the failure to intervene more forcefully; the more cautious response in Cambodia reflects more attenuated interests.

More generally, a realist might emphasize the weaknesses of the atrocities regime in practice. For all the legal instruments signed since 1948, that period has seen scores of bloody conflicts and atrocities, but remarkably few criminal proceedings. There were no international prosecutions until the creation of the ICTY, and most national prosecutions have targeted former Nazis. In Kosovo, as this is written, investigators are uncovering mass graves and civilians are still being killed and driven from their homes, yet most of those indicted by the ICTY remain at large. To a realist, none of these facts is surprising. Yugoslavia will comply with international rules when it calculates that compliance furthers its national interests; Western powers will respond to atrocities by the same calculation. Only the coincidence of power and interest can change this sad scenario.

Liberal and constructivist scholars present a very different picture, emphasizing the emergence of norms through private political action and evolving beliefs and highlighting their subjective effects. In this account, attitudes toward human rights are reconfiguring the norms of sovereignty that have limited international responses to internal atrocities. Simultaneously prohibiting abhorrent conduct and justifying international intervention, these normative changes are reconstituting what it means to be a state. Again, this account suggests concrete political strategies for creating new norms and concrete institutional strategies—centered on modifying normative understandings and beliefs—for designing effective regimes.

Peacetime atrocity norms clearly arose in reaction to historical events—the Holocaust and the abuses by postwar authoritarian governments, especially in Latin America. These events produced cognitive "focal points" around which public attitudes of revulsion could coalesce. But what processes turned them into law? Liberal theory leads us to focus on political activity by individuals and groups. Constructivists emphasize that this is not "politics as usual," but a special politics rooted in values and aimed at changing values. Yet it is still politics, "the strategic activity of actors in an intersubjectively structured political universe."

Individuals have been important catalysts in the emergence of human rights norms. Raphael Lemkin, moved by the Armenian massacres and concerned about Nazi intentions, began to press for international criminalization of racial and religious massacres in 1933. After losing his family in the Holocaust, Lemkin gathered evidence of Nazi atrocities, coined the word "genocide," worked with the Nuremberg prosecutors, and lobbied for adoption of the Genocide Convention.

Human rights NGOs played similar roles. In the 1960s, Amnesty International began its campaign against torture and related abuses. It rallied support by publicizing cases of politically motivated torture in all geographical (and ideological) regions. In the early 1980s, Amnesty helped draft the United Nations Convention against Torture. When Latin American dictatorships turned to "disappearances," Amnesty mobilized around that issue, building support for the 1994 Inter–American Convention on the Forced Disappearance of Persons.

Margaret Keck and Kathryn Sikkink argue that "transnational advocacy networks" (TANs) have been the crucial political actors on human rights. TANs link international NGOs like Amnesty, local NGOs in countries suffering abuses, and supportive officials and agencies within national governments and international organizations. They adopt conscious political strategies, selecting and "framing" issues for maximum political impact, publicizing abuses in dramatic ways, exposing discrepancies between government rhetoric and practice, and seeking material leverage over target countries. Many human rights networks were energized by the 1973 coup in Chile and focused on abuses there. Their contributions to the Torture and Disappearances Conventions were crucial.

This account helps explain why some atrocities have been criminalized and others have not: simply put, TANs and NGOs have worked on those issues that are most conducive to political organization, dramatization and pressure. Keck and Sikkink argue that the most politically potent issues are those involving bodily harm to vulnerable individuals, like torture and disappearances, or the systematic sexual atrocities now addressed by international tribunals in response to pressure from women's groups. Yet they do not explain why other bodily harm issues have not been criminalized. Further research might explain these differences.

As liberal theory would predict, some states appear more vulnerable than others to normative persuasion and pressure. Keck and Sikkink find, for example, that states with liberal, law-based traditions have difficulty resisting legal or normative arguments, even if currently under authoritarian rule (e.g., Argentina). This logic suggests, however, that states without these traditions may resist normative pressures. Indeed, it implies that the widespread ratification of human rights treaties masks widely varying normative views, a form of "organized hypocrisy" inconsistent with legal universality. Realism is also relevant here: Western governments have been reluctant to pressure strategically or economically significant states, while some target countries (e.g., China) are insulated from most forms of leverage.

Those who argue that international norms are transforming sovereignty—including many proponents of international criminal law—must recognize that some states still prefer domestic to international approaches and "truth telling" and reconciliation to prosecution. The Truth Commission in South Africa, with its broad amnesty powers, is the best example. Yet truth-telling institutions themselves reflect new understandings of nationhood and governance. A related development is also significant: international reactions to demands for national autonomy are distinguishing among states on the basis of domestic governance. While virtually everyone accepts South Africa's internal efforts, the Security Council rejected a domestic approach in Yugoslavia (as a sham) and Rwanda (where it might have degenerated into vengeance); legal officials involved in the Pinochet litigation are by and large rejecting it in Chile. IR theory is a valuable aid in mapping these evolving understandings.

Criminal Responsibility and Judicial Implementation

Legal modes of thought and action permeate the atrocities regime. Proscribed conduct is treated as unlawful, not merely unacceptable; it is subject to legal proceedings, not mere political responses. For the most part, moreover, this is relatively "hard" law: the relevant treaties create binding legal obligations; they clearly define the proscribed conduct; and they delegate implementation to judicial institutions—primarily national courts (with universal jurisdiction and prosecute-or-extradite requirements to limit self-serving decisions) but increasingly international tribunals as well. Finally, these agreements incorporate criminal law concepts, not general notions of state responsibility. How would IR theory explain these characteristics?

Realists might argue that legal approaches help powerful states control disfavored conduct. In dealing with Yugoslavia, for example, the threat of prosecution was materially less costly than economic sanctions or military intervention. Governments can also depict such proceedings as apolitical acts, reducing potential political costs. Normatively, realists would support delegation of enforcement decisions to national governments, which can consider national interests; they would accordingly support the U.S. decision not to join the international criminal court (ICC), while doubting the court's practical impact.

For institutionalists like Morrow, legalization enhances the coordinating function of agreements, whatever the underlying power relationships may be. The formality of treaties and their approval and ratification procedures allow states clearly to signal commitments; legally binding commitments raise the political costs of violation, even for powerful states; careful drafting creates common conjectures; independent organizations provide unbiased monitoring; and courts resolve ambiguities and fill gaps.

Regime theory provides an even broader functional account of legalization. Individual criminal responsibility helps deter disfavored conduct, because of its value-laden character as well as the concrete threat of prosecution. Deterrence of individual officials is especially appealing when the alternatives—such as forcible intervention—are costly and difficult to organize. Decentralized enforcement through national prosecute-or-extradite obligations initially enabled regime architects to utilize existing institutions when the creation of new centralized institutions was politically impossible.

Decentralized enforcement, though, presents classic collective-action problems. Few states are materially affected by atrocities committed abroad, so few governments have incentives to prosecute offenders, even if they could obtain jurisdiction. Politically, the benefits of prosecution are limited; the costs may be significant. Material resources are also limited, and governments may choose to devote them to more immediate concerns. Some states may simply be incapable of mounting prosecutions. In spite of the efforts of human rights groups, then, national prosecutions have been few in number and narrowly targeted. The public goods of prosecution and deterrence are undersupplied.

Two kinds of institutions can address such disjunctions between national and community incentives. One is a transnational enforcement process open to private complainants, which allows individuals and activist groups to vindicate international norms. Helfer and Slaughter have detailed how such "supranational" procedures spurred legal development under the European Convention on Human Rights and within the European Community. Human rights plaintiffs have sought similar results through civil actions in national courts. The atrocities regime includes no formal private access procedure. Informally, however, private groups supply information to international prosecutors, serving similar functions.

The second alternative is a public institution empowered to initiate cases on behalf of the community. Examples here are even rarer; the Advocates General of the European Court of Justice (ECJ) come closest, but they cannot initiate litigation. Thus, while most commentators have emphasized the creation of international criminal courts, this analysis suggests that international prosecutors are equally significant, for they can resolve the collective-action problem of enforcement.

To vindicate international norms effectively, however, prosecutors and courts must be structured not only for impartiality and expertise, but also for political independence. Independence depends importantly on the provision of sufficient resources for factfinding and other judicial functions, and for administrative functions like imprisonment. It also turns on details of staffing, structure and procedure—the selection of judges, tenure, compensation, docket control, decision-making procedures—as in domestic legal systems.

These considerations must be weighed against what Duncan Snidal and I term "sovereignty costs," the symbolic and material costs of diminished national autonomy. Independent institutions are a major source of sovereignty costs, in part because their actions are inevitably somewhat unpredictable. The balancing of benefits and costs can be seen in the ICC statute, which gives priority to national prosecutions and limits the tribunal's independence, notably by authorizing the Security Council to delay proceedings.

Liberals would highlight the prominent role of lawyers and legal groups in creating the criminal responsibility system. It may be natural for lawyers to characterize acts like torture and genocide as crimes, and then to address them through prosecutors and courts. In this sense, lawyers operate as a transnational, knowledge-based "epistemic community," framing problems and solutions in legal terms for action by political institutions. Legal approaches also serve political purposes. Characterizing conduct as criminal links emerging norms to established legal values, increasing their legitimacy; it motivates individuals and groups attuned to legal issues, including national judges; and it gives politicians neutral "cover" for potentially unpopular actions. Criminalization also supports the penetration of international norms into national legal systems.

Constructivists would go further, emphasizing the value-laden quality of criminal law. Criminalization—the strongest form of social condemnation—reflects public revulsion. At the same time, international legal institutions can be "teachers of norms," shaping how governments and citizens perceive particular conduct. Actions like the Rwanda Tribunal's genocide conviction of a former mayor, Jean-Paul Akayesu, and the guilty plea of former Prime Minister Jean Kambanda, feed back into society to reshape how individuals view governance, the duties of states and citizens, even the meaning of statehood and citizenship. Social and psychological forces like these may well be influential, but their influence will not be equally deep in all parts of the world. Further study of the processes of normative change seems essential.

Looking Forward

The visions of international relations and international law presented here have significant implications for the future of the atrocities regime. Normative decisions on the content of the regime must be made through legitimate processes of government. IR theory cannot dictate those decisions, but it can inform them with an understanding of what is politically likely, and politically possible. Once the normative decisions are made, moreover, IR can help structure rules and institutions to achieve the agreed ends.

Space precludes anything like a full exposition of these issues. This section summarizes the engines of change identified by the leading schools of IR theory, then considers the special role of legal institutions in the evolution of the regime.

Engines of Change

Realists see the interests of powerful states as the principal force behind—and the major constraint on—change. This need not imply a gloomy future. To some extent, at least, the major Western powers have come to view nondemocratic regimes as political liabilities and serious human rights abuses as undermining stability.

Yet realists would expect political considerations to continue constraining national decisions in this area. Realists would also expect powerful states to influence the design of international rules and institutions in ways that preserve their own flexibility, a prediction borne out in the ICC negotiations. Normatively, of course, most realists would argue that states should act in these ways, to protect their national interests.

Finally, in response to the idealism of some approaches, realists offer cautionary advice. For one thing, legal institutions alone will not bring an end to atrocities. More fundamental approaches, some quite costly, will also be required. In particular, major states may have to apply economic or military power to produce changes in behavior, as chancy as these tactics are. Yugoslavia illustrates the point: with the NATO Stabilization Force generally unwilling to act, the Serbian-dominated nation, only a middling power, has maintained sufficient control on the ground to frustrate the ICTY and commit new atrocities in the face of worldwide condemnation.

Institutionalists typically agree that states are major engines of change, but they emphasize the ability of international rules and institutions to change the context of interaction and facilitate cooperative action. The post-Cold War Security Council, for example, enabled states to establish ad hoc international tribunals with broad legitimacy. When such a tribunal (the ICTY) can call on a major nation (Germany) to render up an accused individual (Dusko Tadic) for trial, who can doubt that international politics has changed? Other legal institutions, from the International Law Commission to the ICC, can also play important roles.

Yet institutionalists would agree that legal arrangements are only part of the solution. An effective atrocities regime must include new or improved institutions for monitoring abuses, avoiding conflict, making and keeping peace, protecting minority rights, supervising elections, and performing many other functions. Political organizations like the Security Council and the Organization for Security and Co-operation in Europe will necessarily be central players.

Liberal theorists stake out a strong predictive/normative position: the distinctions between international, transnational and domestic politics and law are artificial, inappropriate and crumbling in practice. Thus, liberals would predict and support increasing resort to individual criminal responsibility and the demise of the distinction between international and internal conflicts, on political as well as legal grounds.

Liberals see political action by individuals and private groups as the major force behind such changes. They would expect sympathetic national and supranational agencies to cooperate in these efforts. For liberals, the Pinochet litigation is a defining episode: a single Spanish magistrate single-handedly revitalizing the extradite-or-prosecute regime, in a case mingling abuses of citizens and foreign nationals during a predominantly internal conflict. Moreover, neither Judge Garzon's actions nor the responses of the British courts and Home Secretary are the actions of "states"; they are the law-governed actions of independent officials and organs of government.

Constructivists see numerous engines of change: historical events like the Kosovo massacres, political activity by human rights groups and TANs, governmental actions like those in the Pinochet case, judicial decisions like the Akayesu verdict.[6] All of these provide cognitive and moral focal points for social consensus and action. Political activists are expert at framing issues in ways that mobilize political support, resonating with broadly held cognitive and ideological principles. The key for constructivists is the transformative impact such actions have on subjective understandings of interest, appropriate behavior and identity.

Legal Institutions as Political Actors

Lawyers typically view courts and other legal institutions—even in politically charged areas like human rights—as "apolitical"; this is their special virtue. To differing degrees, both positivist and legal process scholars often build on this assumption. Recent IR scholarship, however, sees international legal institutions as intensely political actors, albeit in a special kind of politics. In this account, originally inspired by the ECJ, the political acumen of legal actors is among their most important traits, one that significantly influences the development of law and politics.

Anne–Marie (Slaughter) Burley and Walter Mattli developed a "neo-functionalist" account of legal development, focusing on the actions of individual judges, lawyers, legal scholars and others associated with supranational courts. All these individuals use their positions to pursue particular goals. These may include idealistic values, the interests of certain social groups, or particular legal outcomes, but they are also likely to include pure self-interest, such as professional prestige and

6. [Editors' Note: The International Criminal Tribunal for Rwanda found Jean–Paul Akayesu guilty of engaging in war crimes against Tutsis. The verdict is widely regarded as having influenced understanding of sexual violence as a war crime.]

power. One need not posit special commitments to community interests to explain, e.g., the role of the ECJ in expanding European law; "ruthless egoism does the trick by itself."

Professional norms and institutional rules prevent legal actors from utilizing direct political strategies like threats and bribes. But the law offers more subtle tools. Supranational judges, for example, can utilize standing rules and other access doctrines to acquire a caseload and build a supportive constituency of litigants and lawyers. They can render decisions and craft opinions that encourage national judges to view development of supranational law as a common project, while reassuring them that their own jurisdiction will be respected. (ECJ judges courted national counterparts even more directly, through seminars, dinners and other personal contacts.) They can select cases and interpret agreements in ways that develop doctrine in desired directions. Over time, as the increasing integration of Europe demonstrates, such actions can reshape politics as well as law. Political actors will generally acquiesce so long as judges remain within the seemingly neutral and apolitical domain of law—an image that judicial craftsmanship can help maintain.

Actors associated with international criminal tribunals will undoubtedly pursue similar strategies. Some of their strongest political tools lie in the flexible doctrines of customary international law. The ICTY appellate chamber decision in Tadic, for example, expanded its own jurisdiction and that of other tribunals by enunciating a customary law of war crimes in internal conflicts. Decisions accepting or rejecting indictments, interpreting substantive bases of jurisdiction, and fleshing out relationships to national institutions can develop doctrine, build constituencies, reassure skeptical politicians, and increase institutional legitimacy. By citing each other's decisions and those of national courts, each tribunal can enhance the authority of the entire regime.

Although access by individual litigants is limited, international prosecutors and judges can forge cooperative relationships with national prosecutors and courts, international institutions (like the NATO Stabilization Force in the former Yugoslavia), human rights NGOs with information on pending and potential cases, and other outside groups. Through speeches, articles and personal contacts as well as formal decisions, Judge [Richard] Goldstone, Judge [Louise] Arbour and others associated with the Yugoslavia and Rwanda Tribunals have worked tirelessly to create an international "community of law" around those institutions. Lawyers and legal scholars are significant players in this scenario. In human rights and humanitarian law, as in other specialized areas, lawyers and academics with expertise argue for the creation of particular rules and institutions, help draft the necessary agreements, serve on the institutions they help create or argue before them, and write approvingly of the results. Politically savvy judges will take full advantage of such individuals.

Realist scholars are suspicious of this approach. They argue that states are unlikely to be fooled by legal stratagems, and retain the power to overturn by treaty or supranational legislation any decisions they dislike. If the ECJ promoted European integration, for example, it was because the member states wished it to. Recent analyses see value in both positions. Scholars are developing more sophisticated theories spelling out the conditions under which national and international judges, lawyers, litigants and other actors can cooperate to expand the influence of supranational law, and under which states and other "legislators" will acquiesce.

Conclusion

The atrocities regime is a rich and fascinating area of study. Yet it is not the bare rules of the Geneva Conventions or the procedures of the ICTY that create this fascination; it is the political conflict played out in their creation and design, the struggle to imbue them with meaning, the effort to use them to modify undesirable behavior. As this symposium makes clear, many intellectual approaches can shed light on such complex social phenomena. Yet IR theory (a rich and multifaceted creation) has a particularly important contribution to make, for it has been developed—and is evolving—to illuminate just this kind of issue. IR is not a "legal method" in the narrow sense. Coupled with the study of law and legal institutions, though, it can be the cornerstone for a deeper understanding of international governance.

Notes and Comments

1. The Abbott article, and the article by Mary Ellen O'Connell on the New International Legal Process in Part III.C. are part of a symposium on international legal methodology in 93 AMERICAN JOURNAL OF INTERNATIONAL LAW (1999). Each of these methodological pieces also offer thoughts on the relationship between the methodology being discussed and the Kosovo intervention. Which of these approaches best explains the decision of the United States to intervene in Kosovo?

2. Although they take differing perspectives on the NATO action in Kosovo, both Henkin and Lobel view the intervention as illegal under the UN Charter. This view is not universally held among international lawyers. For example, Bartram Brown argues that:

> The argument for humanitarian intervention assumes that, at least in appropriate cases, the protection of human rights is a higher priority than the defense of national sovereignty from armed intrusion. It follows that when the human rights situation is serious enough, the proportionate use of armed force to remedy this problem should be legal. Article 2(4) of the U.N. Charter prohibits the use of force only "against the territorial integrity or political independence of any state, or in any other manner inconsistent with the Purposes of the United Nations." It therefore can be argued that the Charter allows the use of force to halt massive violations of human rights, as long as the prohibited purposes listed are not also involved.

Bartram S. Brown, *Humanitarian Intervention at a Crossroads*, 41 William & Mary Law Review 1683, 1697 (2000). Brown goes on to argue that "It is far from clear that there was anything illegal about NATO's Kosovo mission. Because of the underdeveloped state of the law, however, it is also far from clear that the operation was conducted in an entirely legal manner." *Id.* at 1740. What role does (and should) law play in determining whether states engage in humanitarian interventions? Could it be argued that there is an emerging "justified intervention" exception, under which humanitarian intervention that is limited in scope and duration is considered lawful? See generally Emerging Norms of Justified Intervention (Laura W. Reed & Carl Kaysen, eds., 1993).

3. As noted in the introduction, humanitarian intervention often involves intervention in a sovereign state without the consent of the government of that state. Such intervention appears to undermine the principle of state sovereignty and mutual respect for other state entities that undergirds the international community. On a related note, some argue that the wariness of states to intervene in other states' affairs stems at least in part from a reaction to colonial history. See, e.g., Neta C. Crawford, *Decolonization as an International Norm: The Evolution of Practices, Arguments and Beliefs*, *in* Emerging Norms of Justified Intervention (Laura W. Reed & Carl Kaysen, eds., 1993). Can principles of state sovereignty be reconciled with humanitarian intervention? Have recent interventions changed conceptions of the bounds of state sovereignty? In this respect, consider the following statement by Kofi Annan, Secretary General of the United Nations:

> State sovereignty, in its most basic sense, is being redefined—not least by the forces of globalisation and international co-operation. States are now widely understood to be instruments at the service of their peoples, and not vice versa. At the same time individual sovereignty—by which I mean the fundamental freedom of each individual, enshrined in the charter of the UN and subsequent international treaties—has been enhanced by a renewed and spreading consciousness of individual rights. When we read the charter today, we are more than ever conscious that its aim is to protect individual human beings, not to protect those who abuse them.

Kofi Annan, *Two Concepts of Sovereignty*, The Economist (September 18, 1999). Can the Secretary–General of the United Nations bless interventions that are formally in violation of the United Nations Charter? If he does, does that alter their legality? Their political legitimacy?

4. As of this writing, there are currently reports of massive human rights abuses in the Sudan. The government has reportedly armed and supported militias known as the Janjaweed (armed men on horseback) which have engaged in ruthless brutality against the civilian population in Darfur. The resulting crisis has reportedly led to some 30,000 people killed, 1.2 million internally displaced, and at least 130,000 living as refugees on the Chad border. Yet there have been no moves toward international military intervention. International involvement has instead focused on encouraging the Sudanese government to bring the militias under control and to engage in a peace process with the insurgent group, the Sudan People's Liberation Army. Why has the international community not intervened in the Sudan, like it did in Kosovo? (Similar questions have been raised about the failure of the international community to intervene in Rwanda to prevent genocidal actions there.) What do these differences suggest about what motivates states to engage or not engage in humanitarian intervention? Which of the theoretical perspectives outlined in this reader best explains state decisions to intervene or not intervene? Would the international community be well served by a hardening of the duty to prevent genocide? See Note 10 in Part IV.A. above.

5. Much of the recent scholarly writing on humanitarian intervention has happened in the wake of the Clinton Administration's interventions in Bosnia, Kosovo, and East Timor, and its conspicuous failure to intervene in Rwanda. Since then, in April 2003, the Administration of President George W. Bush famously led a "coalition of willing nations" to attack and occupy Saddam Hussein's Iraq. Although the invasion was initially justified as necessary to eliminate weapons of mass destruction, at this writing, none have been found. All agree that Saddam Hussein's regime was a gross violator of human rights. Which of the theories in Parts II and III best explain the invasion? Can the invasion and occupation be justified after the fact on humanitarian intervention grounds? What are the dangers of such *post hoc* justification? Did the Bush Administration unnecessarily forego other policy options, for example, seeking to disarm Saddam Hussein without attack? For a transnational legal process argument answering that question in the affirmative, see Harold Hongju Koh, *On American Exceptionalism*, 55 Stanford Law Review 1479, 1515–26 (2003).

6. As should be apparent by now, the law of humanitarian intervention raises many difficult dilemmas. What should be required to authorize humanitarian intervention? Who should decide if the relevant preconditions have been met? Is it possible to create a system that will authorize those interventions that are warranted and prevent those that are not? Should the motives of the intervening state matter in determining whether intervention in another state is warranted? Is a humanitarian intervention less legitimate if the intervening state acts for largely self-interested reasons? What would Carr (Part II.A.) say about what motivates states to engage in humanitarian intervention? Do you agree?

7. What is the relationship between legality and morality in the area of humanitarian intervention? Can an intervention be illegal and yet legitimate? And can an intervention be legal and yet illegitimate? How does your view compare with the legitimacy-centered theories discussed in Part III.B.?

E. Crime

Modern international criminal law has its foundations in the trials of Nazi leaders at Nuremburg after the close of the Second World War.

The trials—which resulted in the prosecution and eventual execution of many of the top German commanders—established a precedent for the prosecution of international crimes by the world community. The record in the years since, however, has been mixed. Horrific crimes in Cambodia, El Salvador, Iraq, East Timor, and elsewhere have—until recently—gone almost entirely unpunished. It was not until the mid-1990s that the United Nations, faced with genocidal acts in the former Yugoslavia and Rwanda, established new international fora for adjudicating war crimes—the International Criminal Tribunal for the former Yugoslavia (ICTY) and the International Criminal Tribunal for Rwanda (ICTR). The tribunals contributed to a renewed commitment to the goal of establishing an international court for the adjudication of violations of the growing body of international criminal law. As we shall see, however, this movement has been far from uncontested.

The readings in this section focus attention on the most recent efforts at providing international criminal justice: the International Criminal Court (ICC) and the two international tribunals that preceded it, the ICTY and ICTR. Taking an ideas-centered perspective, Payam Akhavan argues that the ICTY and ICTR have helped to transform a culture of impunity. This transformation, he argues, has been and will continue to be furthered by the forthcoming International Criminal Court (at the time Akhavan wrote, the statute had not yet entered into force; it subsequently entered into force in July 2002). In the following excerpt, published not long after the ICC entered into force, Jack L. Goldsmith and Stephen D. Krasner take a more skeptical interest-based perspective on the new Court. They argue that much as in the interwar period that led to E.H. Carr's disaffection over a half-century earlier, the idealism of the ICC's advocates is likely to be self-defeating.

Beyond Impunity: Can International Criminal Justice Prevent Future Atrocities?*

PAYAM AKHAVAN

Although still in the early stages of their institutional life, the International Criminal Tribunals for the former Yugoslavia (ICTY) and for Rwanda (ICTR) provide a unique empirical basis for evaluating the impact of international criminal justice on postconflict peace building. The pursuit of justice may be dismissed as a well-intentioned, but futile, ritualistic attempt to restore equilibrium to a moral universe overwhelmed by evil. Moreover, measuring the capacity of punishment to prevent criminal conduct is an elusive undertaking, especially when a society is gripped by widespread habitual violence and an inverted morality has elevated otherwise "deviant" crimes to the highest expression of group loyalty. Yet an appreciation of the determinate causes of such large-scale violence demonstrates that stigmatization of criminal

* Reprinted by permission from 95 American Journal of International Law 7 (2001). © The American Society of International Law.

conduct may have far-reaching consequences, promoting postconflict reconciliation and changing the broader rules of international relations and legitimacy.

Contrary to the simplistic myths of primordial "tribal" hatred, the conflicts in the former Yugoslavia and Rwanda were not expressions of spontaneous blood lust or inevitable historical cataclysms. Both conflicts resulted from the deliberate incitement of ethnic hatred and violence by which ruthless demagogues and warlords elevated themselves to positions of absolute power. At a volatile transition stage, the calculated manipulation of fears and tensions unleashed a self-perpetuating spiral of violence in which thousands of citizens became the unwitting instruments of unscrupulous political elites questing after supremacy. Against such a backdrop, the removal of leaders with criminal dispositions and a vested interest in conflict makes a positive contribution to postconflict peace building. In concert with other policy measures, resort to international criminal tribunals can play a significant role in discrediting and containing destabilizing political forces. Stigmatizing delinquent leaders through indictment, as well as apprehension and prosecution, undermines their influence. Even if wartime leaders still enjoy popular support among an indoctrinated public at home, exclusion from the international sphere can significantly impede their long-term exercise of power. Failure to deliver on promises of economic growth and prosperity, together with the humiliation of pariah status in an interdependent world community, eventually exacts a cost on such leaders' influence and authority. Moreover, political climates and fortunes change, and the seemingly invincible leaders of today often become the fugitives of tomorrow. Whether their downfall comes through political overthrow or military defeat, the vigilance of international criminal justice will ensure that their crimes do not fall into oblivion, undermining the prospect of an easy escape or future political rehabilitation. A postconflict culture of justice also makes moral credibility a valuable political asset for victim groups, rendering vengeance less tempting and more costly. Of course, the preventive effects of international criminal justice can extend beyond postconflict peace building in directly affected countries. The prosecution and related political demise of such leaders sends a message that the cost of ethnic hatred and violence as an instrument of power outweighs its benefits. Precedents of accountability, however selective and limited, contribute to the transformation of a culture of impunity that has hitherto implied the political acceptability of massive human rights abuses.

. . .

Now that a mounting number of wartime leaders are in the dock or on the run, one can fairly say that both the ICTY and the ICTR have become viable international judicial institutions. The ICTY survived a potential amnesty deal in the Dayton peace process.[1] The ICTY and the

1. [Editors' Note: The Dayton Peace Accords were signed in Dayton, Ohio on November 21, 1995. The Accords between the warring parties ended fighting in Bosnia and Herzegovina and maintained Bosnia and Herzegovina as a single state.]

ICTR have gained financial support from the international community and surmounted significant operational difficulties, demonstrating a capacity to hold fair (if not always expeditious) trials. Nonetheless, even if all the senior accused are arrested and prosecuted, the hardest test of their effectiveness is whether the tribunals have contributed to postconflict peace building and reconciliation. Beyond dispensing retributive justice and vindicating the suffering of victims, have these institutions proved to be an effective instrument for preventing further interethnic violence and human rights abuses? This consideration is particularly relevant to the ICTY and the ICTR since the Security Council established both as measures for the restoration of peace and security under Chapter VII of the United Nations Charter.[2]

The empirical evidence suggests that the ICTY and the ICTR have significantly contributed to peace building in postwar societies, as well as to introducing criminal accountability into the culture of international relations. Both institutions have helped to marginalize nationalist political leaders and other forces allied to ethnic war and genocide, to discourage vengeance by victim groups, and to transform criminal justice into an important element of the contemporary international agenda. In Bosnia–Herzegovina, the work of the ICTY has dramatically changed the civic landscape and permitted the ascendancy of more moderate political forces backing multiethnic coexistence and nonviolent democratic process. In Yugoslavia, the ICTY helped to delegitimize Milosevic's leadership, as revealed by his attacks on the Tribunal prior to his overthrow, as well as the later calls for his prosecution by the Serb and Montenegrin public. In Kosovo, the ICTY indictment did not stem the deportation and abuse of ethnic Albanians during the NATO campaign, but it has at least marginally discouraged anti-Serb vengeance by the Kosovo Liberation Army (KLA). In Croatia, cooperation with the ICTY has facilitated steps toward international integration, discrediting extremist elements and encouraging liberal political forces to consider the initiation of complementary war crimes prosecutions before national courts. In Rwanda, the ICTR has undermined the capacity of Hutu extremists to rehabilitate the remnants of their leadership abroad, and mitigated the severity of Tutsi reprisals against the Hutu by making accountability an important and constant political factor.

The impact of the ICTY and the ICTR is not necessarily limited to postconflict peace building in the former Yugoslavia and Rwanda. Nor should the prevention of future atrocities be measured solely by the effects of punishment on directly involved countries recovering from ethnic wars. Despite their ad hoc mandates, the ICTY and the ICTR directly influenced the adoption of the statute of the international criminal court (ICC) at the 1998 Rome Diplomatic Conference. Together

2. [Editors' Note: Chapter VII of the United Nations Charter is entitled "Action with Respect to Threats to the Peace, Breaches of the Peace, and Acts of Aggression," and authorizes the Security Council to "determine the existence of any threat to the peace, breach of the peace, or act of aggression" and "make recommendations, or decide what measures shall be taken ... to maintain or restore international peace and security."]

with the ICTY and ICTR precedents, the ICC blueprint for a future international criminal justice system, however weak and limited, has raised accountability to unprecedented prominence in the politics of international legitimacy. Criminal accusations increasingly constitute a serious political impediment to the ambitions of existing or aspiring leaders. In the calls for the establishment of further ad hoc international criminal tribunals, mixed tribunals, and prosecutions before national or foreign courts, in places as diverse as East Timor and Sierra Leone, Senegal, and Chile, one finds an unmistakable contagion of accountability. This spread of accountability reflects the early glimmerings of an international criminal justice system and the gradual emergence of inhibitions against massive crimes hitherto tolerated or condoned by the international community.

Prevention of Aberrant Contexts: Instilling Inhibitions Against Genocide

Evaluating the contribution of the ICTY and the ICTR to postconflict peace building depends on how prevention is defined in the context of large-scale violence. It is unrealistic to suppose that the ICTY could have instantaneously deterred crimes in the midst of a particularly cruel interethnic war in the former Yugoslavia. Hastily erected bulwarks cannot be expected to save lives when the deluge has already begun. The threat of punishment—let alone an empty threat—has a limited impact on human behavior in a culture already intoxicated with hatred and violence. Similarly, to expect that the ICTR would have brought immediate relief and reconciliation to the survivors of the massacres in Rwanda misapprehends the social devastation left in their wake. In both the former Yugoslavia and Rwanda the impact of postconflict justice was diluted by unwillingness to intervene in a timely way to stop ongoing atrocities. Against this backdrop, the first experiments in international accountability could not have been expected to instantly transform an entrenched culture of impunity into an abiding respect for the rule of law.

Illusory closure can easily be sought through the ritual of legal process. To imagine that the horrors of genocide can be contained within the confines of judicial process is to trivialize suffering that defies description. Yet the potential impact of the ICTY and the ICTR on political behavior is subtle and long-term, profound and lasting. Publicly vindicating human rights norms and ostracizing criminal leaders may help to prevent future atrocities through the power of moral example to transform behavior. "Realism" is not founded on the appeasement of power, and ideals are not irrelevant to "pragmatic" considerations. Beyond retribution and the moral impulse to vindicate humanitarian norms, individual accountability for massive crimes is an essential part of a preventive strategy and, thus, a realistic foundation for a lasting peace.

The proposed conceptual framework for considering the deterrent effect of the ICTY and the ICTR focuses on violence that is extreme and unrestrained, but deliberate and systematically induced. Once mass violence has erupted, threats of punishment can do little to achieve immediate deterrence. However, the outbreak of such violence can be inhibited, and its resumption in postconflict situations prevented—because it often results from an elite's deliberate political choices. Both conflicts were the product of deliberate incitement to socio-ethnic hatred and violence—albeit within societies undergoing a volatile stage of political transition or dislocation. Through systematic indoctrination and misinformation, political leaders created an aberrant context of inverted morality in which dehumanization and violence against members of the "enemy" group were legitimized as purported acts of self-defense. The delicate fabric of interethnic coexistence was gradually torn apart and otherwise shameful and reprehensible behavior elevated to the status of heroism and group solidarity. The homogenization of the masses through collective hysteria, allowing for no dissent, was an expedient political instrument for leaders whose primary concern was to consolidate their power, as well as for those who aspired to a position of leadership and authority. Prevention and punishment should focus primarily on those unscrupulous leaders who goad and exploit the forces advocating a spiral of violence.

. . .

The focus of punishment should be the prevention of . . . deliberately induced aberrant contexts, within which habitually lawful social relations degenerate into unrestrained violence. Once the population has fallen prey to a collective psychosis of ethnic fear and hatred, violent behavior becomes exceedingly difficult to circumscribe through threats of punishment. In this delusional context, criminal conduct that is normally characterized as "deviance" is transformed into acceptable, even desirable, behavior. As Michael Reisman astutely observes:

> In liberal societies, the criminal law model presupposes some moral choice or moral freedom on the part of the putative criminal. In many of the most hideous international crimes, many of the individuals who are directly responsible operate within a cultural universe that inverts our morality and elevates their actions to the highest form of group, tribe, or national defense. After years or generations of acculturation to these views, the perpetrators may not have had the moral choice that is central to our notion of criminal responsibility.

Moral choice in such cases may be limited rather than nonexistent. Many examples can be found of courage and valor indicating a capacity for choice, even in the most extreme circumstances. ICTR deputy prosecutor Bernard Muna relates that "within the drama" of the Rwandese genocide, "those who were close . . . know there were heroes. There were those who hid their friends, those who tried to save some of them by taking them to safe houses." Yet individuals are not likely to be easily deterred from committing crimes when engulfed in collective hysteria and routine cruelty. The central issue is whether and how punishment can prevent such aberrant contexts prior to their occurrence, or prevent their recurrence in postconflict situations.

Prevention of elite-induced mass violence can operate through both conscious and unconscious responses to punishment. Where leaders engage in some form of rational cost-benefit calculation, the threat of punishment can increase the costs of a policy that is criminal under international law. Leaders may be desperate, erratic, or even psychotic, but incitement to ethnic violence is usually aimed at the acquisition and sustained exercise of power. As Professor Ehrlich suggests, "willful engagement in even the most reprehensible violations of legal and moral codes does not preclude an ability to make self-serving choices." Momentary glory and political ascendancy, to be followed by downfall and humiliation, are considerably less attractive than long-term political viability. Furthermore, in an integrated world community, international legitimacy is a valuable asset for aspiring statesmen, no matter how remote their fiefdoms may be. Even an isolated Somali or Afghan warlord cannot entirely disregard the relation between international acceptance and long-term survival. The stigmatization associated with indictment, as much as apprehension and prosecution, may significantly threaten the attainment of sustained political power.

The prevention of aberrant contexts through "deterrence" or conscious responses to threats of punishment can be both specific and general. Punishment of unlawful conduct can be directed against leaders who actually contemplate or are engaged in the pursuit of criminal policies and, generally, against other leaders who might be tempted absent a credible threat of punishment. In both scenarios, the threat of punishment may persuade potential perpetrators to adjust their behavior. This cost-benefit calculation has implications for preventing conflicts, and also for preventing their resumption. In preconflict scenarios, it may discourage decisions to foment ethnic hatred and violence, since power thus accrued would be undermined by international isolation and accountability. In postconflict scenarios, leaders may be incapacitated outright (by arrests or being forced to flee), and the message conveyed that further incitement and violence will incur a high political cost. The credible threat of punishment through vigorous arrests and prosecutions removes impediments to stability from the political stage, and provides an incentive for constructive political behavior.

Besides the conscious fear of punishment, there is another, more subtle, dimension to general prevention—almost "constructivist," if you will—that operates to prevent aberrant contexts by instilling "unconscious inhibitions against crime" or "a condition of habitual lawfulness" in society. As Professor Andenaes has argued,[3] the expression of social disapproval through the legal process may influence moral self-conceptions so that "illegal actions will not present themselves consciously as real alternatives to conformity, even in situations where the potential

3. [Editors' Note: The author refers here to Johannes Andenaes, *The General Preventive Effects of Punishment*, 114 University of Pennsylvania Law Review 949, 949 (1966).]

criminal would run no risk whatsoever of being caught." Although leadership roles in preventing future atrocities are emphasized here, the progressive entrenchment of a more lawful self-conception can occur among a wider public, which could stiffen resistance to the blandishments of a leader seeking to exploit ethnic enmity and thereby reduce the prospect of renewed violence after a conflict. Even where public access to unadulterated sources of information is restricted, leaders may be influenced by "moral propaganda" emanating from the implementation of international criminal justice, and understand how the rules of legitimacy are transformed among international elites. Despite the adoption of numerous international instruments affirming human rights and humanitarian standards, international relations in the modern age have perpetuated a culture of virtually complete immunity. Idi Amin, Mengistu Haile Mariam, Pol Pot, and a litany of other tyrants have never been held accountable for their deeds. Notwithstanding the plethora of pious resolutions, solemn declarations, and legally binding treaties, the international community has accepted international crimes committed as an instrument of statecraft and political control. The long-term consequences of such a culture of impunity cannot be underestimated. The failure to uphold elementary international norms has created a political climate in which extermination, deportation, and wanton destruction lie within the range of options available to rulers—not only as conscious decisions, but as a subliminal conception of viable conduct. Impunity erodes the inhibitions and restraints against such behavior, permitting an amoral account of raison d'etat. Reversing this entrenched culture of impunity is a gradual and incremental process. By instilling such unconscious inhibitions in the international community over time, and gradually but definitively transforming the rules for the exercise of power, a new reality of habitual lawfulness may take root and develop.

. . .

Making Accountability Fashionable: Changing the Rules of Legitimacy

Beyond the former Yugoslavia and Rwanda, the broader impact of the ICTY and the ICTR on transforming a culture of impunity should not be overlooked. These institutions have "mainstreamed" accountability in international relations and thus instilled long-term inhibitions against international crimes in the global community. The establishment of the ICTY and the ICTR helped to revive the process of adopting a statute for an international criminal court. Despite its limited jurisdictional reach, the ICC will make it increasingly difficult for states to avoid their obligations to impose individual accountability for international crimes. Pending the entry into force of the ICC statute, the relative success of the two international criminal tribunals has brought calls for ad hoc judicial intervention in response to other large-scale atrocities. The increased national prestige associated with accountability and the stigma attached to the failure to prosecute international crimes have also encouraged third-party states to use their courts to assert universal jurisdiction over accused war criminals. Several states have prosecuted

Yugoslav or Rwandese perpetrators, even when no international indictments had been issued. In the Pinochet national case, proceedings before English and Spanish courts gave impetus to renewed proceedings before the Chilean courts, despite once insurmountable political obstacles.

The impact of the ICC on the prevention of international crimes can only be surmised since its statute has not yet entered into force. The states most likely to commit themselves to scrutiny are those least likely to violate human rights. But even states with a good human rights record may backslide during a change of regimes. Indeed, that is what happened in the former Yugoslavia, which ratified major human rights treaties before the outbreak of ethnic war in the 1990s. The Application of the Genocide Convention case, initiated by Bosnia–Herzegovina against the Federal Republic of Yugoslavia before the International Court of Justice, was made possible because of Yugoslavia's acceptance of international jurisdiction at a time when such a case could not have been envisaged. Members of the international community may also exert pressure on reluctant states to ratify the ICC statute as a rite of passage to international respectability and credibility. This tactic could be applied not only to so-called pariah states, but also to more influential states with leadership aspirations. One can safely assume, however, that selective Security Council enforcement action under Chapter VII of the Charter—whether in the form of further ad hoc tribunals like the ICTY and the ICTR or referrals to the ICC—will continue to be the mainstay of international criminal prosecutions for the foreseeable future. As Louise Arbour and Morten Bergsmo have observed, "It may be a more accurate proposition that the restrictive jurisdictional regime of the ICC Statute will make effective investigation and prosecution by the Court very difficult as long as a situation has not been referred by the Security Council under Chapter VII of the UN Charter. . . ."

The process leading to the adoption of the ICC statute constituted an important exercise in acculturation engaging thousands of diplomats, advisers, academics, and activists who represented states, international organizations, and NGOs. This process has resulted in greater exposure to and familiarity with the basic principles and procedures of international criminal law, strengthening the idea of accountability in a system of sovereign states. The negotiations leading to the adoption of the ICC statute have made an important contribution to the internalization of relevant human rights and humanitarian law norms, instilling inhibitions against international crimes and making them less acceptable in the community of nations. A significant number of the "like-minded" states that supported a strong and effective ICC have felt impelled to assert national-court jurisdiction over crimes of universal significance.

. . .

The mainstreaming of criminal justice in international relations has created an incentive in some instances for "preemptive" national proceedings, strengthening moderate political forces committed to reconciliation. For example, despite considerable resistance, President Abdurrahman Wahid of Indonesia has shown an unprecedented willingness to investigate the atrocities committed by military and paramilitary forces in East Timor before and after the population voted in favor of independence on August 30, 1999. The UN Commission on Human Rights established an International Commission of Inquiry on East Timor, which found "patterns of gross violations of human rights and breaches of humanitarian law" and recommended the establishment of an "international human rights tribunal .... to try and sentence those accused." In response to these demands, President Wahid indicated his preference for trials "to take place at home." UN Secretary–General Kofi Annan supported Wahid and emphasized that an international tribunal would not be established if the legal proceedings in Indonesia were "fair and transparent."

. . .

President Wahid embraced accountability not just to appease the international community, but also to check the power of the military, strengthen democracy, and promote national reconciliation. Changes in the military command, including Wahid's order for the resignation of General Wiranto, were partially linked with international pressures but clearly served his democratic and reformist agenda. One commentator observed that, from the time of his election in October 1999, Wahid had "set about loosening the Indonesian military's well-fortified power base, brick by cautious brick," including through prosecutions for abuses. "It will help him ... that unless Indonesia proceeds with its own trials, the UN is ready to create an international criminal tribunal on East Timor." Accountability for atrocities and corruption, it was noted, "is the key to obtaining the international investment and aid Indonesia desperately needs. Mr. Wahid is playing his aces—democratic legitimacy and international support—to break with the past."

. . .

Despite political limitations, Wahid's efforts suggest that international demands for criminal justice can inspire action by national courts, and that such pressures can be used to weaken the grip of militarist elements with a view to strengthening democratic forces and promoting national reconciliation.

Accountability and the "New Realism": Toward "Pragmatic Idealism"

The current prominence of accountability, and its emergence as a significant element of international relations, is a reflection of a desire for justice, as well as utilitarian objectives of postconflict peace building and the long-term prevention of mass violence. Impunity is often a recipe for continued violence and instability. The examples of the former Yugoslavia, Rwanda, Sierra Leone, and other transitional situations demonstrate how hard it is becoming even for realpolitik observers and diehard cynics to deny the preventive effects of prosecuting murderous rulers. Indeed, the rules of legitimacy in international relations have so dramatically changed since the inception of the ICTY, the ICTR, and the

ICC during the 1990s that accountability is arguably a reflection of a new "realism." A past view of policy based on principles of justice as naive and unrealistic has been seriously challenged by the convergence of realities and ideals in postconflict peace building and reconciliation.

Accountability is ultimately effective when it conforms with the broader policy context within which it operates. In contrast to the prevention of ongoing atrocities through military intervention or peacekeeping, and substantial postconflict economic assistance and social rehabilitation, resort to international tribunals incurs a rather modest financial and political cost. However, the attractive spectacle of courtroom drama, which pits darkness against the forces of light and reduces the world to a manageable narrative, could lead international criminal justice to become an exercise in moral self-affirmation and a substitute for genuine commitment and resolve. Postmortem justice without a corresponding commitment of military, political, and economic resources significantly dilutes the message of accountability and undermines its long-term viability in preventing crimes.

International criminal justice also cannot enjoy long-term credibility if it becomes an instrument of hegemony for powerful states. Understandably, in a slightly primitive international order built on the anarchy of power and state sovereignty, the early glimmerings of international criminal justice manifest themselves in selective ad hoc accountability. It is reasonable to assume that the progressive internalization of international criminal justice will gradually spread from the periphery to the center and give rise to a more inclusive universal framework, possibly through a widely ratified ICC statute together with vigilant and invigorated national or foreign courts. If the international community is to move beyond the currently fragmented assortment of jurisdictions to a coherent system of justice, a great burden falls on the shoulders of influential states to set a fitting moral example.

No one should entertain the illusion that the relative success of the ICTY, the ICTR, and the ICC process, or the engagement of national and foreign courts, has somehow exorcised the specter of genocide and other massive crimes from our midst. The reality of widespread atrocities in Africa and elsewhere leaves little room for judicial romanticism and even less for moral triumphalism. Achieving effective prevention against an entrenched culture of impunity, and fostering inhibitions against widespread rape, pillage, and murder in a context of habitual violence, cannot be realized through the efforts of a few ad hoc tribunals and national trials here and there. As Professor David Wippman has observed, international criminal prosecutions may "strengthen whatever internal bulwarks help individuals obey the rules of war, but the general deterrent effect of such prosecutions seems likely to be modest and incremental, rather than dramatic and transformative." Yet, in contrast with the gloom that encircled those seeking justice in the not-so-remote past, even these modest and early glimmerings of international criminal justice may be dramatic and transformative.

The Limits of Idealism*

JACK L. GOLDSMITH and STEPHEN D. KRASNER

In 1939 E. H. Carr published what was to become a modern classic on international relations, The Twenty Years Crisis, 1919—1939.[4] Carr has usually been seen as a defender of realism and a debunker of idealism, but his thinking was much more subtle. He believed that power and interest—the bread and butter of realism—were the primary determinants of state behavior. But he also believed that peoples and their nations were motivated by normative values and aspirations, not merely by a desire to marshal power and defend material interests. Carr concluded that "Utopia and reality are thus the two facets of political science. Sound political thought and sound political life will be found only where both have their place."

For Carr the problem of the interwar years was not international idealism itself, but rather international idealism run amuck. At the core of the international idealism he criticized was the assumption that right-minded human beings could agree on abstract normative principles to guide national behavior, and that these principles, once understood and embodied in international law, would influence nations to act with greater justice. By his account, international idealism discounted other factors, including the distribution of power and economic and political interests.

Carr famously argued that such idealism was self-defeating. Some nations, such as Germany, failed to comply with the principles of reason embodied by the League of Nations and similar institutions, and appealed instead to competing principles of law and morality to justify their self-interested and rapacious acts. Other nations, such as Britain and France, relied too heavily on the paper guarantees of international law, and not on a clear-eyed analysis of power and interest (both their own and Germany's), to secure international harmony. Carr attributed the growing international crisis in 1939 (his book was sent to the printer in July of that year) to the idealistic international institutions that were supposed to make a second world war impossible.

The kind of idealism that Carr understood to be so damaging to international peace and stability in the interwar years is again informing many aspects of international politics.... Supporters of ... institutions and policies [like universal jurisdiction and the International Criminal Court] tend to believe that justice is best served when it is isolated from politics and power. Only by insulating international institutions and practice from the bargaining and compromise that characterize political decision-making, and from the domestic political pressure to which politicians must always be alert, can justice be fully realized. On this view, institutions and principles that minimize the influence of power better achieve justice than those in which power plays an important role;

* Reprinted by permission from 132 DAEDALUS 47 (2003).

4. [Editors' Note: *The Twenty Years' Crisis* is excerpted in Part II.A. of this reader.]

and decisions made by unaccountable actors, especially judges, are more likely to be just than decisions made by political leaders responsible to their electorates.

We believe the new international idealism suffers from four fundamental flaws:

- First, it assumes the utopian premise that a global consensus can be reached, not just on normative principles, but also on when and how they should be applied.
- Second, it minimizes considerations of power, and assumes that norms of right behavior can substitute for national capabilities and material interests.
- Third, it neglects political prudence: it offers a deontological rather than a consequentialist ethics.
- Fourth, it consistently slights the value of democratic accountability.

Our claim is not that idealism in international politics is irrelevant or inherently harmful. With Carr, we believe that normative ideals can provide a hope for progress, an emotional appeal, and a ground for international action. But we also agree with Carr that ideals can be pursued effectively only if decisionmakers are alert to the distribution of power, national interests, and the consequences of their policies. The lesson Carr teaches is that when idealism is not tempered by attention to these factors, the best can become the enemy of the good, and aspiration the enemy of progress.

1

Universal jurisdiction is the power of a domestic court to try foreign citizens, including government officials, for certain egregious international crimes committed anywhere in the world. This authority is premised on the idea that human rights violations are an affront to all humanity and thus may be punished anywhere, regardless of the defendants' nationality or the place of the crime. Universal jurisdiction aims to strengthen international human rights law by marshaling politically independent domestic courts to enforce that law. The classic modern example is the *Pinochet* case, in which Spain attempted to extradite Pinochet from England (where he was undergoing back surgery) to stand trial in Spain for torture and related international crimes he allegedly committed in Chile. (The extradition request originally charged Pinochet with crimes against Spaniards as well, but these charges were deemed inadmissible, thus making the case one of "pure" universal jurisdiction.) The House of Lords ruled that international law required England to extradite Pinochet to Spain for these crimes, but the government of Great Britain eventually sent Pinochet back to Chile after determining that he was unfit to stand trial.

The Princeton Principles of Universal Jurisdiction, a document drafted by leading scholars and jurists from around the world, are a comprehensive statement of the nature and scope of universal jurisdiction. The Principles extend universal jurisdiction to piracy, slavery, war crimes, crimes against peace, crimes against humanity, genocide, and torture. They specify that "national judicial organs may rely on universal jurisdiction even if their national legislation does not specifically provide for it." They strip all defendants—including sitting heads of state—of any official immunities. And they maintain that amnesties in particular "are generally inconsistent with the obligation of states to provide accountability for serious crimes under international law." In short, the Princeton Principles aim to replace impunity with accountability by extending universal jurisdiction as broadly as possible.

The Princeton Principles reflect conventional wisdom among idealists about the shape and direction that international law should take. The Principles will likely influence future universal jurisdiction prosecutions, because national courts interpreting international law give special deference to the views of scholars and jurists. In our view, however, the Princeton Principles are an unfortunate development that exemplifies the new idealism's failure to take seriously the contested nature of international norms, the importance of prudence, and the possibility of abuse exacerbated by the absence of democratic accountability.

International criminal law is extraordinarily vague. Virtually everyone agrees that genocide and torture and crimes against humanity are international crimes. But when we attend to the details of what acts constitute these crimes, and of when these crimes can properly be tried by courts, there is much dispute and little definitive guidance. Consider three of many examples:

- Among the most clearly defined of international crimes is torture, which the Torture Convention defines to include any act inflicted by a public official "by which severe pain or suffering, whether physical or mental, is intentionally inflicted on a person" to obtain information, punish, or intimidate. Amnesty International claims that the United States violates this principle when its police use stun guns, pepper sprays, and restraint chairs, and when its prison officials use solitary confinement and related maximum security detention techniques. The United States disagrees; it believes these practices are legitimate and do not constitute torture within the meaning of the Torture Convention. There is no definitive source or judicial decision that can resolve this disagreement. Under universal jurisdiction, any national court could try these U.S. officials if it, like Amnesty International and many other human rights groups, viewed these police practices as torture.
- A crucial issue in any universal jurisdiction prosecution is whether the defendant has an official immunity from prosecution under international law. The existence and scope of these immunities as they apply to universal jurisdiction prosecutions are contested and unsettled. The House of Lords interpreted international law to lift Pinochet's immunity as a former head of state. More recently, the International Court

of Justice (ICJ) interpreted international law to hold that the Congolese foreign minister was immune from a universal jurisdiction prosecution in Belgium for alleged war crimes and crimes against humanity he committed in his country. The ICJ decision technically has no precedential effect beyond the case it decided. So the scope of official immunity from a universal jurisdiction prosecution remains an open question. Under universal jurisdiction, each national court gets to determine the proper scope for itself.

- When the United States and its NATO allies bombed Yugoslavia in 1999, they violated the UN Charter's prohibition on the use of force against sovereign nations in the absence of Security Council authorization. Under the Princeton Principles, NATO officials might be subject to universal jurisdiction prosecutions for "crimes against peace." But they might not; many international lawyers believe there is a developing customary exception to the UN Charter for certain humanitarian interventions. In addition, Amnesty International and an independent group of law professors have concluded that NATO countries committed "serious violations of the laws of war" when they purposefully destroyed civilian targets (such as a television station and electricity grids) and when they killed civilians by dropping bombs from no lower than fifteen thousand feet. The prosecutor at the International Criminal Tribunal in The Hague investigated these allegations and concluded, after much internal wrangling, that they did not warrant prosecution. Under a regime of universal jurisdiction, a court in any nation of the world could prosecute NATO leaders and military members and decide whether such actions constitute acceptable humanitarian intervention or criminal acts.

Because the content of international human rights law is so contested, courts exercising universal jurisdiction in good faith are likely to interpret and enforce this law in ways that affected groups will view as unconvincing, self-serving, and discriminatory. A universal jurisdiction prosecution can do more than provoke resentment among the affected groups; it can also provoke domestic unrest or international conflict. Until recently, Belgium was considering universal jurisdiction charges against both Ariel Sharon and Yassar Arafat for human rights violations each allegedly committed in the Middle East. (Such a prosecution remains a possibility.) A decision by a Belgian court that Sharon or Arafat, or both, are war criminals will not likely dampen discord in the Middle East. It is much more likely to make matters worse by legitimizing views of extremists on both sides.

Proponents of universal jurisdiction claim that these leaders should be held accountable for their international crimes, no matter what the consequences. This argument presupposes a consensus on the nature of the international crimes we have just questioned. The argument also overlooks the possibility that a universal jurisdiction prosecution may cause more harm than the original crime it purports to address. Universal jurisdiction courts and prosecutors possess neither the competence nor the incentive to fully consider these harms. They are doubly unaccountable in the sense that they are relatively unaccountable to their own government (to the extent that they are politically independent), and they are completely unaccountable to the citizens of the nation whose fate they are ruling upon. It doesn't matter that they act with benevolent intent. What matters is that they may do something that harms people to whom they have no real connection and whose interests they are poorly positioned to assess. Because relevant constituencies cannot hold courts exercising universal jurisdiction accountable for the negative consequences of their rulings, the courts themselves will invariably be less disciplined and prudent than would otherwise be the case.

The inability of universal jurisdiction courts to consider the consequences of their actions in affected countries is a particular threat to amnesties, reconciliations, truth commissions, and similar programs that can successfully facilitate transitional justice. Modern international idealists tend to see these programs as a rejection of accountability. In fact, such programs often contain elements of individual accountability. More importantly, these programs are best viewed as prudential arrangements that sacrifice some benefits—such as punishment of the guilty and restoration of the respect and integrity of victims—for the sake of other values, including the minimization of human suffering, closure, a stable peace, and the like. In recent years, amnesties have been an important component in several peaceful settlements of bloody civil conflicts, including ones in Chile, Haiti, Sierra Leone, and South Africa.

As Michael Scharf correctly notes, a rejection of amnesty and an insistence on criminal prosecutions "can prolong ... conflict, resulting in more deaths, destruction, and human suffering." Consider the Truth and Reconciliation process in South Africa. Under the Princeton Principles, this process would not preclude a universal jurisdiction prosecution, in a court outside South Africa, of Apartheid-era governmental officials. This insistence on individual accountability at any cost could have terrible effects on the still-fragile South African reconciliation. And it might have precluded the reconciliation altogether (or at least made it even more rocky) had universal jurisdiction been widely practiced in the 1990s. In this way, universal jurisdiction can make political solutions to already difficult transitions to peace and democracy even more difficult.

The inability of universal jurisdiction prosecutors to weigh judiciously the consequences of their actions distinguishes them from purely domestic prosecutors, and attests to the importance of democratic accountability in the enforcement of criminal law. In a domestic prosecution, at least in the United States, the prosecutor is accountable to the community in which she serves in the sense that she is either elected (as in many states) or (as in the federal system) appointed and subject to removal by elected officials. As a result, in deciding whether and how to prosecute a crime, a domestic prosecutor will often take into account the consequences of the prosecution for community health, safety, and morale. In many instances the adverse community consequences of holding an individual accountable for a past crime can lead prosecutors to forgo prosecution, or to strike a plea deal favorable to the accused. (And of course political accountability also dampens the likelihood that this discretionary process will be abused.) Because universal jurisdiction prosecutions take place outside affected communities, universal jurisdiction courts and prosecutors lack the incentive, or the institutional capacity, to consider such tradeoffs.

The discussion thus far has proceeded on the optimistic assumption that nations will apply universal jurisdiction principles in good faith. But there is no reason to believe this will be true. It is not only the House of Lords and the Belgian courts that can prosecute under universal jurisdiction. Corrupt courts that lack political independence can as well. And many nations will have incentives to engage in politically motivated universal jurisdiction prosecutions.

The Princeton Principles rely on legal norms to preclude such prosecutions. They insist that a "state shall exercise universal jurisdiction in good faith," and add that a "state and its judicial organs shall observe international due process norms, including . . . the independence and impartiality of the judiciary." The reliance on legal norms in this context is wholly unconvincing. The Principles fail to consider why a nation with bad-faith motives to prosecute a universal jurisdiction crime would care about such due process principles—principles that, in any event, are manipulable in opportunistic ways.

To date, the costs of universal jurisdiction have not been obvious—at least in the United States and Europe—because most universal jurisdiction prosecutions have been brought by Atlantic alliance nations against offenders in weak countries. But there is no reason to think this pattern will continue. The rate of universal jurisdiction prosecutions has increased in recent years. And, as their potential and scope become clear, as human rights groups continue to pressure nations to bring such prosecutions, and as weaker countries realize that universal jurisdiction can be a tool for creating political mischief on the international stage, especially against more powerful countries, such prosecutions will increase. Enthusiasm for universal jurisdiction might dampen in light of the ICJ's recent ruling on immunity for the Congolese foreign minister. If not, we expect that the many adverse consequences of universal jurisdiction we have discussed will become more apparent.

2

In July of 2002, international idealists realized a long-held dream: the creation of an International Criminal Court (ICC) with jurisdiction over genocide, crimes against humanity, war crimes, and, potentially, the crime of aggression.

In some respects, the ICC is an improvement over a regime of universal jurisdiction by national courts. The ICC is a centralized institution. Its treaty defines the international crimes within its jurisdiction. It also rejects universal jurisdiction, requiring instead a nexus to the territory or persons of a treaty signatory.

And yet the ICC has most of the other characteristics—and flaws—of universal jurisdiction. Its norms are still much too open-ended and contested to permit a consensus on proscribed behavior; it suppresses considerations of power; it lacks democratic accountability; and it cannot reliably balance legal benefits against possible political costs.

The ICC defines the crimes within its jurisdiction. But these definitions rely a great deal on contested international law norms, and they leave the ICC great interpretive flexibility. For example, "crimes against humanity" include "imprisonment or other severe deprivation of physical liberty in violation of fundamental rules of international law." Unfortunately, international law provides little concrete guidance about what these fundamental rules require. After listing other examples of crimes against humanity, the ICC treaty describes as a final one "other inhumane acts of a similar character intentionally causing great suffering, or serious injury to body or to physical or mental health." Such a criminal prohibition would almost certainly be void for vagueness under U.S. law.

To take another example, the ICC includes dozens of prohibitions under the heading of "war crimes," including "willfully causing great suffering, or serious injury to body or health" of civilians, and "destroying or seizing the enemy's property unless ... imperatively demanded by the necessities of war." The scope of these prohibitions is obviously uncertain, but it is easy to imagine them being applied to NATO actions in Kosovo and U.S. actions in Afghanistan. The ICC treaty is chock-full of many similarly vague and indeterminate criminal prohibitions.

One reason these vague norms are particularly troublesome is that the ICC prosecutor and court are unaccountable to any democratic institution or elected official. The ICC prosecutor is, to be sure, elected by a secret ballot by a majority of the signatory nations, each of which gets a single vote. But such an electoral system is problematic because, among other things, the vast majority of ICC ratifiers are weak nations that are never seriously involved in international police actions and thus have no incentive to consider the costs of zealous prosecutions. Even more importantly, the prosecutor can initiate investigations and prosecutions on his own, or at the suggestion of the UN or any signatory nation—all without review, or the threat of review, by political actors. His prosecutions are subject to legal review by the trial and appellate courts of the ICC, but these courts are similarly unaccountable to any democratic institution.

This lack of accountability means that the ICC presents many of the dangers of universal jurisdiction. Its structure is remarkably similar to the much-maligned U.S. Independent Counsel statute. By guaranteeing independence at the price of political control, it invites questionable and even politically motivated prosecutions. Legal restrictions and definitional limitations are not likely to provide real checks on the ICC's behavior, for the ICC itself is the ultimate interpreter of these norms. Experiences with the more accountable international tribunals in The Hague and

Rwanda have shown that international courts will not be bound by the letter of their governing rules when justice as they conceive it requires otherwise. ICC jurisdiction can only be expected to expand.

In addition, the ICC, like a universal jurisdiction court, lacks the institutional capacity to identify and balance properly the consequences of a prosecution on potentially affected groups. The ICC treaty insists that "the most serious crimes of concern to the international community as a whole must not go unpunished and their effective prosecution must be ensured." Here again we see modern international idealism's commitment to individual accountability at the expense of national amnesties and other forms of political reconciliation. The ICC theoretically permits the prosecutor to decline to investigate when there are "substantial reasons to believe that an investigation would not serve the interests of justice." But the final call rests with the prosecutor, who there is no reason to think has the perspective, information, or incentives to make this decision wisely. (When Richard Goldstone, the Yugoslav Tribunal's first prosecutor, was asked if he "worr[ied] about the consequences to the Bosnian peace process of indicting Radovan Karadzic and Ratko Mladic," he responded that the indictment "was really done as, if you like, as an academic exercise... because our duty was clear.")

It is true that the ICC treaty requires the court to dismiss a case if it is already under investigation in national court, "unless the State is unwilling or unable to genuinely carry out the investigation or prosecution." But the ICC has the final word on what counts as a genuine investigation based on its perception of whether the domestic proceedings are "inconsistent with an intent to bring the person concerned to justice," a provision that opens the possibility of double jeopardy if the prosecutor decides that a national conviction or investigation is too lenient and therefore not genuine. It is natural to expect the ICC to interpret its charter in ways that support its jurisdiction.

Perhaps the most troubling element of the ICC is its relationship to the UN Security Council. The United States argued that the ICC should prosecute only on the basis of referrals from the Security Council. The ICC drafters rejected the U.S. proposal on the grounds that it would inject international power politics into the decision whether to prosecute, and would give each of the Big Five powers a veto over any prosecution. The drafters viewed power politics, and the opportunistic use of Security Council vetoes, as an obstacle to individual accountability under international human rights law.

The ICC in its final form does permit the Security Council to delay a prosecution for twelve-month renewable terms. But this just means that an ICC case can go forward so long as a single permanent member vetoes a resolution of delay. And even if the Security Council votes to delay an ICC initiative (as it did when it granted UN peacekeepers a twelve month immunity from prosecution in July of 2002), many commentators believe the ICC has the power to engage in "judicial review" of the Security Council and possibly to disregard its decision.

There are at least two problems with this attempt to eliminate power politics from the enforcement of international criminal law and to subvert the recognition of national power incorporated in the UN Security Council. The first parallels a problem with universal jurisdiction: the ICC could initiate prosecutions that aggravate bloody political conflicts and prolong political instability in the affected regions. Relatedly, the possibilities for compromise that exist in a political environment guided by prudential calculation are constricted when political deliberation must compete with an independent judicial process. Many believe that the threat of prosecution by the international tribunal in The Hague made it practically impossible for NATO to reach an early deal with Milosevic, thereby lengthening the war and the suffering in the Balkans in the summer of 1999. The best strategy for stability often depends on context and contingent political factors that are not reducible to a rule of law. There is no reason to think that a politically unaccountable prosecutor and court will make such difficult, context-specific calls wisely, even assuming they had the discretion to do so.

The second problem results from what Carr would have described as a chasm between theory and practice. Proponents of the ICC believe that it may, in the words of Human Rights Watch's Kenneth Roth, "save many lives." This is wishful thinking. Even if the ICC turns out not to have the disruptive effects described above, and even if it is somehow able to prosecute low-level human rights abusers, it is hard to see how the ICC can stop, or even affect, persons responsible for large-scale human rights abuses.

The main reason for this conclusion is that the ICC can only prosecute persons it can get custody over. The Milosovics, Mullah Omars, and Pol Pots of the world, however, tend to hide behind national borders, where they are hard to reach. Moreover, the most notorious human rights abusers have been motivated by their own sense of mission and justice. They have seen themselves as saviors, not sinners. They have been determined to cling to power and they believe, as all leaders with a mission do, that they can reshape the world in their own image. If they have not been deterred by the threat of U.S. military intervention, they are unlikely to worry much about an ICC that lacks any real enforcement mechanism of its own and that must depend on its members, whose decisions are uncertain, to arrest and surrender suspects.

This brings us to the U.S. refusal to participate in the ICC. There are many reasons for the U.S. stance, most notably the perception that the United States's disproportionate share of international policing responsibilities exposes it to a disproportionate risk of politically motivated charges being brought before the ICC.

It may seem odd that an institution that will have little effect on rogue human rights abusers could so concern the world's greatest power. But U.S. troops, unlike rogue government officials, do not hide behind national borders. Hundreds of thousands of them are deployed around the globe, making them potentially easy to grab and bring to The Hague.

(The United States is trying to counter this danger by signing bilateral agreements in which the signatories agree not to surrender nationals of the other to the ICC.)

Even if no U.S. defendant is brought before the ICC, it can still cause mischief for the United States by being a public forum for official criticism and judgment of U.S. military actions. For all these reasons, the ICC will more likely affect the activities of the generally human-rights-protecting but militarily active United States than rogue state actors who hide behind walls of sovereignty (or in ungoverned areas) and care little about world public opinion and international legitimacy.

Despite his opposition to the ICC treaty, President Clinton signed it in 2001, just before he left office, so that the United States could participate in ongoing negotiations. In May of 2002, however, the Bush administration officially notified the United Nations that "the United States does not intend to become a party to the treaty." In August of 2002, President Bush signed the American Servicemen's Protection Act (ASPA), a statute that enjoyed broad bipartisan support. ASPA is sometimes called the Hague Invasion Act because it authorizes the president to use all necessary means to release U.S. officials from ICC captivity. It also bars military aid to some nations that support the ICC, and it requires the president to certify that U.S. peacekeepers will be immune from ICC prosecution.

U.S. opposition to the ICC is important because U.S. military and financial backing have been crucial to the operation of ad hoc international criminal tribunals. Consider how Milosevic wound up in The Hague. It was not the gravitational pull of international norms that brought him there. Rather, the United States wielded enormous diplomatic and military power to oust him from office, and then threatened to withhold some $50 million in aid to the successor regime in Yugoslavia until it turned over Milosevic to the Yugoslav tribunal.

The Milosevic episode teaches a general lesson. The ICC simply cannot, without U.S. support, fulfill its dream of prosecuting big-time human rights abusers who hide behind national borders. This is why the ICC's alienation of the United States may actually hinder rather than enhance human rights enforcement. We have already seen this effect on peacekeeping and ad hoc international tribunals. And of course the ICC will most likely chill U.S. military action not when central U.S. strategic interests are at stake (as in Afghanistan), but rather in humanitarian situations (like Rwanda and perhaps Kosovo) where the strategic benefits of military action are low, and thus even a low probability of prosecution weighs more heavily. In this way, the ICC may ironically increase rather than decrease impunity for human rights atrocities.

The establishment of an ICC that is unacceptable to the world's most powerful nation (and also to other large and powerful nations, including Russia, China, Indonesia, and India) represents a folly reminiscent of the League of Nations, and portends a similar fate. The international idealists who rejected U.S. demands for Security Council control over ICC prosecutions aimed to decouple the enforcement of international criminal law from international politics. They wanted "equal justice under law"—the equal application of international human rights law to weak and powerful nations alike. Both aims are a fantasy strongly reminiscent of the interwar idealism that Carr so effectively and presciently criticized. In demanding a full loaf of neutral justice rather than a half loaf of justice that accords with the interests of nations that can enforce it, and in creating an institution that relies on legal norms wholly removed from considerations of power, international idealists may diminish rather than enhance the protection of human rights. . . .

4

We have offered reasons to be pessimistic about the efficacy of . . . regimes [like] universal jurisdiction [and] the ICC . . . that aim to enforce international human rights norms. Our point is not to criticize the norms themselves, but to focus attention on pathologies that may result from the inadequate institutions in which they are embedded. International institutions can damage rather than promote international ideals if they are incompatible with the interests of those states whose support is needed for their success.

. . .

Universal jurisdiction and the ICC . . . can matter, because they establish judicial procedures that rely on the authority and policing powers of national states for enforcement. The problem here is not that such institutional arrangements will be ineffectual. As we have suggested, these institutions can affect the costs of political action, and can have a special impact on nations like the United States that are globally active and care about public opinion and international legitimacy. The problem with these institutions is that they can do more harm than good.

The ICC and universal jurisdiction assume a consensus on human rights ideals and their applicability, and expect that compliance will follow. But no such consensus exists; non-national judicial proceedings will always be open to charges of bias, an ambiguity that Milosovic has exploited in his trial before the International Criminal Tribunal for the Former Yugoslavia (an institution that avoids many of the pitfalls of the ICC). The ICC and universal jurisdiction sever the link between norm enforcement and political accountability. One consequence of this separation is that the institutions are practically, and in some circumstances legally, discouraged from engaging in assessments of costs and benefits that are often so important for the prevention of human suffering. As a result, such institutions may worsen rather than alleviate human rights catastrophes.

Notes and Comments

1. The ICTY and ICTR have come to be viewed as invaluable case studies for the International Criminal Court. Some argue that the tribunals have proven the limitations of international criminal law in its current form. In describing lessons from the Yugoslav tribunal, Michael Scharf notes that:

> Like the ICTY, the inherent weakness of the ICC will be the need often to rely on the voluntary cooperation of the very governments whose officials and personnel it seeks to prosecute. In the absence of voluntary cooperation, [however] the international community has generated an impressive arsenal of indirect enforcement mechanisms for the ICTY, which are potentially of great use to the ICC. . . . [T]hese include condemnation by the Assembly of State Parties or the U.N. Security Council; offers of individual cash rewards for assistance in locating and apprehending indicted war criminals; use of luring to obtain custody over indicted war criminals by deception; freezing the assets of indicted war criminals; offers of economic incentives to governments to induce cooperation; imposition of diplomatic and economic sanctions on non-cooperating governments; and use of military force to effectuate apprehension.
>
> Yet, owing to a lack of political will and divergent interests of key states, the international community has to date not sufficiently employed these enforcement tools, prompting the ICTY to warn the U.N. General Assembly that "the potential benefits of the Tribunal's work can not be realized until the international community demonstrates the same commitment to empower the Tribunal as it had shown when it established it." The ICTY has struggled with funding, with lack of support from the U.N. Security Council, and above all with arrests.
>
> As a result, seven years after its establishment, the ICTY still has not obtained custody over the major war criminals most responsible for the Balkan atrocities. The failure to bring these indicted leaders to justice has severely damaged the goal of peace-building in the former Yugoslavia, subverted the credibility of the ICTY, and undermined any deterrent value the ICTY might have had both in the former Yugoslavia and around the world.
>
> Given the impressive array of enforcement mechanisms which have been employed in connection with the ICTY, one might have high hopes for the success of the ICC. Yet, in light of the ICTY's limited success with these mechanisms, one must temper those hopes with modest expectations. In the end, the ICC will succeed only where international justice and power can be brought together.

Michael P. Scharf, *The Tools for Enforcing International Criminal Justice in the New Millennium: Lessons from the Yugoslavia Tribunal*, 49 DePaul Law Review 925 (2000). What lessons does the example of the ICTY offer for the ICC? Is there any reason to expect that countries would act differently with regard to the ICC than they have with the ICTY? Why would states create a system for prosecuting crimes at the international level, but then fail to enforce its orders?

2. As already noted, the ICTY has been far from an unadulterated success. The trial of Slobodan Milosovic, in particular, has been drawn out and highly politicized, with Milosovic using his trial as an opportunity to grandstand (the trial is televised in the former Yugoslavia). For a thoughtful discussion of the history and politics of the war crimes tribunals, see GARY JONATHAN BASS, STAY THE HAND OF VENGEANCE: THE POLITICS OF WAR CRIMES TRIBUNALS (2000). See also INTERNATIONAL WAR CRIMES TRIALS: MAKING A DIFFERENCE? (2003 Steven R. Ratner & James L. Bischoff, eds.); Patricia Wald, *The International Tribunal for the Former Yugoslavia Comes of Age*, 5 WASHINGTON UNIVERSITY JOURNAL OF LAW & POLICY 113 (2001). Bass concludes his book by considering whether such war crimes tribunals work. He writes:

> Do war crimes tribunals work? The only serious answer is: compared to what? No, war crimes trials do not work particularly well. But they have clear potential to work, and to work much better than anything else diplomats have come up with at the end of the war. A well-run legalistic process is superior, both practically and morally, to apathy or vengeance. True, the track record of war crimes tribunals so far has not been particularly impressive, except—and this is a big exception—for Nuremberg. But the track record of other approaches to defeated foes leaves even more to be desired. The task is to do a tribunal, and to do it properly. If at first you don't succeed, try again.

BASS, *supra*, at 310. Do you agree with Bass? Are international tribunals such as the ICTY and the ICC the worst means for dealing with massive violations of international law except for all the others? Do such tribunals simply offer a form of victor's justice (as Milosovic has alleged), or are they something more?

3. Much of the debate surrounding the ICC has centered on the role of the prosecutor. Unlike the ICTY and ICTR, the ICC will operate largely independently of the United Nations Security Council. Some have expressed the concern that this independence could allow for abuse of the discretion necessarily granted to members of the Court, including the prosecutor. Allison Marston Danner has written an excellent account of the dilemma, and proposes a solution based on, as she puts it "good process." She argues that by articulating "prosecutorial guidelines that will shape and constrain his discretionary decisions," the prosecutor can help shield himself and the Court against charges of politically driven prosecutions and thereby enhance their legitimacy and effectiveness. See Allison Marston Danner, *Enhancing the Legitimacy and Accountability of Prosecutorial Discretion at the International Criminal Court*, 97 AMERICAN JOURNAL OF INTERNATIONAL LAW 510 (2003). Are such protections necessary? Are they likely to work? How would you answer these questions from the interest-based perspectives and norm-based approaches discussed in Parts II and III of this book?

4. The trial of Saddam Hussein is taking place not before an international tribunal but before an Iraqi tribunal, supported by (some say orchestrated by) the international community, particularly the United States. Is this a better or worse alternative than the ICC or the ICTY? Is it workable as a general solution to the dilemma of how best to deal with massive violations of international law? Another alternative sometimes used in cases of massive past human rights violations is a truth and reconciliation process, of which the South African Truth and Reconciliation Commission—set up by the South African Government of National Unity to address crimes committed during apartheid—is the best known. The South African Commission focused on gathering information and offering victims and perpetrators the chance to testify about their experiences. Perpetrators that chose to testify about their actions were offered immunity from prosecution. For more on different forms of transitional justice, see, e.g., MARTHA MINOW, BETWEEN VENGEANCE AND FORGIVENESS: FACING HISTORY AFTER GENOCIDE AND MASS VIOLENCE (1998); RUTI G. TEITEL, TRANSITIONAL JUSTICE (2000).

5. What kinds of criminal acts should be considered "international crimes"? In *Prosecutor v. Tadic*, the ICTY appeals chamber devised a four-part test to determine the existence of an "international crime":

a. The infringement of a rule of international humanitarian law
b. The customary or treaty law character of the crime
c. The "seriousness" of the violation of humanitarian law
d. The establishment of individual criminal responsibility by the rule in question

Bruno Simma & Andreas L. Paulus, *The Responsibility of Individuals for Human Rights Abuses in Internal Conflicts: A Positivist View*, 93 AMERICAN JOURNAL OF INTERNATIONAL LAW 302 (1999) (describing *Prosecutor v. Tadic*, Appeal on Jurisdiction, No. IT–94–1–AR72, para. 94 (Oct. 2, 1995), 35 ILM 32 (1996)); see Jeffrey L. Dunoff & Joel P. Trachtman, *The Law and Economics of Humanitarian Law Violations in Internal Conflict*, 93 AMERICAN JOURNAL OF INTERNATIONAL LAW 394 (1999). Is this definition too inclusive? Too restrictive? How do you decide what kind of crimes should be prosecuted at the international level and which should be dealt with only on the domestic level? And, relatedly, how do you decide whom to prosecute at the international level? Should lower-level personnel be prosecuted at the international level, or should such prosecutions be limited to those who give the orders that cause war crimes to happen?

6. The United States has gone from being a major proponent of international adjudicatory bodies to a major opponent of the ICC. Many have argued that the new position is ill-advised. For example, David J. Scheffer, a U.S. Ambassador at Large for War Crimes Issues under the Clinton Administration, wrote:

> For the United States to position itself as the enemy of the rule of law would be a remarkable reversal of American international law enforcement policy sustained throughout the 20th century. In fact,

> the consequences for U.S. national interests in pursuing a rejectionist strategy of the ICC would be exceptionally negative and far-ranging. This is particularly so in the wake of the September 11, 2001, terrorist attacks on the United States and the creation of an anti-terrorism coalition under U.S. leadership.

David J. Scheffer, *Staying the Course with the International Criminal Court*, 35 CORNELL INTERNATIONAL LAW JOURNAL 47 (2001); see also TOWARD AN INTERNATIONAL CRIMINAL COURT? THREE OPTIONS PRESENTED AS PRESIDENTIAL SPEECHES (Alton Frye, ed., 1999). How would scholars from the various schools studied in Parts II–III of the book account for this change of heart? Does it simply reflect a change of administration (from the Clinton to the Bush Administration) or a deeper shift? Do you agree with Akhavan's statement above that, "The establishment of an ICC that is unacceptable to the world's most powerful nation (and also to other large and powerful nations, including Russia, China, Indonesia, and India) represents a folly reminiscent of the League of Nations, and portends a similar fate"? Can the ICC operate effectively without the support of the United States?

7. Harold Hongju Koh places recent developments in international criminal law into a broader frame:

> In retrospect, the early post-Cold War years revived and rejuvenated the Nuremberg concept of adjudication of international crimes. That rejuvenation found particular expression during [a] period of global optimism ... from 1989 to 2001. The revival could be seen in the International Criminal Tribunals for the Former Yugoslavia and Rwanda, the Lockerbie trial, the move to create mixed international-domestic tribunals in Cambodia and Sierra Leone, the Pinochet prosecution in Spain and Chile, and the civil adjudication of international human rights violations in U.S. courts under the Alien Tort Claims Act. From the U.S. perspective, the symbolic high-water mark came on December 31, 2000, when President Clinton signed the International Criminal Court Treaty during his last days in office, a treaty that entered into force in July 2002.
>
> But in the wake of September 11, every one of these hallmarks of the age of optimism about global justice has been placed under stress. With the trial of Slobodan Milosevic, the Yugoslav Tribunal faces its make-or-break case. The Rwanda Tribunal has been singularly unsuccessful, and the Lockerbie result disappointed many Western governments. For a time, the United Nations pulled out of the Cambodia tribunal, and the Sierra Leone tribunal has yet to decide any case. Pinochet was never tried and a follow-on effort to try Chadian dictator Hissene Habre in Senegal stalled. Academic commentators and some judges have started to challenge the rise of human rights litigation in U.S. courts. With the global justice system teetering, enter the Bush Administration. The new administration faced four options: first, supporting the growth and development of the global justice system; second, constructive engagement with that system, to try selectively to encourage it to develop in a

manner that served long-term American accountability interests; third, benign neglect—to leave the system alone to evolve its own way; or fourth, declaring hostility to that system and placing the United States outside of it, in effect adopting a double standard toward global adjudication.

Although Colin Powell initially signaled his preference for benign neglect, the Bush Administration has now opted, with four decisive measures, to pursue a hostile course. First, the United States announced that it would cease funding the Yugoslav and Rwanda tribunals by 2008, but failed to specify clearly that this defunding would be conditioned upon participating countries cooperating fully with those tribunals, thus potentially encouraging defendants to pursue foot-dragging measures that would wait out the tribunals. In effect, this decision gave every defendant currently before the tribunal an incentive to stall until 2008 to avoid getting tried. Second, at a time when a logical strategy for a country seeking allied support for a war on terror was to treat President Clinton's December 2000 signature of the International Criminal Court Treaty with benign neglect, in May 2002, the Bush Administration took the surprising step of sending U.N. Secretary–General Kofi Annan a letter seeking to undo that signature, effectively declaring war on the ICC. Third, the administration initially vetoed extension of the U.N. law enforcement assistance mission in Bosnia. The United States objected because the Security Council would not grant an indefinite and universal exemption from ICC jurisdiction for all U.S. officials engaged in peacekeeping operations, but ultimately consented to continuation of the mission in exchange for a one-year exemption (the maximum the Security Council could provide under the Rome Statute). Fourth, the much-criticized U.S. proposal to try certain foreign terrorist suspects for war crimes before ad hoc domestic military commissions has signaled a symbolic decoupling from international criminal adjudication. For the military commission proposal de facto "unsigns" our commitment to a global adjudication system by declaring that claims involving international crimes of terrorism should henceforth be heard not in international court, or even in U.S. civilian or military courts, but rather, in ad hoc military commissions under the control of the U.S. military, and set up at the U.S. Naval Base in Guantanamo Bay, Cuba.

Harold Hongju Koh, *On American Exceptionalism*, 55 Stanford Law Review 1479, 1503–05 (2003). Under what conception of national interest would it make sense for the United States government to oppose the global system of adjudication that it helped to create? Under a legal process approach, is the United States already too deeply enmeshed in supporting a global justice system to switch positions at this stage of the game? How would Liberal theory explain the change? Has domestic legal structure in the United States changed from administration to administration? And does a legal process approach suggest a strategy that human rights activists and other actors opposed to the switch in policy might pursue?

F. War

International law has enjoyed its greatest impotence—and arguably its greatest influence—on the battlefield of war. Classical international law distinguished between *jus ad bellum* (the law governing decisions to go to war) and *jus in bello* (the law governing the conduct of warfare). Both bodies of law have been "positivized," formalized and embedded into formal treaty arrangements. The primary body of law governing *jus ad bellum* may now be found in Article 2(4) of the United Nations Charter, discussed in Part IV.D. above. Meanwhile, the body of law governing *jus in bello* has been profoundly shaped by modern human rights law and humanitarian law, principally the Geneva Conventions. The post-September 11 war on terrorism, and the 2003 war in Iraq severely tested both bodies of international law. The United States' decision to go to war without explicit Security Council approval tested the limits of Article 2(4), particularly when combined with murky preemptive self-defense and humanitarian intervention rationales. Meanwhile, the treatment of detainees—on the battlefield, in Iraq (particularly at the now-infamous Abu Ghraib prison), at the U.S. Naval Base in Guantanamo Bay, Cuba, and in U.S. military facilities, where detainees who had been designated as "enemy combatants" were held incommunicado for months—raised the question whether and to what extent the Geneva Conventions apply to these post-9/11 situations.

The readings that follow—two of which are drawn from an Agora by the *American Journal of International Law* on the Iraq Conflict—focus on *jus ad bellum*: When is it lawful for nations to go to war? In the first reading, international law scholar John Yoo, who served as Deputy Assistant Attorney General, Office of Legal Counsel, U.S. Department of Justice, from 2001–2003, lays out the international law arguments favoring the U.S. conduct of the war in Iraq. In his piece, Thomas Franck, who worked in the United Nations and who has enjoyed an extended career as an international legal scholar, challenges the United States' justification for the Iraq war and argues that the controversy has confirmed that Article 2(4) of the United Nations Charter is effectively dead as a legal constraint on great-power warmaking. Finally, in an article on American exceptionalism, Harold Hongju Koh challenges the validity of the U.S. decision to go to war in Iraq on transnational legal process grounds.

International Law and the War in Iraq*

JOHN YOO

In his speech before the United Nations (UN) in September 2002, President George W. Bush characterized the possible use of force against

* Reprinted with permission from John Yoo, *International Law and the War in Iraq*, 97 American Journal of International Law 563 (2003). © The American Society of International Law.

Iraq as necessary to enforce existing Security Council resolutions and to eliminate a dangerous threat to international peace and security. The Security Council responded by adopting Resolution 1441, which found Iraq to be in material breach of previous Security Council resolutions and threatened serious consequences for further intransigence. When Iraq refused to fully comply with these resolutions, the United States led an ad hoc "coalition of the willing" that invaded Iraq on March 19, 2003, quickly defeated Iraq's armed forces, and ended the regime of Saddam Hussein and the Ba'ath party. On May 1, 2003, President Bush announced that major combat operations in Iraq had ended. At the time of this writing, the United States has assumed the position of an occupying power that is responsible for rebuilding Iraq, as recognized by the Security Council in Resolution 1483.

Despite these actions, other leading nations (primarily France, Germany, and Russia) and many international scholars have argued that international law did not justify the war in Iraq. The first part of this paper will explain why their view failed to properly read existing Security Council resolutions to authorize the use of force. Even putting the United Nations to one side, the war was further justified as an exercise of self-defense. Under basic notions of customary international law, properly understood, the United States could have attacked Iraq even without Security Council authorization. The second part of this paper will discuss why the toppling of Saddam Hussein's regime was justified as an exercise of anticipatory self-defense.

. . .

I. Background

Examination of the factual and legal setting leading up to the Iraq war will show that sufficient legal authority existed for the 2003 conflict with Iraq. On August 2, 1990, Iraq invaded Kuwait. The next day, the Security Council adopted Resolution 660, the first of many resolutions to condemn Iraq's actions and demand withdrawal from Kuwait. After diplomacy failed, the Security Council adopted Resolution 678, which gave Iraq until January 15, 1991, to implement Resolution 660 fully. Paragraph 2 of Resolution 678 authorizes member states "to use all necessary means to uphold and implement resolution 660 (1990) and all subsequent relevant resolutions and to restore international peace and security in the area." Iraq refused to withdraw from Kuwait before the January 15th deadline, and Operation Desert Storm began the next day. Iraq was expelled from Kuwait on February 27, 1991.

On April 3, 1991, the Security Council adopted Resolution 687, which established the conditions for a formal cease-fire suspending hostilities in the Persian Gulf. Resolution 687 required Iraq to: (1) destroy its chemical and biological weapons and ballistic missiles and agree to on-site inspections; (2) not use, develop, construct, or acquire such WMD and their delivery systems; (3) not acquire or develop nuclear weapons or nuclear-weapons-usable material or components; and (4) accept on-site inspection and destroy nuclear-related weapons or materials. To carry out the inspections, the resolution established a United Nations Special Commission (UNSCOM) to cooperate with the International Atomic Energy Agency (IAEA), which was to take custody of all of Iraq's nuclear-weapons materials. On April 6, 1991, Iraq officially accepted the terms, and a formal cease-fire went into effect between Iraq, Kuwait, and the nations that had cooperated with Kuwait, including the United States.

From the beginning, Iraq resisted UNSCOM's efforts to perform its mandate. On August 15, 1991, little more than four months after the adoption of Resolution 687, the Security Council "condemn[ed]" Iraq's "serious violation" of a number of its obligations regarding the destruction and dismantling of its WMD program and of its agreement to cooperate with UNSCOM and the IAEA and stated that the violation "constitutes a material breach of the relevant provisions of [Resolution 687] which established a cease-fire and provided the conditions essential to the restoration of peace and security in the region." Iraq's intransigence continued for years. In June of 1996, the Security Council "deplored" the refusal of Iraq to allow access to UNSCOM inspectors and Iraq's "clear violations" of its resolutions. In June 1997, the Council again "condemn[ed] repeated refusal of Iraqi authorities to provide access" to UNSCOM inspectors as a "clear and flagrant" violation of its resolutions and demanded full, immediate, and unconditional compliance. In the fall of 1997, Resolution 1137 "condemn[ed] ... the continued violations by Iraq of its obligations under the relevant resolutions to cooperate fully and unconditionally with [UNSCOM]," found that the situation continued to constitute a threat to international peace and security, and warned that "serious consequences" would result if Iraq failed to comply with its international obligations.

In February 1998, UN Secretary–General Kofi Annan secured a memorandum of understanding confirming Iraq's acceptance of all relevant Security Council resolutions and its reaffirmation to cooperate fully with UNSCOM and the IAEA. Nonetheless, Iraq formally halted all cooperation with UNSCOM at the end of October. The Security Council responded by condemning Iraq's decision as a "flagrant violation of resolution 687 ... and other relevant resolutions." On December 15, UNSCOM reported that it could not complete its mandate due to Iraq's obstructionism. The next day, the United States and Britain launched a seventy-hour missile and aircraft bombing campaign against approximately one hundred targets in Iraq. For the next four years, Iraq refused to permit UN inspections. In December 1999, the Security Council decided to disband UNSCOM and replace it with the United Nations Monitoring, Verification and Inspection Commission (UNMOVIC).

The terrorist attacks on September 11, 2001, and the United States' military response in Afghanistan against the Qaeda terrorist organization and the Taliban militia that harbored it, led to a sharper focus on the Iraq problem. The attacks on the World Trade Center and the Pentagon, carried out by Al Qaeda operatives trained and led from their bases in Afghanistan, demonstrated the threat posed by terrorists who could seek safe haven in rogue nations with potential access to WMD. As President Bush said in his January 2002 State of the Union address:

> States like these, and their terrorist allies, constitute an axis of evil, arming to threaten the peace of the world. By seeking weapons of mass destruction, these regimes pose a grave and growing danger. They could provide these arms to terrorists, giving them the means to match their hatred. They could attack our allies or attempt to blackmail the United States. In any of these cases, the price of indifference would be catastrophic.

On September 12, 2002, President Bush challenged the United Nations to address the threat posed by Iraq as highlighted by its continuing defiance of the Security Council. On November 8, the Security Council unanimously approved Resolution 1441 to address "the threat Iraq's non-compliance with Council resolutions and proliferation of weapons of mass destruction and long-range missiles poses to international peace and security." The resolution "deplor[es]" the absence of international inspections in Iraq since December 1998 and Iraq's continued failure to renounce international terrorism and cease the repression of its civilian population, and gives Iraq "a final opportunity to comply with its disarmament obligations under relevant resolutions of the Council." It reminded Iraq that the Security Council has repeatedly warned that "serious consequences" would result from the continued violation of its obligations.

Although Iraq responded to the resolution by permitting the resumption of inspections, it never took advantage of its final opportunity to comply with its international obligations. Iraq submitted a declaration on December 7, 2002, but the declaration was incomplete, inaccurate, and composed mostly of recycled information. Iraq's declaration clearly failed to address any of the outstanding disarmament questions that previous disarmament inspectors had publicly documented. The reports submitted by UNMOVIC to the Council confirmed these shortcomings. Iraq's submission of a declaration that did not comply with Resolution 1441 was a further material breach of its obligations. As President Bush stated on March 6, 2003, Iraq continued to produce missiles that violate the restrictions in Resolution 687 and to hide biological and chemical agents to avoid detection by international inspectors. No permanent member of the UN Security Council claimed that Iraq had lived up to its obligations in Resolution 1441. On February 5, 2003, Secretary of State Colin Powell delivered a comprehensive presentation to the Security Council demonstrating Iraq's ongoing WMD efforts and their concealment from UN inspectors. As Dr. Blix indicated to the Security Council on January 27, 2003, Iraq had not come "to a genuine acceptance, not even today, of the disarmament which was demanded of it."

The conclusion is inescapable that at the time of the outbreak of the 2003 conflict, Iraq had decided to refuse to comply with its disarmament obligations. This placed Iraq in material breach of Resolution 1441 as well as Resolution 687. At the time of this writing, coalition forces in Iraq continue to search for WMD sites; while no weapons have yet been discovered, it may take months if not years to learn the fate of Iraq's WMD stockpile. It has become clearer since the war that Saddam Hussein had allowed Al Qaeda-linked terrorists to operate from Iraq. Nonetheless, these ex post developments do not directly bear on the justification for the use of force ex ante. What is important for jus ad bellum purposes is what the United States and its allies reasonably understood the facts to be at the start of hostilities, not what turned up afterwards.

II. UN Security Council Authorization for the Use of Force Against Iraq

In light of this background, two independent sources of law provided the United States and its allies with authority to use force in Iraq: UN Security Council resolutions and the right to self-defense. Resolution 678 authorized member states "to use all necessary means to uphold and implement resolution 660 (1990) and all subsequent relevant resolutions and to restore international peace and security in the area." One of the most significant "subsequent relevant resolutions" was Resolution 687. Pursuant to Resolution 678, the United States could use force not only to enforce Resolution 687's cease-fire, but also to restore "international peace and security" to the region. In Resolution 1441, the Security Council unanimously found that Iraq was in material breach of these earlier resolutions and that its continuing development of WMD programs, its support for terrorism, and its repression of the civilian population presented an ongoing threat to international peace and security.

These findings triggered Resolution 678's authorization to use force in Iraq. Suspending the cease-fire and resuming hostilities with Iraq was an appropriate response to Iraq's material breaches of Resolution 687. Over the years, Iraq repeatedly refused to respond to diplomatic overtures and other nonmilitary attempts to force compliance with its obligations to disarm and to permit full UN inspections of its WMD program. Military force was necessary to obtain Iraqi compliance with the terms of the cease-fire and to restore international peace and security to the region.

Some have argued, however, that, Resolution 678's authorization had expired. Representatives from France, Germany, and Russia, for example, seemed to take the position that because the current members of the Security Council would not agree to the use of force in the spring of 2003, the 1991 resolution's broad authorization was somehow extinguished. That view is simply wrong as a matter of UN practice and as a matter of law. The UN Security Council has not readily authorized the use of force in the past (indeed, it appears to have done so only in the context of seven conflicts), nor has it rescinded those decisions lightly. When the Security Council has taken the serious step of ending its authorization to use force, it has only done so in one of two ways: either by expressly terminating the prior authorization or by setting an up-front time limit on the authorization. With regard to Bosnia, for example, the Security Council ended the legal authority for the use of force by expressly terminating the previous authorization in a separate resolution, while in Somalia, the Security Council explicitly established a sunset date when it extended the authorization. In fact, when the Security Council has wanted to reserve for itself whether the conditions for termination of its authorization have been met rather than leave the matter to the member states, it has explicitly done so. Security Council practice has been consistent on this point over a substantial period of time. Resolution 678, by contrast, contains no self-imposed time limit, and none of the resolutions relating to Iraq, including Resolution 1441, explicitly terminated the resolution's endorsement of the use of force. Unless the Security Council had clearly stated, using the same language that it has in the past, that it has terminated Resolution 678's authorization for the use of force, any such authorization continued.

In fact, the view of France, Germany, and Russia directly undermines the idea that UN Security Council enactments are law at all. In 1991, the members of the Security Council unanimously agreed to authorize the use of force against Iraq, and reduced that agreement into the written text of Resolution 678. That text has not been subsequently changed, and the conditions for its authorization continued. If the current members of the Security Council disagreed with Resolution 678, they could have repealed it. To argue that Resolution 678's authorization had somehow dissipated, despite its clear text, simply because some of the current members of the Council no longer agreed with it treats Council resolutions as if they merely recorded temporary diplomatic agreement rather than enacted enduring legal texts. The French, German, and Russian view considers Security Council resolutions to be ad hoc executive edicts, rather than legislative acts—a result that would cause considerable uncertainty about their legal force and when they expire.

Some nations attempted to sidestep the inevitable conclusion to this argument by claiming that Resolution 1441 itself somehow eclipsed Resolution 678's authorization to use force. Resolution 1441, however, twice "[r]ecall[ed]" Resolution 678 and explicitly restated that Resolution 678 referred to the ability of member states "to use all necessary means to uphold and implement resolution 660 (1990) and all subsequent relevant resolutions and to restore international peace and security in the area." In fact, rather than negate earlier authorizations, Resolution 1441 instead triggered them. Resolution 1441 "[d]ecides" that Iraq "has been and remains in material breach of its obligations under relevant resolutions," in particular the obligations in Resolution 687 regarding Iraq's WMD program. In addition, the resolution specifies that any false statements or omissions with respect to Iraq's WMD program "shall constitute a further material breach of Iraq's obligations." The resolution also reminds Iraq that the Security Council has repeatedly warned that "serious consequences" will result from the continued violation of its obligations. No member of the Security Council found that Iraq had been in compliance with Resolution 1441, Resolution 678, or Resolution 687.

Resolution 1441's finding that Iraq was in material breach allowed the United States and its allies to terminate the cease-fire created by Resolution 687 and resume the use of force as authorized by Resolution 678. In the multilateral context, it is well-established that a material breach of a treaty by one of the parties entitles a party "specially affected" by the breach to suspend the operation of the treaty in whole or in part vis-à-vis the defaulting state. Even if a state party were not "specially affected," however, a material breach that "radically changes" the position of the parties also permits complete or partial suspension. Resolution 687 explicitly established "a formal cease-fire ... between Iraq and Kuwait, and the [UN] Member States cooperating with Kuwait in accordance with resolution 678 (1990)." The state parties to the cease-fire agreement were Iraq, Kuwait, the United States, and the other members of the coalition in the Gulf war but not the United Nations itself. During the decade after the end of the first Gulf war, Iraq committed numerous material breaches of the cease-fire, in particular by continuing to develop weapons of mass destruction. Iraq's material breaches of the cease-fire entitled the United States, as a party to the cease-fire, unilaterally to suspend its operation. Under accepted principles of international law, the United States did not need the concurrence of the other parties. Once the cease-fire was suspended, the United States could rely on Resolution 678 to use force against Iraq to implement Resolution 687 and to restore international peace and security to the area.

The March 2003 attack was also justified under the law governing armistices. Resolution 687 was basically an armistice—unlike a peace treaty, it did not terminate the state of war, but merely "suspend[ed] military operations by mutual agreement between the belligerent parties." A cease-fire allows a party to a conflict to resume hostilities under certain conditions. Under the Hague Regulations, "[a]ny serious violation of the armistice by one of the parties gives the other party the right of denouncing it, and even, in cases of urgency, of recommencing hostilities immediately." The missile strikes in 1993 and 1998 serve as clear examples of the suspension of a cease-fire and a resumption of hostilities due to serious violations by Iraq. Because the initial use of force in response to the invasion of Kuwait—Operation Desert Storm—was authorized under Resolution 678, subsequent uses of force against Iraq in response to serious violations of the terms of the cease-fire established by Resolution 687 are authorized as well. Thus, because Iraq refused to fully comply with Resolution 687, such as by destroying fully its WMD and their delivery systems, it was in "serious violation" of the cease-fire and the United States was justified in resuming the use of force under Resolution 678.

This understanding of the interaction between Resolution 678 and 687 is supported by state practice in the decade following the end of the first Gulf war. The consistent position of the United States had been that Resolution 678's authorization continued. The United States and Britain, for example, used force against Iraq in 1993 and 1998 in response to Iraq's material breach of Resolution 687. On January 17, 1993, President George H. W. Bush ordered missile strikes against a nuclear facility near Baghdad due to Iraqi infringements of the terms of the cease-fire. Just four days before, President Bush had ordered air attacks on surface-to-missile sites and related facilities in the southern no-fly zone. These attacks, which were joined by Britain and France, appear to have been primarily in response to Iraqi violations of the southern no-fly zone—Iraq had moved surface-to-air missiles into the zone to threaten coalition aircraft—but President Bush also pointed to Iraq's " 'failure to live up to the resolutions.' " The president's report to Congress on the attack takes note of a statement by the UN secretary-general explaining that " 'the forces that carried out the [January 13th] raid have received a mandate from the Security Council, according to Resolution 687, and the cause of the raid was the violation by Iraq of Resolution 687 concerning the cease-fire.... [T]his action ... conformed to the Charter of the United Nations.' "

... In sum, well-established principles of UN Security Council practice, treaty law, and armistice law allowed the United States to suspend the cease-fire in response to Iraq's material breaches of Resolution 687. The United States then could rely on Resolution 678 to use "all necessary means" to bring Iraq into compliance. Nothing in Resolution 1441 suggested that the Security Council needed to adopt any additional resolution to establish the existence of further material breaches to provide the basis for the use of force under Resolution 678. Indeed, Resolution 1441 left intact Resolution 678's reference to the use of force. Resolution 1441 neither revoked Resolution 678's language concerning the use of "all necessary means" against Iraq, nor terminated its effect in any way.

III. Use of Force Against Iraq in Anticipatory Self–Defense

Independent of the support provided by UN Security Council resolutions, authority for the armed intervention in Iraq stemmed from the national right of self-defense. Article 51 of the UN Charter recognizes and affirms, but does not limit, that "inherent" right under international law:

> Nothing in the present Charter shall impair the inherent right of individual or collective self-defense if an armed attack occurs against a Member of the United Nations, until the Security Council has taken measures necessary to maintain international peace and security.

Despite the long-standing recognition of a nation's right to self-defense, some argue that Article 51 has limited the right to permit only a response to an actual "armed attack." Some even argue that an armed attack must occur across national borders to trigger Article 51. Under this interpretation, the UN Charter superseded the existing right under customary international law to take reasonable anticipatory action in self-defense. There is no indication that the drafters of the UN Charter intended to limit the customary law in this way, nor that the United States so understood the Charter when it ratified. Instead, Article 51 merely partially expressed a right that exists independent of the UN Charter.

The customary international law right to use force in anticipatory self-defense is a well-established aspect of the "inherent right" of self-defense. Leading up to the Cuban missile crisis, the Office of Legal Counsel of the Department of Justice explained in an internal memorandum:

> The concept of self-defense in international law of course justifies more than activity designed merely to resist an armed attack which is already in progress. Under international law every state has, in the words of [then-Secretary of State] Elihu Root, the right ... to protect itself by preventing a condition of affairs in which it will be too late to protect itself.

The classic formulation of the right of anticipatory self-defense arose from the Caroline incident. In 1837, the steamer Caroline had been supplying armed insurgents against British rule in Canada with reinforcements of men and materials from the United States. In response, a British force from Canada entered U.S. territory at night, seized the Caroline, set the ship on fire, and launched it down Niagara Falls, killing two U.S. citizens in the process. The British claimed that they were acting in self-defense, and Secretary of State Daniel Webster called upon the British to show that the necessity of self-defence [was] instant, overwhelming, leaving no choice of means, and no moment for deliberation ... [and that the British force], even supposing the necessity of the moment authorized them to enter the territories of the United States at all, did nothing unreasonable or excessive; since the act, justified by the necessity of self-defence, must be limited by that necessity, and kept clearly within it.

The next year, Lord Ashburton, who had been sent by the British as a special minister to resolve the Caroline dispute and other related matters, implicitly accepted this test by justifying Britain's actions in these terms. Webster's formulation was reaffirmed a century later by the International Military Tribunal at Nuremberg, when it ruled that the German invasion of Norway in 1940 was not defensive because it was unnecessary to prevent an "imminent" Allied invasion.

The Caroline test has been distilled into two principal requirements. First, the use of force must be necessary because the threat is imminent and, thus, pursuing peaceful alternatives is not an option. Second, the response must be proportionate to the threat. International law does not supply a precise or detailed definition of what it means for a threat to be sufficiently "imminent" to justify the use of force in self-defense as necessary. Although the dictionary definition of "imminent" focuses on the temporal, under international law the concept of imminence must encompass an analysis that goes beyond the temporal proximity of a threat to include the probability that the threat will occur.

In addition to the probability of the threat, the threatened magnitude of harm must be relevant. The advent of nuclear and other sophisticated weapons has dramatically increased the degree of potential harm, and the importance of the temporal factor has diminished. Weapons of mass destruction threaten devastating and indiscriminate long-term damage to large segments of the civilian population and environment. In addition, the danger posed by WMD is exacerbated by the possibility that the means of delivery may be relatively unsophisticated—for example, a "dirty bomb" driven into a building by a suicide bomber, or the spread of a biological agent with an ordinary crop duster. At the same time, the development of advanced missile technology has vastly improved the capability for stealth, rendering threats more imminent because there is less time to prevent their launch.

State practice since the development of nuclear weapons and sophisticated delivery systems demonstrates the evolution of the concept of imminence. During the Cuban missile crisis, for example, the United States labeled the secret establishment of long-range nuclear missile bases in Cuba by the Soviet Union as an "immediate" threat to U.S. security and imposed a quarantine on offensive military equipment to Cuba in self-defense. Although the sudden and secret preparation of the missile bases undoubtedly "add[ed] to an already clear and present danger," their positioning in Cuba constituted a less immediate temporal threat of armed attack on the United States than that contemplated by previous applications of the Caroline test. There was no indication that the Soviet Union would use them either immediately, or even in the near term.

In the past two decades, the United States has used military force in anticipatory self-defense against Libya, Panama, Iraq, Afghanistan, and the Sudan.... Self-defense has served specifically as a justification for strikes against Iraq in the decade preceding the March 2003 conflict. In June 1993, for example, the United States justified its strike on Iraqi intelligence headquarters as self-defense because of "compelling evidence" that Iraq had attempted to assassinate President George H. W. Bush. As President Clinton explained:

> The evidence of the Government of Iraq's violence and terrorism demonstrates that Iraq poses a continuing threat to United States nationals and shows utter disregard for the will of the international community as expressed in Security Council Resolutions and the United Nations Charter. Based on the Government of Iraq's pattern of disregard for international law, I concluded that there was no

reasonable prospect that new diplomatic initiatives or economic measures could influence the current Government of Iraq to cease planning future attacks against the United States.

The objective of the strikes was to diminish Iraq's capability to support violence against the United States and others, and "to deter Saddam Hussein from supporting such outlaw behavior in the future." The Security Council rejected the plea of the Iraqi ambassador to condemn the U.S. action as an act of aggression. . . .

The use of force in anticipatory self-defense must be necessary and proportional to the threat. At least in the realm of WMD, rogue nations, and international terrorism, however, the test for determining whether a threat is sufficiently "imminent" to render the use of force necessary at a particular point has become more nuanced than Secretary Webster's nineteenth-century formulation. Factors to be considered should now include the probability of an attack; the likelihood that this probability will increase, and therefore the need to take advantage of a limited window of opportunity; whether diplomatic alternatives are practical; and the magnitude of the harm that could result from the threat. If a state instead were obligated to wait until the threat were truly imminent in the temporal sense envisioned by Secretary Webster, there is a substantial danger of missing a limited window of opportunity to prevent widespread harm to civilians. Finally, in an age of technologically advanced delivery systems and WMD, international law cannot require that we ignore the potential harm represented by the threat.

Applying the reformulated test for using force in anticipatory self-defense to the potential use of force against Iraq reveals that the threat of a WMD attack by Iraq, either directly or through Iraq's support for terrorism, was sufficiently "imminent" to render the use of force necessary to protect the United States, its citizens, and its allies. The force used was proportionate to the threat posed by Iraq; in other words, it was limited to that which is needed to eliminate the threat, including the destruction of Iraq's WMD capability and removing the source of Iraq's hostile intentions and actions, Saddam Hussein . . . . .

What Happens Now? The United Nations After Iraq*

THOMAS M. FRANCK

I. Who Killed Article 2(4) Again?

Thirty-three years ago I published an article in this Journal entitled Who Killed Article 2(4)? or: Changing Norms Governing the Use of Force by States, which examined the phenomenon of increasingly frequent resort to unlawful force by Britain, France, India, North Korea, the

* Reprinted with permission from Thomas M. Franck, *What Happens Now? The United Nations After Iraq*, 97 AMERICAN JOURNAL OF INTERNATIONAL LAW 607 (2003). © The American Society of International Law.

Soviet Union, and the United States. The essay concluded with this sad observation:

> The failure of the U.N. Charter's normative system is tantamount to the inability of any rule, such as that set out in Article 2(4), in itself to have much control over the behavior of states. National self-interest, particularly the national self-interest of the super-Powers, has usually won out over treaty obligations. This is particularly characteristic of this age of pragmatic power politics. It is as if international law, always something of a cultural myth, has been demythologized. It seems this is not an age when men act by principles simply because that is what gentlemen ought to do. But living by power alone . . . is a nerve-wracking and costly business.

The recent recourse to force in Iraq recalls this observation, which again seems all too apt. All that has changed is that we now have on offer proposed models for interstatal relations that seem even worse than the dilapidated system to which, by 1970, state misbehavior had reduced the postwar world. That once shiny new postwar system, embodied in the United Nations Charter, had been based on the assumption of states' reciprocal respect for law as their sturdy shield against the prospect of mutual assured destruction in an uncharted nuclear era. The 1970 essay regretted the loss of that vision in a miasma of so-called realpolitik.

Should international lawyers guard their faith in such circumstances? Or should we cut our coats according to the cloth? Si non possis quod velis, velis id quod possis. Perhaps. But, then, for one dazzling moment in the 1990s, the end of the Cold War seemed to revive faith in the Charter system, almost giving it a rebirth. Now, however, in the new millennium, after a decade's romance with something approximating law-abiding state behavior, the law-based system is once again being dismantled. In its place we are offered a model that makes global security wholly dependent on the supreme power and discretion of the United States and frees the sole superpower from all restraints of international law and the encumbrances of institutionalized multilateral diplomacy.

There is one major difference, however, between then and now. The unlawful recourses to force, during the period surveyed in the 1970 essay, were accompanied by a fig leaf of legal justification, which, at least tacitly, recognized the residual force of the requirement in Charter Article 2(4) that states "refrain in their international relations from the threat or use of force against the territorial integrity or political independence of any state." Then, the aggressors habitually defended the legality of their recourse to force by asserting that their actions, taken in response to an alleged prior attack or provocation, were exercises of the right of self-defense under the terms of Charter Article 51. Now, however, in marked contrast, they have all but discarded the fig leaf. While a few government lawyers still go through the motions of asserting that the invasion of Iraq was justified by our inherent right of self-defense, or represented a collective measure authorized by the Security Council under Chapter VII of the Charter, the leaders of America no longer much bother with such legal niceties. Instead, they boldly proclaim a new policy that openly repudiates the Article 2(4) obligation. What is remarkable, this time around, is that once-obligatory efforts by the aggressor to make a serious effort to stretch law to legitimate state action have given way to a drive to repeal law altogether, replacing it with a principle derived from the Athenians at Melos: "the strong do what they can and the weak suffer what they must."

In this essay I will attempt to examine whether this neo-Melian doctrine will make any difference to the way the international system works, or whether our government, by dispensing with the lawyers' shopworn casuistry, is just being realistic in exposing the yawning gap between what states always do in their ambitious pursuit of power and what they are permitted to do by the fragile normative structure. . . .

III. The Optimistic 1990s

After the Soviet side of bipolarity crumbled, the logic of the 1970s' normative balance-of-power system ceased to be convincing. Then, in the wake of our unchallenged primacy, a reasonable expectation arose that, with America's new-found muscle, a different, more enduring, and more noble stability would be achieved in international relations and, moreover, that this could be brought about by rediscovering the Charter's founding principle: that force would be used only in self-defense against an actual armed attack; or after a threat to the peace had been determined by the collective decision-making process of the Security Council acting under Chapter VII of the Charter; or, exceptionally, if the General Assembly, proceeding in accordance with the "Uniting for Peace" resolution, had determined the existence of a "threat to the peace, breach of the peace or act of aggression."

For about a decade, the international system seemed to be moving in this direction, with Article 2(4) miraculously reborn in a post-Cold War order underwritten by a return to the law of the long-languishing Charter. This expectation was reinforced, and was facilitated by, UN-organized or- authorized military deployments in the first Gulf war, the former Yugoslavia, Somalia, and Haiti. In 1989 the United States briefly reverted to the Cold War model by invading Panama and doing so under cover of a claim to be acting in self-defense. By and large, however, the decade after the Soviet collapse seemed to presage a resurrection of Article 2(4), albeit with some flexible adaptation in practice to reflect changes of circumstance.

This ebullient period reached its high-water mark on September 12, 2001, when the Security Council unanimously passed the resolution in reaction to the attacks on the World Trade Center and the Pentagon. This resolution demonstrated not only the goodwill and collective wisdom of the Council as global decision-making forum, but also the flexibility of the Charter system in adapting old text to new exigencies. It construed the Charter-based right of self-defense to include authority to use force against nonstatal terrorist organizations, as well as "those responsible for aiding, supporting or harbouring the perpetrators, organizers and sponsors of ... acts" of terrorism. Two weeks later, the Council created mandatory global controls to prevent the financing of terrorism and the recruiting of terrorists, while adding procedures for monitoring and enforcing state compliance. It appeared that the long dormant Charter rules regarding recourse to force not only were starting to revive—that I had reported their death prematurely—but were exhibiting an altogether-unexpected capacity to grow and adapt. In a rapidly changing world, the Security Council was proving itself able to interpret and apply the rules in such a way as to make them responsive to new dangers posed by nongovernmental terrorism and terrorism-harboring states, treating these as bona fide threats to the peace against which resort to force in collective self-defense is not merely necessary but also permissible.

IV. The Relapse of 2003

The invasion of Iraq in March of 2003, and a penumbra of policy statements made concurrently by the United States, have succeeded in changing all that. Article 2(4) has died again, and, this time, perhaps for good.... Article 2(4) taken another hit; this time, however, as part of a much broader plan to disable all supranational institutions and the constraints of international law on national sovereignty. If, as now seems all too possible, this campaign succeeds within the life span of the present U.S. administration, what sort of world order will emerge from the ruins of the Charter system?

V. Did the Iraq Invasion Violate the Charter?

Any prognosis regarding the future of world order must begin by addressing the question whether recent events have indeed had a transformative effect on the law of the international system and, if so, what that transformation portends. As in 1970, one must begin by making a clear-eyed appraisal of what has been happening. If the invasion of Iraq was nothing but an act of self-defense by the United States and its allies, or merely an exercise of police power previously authorized by the Security Council, these events would serve only to verify the continued efficacy of the Charter system. There would have been no violation of the cardinal principle of Article 2(4), as that no-first-use pledge is always subordinate to both the right of self-defense recognized by Article 51 and the right of the Security Council, under Chapter VII, to authorize action against a threat to the peace. If, however, the invasion cannot thus be reconciled with the rules of the Charter, does the invasion of Iraq constitute a simple violation of the rules—one of many and thus of no more legal significance than a holdup of the neighborhood grocery—or should it be celebrated as a deliberate and salutary move toward UN reform? Or should these recent events be understood, more apocalyptically, as the final burial of the Charter's fundamental rules? At this point in our analysis of the systemic significance of these events, it becomes essential to focus not only on facts but also on motives for action. Needless to say, this is swampy terrain; but one must try.

The invasion of Iraq can be positioned in each of these explanatory contexts, but just barely. It can be argued that the invasion was lawful (and thus neither violative nor transformative of the Charter). It can also be argued that, while the attack on Iraq may have been technically illegal, its transformative effect on the law has been wholly benevolent. Finally, it can be argued that these events have repealed a legal regime far beyond its prime and, at last, have ushered in a new doctrine of preventive use of force that is far more responsive to the real dangers of our times.

The argument that recent events have not challenged, or have violated only de minimis, the Charter law pertaining to recourse to force is very difficult to sustain, although it enjoys the enthusiastic support of some American academics and the rather less enthusiastic support of State Department lawyers. Abroad, it has been advanced only by the British attorney general, supported by a prominent academic lawyer. As enunciated by Legal Adviser William Howard Taft IV of the Department of State, the argument has two prongs. The first is that the president may, "of course, always use force under international law in self-defense." The problem with that rationale is that, even if it were agreed that the right of self-defense "against an armed attack" (Charter, Art. 51) had come, through practice, to include a right of action against an imminent (as opposed to an actual) armed attack, the facts of the situation that existed in March 2003 are hard to fit within any plausible theory of imminence. This was a time, after all, when UN and International Atomic Energy Agency inspectors were actively engaged in situ in an apparently unrestricted search for weapons of mass destruction (WMDs) undertaken with full authorization by the Security Council. Whatever the inspectors did or did not learn about Iraqi WMDs, nothing in their reports lends any credibility to the claim of an imminent threat of armed aggression against anyone. Indeed, the memorandum of the attorney general of the United Kingdom, while supporting the right to use force, wisely omits all reference to this rationale for its exercise.

The second prong of the de minimis argument is more sophisticated than the plea to have acted in self-defense. It avers that the attack led by Britain and the United States had already been sanctioned by the Security Council. Essential to the success of this assertion is a creative, and ultimately unsustainable, reading of three Security Council resolutions—678, 687, and 1441—and of their "legislative history." According to Legal Adviser Taft, Resolution 678 was the authorization to use force for the Gulf War in January 1991. In April of that year, the Council imposed a series of conditions on Iraq, including most importantly extensive disarmament obligations, as a condition of the ceasefire declared under UNSCR 687. Iraq has "materially breached" these disarma-

> ment obligations, and force may again be used under UNSCR 678 to compel Iraqi compliance.
>
> ... Just last November, in resolution 1441, the Council unanimously decided that Iraq has been and remains in material breach of its obligation. 1441 then gave Iraq a "final opportunity" to comply, but stated specifically that violations of the obligations, including the obligation to cooperate fully, under 1441 would constitute a further material
> 612 breach. Iraq has clearly committed such violations and, accordingly, the authority to use force to address Iraq's material breaches is clear.

The British government developed this same thesis, claiming that, by Resolution 678 the Security Council had authorized "Member States to use all necessary means to restore international peace and security in the area" and that, while that authorization "was suspended but not terminated by Security Council resolution (SCR) 687 (1991)," it was "revived by SCR 1441 (2002)."

This version of the meaning and intent of these three resolutions is highly problematic, and appears to have caused the resignation, on a matter of principle, of the deputy legal adviser of the British Foreign Office. Resolution 678 culminated a series of resolutions by the Security Council that condemned Iraq's invasion of Kuwait, called for the immediate withdrawal of the aggressor, imposed mandatory sanctions on Iraq until Kuwaiti sovereignty was restored, and declared the Iraqi annexation of Kuwait to be null and void. In each instance, the purpose of the resolution was solely to liberate Kuwait. Only when these measures failed to secure Iraqi withdrawal did the Council in Resolution 678, citing Chapter VII of the Charter, "authorize[ ] Member States cooperating with the Government of Kuwait ... to use all necessary means to uphold and implement resolution 660 (1990) and all subsequent relevant resolutions and to restore international peace and security in the area."

This sequence readily demonstrates that the restoration of Kuwaiti sovereignty was the leitmotif of Council action. That the authorization of collective measures by Resolution 678 additionally refers to the restoration of "international peace and security in the area" does not connote some expansive further mandate for contingent action against Iraq at the discretion of any individual member of the coalition of the willing. President George Bush Sr. acknowledged as much in explaining why the American military had not pursued Saddam Hussein's defeated forces to Baghdad. They were not authorized to do so.

The resolution, however, certainly does signal that Iraq was to be subject to further post-conflict intrusive controls: those imposed by the Council in Resolution 687, as part of the cease-fire. These additional obligations are made binding by reference to Chapter VII of the Charter and they were designed, implemented, and meant to be monitored by the Security Council as a whole, not by any individual member acting at its own pleasure. Resolution 687, sometimes referred to as the "mother of all cease-fires," is not only a binding decision of the Security Council, but also an international agreement between the United Nations and Iraq, made effective only "upon official notification by Iraq to the Secretary–General and to the Security Council of its acceptance" of the provisions set out therein. In legal form, then, as also in substance, this proviso manifests that it is the Security Council and the United Nations, and not individual members, who are the parties, with Iraq, to the cease-fire agreement. It is they who are entitled in law to determine whether Iraq is complying with its commitments to the Council, how long these are to remain in effect, and what is to be done in the event of their violation.

The obligations imposed by Resolution 687 are certainly onerous, and encompass everything that Iraq, thereafter, has been accused of failing to do. Baghdad had to agree to the verified destruction of its weapons of mass destruction and any industrial capacity to produce them, as well as of its medium and long-range delivery systems. Monitoring of compliance, both by a special commission to be created by the Secretary–General and by inspectors of the International Atomic Energy Agency, became mandatory. Baghdad was also required "to inform the Security Council that it will not commit or support any act of international terrorism or allow any organization directed towards commission of such acts to operate within its territory." What if Iraq failed to carry out these commitments to the Council and the United Nations? Clearly, this determination was to be made by the collective security process of the Organization. To ensure such follow-up, the Council, in Resolution 687, was "to remain seized of the matter and to take such further steps as may be required for the implementation of the present resolution and to secure peace and security in the area." It would take further steps, not individual member states acting without further authorization.

Neither the text nor the debates on the adoption of Resolution 687 reveal the slightest indication that the Council intended to empower any of its members, by themselves, to determine that Iraq was in material breach. Much less can the resolution be read to authorize any state to decide unilaterally to resume military action against Iraq, save in the event of an armed attack. That deduction is supported by the architecture of the Charter. For the Council to have made a prospective grant of unilateral discretion to states to deploy armed force, in the absence of an actual (or imminent) armed attack, would have been an unprecedented derogation from the strictures of Article 2(4). At the least, to be plausible, such a derogation would have had to be explicit. Moreover, such a delegation of unlimited discretion to individual states cannot be assumed because it could not have been implemented alongside the Council's institution of an extensive system of inspections under its authority and control.

The UK attorney general cannot overcome these objections by an unsupported averral that a "material breach of resolution 687 revives the authority to use force under resolution 678." As we have noted, the authority to use force under Resolution 678 extended exclusively to the liberation of Kuwait and to restoring peace and security in the region. In

March 2003, the peace and security of the region did not require recourse to force, and the Council plainly did not think otherwise. What the Council thought is crucial. Resolution 687 would not have explicitly reserved sole discretion to the Council "to take such further steps as may be required for [its] implementation" if the Council had simultaneously intended to delegate that function to the sole discretion of member states.

Thus, neither Resolution 678 nor Resolution 687 helps Washington or London make a convincing case that they acted with, rather than against, the law. Nor are their difficulties in any way alleviated by Resolution 1441. While that instrument does deplore "that the Government of Iraq has failed to comply with its commitments pursuant to resolution 687," it addresses that failure exclusively by deciding "to set up an enhanced inspection regime." Anticipating further Iraqi noncompliance, the resolution makes provision for the Council to be convened immediately "in order to consider the situation and the need for full compliance ... in order to secure international peace and security," and it warns Iraq "in that context ... that it will face serious consequences as a result of its continued violations of its obligations." It once again decides that the Council will "remain seized of the matter." The British attorney general somehow concluded from these words that even though the Council is to convene to "consider the matter before any action is taken," no matter what the Council does or does not do, "further [military] action can be taken [by a member] without a new resolution of the Council." From this he deduces that "all that resolution 1441 requires is reporting to and discussion by the Security Council of Iraq's failures, but not an express further decision to authorise force." This conclusion is at best a creative interpretation. In fact, what Resolution 1441 did was to purchase unanimity for the return of the inspectors by postponing to another day, which the sponsors hoped might never be reached, the argument as to whether Resolutions 678 and 687 had authorized further enforcement at the sole discretion of one or more of the Council's members.

Perhaps to its credit, the Taft statement does not tread this tortuous path. Instead, it argues that since the Council had recognized several times that Iraq had committed a "material breach" of Resolution 687, recourse to force rested within the sole discretion of each Council member in accordance with the provision of the law of treaties on the consequences of such a "material" violation of obligations. This tack moves the argument away from a parsing of Council resolutions to the Vienna Convention on the Law of Treaties. But it is the United Nations, not the United States, that is the offended "party" to Resolution 687, and thus it is the Council, not the United States, that has the option under the Convention to regard the resolution as voided by Iraq's material breaches. Additionally, even if the United States were regarded as a "party" to the commitments made by Iraq in agreeing to Resolution 687, a material breach would not release Washington, as the offended party, from the obligation under the Vienna Convention "to fulfil any obligation embodied in the treaty to which it would be subject under international law independently of the [materially breached] treaty." That provision, it would appear, places the United States squarely back under the obligation of Charter Article 2(4), which, in the absence of any provision in Resolution 687 to the contrary, must be regarded as an essential part of its legal context and which requires states to abstain from the use of force in the absence either of an armed attack or of prior authorization by the Security Council.

These British and U.S. justifications do not fare well under close examination, however benevolent their intent to demonstrate compliance with the Charter. Consequently, the effect of those nations' unauthorized recourse to force against Iraq must be seen as either revising or undermining the provisions limiting the discretion of states to resort to force.

VI. A Charter Revisited

Well, if the Iraq invasion did not exactly conform with the law of the Charter, should it not, at least, be celebrated as a violation that has the capacity to reform the law and make it more realistic?

In international law, violators do sometimes turn out to be lawgivers. I have argued elsewhere that the Charter, as a quasi-constitutional instrument, is capable of evolving through the interpretive practice of its principal organs. That interpretive practice may sometimes be led by states with an interest in outcomes that cannot be legitimated by a narrowly originalist reading of the text. In such circumstances, violation shades into revision, sometimes to the benefit of the law and the institution charged with its implementation. The phenomenon is not unknown, also, to domestic law, though it occurs much more frequently in the international arena. The International Court has confirmed, for example, that the abstention of a permanent member of the Security Council in a vote on a substantive resolution is no longer to be taken to constitute a veto as a result of "abundant evidence" of members' practice to that effect. The Court reached this conclusion despite the text of Charter Article 27(3), which requires that substantive resolutions receive "the concurring votes of the permanent members." In a similar example of the interpretive power of institutional practice, extensive UN peacekeeping operations have long been based on an evolutionary reading of the Charter's imagined "Chapter 6 1/2." Nothing in the text actually authorizes these by-and-large salubrious activities. In recent years, too, practice has seemed to legitimate such humanitarian interventions as those undertaken by regional organizations in West Africa and Kosovo, even though they had not received the requisite (Art. 53) prior authorization of the Security Council. Further evidence of this important interpretive change is afforded by the Constitutive Act of the African Union, Article 4(h) of which recognizes "the right of the Union to intervene in a Member State pursuant to a decision of the Assembly in respect of grave circumstances, namely: war crimes, genocide and crimes against humanity," when such intervention is authorized by two-thirds of the members.

Even allowing that the Charter text is subject to reinterpretation in practice, it is difficult to chart the direction in which it could be said to be evolving under the impetus of the Middle Eastern events of March and April, 2003....

In essence, the Iraqi crisis was not primarily about what to do but, rather, who decides. There is an answer to that problem, of course, one clearly set out in Article 27 of the Charter. Through the veto, the United States, with the other four permanent members, has the right to block collective action and it takes frequent advantage of this prerogative. On the other hand, the Charter does not give the United States, or any other state, sole power to initiate action, except in response to an armed attack. While this deal may have seemed acceptable to America in 1945, it is apparently no longer satisfactory to the protectors of American preeminence. Nowadays, the U.S. government does not wish to be limited in this way. Thus, the invasion of Iraq is more accurately seen as a repudiation of the central decision-making premise of the Charter system than as a genuine opening to reform, unless by reform is meant the reconstitution of the international system along the lines of an American global protectorate.

This is a sad conclusion to offer well-meaning champions of the Charter system. Unfortunately, however, this is not a time for optimistic speculation about how to make the United Nations more responsive to new challenges. Rather, reformers need first to understand that the system stands in mortal jeopardy of being destroyed altogether. If, and only if, something can be done about that will there be another time to talk about improving the rules.... "While the United States will constantly strive to enlist the support of the international community," Mr. Bush said, "we will not hesitate to act alone, if necessary, to exercise our right of self-defense by acting preemptively against such terrorists, to prevent them from doing harm against our people and our country...."

In this key sentence, he conflates an expanded, if perhaps necessary, concept of anticipatory self-defense with a militant and highly transformative assertion of a right by the United States to determine for itself whether, and when, the conditions exist to justify recourse to this expanded right. The sum of the two assertions is far greater than the parts, for, together, they set out the doctrine that the nation is free to use force against any foe it perceives as a potential threat to its security, at any time of its choosing and with any means at its disposal. This would stand the Charter on its head.

The point is a subtle, but important one. To the extent a state acts in "self-defence if an armed attack occurs," Article 51 of the Charter does, indeed, entitle it to decide, unilaterally, when and how to deploy military force. In that sense, Article 51 is unique in the Charter scheme, for it permits each state to decide for itself whether to use force, limited only by the conditionality "if an armed attack occurs." That terminology was intended to preclude the kind of bogus claim to be acting in self-defense that Germany used to justify its invasion of Poland in 1939. No such qualification applies to collective measures taken by the Security Council under Chapter VII of the Charter. Notably, these provisions permit the use of force against many kinds of "threats to the peace" that do not take the form of an actual armed attack. Such action, however, must first be authorized by the Council, as it was in response to such threats to the peace as the military coup in Haiti, the disintegration of civil governance in Somalia, and the humanitarian crises in the former Yugoslavia, Albania, and Rwanda. In each instance, the decision to authorize resort to force was made collectively.

In the case of Iraq, the Council, instead of approving the use of military force, unanimously, in Resolution 1441, authorized an extensive system of international inspections. Three months on, most states seemed to think this inspection regime was working well enough to obviate, at least for the time being, any further preemptive action. The presidential policy set out in the NSS [National Security System] seeks to ensure that this sort of thing does not happen. It aims at ending all collective control over the U.S. recourse to force. This is not system transformation but system abrogation. Instead of the law of the Charter, we find an unabashed return to the Melian principle.

IX. What Can Be Done?

It is not within the purchase of the lawyer to make, or to change, national policy. That, in a democracy, falls within the purview of the voters and their representatives. If the voters want the United States to play the imperial superpower, it is for the historians to warn of the discouraging precedents and for the economists to count the costs. It is for the press to portray fairly and fearlessly how that policy affects the people and societies at which it is directed.

What, then, is the proper role for the lawyer? Surely, it is to stand tall for the rule of law. What this entails is self-evident. When the policymakers believe it to society's immediate benefit to skirt the law, the lawyer must speak of the longer-term costs. When the politicians seek to bend the law, the lawyers must insist that they have broken it. When a faction tries to use power to subvert the rule of law, the lawyer must defend it even at some risk to personal advancement and safety. When the powerful are tempted to discard the law, the lawyer must ask whether someday, if our omnipotence wanes, we may not need the law. Lawyers who do that may even be called traitors. But those who do not are traitors to their calling. Ordinarily, however, the role of the lawyer is more positive: to help design the framework of rules, procedures, and institutions within which persons and peoples can live productively at peace with one another.

This may not be a moment in which that positive role can come to the fore, not a time when lawyers, particularly international lawyers, can flourish. In a sense, the "realists" are right. In the circumstances of the present power disequilibrium, it may be inevitable that those who have the power will sometimes seek to take advantage of it without much regard for such ephemera as respect for neutral and reciprocal principles. It is understandable that some politicians should behave in this way, but lawyers must not. Rather, they should zealously guard their professional integrity for a time when it can again be used in the service of the common weal.

On American Exceptionalism*

HAROLD HONGJU KOH

In January 1991, through an impressive diplomatic effort that led then-Secretary of State James Baker to more than forty nations, the United States obtained a U.N. Security Council resolution authorizing member nations to "use all necessary means" after January 15, 1991 to drive Iraq from Kuwait. Soon thereafter, the first President Bush announced his commitment to "a new world order—where diverse nations are drawn together in common cause, to achieve the universal aspirations of mankind: peace and security, freedom and the rule of law."

This time, the Bush Administration first secured sweeping congressional authorization to use force, then bluffed down the unilateralist path. Pressed principally by Secretary of State Colin Powell and British Prime Minister Tony Blair, however, the United States eventually brought the use of force issue back into the U.N. Security Council framework. With United Nations Security Council Resolution 1441, the United States achieved a significant and unanimous diplomatic success. Resolution 1441: (1) decided that "Iraq has been and remains in material breach of its obligations" through its failure to cooperate with inspectors and its failure to disarm; (2) afforded Iraq "a final opportunity to comply with its disarmament obligations under relevant resolutions" by setting up an enhanced inspection regime and ordering Iraq to submit an accurate and complete declaration of its chemical, biological, and nuclear weapons programs; and (3) "warned Iraq that it will face serious consequences as a result of its continued violations of its obligations." Seven days after, Iraq reluctantly confirmed its intent to comply with the resolution.

Thereafter ensued a four-month public "trial" of disarmament facts à la the Cuban Missile Crisis. During these months, U.N. inspectors combed through Iraq, even while Iraq was supposedly developing a "currently accurate, full and complete declaration of all aspects of its programmes" to develop chemical, biological, and nuclear weapons and long-range missile programs. Throughout this period, the administration waffled on three points: whether it would seek a second Security Council resolution before using military force; whether its real goal in Iraq was

* Reprinted with permission from Harold Hongju Koh, *On American Exceptionalism*, 55 Stanford Law Review 1479, 1516–24 (2003).

disarmament, regime change, or democracy-promotion; and whether its ultimate rationale for use of force would be breach of past Security Council resolutions, the continuing threat posed by Saddam Hussein to peace and security, preemptive self-defense, or human rights.

At the same time, however, the transnational legal process framework clearly pushed the [Bush] administration further than it preferred down a U.N. path. First, the President's advisers said they didn't need any new Security Council resolution, but then they got resolution 1441. Then they said they didn't need any inspections, but for four months they pursued inspections. Then they said they didn't need a second resolution, but in March 2003, at Tony Blair's urging, they pursued a second one.

By March 2003, however, the administration was feeling the pinch of its own military timetable, which called for any invasion to begin before late spring. After initial wrangling over the second resolution, President Bush and French President Chirac issued incompatible pronouncements. Chirac announced that the French would veto any resolution calling for force; Bush retorted that the United States would go to war, along with the United Kingdom, whether it secured a second resolution or not. The two announcements unnecessarily created a zero-sum situation in which the only second resolution the United States deemed relevant (one supporting rapid attack) was one that the French were precommitted to veto. By framing the issue this way, the United States also virtually guaranteed its own inability to secure the nine votes necessary to pass a second resolution in the absence of a veto. For even close U.S. allies, such as Mexico and Chile, were not willing to subject their citizens to a controversial vote for war, when both the United States and the French had made it clear that that vote would not matter.

Diplomatic historians will long revisit the missed steps that led to the messy start of the second Gulf War. My view is that a transnational legal process solution—the exercise of multilateral coercive power, led by the United States through the U.N. mechanism—was available, but tragically bungled. Saddam's venality, Chirac's obstinacy, and the United Nations's fecklessness all deserve a good share of the blame. Perversely, Chirac's overbroad veto threat virtually ensured the future weakening of the Security Council, the only U.N. organ in which his country holds disproportionate power.

... [Much] of the blame must also go to the Bush Administration's decision to frame the issue in bipolar terms—either attack, or accept a status quo in which Saddam builds unconventional weapons and brutalizes his own citizens without sanction. By flattening the issue in this way, the Bush Administration discouraged examination of a meaningful third way: to *disarm Iraq without attack* through a multilateral strategy of disarmament plus enhanced containment plus more aggressive human rights intervention. That strategy would have supported continuation of the initial Bush approach of diplomacy backed by threat of force: restoring effective U.N. weapons inspections, disarming and destroying

Iraqi weapons of mass destruction, and cutting off the flow of weapons and weapons-related goods into Iraq. At the same time, however, this strategy would have also pressed more aggressively for the insertion of human rights monitors, supporting the forces of peaceful democratic opposition in Iraq, as well as developing the "Milosevic-type" possibility of diplomatically driving Saddam and his top lieutenants into exile and bringing them to justice before an appropriate international tribunal. That strategy would have pursued disarmament and regime change not simply through coercion, but rather, through a transnational legal process solution, whereby the United States would have used the threat of U.N.-authorized force to demand that Saddam and his sons leave Iraq to face prosecution before either the International Criminal Court or an ad hoc tribunal.[1] Although the Bush Administration ultimately offered this option on the eve of war, it was not a credible one, because the United States had rejected the International Criminal Court and had not invested enough in an alternative legal process solution to make coerced departure plus prosecution a realistic means of regime change.

Such a strategy would have had obvious advantages: It would have avoided a bloody war, the financial and symbolic costs of that war, and the thousands of combatant and civilian deaths that war has entailed. More fundamentally, it would have secured Iraq's compliance with international law at no cost to the United States's own appearance of compliance. It would have strengthened the United States's capacity to return to the U.N. Security Council for the lifting of Iraqi sanctions, to secure the support of the United Nations in identifying and destroying any unconventional weapons still in Iraq, to secure a United Nations-supervised civilian reconstruction mission in Iraq, and to create an ad hoc criminal tribunal to prosecute apprehended Iraqi war criminals. But that strategy would have required genuine strategic multilateralism. It would have required the United States to work with other global democracies to fight global terrorism. Instead, the United States chose to ignore the very global partners who had helped it create the postwar system of international law and institutions precisely to provide nonmilitary multilateral options that did not exist during World War II.

Hot debate still rages over the legal justification of the Iraq war. At this writing, the U.S. government has yet to issue its own definitive legal justification for the war. Although some American officials have suggested preemptive self-defense as an additional legal basis for the war, the core U.S. claim rests not on that murky ground, but on the much narrower claim that Iraq was in material breach of U.N. Security Council Resolutions 678, 687, and 1441. Similarly, the contested British legal opinion justifying the war relies at bottom not on broad customary

1. Indeed, a Milosevic-type solution was available even at the end of the first Gulf War, when the United States could have concluded that Saddam Hussein's continuation in power was a continuing threat to peace and security in the region. Had it done so, the first Bush Administration could have refused to endorse U.N. Security Council Resolution 687 of April 3, 1991, which declared a formal cease-fire in effect, until Saddam and his sons had actually left Iraq. With hundreds of thousands of U.S. troops still in Iraq, and Saddam's forces in shambles, it seems likely that Saddam would have eventually complied.

law arguments about preemptive self-defense or humanitarian intervention, but on two narrow resolution-based arguments. First, the opinion argues, the U.N. Security Council's explicit authorization of force in resolution 678, which was suspended by the cease-fire of April 1991 that ended the first Gulf War, "revived" upon Iraq's recent failures to meet its disarmament obligations. Second, the opinion suggests resolution 1441 was effectively self-executing, with individual U.N. members entitled to determine whether to use force against Iraq as part of the "serious consequences" Iraq should face for noncompliance.

In my view, the Iraq invasion was illegal under international law.[2] While justifying the war through narrow parsing of U.N. Security Council resolutions is far preferable to unmoored claims of "preemptive self-defense," the legal arguments based on "revived force" under resolution 678 and "serious consequences" under resolution 1441 still strike me as unpersuasive. The problem with both arguments is that they disdain the need for political legitimacy in a strained quest for legal authority. The "revived force" argument relies on twelve-year-old resolutions passed by earlier Security Councils at a time when the United States demonstrably cannot muster nine votes for war in the current Security Council. Invoking that argument to justify force tells current U.N. members that their current votes and opinions don't really matter. The only Security Council resolution explicitly authorizing the use of force against Iraq was resolution 678, passed in November 1990 shortly after the invasion of Kuwait. The only military action it explicitly authorized was such force as was necessary to restore Kuwait's sovereignty and to restore peace and security to the region (as was later done, for example, through the creation of northern and southern "no-fly zones"). Similarly, U.N. Security Council Resolution 687, which declared the 1991 ceasefire to the Gulf War, required Iraq to destroy its weapons of mass destruction. But at this writing, the United States still has not demonstrated that such destruction was not finally occurring under the U.N. inspections regime in operation at the time when the United States launched its invasion.

Similarly, resolution 1441 gave Iraq "a final opportunity to comply with its disarmament obligations" and warned Iraq of "serious consequences" if it did not comply. But by choosing the words "serious consequences," not authorizing the member states to use "all necessary means"—the term of art used to authorize the use of force under Security Council resolutions authorizing intervention in Rwanda, Bosnia, Somalia, Haiti, and Iraq itself—resolution 1441 deliberately *avoided* authorizing force, apparently hoping that, when the time came, there

2. To the extent that the military action exceeded the authorization provided by the U.N. Charter and existing Security Council resolutions, it also ran afoul of Article II of the Constitution's directive that the President "take Care that the Laws be faithfully executed" and enforce the United Nations Charter, a treaty duly approved by the Senate, as the "supreme Law of the Land." U.S. Const. art. II, § 3; *id.* art. IV. As a matter of domestic law, however, the President's decision is almost certainly immunized from legal challenge by the sweeping terms of the congressional resolution [passed in November 2001 to authorize use of military force].

would be a clearer political consensus to do so. It seems highly unlikely that the Security Council members who voted unanimously for resolution 1441, including permanent members France and Russia and such other members as Syria, intended by so voting to authorize a future use of force without further explicit U.N. action. It is thus disingenous to pretend that these past legal instruments somehow created a present political consensus within the United Nations that legally authorized the war, when recent events had made manifestly clear that in fact, there was none.

Notes and Comments

1. As noted above, John Yoo and Thomas Franck's articles were first printed in an Agora on the Iraq conflict, "Future Implications of the Iraq Conflict," published by the *American Journal of International Law* in July 2003. For more articles in the Agora, see Volume 97, Issue 3 of the *Journal*. Another piece in that Agora, by Richard Falk, adds yet another distinct perspective to the discussion of the conflict. In a section entitled, "A Constructivist Future for the UN Charter System," Falk writes:

> The position favored here is that the United States would be best served by adhering to the UN Charter system. This system is flexible enough to accommodate new and genuine security imperatives as well as changing values, including a shifting balance between sovereign rights and world community responsibilities. In both settings of humanitarian intervention and responses against mega-terrorism the Charter system can be legally vindicated in appropriate factual circumstances.
>
> From this perspective recourse to war against Iraq should not have been undertaken without a prior mandate from the Security Council, and rather than "a failure" of the United Nations, the withholding of such a mandate represented a responsible exercise of constitutional restraint. The facts did not support the case for preemption, as there was neither imminence nor necessity. As a result, the Iraq war seemed, at best, to qualify as an instance of preventive war, but there are strong legal, moral, and political reasons to deny both legality and legitimacy to such a use of force. Preventive war is not an acceptable exception to the Charter system, and no effort was made by the U.S. government to claim such a right, although the highly abstract and vague phrasing of the preemptive war doctrine in the National Security Strategy of the United States of America would be more accurately formulated as a "preventive war doctrine." But even within this highly dubious doctrinal setting, to be at all convincing the evidence would at least have to demonstrate a credible future Iraqi threat that could not be reliably deterred, and this was never done.
>
> My legal constructivist position is that the United States (and the world) would benefit from a self-imposed discipline of adherence to the UN Charter system governing the use of force. Such a voluntary

discipline would overcome the absence of geopolitical limits associated with countervailing power in a unipolar world. It would also work against tendencies of the United States and others to rely too much on military superiority, which encourages the formation of defensive alliances, and possibly arms races. International law is flexible enough to allow the United States, and other countries, to meet novel security needs. Beyond this, neither American values nor strategic goals should be construed to validate uses of force that cannot win support in the UN Security Council. If one considers the course of American foreign policy over the course of the last half century, adherence to the Charter system with respect to the use of force would have avoided the worst policy failures, including that of Vietnam. Deviations from the Charter system of prohibitions on the use of force can be credited with no clear successes.

It is not the Charter system that is in disarray, providing sensible grounds for declaring the project of regulating recourse to war by states a failed experiment that should now be abandoned. It is rather leading states, and above all the United States, that need to be persuaded that their interests are served and their values realized by a more diligent pursuit of a law-oriented foreign policy. The Charter system is not a legal prison that presents states with the dilemma of adherence (and defeat) and violation or disregard (and victory). Rather adherence is the best policy, if understood against a jurisprudential background that is neither slavishly legalistic nor cynically nihilistic. The law can be stretched as new necessities arise, but the stretching must to the extent possible be in accord with procedures and norms contained in the Charter system, with a factually and doctrinally persuasive explanation of why a particular instance of stretching is justified. Such positive constructivist attitudes will renew confidence in the Charter system. It is also true that constructivism can work negatively, and so if the disregard of the legal framework, public opposition, and governmental resistance present in the Iraq case is repeated in the future, then indeed the Charter system will be in a shambles before much longer.

Richard A. Falk, *What Future for the UN Charter System of War Prevention?*, 97 American Journal of International Law 590 (2003). Richard Falk labels his position a "legal constructivist" view, but he uses this term differently from the constructivist theorists of international relations discussed in Part III.A. Falk's work is instead often associated with the New Haven School described in Part III.C. How does Falk's position compare with the political science constructivist position? How does it compare with the other theories outlined earlier in this book?

2. Compare John Yoo's approach with Harold Hongju Koh's transnational legal process approach. On what points of legal interpretation do the two analyses differ? Do these differences appear to reflect different underlying theoretical perspectives regarding what does (and should) motivate states to act?

3. Can preemptive self-defense be subjected to meaningful limits? If so, does Yoo's approach succeed in imposing such limits? What would a realist say the limits can and should be on the use of preemptive self-defense? Do you agree?

4. Is Thomas Franck correct in saying that "Article 2(4) has died again, and, this time, perhaps for good?" If Article 2(4) has been so consistently under siege since the 1970s, does it have the kind of "compliance pull" that Franck finds necessary for it to achieve international legitimacy? Does Franck's interpretation of recent events call into question the view of international law he offers in his other writings or does it instead validate it (see Part III.B.)?

5. Think back to the discussion of humanitarian intervention (Part IV.D.). Do states make the decision to go to war differently when the aim is humanitarian than when the aim is (primarily) to eliminate a perceived security threat? Do norms play a greater role in one context than in the other? Are theories that are persuasive in one situation less so in the other? And, finally, does law play a greater role in shaping state decisions to use military force for humanitarian reasons than it does in shaping decisions to use force to address perceived threats to national security? Why or why not?

6. There is a rich body of scholarship on the question, not directly addressed here, of why states do or do not observe the law governing the conduct of war (*jus in bello*). See, e.g., Jeffrey W. Legro, *Which Norms Matter? Revisiting the "Failure" of Internationalism*, 51 INTERNATIONAL ORGANIZATION 31 (1997); Catharine A. MacKinnon, *Crimes of War, Crimes of Peace*, 4 UCLA WOMEN'S LAW JOURNAL 59 (1993); Jacques Meurant, *Inter Arma Caritas: Evolution and Nature of International Humanitarian Law*, 24 JOURNAL OF PEACE RESEARCH 237 (1987); Oliver Durr, *Humanitarian Law of Armed Conflict: Problems of Applicability*, 24 JOURNAL OF PEACE RESEARCH 263 (1987); MARTHA FINNEMORE, NORMS AND WAR: THE INTERNATIONAL RED CROSS AND THE GENEVA CONVENTIONS, IN NATIONAL INTERESTS IN INTERNATIONAL SOCIETY (1996). (For contrasting views regarding recent violations of the laws of war, see Steven R. Ratner, Jus ad Bellum *and* Jus in Bello *After September 11*, 96 AMERICAN JOURNAL OF INTERNATIONAL LAW 905 (2002); Jeremy Rabkin, *After Guantanamo: The War Over the Geneva Convention*, THE NATIONAL INTEREST 15 (Summer 2002); Kenneth Roth, *After Guantanamo: A Reply*, THE NATIONAL INTEREST (Winter 2002)(Letter to the editor).) Most agree that while not all states always observe the laws of war, most do observe them most of the time. How would you explain this? Is it the result of an expectation of reciprocity? The operation of norms? Simple self-interest (e.g., states only comply with the laws of war because violating them does not prove to be more effective)? Which of the theories you have studied provide the most useful guidance in thinking about these questions?